Harford County Maryland Marriage Licenses

1777–1865

Compiled by
Jon Harlan Livezey
and
Helene Maynard Davis

HERITAGE BOOKS
2010

HERITAGE BOOKS
AN IMPRINT OF HERITAGE BOOKS, INC.

Books, CDs, and more—Worldwide

For our listing of thousands of titles see our website
at
www.HeritageBooks.com

Published 2010 by
HERITAGE BOOKS, INC.
Publishing Division
100 Railroad Ave. #104
Westminster, Maryland 21157

Copyright © 1993 Jon Harlan Livezey
and Helene Maynard Davis

All rights reserved. No part of this book may be reproduced or transmitted in any form or by any means, electronic or mechanical, including photocopying, recording or by any information storage and retrieval system without written permission from the author, except for the inclusion of brief quotations in a review.

International Standard Book Numbers
Paperbound: 978-1-58549-263-3
Clothbound: 978-0-7884-8509-1

INTRODUCTION

This book is a compilation of extant records of marriage licenses issued in Harford County, Maryland, from 1777 to 1865, augmented with useful cross references. The information has been extracted from the *original* records, as available, and from the courthouse transcription, where not, and is supplemented by early minister's returns. The records and the arrangement employed herein are fully described hereafter in the "Researcher's Guide."

Official marriage license records are a particularly valuable genealogical source. Often the primary means of identifying a maiden surname, the license may be the only or at least the most definitive record of an individual's existence, especially for people of limited means. Researchers sometimes lend them too much credence, ignoring the possibility of errors somewhere in the record-making process. One should bear in mind that occasionally a license was issued but no marriage took place, and also that the bride's surname may not be her maiden name, but that from a prior marriage.

There were sporadic experiments with licensing marriages in colonial Maryland, but it was Chapter 12 of the 1777 Session Laws that authorized the regular issuance of licenses by the clerks of the county courts. The clerks were directed to forward to the Treasurer of their Shore an annual record of licenses issued; ministers were required to report marriages performed [See Appendix A]. In 1865, Chapter 130 of the Session Laws provided for local registration of ministers' returns. Maryland had special provisions for Friends (Quakers) and for marriages where banns had been announced. Until 1964, only a clergyman could perform a Maryland marriage ceremony.

The record of antebellum marriage licenses available to the public and the clerk's staff in the Harford County Court House is in fact a *transcription* made by the clerk in 1888 from the various booklets that had been employed to record licenses as issued. At that time, the original records covering the periods 1777-1778 and 1786-1791 apparently were missing, perhaps lost in the 1858 fire that consumed part of the courthouse. The larger part of the original records remain in the possession of the court. They are extracted here.

Comparison of the originals with the transcription revealed numerous errors, most minor. In some cases the name had been misinterpreted beyond recognition, as when "Anderson" was read as "Aprioson." A few licenses had been entirely overlooked. The transcription omitted the names of the ministers to whom the licenses were directed, and misstated the dates of the earliest licenses by one year.

The compilers have recorded names here exactly as found in the original to the extent discernible, notwithstanding "corrections" made in the transcription. Researchers should examine possible variant spellings. Parts of the originals, particularly in the mid 1840s, are now very difficult or impossible to read because of fading or damage as well as indecipherable penmanship, and the transcript was relied upon in such cases. Where capitals I and J could not be distinguished, the form I/J. or J/I. was employed here. A question mark, in brackets where space permitted, has been inserted in cases of doubtful interpretation. Dates are presented uniformly, irrespective of the actual form in the record.

When no originals were available, the transcription entries were simply copied. In those cases, there was no means for correcting transcription errors, which certainly did occur. For example, the transcription as faithfully recorded here shows a license issued to James W. Livezey and Frances F. Everett, but it is well-documented that *Joseph* Waterman Livezey married Frances *Edna* Everist. The original probably was written "Jos.," easily misread in handwriting as "Jas.," which the transcriber wrote out in full as "James." The discrepancies in the bride's name could have several explanations.

Our purpose is to provide a carefully compiled record standing on its own, as there is presently no convenient access to the originals for comparison, the hallmark of sound genealogical research. This project had its genesis over twenty years ago, and was recently taken up again. The tedious work of comparisons with the originals, alphabetical arrangement, and entry into the word processor, and the addition of the appended materials having been completed, we are pleased to present it to the Harford County researcher. The considerable assistance of Caroline Borman and Julia Frazer and the courtesies of Clerk of the Circuit Court Charles G. Hiob, III, and his predecessor, the late H. Douglas Chilcoat, are very much appreciated.

In addition to noting the size of each surname's representation in the community, it is interesting to observe unusual names encountered, such as Christian Blessing, Kilian Kub, Randsome Fayerweather, Peen Bartonslade, Solivia Scheckle, and Amanda A. C. Pepoo. Here also are records of Chas. Frederick Egidius Shultz, the locally well-known Zacheus Onion Bond, and Baltis Fie and his three brides, one of whom was Artreque (Cannon) Rider, widow of Noble Rider. May all these now departed souls find an honored place in a descendant's ancestor chart.

Harford County, 1993   Jon Harlan Livezey
                            Helene Maynard Davis

RESEARCHER'S GUIDE

I. Arrangement

The marriage license records are entered by both bride and groom under the surname (in all capitals) as spelled in the original. The surnames are arranged alphabetically, with "Mc" treated as "Mac" and "St." as "Saint." Editorial cross-references enclosed in brackets may follow, showing use of the surname as a given or middle/maiden name, or alternate spellings. Selection of given names which may represent family connections was of necessity somewhat arbitrary. For example, Washington was deemed of no likely value, but instances of Jefferson are noted. Jarrett, Corbin, and Nelson are cross-referenced, but Oliver, Lewis, and Martin are not.

The given name of the groom or bride is in the first column, listed alphabetically under the surname. In cases where both names were judged of ambiguous gender, the bride and groom are so identified. In the rare instances of racial identification, the original designation "col'd" is shown.

The other party's name is in the second column.

The third column contains the date of issuance of the license.

The fourth column gives the location of the entry in the original record where one was available (see key on next page).

The fifth column contains the page reference to the entry in the 1888 transcription (volume W.S.F. # 1, indicated by "W").

The sixth column is for remarks - a name standing alone is that of the minister to whom the license was directed. (He was not necessarily the person who actually performed the ceremony - see the license reproduced on page 271 of this book). Otherwise, it may be a note as to residence, a brief editorial comment, or a reference to an appendix. "ALJ1" refers to four instances of marriage returns recorded for these licenses in a later volume. These are set out in Appendix B. [We do not know why the term "wheat" was appended to several early records - perhaps the license was paid for in grain rather than hard currency.]

Longer editorial remarks or quotes may be found directly below the entry. Some of these refer to comparisons with original licenses, copies of a small number of which are deposited in the Genealogical Reference Library of the Historical Society of Harford County.

II. Abbreviations

br = bride; gr = groom; ret = return; cr = couples' residence; gn, bn = groom's, bride's name

III. Key to Extracted Records

[Note: the letters B, C, E, and H are the compilers' arbitrary designations for the separate record booklets; the originals are not so designated nor are their pages numbered unlike the 1888 transcription, Vol. W.S.F. #1 ("W"). For the purpose of this book, the compilers sequentially numbered pages in a photocopy of each original.]

Time Period	Original Record	Transcription (WSF #1)
1777-1778	missing - some returns in Appendix A	
10Nov1778-25Oct1779	B1 - B3	W1 - W2 (misdated)
06Nov1779-07Jan1786	C1 - C10	W3 - W10 (misdated)
1786-1791	missing - some returns in Appendix A	
16Mar1791-25Sep1845	E1 - E88	W21 - W89
01Oct1845-20Nov1851	not located	W89 - W97
01Dec1851-30Nov1857	H1 - H13	W97 - W107
07Dec1857-21Jun1865	not located	W107 - W121

Harford Co. Md. Marriage Licenses, 1777-1865   1

ABBITT
David   Ann Bond   04Sep1783   C7 W9   cr-Salim Co

ABBOTT
Charlotte   John Wood   30Jun1808   E32 W41

ACKERS
Jemima   Jesse Cullum   10Jan1861   W113

ACRES
Isaac   Sarah Gardner   19Oct1857   H13 W107 Hoopman
John   Jemima Andrew   23Apr1824   E58 W62
John Thomas   Caroline A. Allender   27Apr1855   H7 W102 Finney
Lamiania[?]   James Townsley   27Feb1837   E77 W79 Finny
Martha Caroline   George L. Scott   10Feb1863   W117
Samuel   Georgianna Courtney   29Oct1862   W116
Susanna J/I.   David McNutt   27Apr1855   H7 W102 Finney
Thomas   Louisa Preston   18Feb1854   H5 W100 Finney

ADAM
Wilhelm   Mary E. Beck   15May1857   H12 W106 Monroe

ADAMS [see Eliza Adams Gillet]
Agnes   William White   05Sep1797   E11 W26
Alexander S.   Amanda E. Reasin   20Jan1859   W109
Caleb   Sarah Hitchcock   07Dec1819   E51 W57
Hannah C.   Amos H. Hughes   23Feb1841   E83 W84 Wiggins
John P.   Kate Woodhouse   29Nov1859   W111
Mary Ann   Elias Scarborough   14Jan1848   W92
Susan G.   William C. Wilson   28Nov1848   W93
Wm   Eleanore Magnes[?]   12Feb1782   C5 W7
William   Catherine Brown   04Mar1811   E36 W44
William A.   Caroline Howlett   16Feb1855   H7 W102 Collins

ADLUM
Joseph   Ann McPhail   07Nov1798   E15 W27
Thomas   Sarah McCasky   23Mar1799   E15 W28

ADY [see also EDIE]
Caroline   William Ady   29Nov1860   W112
Chloe   John Kean   18Jan1841   E83 W84 Reed
Cloe C.   George Wood   28Nov1848   W93
Elizabeth   Solomon Ady   27Jun1814   E42 W49
Francis   Caroline Wheeler   19Nov1841   E84 W84 Reid
Hannah   James Willson   08Oct1783   C8 W9
Hannah   Aaron Lancaster   28Mar1815   E43 W49
Jonathan   Elizabeth Macatee   04Aug1807   E30 W39
Leonard   Elizabeth Gordon   24Feb1838   E79 W80 Cosgray
Martha   John B. Robinson   14Mar1812   E38 W46
Rachel   John Y. Pierce   09Nov1850   W95
Ralph   Marjarum Pearson   17Nov1812   E39 W47
Rebecca   John Preston   04Oct1804   E25 W35
Samuel   Mary Ayres   21Sep1814   E42 W49
Samuel M.   Cassandra Kean   02Jun1862   W116

2 Harford Co. Md. Marriage Licenses, 1777-1865

ADY, continued
Solomon	Elizabeth Ady	27Jun1814	E42 W49
William	Caroline Ady	29Nov1860	W112

AITKIN
Sarah	James Taylor	25Jan1800	E17 W29

AKENS
William	Sarah Arnold	13May1807	E29 W39

ALBERT
Elizabeth	Hezekiah Scarbrough	01Feb1814	E41 W48

ALDERSON
Abel	Ann Amos	16Feb1804	E24 W35	
Charles D.	Annie P. Hopkins	28Sep1863	W118	
Elizabeth A.	George L. Elgin	13Oct1849	W94	
Jane D.	Joshua B. Morris	20Mar1839	E80 W81	Scott
John D.	Hannah Trego	20Dec1838	E80 W81	Scott
John D.	Anne M. Dunn	27Nov1860	W112	
Lucretia	Richard Mechem	03Dec1835	E76 W77	Scott

ALDRIDGE
Eliza Ann	Sylvester Newgent	13Dec1826	E62 W65	Richardson
Elizabeth	Vincent J. Watkins	16Sep1812	E38 W46	

ALEXANDER [see Francis Alexander Linton]
Andrew	Ann Watson	27Jan1814	E41 W48	
Eliza Jane	Thomas McKinnon	11Feb1834	E74 W75	Parke
Elizabeth	Franklin Ruff	10May1845	E88 W88	Park
James	Mary Clendinen	05May1801	E20 W31	
James	Harriet Wilson	21Dec1839	E81 W82	Keech
Mary G.	John A. Kirkwood	06Mar1832	E70 W72	Sewall
Robert	Jane Clendening	04Sep1800	E18 W30	
William	Maria Cox	27Jan1851	W96	

ALL
Mary	James Hair[?]	07Jan1786	C10 W10
Micajah	Rachel Cannon	04Dec1802	E22 W33

ALLEN
Ann Frances	Walter Jarvis	13Sep1830	E67 W70	Stephenson
Ann Maria	James W. Glanville	23Oct1830	E68 W70	Tippet
Catharine	Stephen Pearce	21Feb1825	E59 W63	Allen
Ebenezer N.	Elizabeth Chauncey	13Feb1816	E44 W51	
Ebenezer N.	Elecia[?] M. Monks	19Nov1821	E54 W59	
Ebenezer N.	Mary Ann Billingslea	02Dec1823	E57 W61	
Ebenezer N.	Martha Dickinson	28May1827	E63 W66	Allen
Edward M.	Sarah E. Wilson	02Dec1852	H2 W98	Keech
Emily Jane	John St. Clair	31Jul1858	W108	
Isaac	Mary Herring	23Dec1800	E19 W30	
James	Sarah Williams	06Jan1781	C4 W5	
John	Phoebe Sheredine	14Nov1805	E27 W37	
John	Sarah C. Heape	24Dec1858	W109	
Kate	Patrick Carroll	13Feb1857	H11 W106	Walter

ALLEN, continued

Margaret B.	Robert Bolton	28Jul1828	E65 W68	McGee
Martha M.	Jacob T. Dickinson	22Jul1837	E78 W79	Collins
Mary Louisa Fell	William A. Lennox	13Apr1835	E75 W76	D. Bond
Nancy	John Sheredine	17Apr1805	E26 W36	
Richard	Sarah Hughes	29Dec1812	E39 W47	
Richard N.	Adeline Miller	02Sep1828	E65 W68	Keeck
Richard Nun	Elizabeth Gittings Gover	17Feb1819	E50 W56	
Robert	Elizabeth Hopkins	17Dec1813	E41 W48	
Robert T. P.	Julian Dickerson	07Jul1834	E74 W75	Dunahay
Sarah	Thomas W. Bond	01Apr1834	E74 W75	Dunahy
Sarah Elizabeth	Charles Y. Haines	12Oct1833	E73 W74	D. Bond
Thomas	Rebecca Willey	09Aug1808	E32 W41	
William	Hannah Bond	12Apr1798	E13 W27	Jno Allen
William H.	Emeline Rickey	22Nov1858	W109	

ALLENDER

Ann	William Turner	13Nov1818	E50 W55	
Caroline A.	John Thomas Acres	27Apr1855	H7 W102	Finney
Edward	Nacky Enlows	21Dec1802	E22 W33	[ret-AppA]
Frances Ann Maximitton	Maxwell Strong	14Sep1825	E60 W64	
[minister - Benjn Richardson]				
George	Mary Ann Ricketts	12Jan1825	E59 W63	Richardson
John J.	Susan Gardner	07Feb1853	H3 W99	Finney
Mary	James Dick	05Sep1830	E67 W70	Tippit
Mary Ann	Robert Boldon	16Nov1858	W109	
Nicholas	Sarah Bradford	26Jun1797	E11 W26	
Nicholas	Elizabeth Morris	29Sep1806	E28 W38	
Nicholas	Martha Lyons	06Oct1823	E57 W61	
Sarah	John Day	m. 1788[?]		[ret-AppA]
Thomas	Sarah Barton	m. 1803		[ret-AppA]
William	Mary Foster	27Jan1810	E34 W43	

ALLISON

Robt	Sarah Turner	09Jul1779	B3 W2

ALLMAN

Mary	Edward Doran	12Sep1801	E20 W31

ALMONY

Benjamin	Jane Gammell[?]	12Apr1854	H5 W100	Smith
Elizabeth	Henry M. Strawbridge	01Jan1851	W96	
Elizabeth Ann	Jacob Bradenbaugh	01Jan1839	E80 W81	Finney
Mary Ann	Benjamin Sutton	01Feb1845	E88 W88	Reid
Mary J/I.	Obed Lowe	20Feb1854	H5 W100	Smith
Sarah Ann	John Houston	02Mar1846	W90	
Sarina C.	William Heaton	31Mar1857	H11 W106	Dumm

AMMONS

Elizabeth	John Dobbins	23Dec1818	E50 W56

AMOS [see also AMOSS]

Ann	James McComas	03Dec1780	C4 W5	
[recorded after 19Dec]				
Ann	Abel Alderson	16Feb1804	E24 W35	
Ann	Zachariah Roberts	09Jun1804	E25 W35	
Ariel	Abraham Rutledge	01Jan1857	H11 W105	
Balinda P.	George W. Kirk	23Aug1841	E38 W84	Keech
Caroline	Adam Hilt	20Oct1851	W97	
Catharine	Aquila Hall	05Nov1822	E56 W60	
Ed. H.	Mary E. Morris	11Nov1864	W120	
Elisha Pearson	Francina H. Wetherall	21Jan1858	W108	
Eliza B.	Jacob Grupy	18Feb1823	E56 W61	
Elizabeth	Annanias Divers	19Feb1828	E64 W67	Keech
Elizabeth	James Logue	02Mar1830	E67 W69	Poteet
Elizabeth	Otho N. Renshaw	02Nov1830	E68 W70	Uwing
Elizabeth	Thomas M. Hope	12Dec1837	E78 W79	Cross
Fredrick T.	Cassandra Adelin Jones	19Jan1837	E77 W78	Reese
John	Elizabeth Jarrett	20Feb1804	E24 W35	
John	Elizabeth Rampley	14Feb1824	E58 W62	
Lydia	Isakah Hughes	16Aug1815	E43 W50	
Margaret	James Worthington	01Jan1838	E78 W80	Park
Martha	John Watt	09Jan1828	E64 W67	Keech
Martha R.	Joseph Hanway	18Feb1851	W96	
Mary	James Watt	08Jul1831	E69 W71	Sewall
Mary	George Smithson	02Mar1842	E84 W85	Cross
Oliver H.	Elizabeth Ann King	16Mar1829	E65 W68	Keech
Phillip	Mary Ann Pocock	29Apr1824	E58 W62	
Robert C.	Hannah Rush	09Dec1846	W90	
Sarah Eliza	Daniel Raymond	18Feb1830	E67 W69	Keech
Susanna	James Garrison	26Jan1825	E59 W63	Richardson
Susannah G.	William A. Lewis	08Mar1842	E84 W85	Keech
Thomas B.	Sarah Ann Maulsby	16Sep1841	E84 W84	Keech
William T.	Helen D. Rigdon	24Jan1857	H11 W105	Wilson

AMOSS [see also AMOS; see William Amoss Carr]

Abraham	Elizabeth Rigdon	19Apr1821	E54 W59	
Ann	Abraham Ditto	23May1796	E8 W25	
Ann	Daniel Cunningham	16Oct1797	E11 W26	[ret-AppA]
Aquila	Elizabeth Montgomery	25Apr1804	E25 W35	
Aquila of Thos	Mary Amoss	16May1809	E34 W42	
Benjamin	Margaret Conn	05Nov1800	E18 W30	
Casandra	Daniel Bay	11Apr1827	E62 W66	Park
Cassandra Ann	Zachariah Stroble	07Jan1794	E5 W23	
Corbin	Amanda Jane Holland	04Sep1861	W114	
Elizth	Robert Amoss	02Jan1792	E2 W21	
Elizabeth	Edward Tracey	03Mar1810	E35 W43	
Hannah	Richd Sampson	03Mar1781	C4 W6	
[same parties 3Feb C4]				
Hannah	James Fulton	01Feb1809	E33 W42	
Hannah	John Smithson	27Mar1811	E36 W44	
Henry C.	Sarah Jane Whiteford	20Oct1860	W112	
Henry R.	Mary Streett	17Mar1803	E23 W33	
James	Jane Bell	20Feb1798	E13 W27	
James of Josha	Mary Amoss	04Dec1799	E17 W28	

Harford Co. Md. Marriage Licenses, 1777-1865

AMOSS, continued

James A.	Eliza K. Watters	19Jan1846		W89
James Bussey	Ann Rigdon	04Jan1808	E31	W40
John	Ruth Wilson	14Jun1810	E35	W44
John M.	Mary Jane Gleem	04Mar1848		W92
Luke	Sarah Gallion	26Nov1794	E6	W23
Martha	Aqª McComas	10Jan1797	E10	W25
Martha	Stephen Rigdon	05Jun1813	E40	W47
Martha	Joshua Glenn	03Apr1845	E88	W88 Park
Mary	Joshua Barton	18Apr1782	C6	W7
Mary	James Amoss of Joshª	04Dec1799	E17	W28
Mary	Francis Howard	21Mar1805	E26	W36
Mary	John Way	22Jun1806	E28	W38
Mary	Aquila Amoss of Thoˢ	16May1809	E34	W42
Mary	William Calwell	01Dec1813	E41	W48
Rachel	Benjamin Standiford	09Jan1798	E13	W27 Jno Coleman
Robert	Elizᵗʰ Amoss	02Jan1792	E2	W21
Robert	Martha Johns	31Mar1808	E31	W40
Sarah	Aqª Parker	03Mar1779	B1	W1
Sarah	Henry Gilbert	25Jul1816	E45	W52
Sarah Ann	Benjamin Rigdon	24Oct1857	H13	W107 Wilson
Thomas	Mary Jane Slade	17Feb1858		W108
Wᵐ	Mary Sinclair	19Nov1778	B1	W1
William	Ruth Sutton	06Jun1799	E16	W28
William of Thos.	Milcah McComas	01Jan1803	E23	W33
William	Susan Richardson	01Nov1815	E43	W50
William	Hannah Streett	05Mar1859		W110
Zachariah	Susanah Mutchmer	23Jan1792	E2	W21

ANDERSON

Agnes	Andrew Humphrey	16Aug1779	B3	W2
Amos	Ann Gilbert	09Apr1821	E54	W59
Anna	Ebenezer Gilbert	26Feb1807	E29	W39
Benjamin F.	Susan Hughes	30Nov1855	H8	W103 Smith
Comfort	Robert L. Plumer	03Dec1859		W111
Danˡ	Rachel Wearim	29Feb1784	C8	W9 cr-Harf
Daniel	Susan S. Gilbert	23Mar1847		W91
David Lee	Phebe Rebecca Ann Clowman	29Dec1851	H1	W97 Robey
Delia	Thomas Lytle	14May1807	E29	W39
Delia	Israel Hitchcock	10Mar1812	E38	W46
Elizabeth	Samuel Whitaker	15Jun1809	E34	W42
Elizabeth	Edward Tredway	20Mar1810	E35	W43
Elizabeth	Bernard Mitchell	19Jun1827	E63	W66 McElhiney
Francis D.	Mary D. Silvers	10Jun1833	E73	W74 Finney
George	Mary E. Keen	22Jan1852	H1	W97 Chapman
George W.	Hannah Norris	22Jul1812	E38	W46
James	Margᵗ McCan	m. 1778		[ret-AppA]
Jaˢ	Sarah Hill	03Apr1780	C1	W3
James	Casandra McComas	12Feb1781	C4	W6
James	Ann Tredway	06Jan1815	E42	W49
James M.	Susan R. Fulton	30Nov1859		W111
Jane A.	James Jeffery	13Sep1830	E67	W70 Finney
John	Eliza Durbin	24Oct1808	E32	W41
John W.	Mary Ann Anderson	06Dec1854	H6	W101 Carter

ANDERSON, continued

John W.	Sarah Ann Kirkwood	29Oct1859	W111	
Joseph	Elizabeth Wilson	11Feb1831	E68 W70	Park
Joshua	Elizabeth Forwood	06Jan1831	E68 W70	Reese
Margaret	Robert Askey	02Oct1824	E58 W62	
[orig. lic. to Webster; cr-Harf]				
Mary	Robert Renshaw	12Feb1781	C4 W6	
Mary	Benjn Ford	01Sep1781	C5 W7	
Mary Ann	John W. Anderson	06Dec1854	H6 W101	Carter
Michael G.	Mary A. Ward	22Nov1862	W116	
Nancy	Aquila Tredway	18Dec1809	E34 W43	
Rachel	William Lofton	31Jan1804	E24 W34	
Robert	Adeline A. Quigly	21Apr1842	E85 W85	Park
Rosetta	Abraham Slade	27Feb1816	E44 W51	
Sarah	John Bowan	13Dec1784	C9 W10	
Sarah	James Ingram	01Nov1828	E65 W68	Richardson
Susan	Thomas Mitchell	04Apr1815	E43 W50	
William	Nancy McVay	17Aug1815	E43 W50	
William	Sarah White	18Feb1818	E48 W54	
William	Mary Land	22Dec1845	W89	
William	Elizabeth Lemmon	27Feb1849	W93	

ANDREW

James R.	Mary E. Divers	20Nov1850	W95	
Jemima	John Acres	23Apr1824	E58 W62	
John	Ruth Spencer	14Mar1826	E61 W65	Finney
Mary A.	Benjamin F. Miller	14Apr1858	W108	
Mary Elizth	George T. Miller	14May1859	W110	
Sarah A.	Benjamin F. Miller	09Jun1847	W91	
William	Catherine Blackburn	26Feb1780	C1 W3	
William G.	Sarah Tolly	11Jun1861	W114	

ANDREWS

Abraham	Mary Hanson	17Mar1779	B1 W1	
Fanny	Thomas Lee	19Dec1805	E27 W37	
John	Ann Gillum	14Feb1811	E36 W44	
John W.	Mary Ann Keen	14Mar1843	E85 W86	Thomas
Kate	Job A. Price	25Feb1858	W108	
Margaretta	William T. Williamson	08Nov1858	W109	
Mary	William Hedric	28Oct1819	E51 W57	
Ruth C.	John A. Greenland	20Feb1855	H7 W102	Dumm
Sarah Ann	Joseph Griffin	05Mar1860	W111	
Syna	William Williams	19Jan1804	E24 W34	
William H.	Alice Amanda Stubbins	04Mar1865	W121	

ANGELL

Mary	Edward Stiles	14Jan1801	E19 W30

ANKRAM

Sam'l J.	Alice R. Lowe	29Dec1863	W118

ANNIS [see ONINS]

Harford Co. Md. Marriage Licenses, 1777-1865

ANTHONY
Eliza	John Roberts	14Jul1813	E40	W48	
Martha	Thomas Stockham	04Jun1831	E69	W71	Sewall

ANTLEY
Ann	Gregory Gallion	16Oct1784	C9	W10

ARCHER [see Archer Lee]
Catherine	Henry Smithson	11Jul1836	E76	W78	Finney
Hannah C.	George L. Van Bibber	05Nov1839	E81	W82	Finney
Hannah S.	Albert Constable	21Dec1829	E66	W69	Finney
Harriet H.	Lewis J. Williams	17Jun1850		W95	
John, Jur.	Ann Stump	15Nov1802	E22	W33	
Laura S.	Joseph A. Turpin	17Oct1836	E77	W78	Finney
Pamelia H.	Chas T. Chamberland	21Nov1843	E86	W87	Finney
Stevenson	Pamelia B. Hays	20Jan1811	E36	W44	
Thomas	Elizabeth Phillips	08Jun1803	E23	W33	
Thomas	Susanna P. Glasgow	16Nov1841	E84	W84	Finney

AREL [perhaps Orel]
George	Sarah Drennen	19Jan1785	C10	W10

ARMITAGE
John	Sarah Givins	03Mar1799	E15	W28

ARMSTRONG
Ann	Reubin Sutton	09Feb1804	E24	W34	
Frances	Johel Tuchstone	25Sep1838	E79	W80	Sheperd
George Sidney	Sarah Catharine Gilbert	09Jan1850		W94	
Hannah	William Monk	04Apr1822	E55	W60	
Isabella	James Price	16Nov1801	E20	W31	
Isabella	Job Everist	11Jun1816	E45	W51	
John*	Elizabeth Edwards	14Aug1791	E1	W21	
[*Solomon crossed out]					
John	Mary Cronin	12Jan1865		W120	
Margaret	William Barnes	m. 1787			[ret-AppA]
Martha	John Phison	16Jun1779	B2	W2	
Robert	Hannah Kimble	28Oct1809	E34	W43	
Susannah	James Olliver	25Feb1780	C1	W3	
Thomas	Lydia Shareswood	29Apr1812	E38	W46	

ARNETT
Thomas	Mary Ann Kelley	26May1830	E67	W69	O'Brion

ARNOLD
Cordelia	John Mitchell	30Apr1828	E64	W67	Webster
[orig. lic. to Webster; cr-Harf]					
Elizabeth	Benjamin Cole	14Feb1815	E42	W49	
Ephraim	Sophia Barnes	20Dec1814	E42	W49	
Harriott	Hanson Courtney	24Dec1816	E46	W52	
Henry F.	Elizabeth Baker	04Mar1829	E65	W68	Webster
[orig. lic. to Webster; cr-Harf]					
Mary	William Mitchell	26Feb1822	E55	W60	
Mary E.	George Dever	08Jan1864		W118	

ARNOLD, continued

Sarah	William Akens	13May1807	E29	W39	
Sophia	Edward Jackson	04Feb1824	E57	W62	
Susan	Hugh Jefferson Dever	02Sep1862		W116	
William	Jane Denison	03Oct1835	E75	W77	Dulany

ARNUTT

Anna B.	Jesse Hughes	02May1859		W110

ARTHER

Joseph	Mary Jane Grier	19Dec1843	E86	W87	Keech

ARTHUR

Anna	Geo. T. Few	23Dec1864		W120
Elizabeth	Jacob Erwin	07Sep1861		W114
John	Susannah Stovir	03Dec1861		W115
Lucretia	Stephen J. Philips	26Aug1861		W114
Samuel	Martha Ayres	25Dec1850		W95
Samuel	Martha Thompson	19Apr1862		W116

ARY

Sarah	Samuel B. Ivans	18Oct1859		W110

ASBERRY [see Asberry Cord]

ASBURY [see Francis Asbury Ruth, Asbury Sheredine]

ASHBERRY [see Ashberry Coard, Ashberry Taylor]

ASHLEY

Margaret	James F. Taylor	21Jun1858		W108	
Rebekah	Joseph Johnson	30Dec1795	E8	W24	
Thomas	Rebecca Grace	02Feb1783	C7	W8	cr-Harf

ASHMEAD

Ann	Nathan Clark	28Apr1803	E23	W33	
Betsey	Wm Sloan	04Oct1795	E7	W24	
John	Catharine Jordon	14Jul1800	E18	W29	

ASHMORE

Margt	Wm Hemphill	10Nov1778	B1	W1

ASHTON [see also ASTON]

Amanda	George Meechem	13Dec1832	E71	W73	Keech
Catharine	Billingslea Bull	17May1808	E31	W40	
Elizabeth	George Jessup	18May1840	E82	W83	Keech
James	Keziah Ashton	07Dec1842	E85	W86	Thomas
James F.	Matilda Lytle	15Jun1864		W119	
John	Susanna Fulton	03May1800	E18	W29	
Joseph	Elizabeth Baldwin	22Sep1810	E35	W44	
Keziah	Glenn Streett	10Feb1826	E61	W64	Keech
Keziah	James Ashton	07Dec1842	E85	W86	Thomas
Mary Ann	Owen Michael	14Jan1839	E80	W81	Keech
Richard	Ruth Love	10Nov1807	E30	W39	
Sarah	David Streett	22Feb1827	E62	W66	Keech

ASHTON, continued
Sarah L.　　　　　　William M. Glenn　　　25Jan1858　　　W108

ASKER
Jane　　　　　　　　Jno Silvers　　　　　　m. 1778　　　　[ret-AppA]

ASKEY
Robert　　　　　　　Margaret Anderson　　　02Oct1824　E58 W62
　[orig. lic. to Webster; cr-Harf]

ASTON
Susan　　　　　　　 Thomas Street　　　　　26Nov1816　E46 W52

ATKINSON
David　　　　　　　 Sarah Spencer　　　　　26Feb1821　E54 E58
Isaac　　　　　　　 Hannah Burnett　　　　 29Mar1809　E33 W42
Israel　　　　　　　Esther Lancaster　　　 21Apr1829　E66 W68　Richardson
John　　　　　　　　 Sarah Kimble　　　　　 19Jan1825　E59 W63　Richardson
　[orig. lic. to Benjn Richardson; cr-Harf]
Mark　　　　　　　　 Eliza Jane Ely　　　　28Oct1851　　 W97

AUSTEN
Rody　　　　　　　　 Thomas Ramsey　　　　　09Jun1807　E36 W39

AUSTIN [see Henry Austin Greenfield]

AYRES [see also HEIRS]
Ann　　　　　　　　　Ezekiel J.[?] Richardson 09Mar1846　　W90
Ann　　　　　　　　　John Wiley　　　　　　 29Jan1857　H11 W105 Lee
Benjamin F.　　　　　Dorcas Ayres　　　　　 13Apr1852　H2 W98　Elderdice
Dorcas　　　　　　　 Jacob Bradenbaugh　　　12Jun1811　E36 W45
Dorcas　　　　　　　 Benjamin F. Ayres　　　13Apr1852　H2 W98　Elderdice
James　　　　　　　　Elizabeth Baldwin　　　06Oct1831　E69 W71　Webster
　[orig. lic. to Webster; cr-Harf]
John　　　　　　　　 Elizabeth Perdue　　　 15Apr1847　　 W91
John T.　　　　　　　Sarah J. Colder　　　　08Dec1862　　 W116
Levitha　　　　　　　Joseph Garner　　　　　01Nov1802　E22 W33
Lorenza　　　　　　　Benjamin Sutton　　　　06Feb1830　E67 W69　O'Brian
Margaret M.　　　　　Elijah Rockhold, Junr　30Dec1851　H1 W97　Elderdice
Martha　　　　　　　 Samuel Arthur　　　　　25Dec1850　　 W95
Martha A.　　　　　　Henry C. Cooper　　　　18Dec1862　　 W116
Mary　　　　　　　　 Samuel Ady　　　　　　 21Sep1814　E42 W49
Matilda　　　　　　　John Patten　　　　　　01May1827　E63 W66　Barton
Richard　　　　　　　Elizabeth Baxter　　　 10Oct1803　E24 W34　[ret-AppA]
Thomas W.　　　　　　Susan Sharp　　　　　　07Nov1820　E53 W58

BACON
Ann　　　　　　　　　Jacob W. Giles　　　　 14May1817　E47 W53
Sarah　　　　　　　　John Wilson　　　　　　17Sep1811　E37 W45

BADDERS
Andrew J.　　　　　　Amanda Scarff　　　　　15Aug1855　H8　W103 Hinsey

BAEHR [See also BAIR, BEAR]
Maria　　　　　　　　Jacob Emrick　　　　　 14Sep1859　　 W110

10   Harford Co. Md. Marriage Licenses, 1777-1865

BAGELEY
John O.	Hannah Husband	05Jun1833	E72 W74	Finney
Mary H.	Francis Asbury Ruth	18Oct1824	E58 W63	
Valeria J.	William Jones	06Mar1855	H7 W102	Lemmon

BAGELY
Samuel H.	Martha Matilda Ewing	20Jun1862	W116	ALJ1-21,34

BAGLEY
Ann H.	Cunningham S. Ramsey	20Apr1825	E59 W63	Sample
Mary	Christopher Wilson	08Jun1852	H2 W98	Cornelius
Philip G.	Ann McFadden	22May1865	W121	
Rachel H.	Henry Conley	13Dec1825	E60 W64	Finney
Samuel	Mary Smith	21Dec1820	E53 W58	

BAILESS
Asael	Sophia Keen	23Feb1809	E33 W42

BAILEY [See Bailey St. Clair; see also BAILY, BALEY, BAYLEY]
Ann Jane	Samuel S. Scarborough	27Feb1860	W111	
Anne	Marshall Lee	10Apr1817	E47 W53	
Aquila	Martha Evans	08Nov1810	E36 W44	
Aquila	Martha Cohen	07Jan1834	E73 W75	Higby
Asael	Mary Barnes	29Feb1808	E31 W40	
Avarilla	Cyrus Courtney	22Dec1812	E39 W47	
Dan¹	Catharine Crosen	27Mar1781	C4 W6	
Daniel L.	Mary Elizth Scarborough	05May1863	W117	
Elizabeth	George Walker	29Jan1806	E27 W37	
Elizabeth	John Coen	07Oct1817	E47 W54	
Elizabeth	Gorard H. Sappington	13Jun1831	E69 W71	Stephenson
Ellen	John S. Loflin	23Mar1844	E87 W87	Finney
Emely	William Lofflin	21Apr1831	E69 W71	Finney
George	Elizabeth Spencer	27Jan1851	W96	
Gerard	Sarah Barnes	15Jun1824	E58 W62	
Harriet	Robert W. Dick	24Oct1859	W111	
Harriett	Alfred Mitchell	09Feb1835	E75 W76	Finney
Helen Dalby	Robert Amos Rigdon	20Feb1852	H1 W97	Wilson
John	Harriot Barnes	24Dec1818	E50 W56	
Jones	Salinah Renshaw	19Dec1780	C3 W5	
Josias	Catharine Vandegrift	24Feb1823	E56 W61	
Mary	Jacob James	12Dec1821	E55 W59	
Mary	William S. Bowman	26Jan1846	W89	
Nancy	John Coen	04Aug1825	E60 W64	Finney
Phebe	William A. Bailey	31Mar1840	E82 W83	Finney
Sarah	Mordecai Barnes	29Dec1817	E48 W54	
Sarah	John R. Spencer	12Jan1848	W92	
Shadrach	Mary Barnes	15Jul1835	E75 W76	Finney
William	Rachel Preston	26Jul1809	E34 W42	
William	Priscilla Boarman	29May1849	W94	
William A.	Phebe Bailey	31Mar1840	E82 W83	Finney
William Lewin	Emeline S. Scarborough	26Dec1860	W113	

BAILISS
Elias	Rachel Barcellay	29Jan1781	C4 W6

Harford Co. Md. Marriage Licenses, 1777-1865   11

BAILY [See Baily Warn]
Nehemiah   Mary Hobbard   m. 1777   [ret-AppA]

BAIR
William A.   Elizabeth Forsythe   13Apr1858   W108

BAITY
Rebecca   John Scott   09Aug1830   E67 W70 Finney

BAKER
*   Morgan Jones   25Jan1798   E13 W27
[*bride's first name not stated]
Agness   James Bonar   01Apr1784   C8 W9   cr-Harf
Ann   John Saunders   25Jun1811   E36 W45
Ann   John Bowman   15Aug1821   E54 W59
Ann Moore   John Crail   04Mar1812   E38 W46
Catharine   Charles Criswell   01Jul1844   E87 W87   Norris
Catherine   Benjamin F. Brown   20Aug1835   E75 W77   Gallion
Charles   Elizabeth Tuder   12Sep1780   C3 W5
Charles   Charlotte Bradfield   11Feb1856   H9 W104 Gallion
Charles G.   Adaline Osborn   22Jan1849   W93
Charlotte   William Smith   22Apr1831   E69 W71   Stephenson
Christian   Margaretta Everist   23Jul1822   E56 W60
Elizabeth   John Baker   06Feb1808   E31 W40
Elizabeth   Henry F. Arnold   04Mar1829   E65 W68   Webster
[orig. lic. to Webster; cr-Harf]
Elizabeth   Peter Stredehoof   22Jan1830   E66 W69   Hewin
Elizabeth   George T. Everist   11Apr1859   W110
Ellen   George W. Courtney, Jr.   28Apr1841   E83 W84   Myers
George   Elizabeth Greenland   26Feb1838   E79 W80   Collins
Henry   Elizabeth Foster   24Sep1838   E79 W80   Collins
Hester   Peter Code   02Sep1854   H6 W101 Gallion
Isaac   Ann Stewart   22Nov1780   C3 W5
James   Jane Wilson   21May1864   W119
John   Delia Presbury   13Aug1779   B3 W2
John   Elizabeth Baker   06Feb1808   E31 W40
John H.   Sarah F. Ruff   19Jan1852   H1 W97   Gibson
Margaret   William Criswell   16Mar1843   E85 W86   Wilson
Martha   James Presbury   23Dec1800   E19 W30
Mary   Mordecai Meade   20Nov1779   E17 W28
Mary   Samuel Webster   03Aug1780   C2 W4
Mary   Israel Day   22Feb1821   E53 W58
Morris   Jane Haithhorn   20Aug1781   C5 W7
Nathan¹   Sarah Daniel   07May1781   C4 W6
Nicholas   Elizabeth Cole   06Jan1801   E19 W30
Nicholas   Elizabeth Carsins   02Nov1837   E78 W79   Colls
Nicholas   Mary B. Greenland   03Mar1856   H9 W104 Reese
Rachel   David Nelson   16Nov1780   C3 W5
Sarah Ann   Hollis Courtney   25Aug1819   E51 W56
Sophia   Taylor Gilbert   12Feb1823   E56 W61

BALDING
Anne   James Brown   04Feb1802   E21 W32

12   Harford Co. Md. Marriage Licenses, 1777-1865

BALDWIN

Anna	Thomas C. Marshall	21Sep1858		W108	
Elizabeth	Joseph Ashton	22Sep1810	E35	W44	
Elizabeth	James Ayres	06Oct1831	E69	W71	Webster
[orig. lic. to Webster; cr-Harf]					
Franklin C.	Laura C. Robinson	21Nov1863		W118	
George	Matilda Elizth Gilbert	12Nov1850		W95	
George	Lucinda A. Walker	25Sep1862		W116	
James	Ruth Ann Sheredine	18Feb1835	E75	W76	Gallion
James	Eliza Shenberger	15Feb1851		W96	
James	Sally Middleditch	18Jan1854	H5	W100	Clay
Jarrett T.	Alisann Keen	24Jan1846		W89	
Jemima	John Ellis	06May1802	E22	W32	
John S.	Rachel C. Bull	03Dec1842	E85	W85	Keech
Margaret J.	Henry C. Payne	26Dec1862		W117	
Marshal	Ruth Watters	14Mar1816	E45	W51	
Mary Ann	John Miller	02Dec1837	E78	W79	Gallion
Ruth Ann	Jacob Briney	20Aug1862		W116	
Samuel	Margarett Kaufman	25Oct1821	E54	W59	
Samuel	Frances Loflin	10Sep1838	E79	W80	Hoopman
Samuel, Jr.	Jane Beggs	15Jul1857	H12	W106	Smith
Sarah	John Deaver	14Nov1864		W120	
Sarah Ann	William Henry Keen	10Jan1849		W93	
Sarah M.	John P. Kirk	03Jan1865		W120	
Silas	Charlotte Street	06Feb1816	E44	W51	
Silas	Mary Gordan	11Feb1852	H1	W97	Robey
Timothy	Mary Ann R. Bowen	14Aug1839	E81	W82	Gallion
Tyler	Sally Keen	20Mar1806	E28	W37	
William	Catharine Middeditch	09May1849		W93	

BALEY

| Sarah | Obediah Pritchard | 22Oct1782 | C6 | W8 | |

BALIES[?]

| Ann | Ja^s Ruck | 01Sep1781 | C5 | W7 | |

BANAR

| George E. | Catharine Grant | 04Oct1852 | H2 | W98 | McNally |

BANE

| Patterson | Rebecca Luckie | 20Aug1800 | E18 | W30 | |

BANKHEAD

| James G. | Mary Demoss | 18Dec1826 | E62 | W65 | Parks |

BANKS

| Elizabeth | William Lindemore | 20Feb1864 | | W118 | |

BANNISTER

| Andrew A. W. | Eliza I/J. Ward | 31Jan1856 | H9 | W104 | Cushing |

BANNON

| Anna | Michael Hayes | 25Jul1859 | | W110 | |

Harford Co. Md. Marriage Licenses, 1777-1865   13

BARBER
Elizabeth B.	Peter F. Calary	31Jan1862	W115	
Joseph	Mary Haroneina	02Aug1851	W96	

BARCELLAY
Rachel	Elias Bailiss	29Jan1781	C4 W6	

BARCLAY [see John Barclay Scarborough]
James	Margaret Fisher	29Nov1803	E24 W34	
James F.	Mary Ann Pool	08Aug1831	E69 W71	Stephenson

BARETT
Sally	James Huggins	m. 1803		[ret-AppA]

BARLIN
Mary Ann	Kasper Smith	23Dec1837	E78 W80	Collins

BARNARD [see also BARNETT, BERNARD, BIRNARD]
J. G.	Ann Eliza Boyd	29Sep1860	W112	
Susan	John B. Botts	16Nov1840	E82 W83	Finney
Thomas P.	Henrietta Dobson	09Feb1846	W90	

BARNES
Alonzo G. W.	Frances L. J. D. Downer	12Oct1836	E77 W78	Crosgrey
Amos	Ann Catherine Mitchell	29Jan1817	E46 W52	
Amoss	Rebecca Wood	12May1782	C6 W7	
Arabella	James Thomas	01Feb1796	E8 W24	
Catherine Ann	William Elliott	10Dec1836	E77 W78	Furlong
Elisha	Ellen S.[?] Ely	10Feb1842	E84 W85	Keech
Elizabeth	John Barnes	17Mar1812	E38 W46	
Elizabeth	Thomas C. Fletcher	17Jan1837	E77 W78	Finney
Elizabeth	Jarrett Ward	03Feb1841	E83 W84	Finney
Foard	Ann Gilmore	30Nov1792	E3 W22	
Ford	Mary Gilbert	m. 1788		[ret-AppA]
Ford	Elizabeth Dutton	22Dec1806	E29 W38	
Ford	Mary Ann Osborn	01Jan1822	E55 W59	
Frances A.	Henry W. Williams	22Jan1844	E86 W87	Reese[?]
George W.	Sarah Jane Heverine	04Sep1848	W93	
Gregory	Elizabeth Osborn	m. 1788		[ret-AppA]
Harriot	William Osborn	30May1809	E34 W42	
Harriot	John Bailey	24Dec1818	E50 W56	
Henry	Sarah B. Whitaker	28Aug1822	E56 W60	
Henry	Eliza Kenley	09Sep1841	E84 W84	Wilson
Hester Ann	John B. Murphy	28Jul1843	E86 W86	Maddox
Hosea	Elizabeth Lester	06Jan1809	E33 W42	
Hosea	Mary Garretson	23Mar1812	E38 W46	
Hosea	Mary Powell	11Nov1815	E44 W50	
Hosea	Sarah Gilbert	14Dec1840	E82 W83	Finny
Hosia	Mary Wood	m. 1788		[ret-AppA]
James	Sarah Fort	22Mar1780	C1 W3	
John	Elizabeth Barnes	17Mar1812	E38 W46	
John	Eleanor Mitchell	29Apr1818	E49 W55	
John	Ann Smith	30Oct1832	E71 W73	Finney
John	Avarilla Fulton	04Feb1847	W91	

BARNES, continued

John R.	Susan H. Duvall	25Nov1839	E81 W82	Hunt[?]
Lavina	John Richie	26Dec1808	E33 W41	
Lydia	Benedict Hanson	24Sep1829	E66 W69	McGee
Margaret	Falix Welsh	27May1781	C5 W6	
Margaret	Henry Ruff Gilbert	29Dec1814	E42 W49	
Martha	Wm. Finney Hanna	29Dec1863	W118	
Mary	James Everett	26Oct1782	C6 W8	
Mary	Asael Bailey	29Feb1808	E31 W40	
Mary	James Stellings	10Mar1813	E40 W47	
Mary	Shadrach Bailey	15Jul1835	E75 W76	Finney
Mordecai	Sarah Bailey	29Dec1817	E48 W54	
Rachael	Aquila Bailey	m. 1787		[ret-AppA]
Rachel	Alex. Ford	m. 1789		[ret-AppA]
Rebecca	George Veazy	05Feb1813	E39 W47	
Rebecca	Edward Evans	03Nov1818	E49 W55	
Richard	Sarah Kidd	17Dec1782	C6 W8	
Richard	Mary Myers	27Sep1808	E32 W41	
Richard	Mary Bayless	22Feb1812	E38 W46	
Richard	Susanna Osborn	21Jan1832	E70 W72	Finney
Richard A.	Mary F. Noble	13Mar1861	W113	
Robert A.	Avarilla Gilbert	28May1846	W90	
Rosa	Chas. Frederick Egidius Schultz	07Oct1853	H4 W100	McNally
Ruth	Wm Williams	m. 1778		[ret-AppA]
Sallie E.	James Hopper	28Jan1861	W113	
Sarah	Thomas Cowan	m. 1790		[ret-AppA]
Sarah	Thomas Knight	20Jan1804	E24 W34	
Sarah	Gerard Bailey	15Jun1824	E58 W62	
Sarah A.	Aquila E. Tredway	13Jun1855	H7 W103	Finney
Sophia	Ephraim Arnold	20Dec1814	E42 W49	
William	Margaret Armstrong	m. 1787		[ret-AppA]
William	Ann Johns	12Mar1813	E40 W47	

BARNET [see Barnet Harper, Barnet Johnson]

George	Annetta Miller	27Jun1828	E65 W67	Keeck
[orig. lic. to Keeck, 28Jun1828; cr-Harf]				
John	Elizabeth Hill	m. 1777		[ret-AppA]

BARNETT [see Barnett Clark; see also BARNARD, BURNETT]

Charles	Ann Burton	24Mar1795	E7 W24	
James, Junr	Margaret Rigbie	04Nov1805	E27 W36	
Joanna	Hugh Johnson	08Jun1822	E55 W60	
John A.	Elizabeth Fullard	01Feb1834	E73 W75	Parke

BARNEY

John Holland	Margaret Webster	05Nov1825	E60 W64	Finney

BARNHOUSE

Mary	Thomas Stroud	16Mar1779	B1 W1	

BARNS
Adelia	Alexander Jeffery	07Apr1802	E22 W32	
Elen	William F. Evans	22Jan1838	E78 W80	Finney
Emily W.	Samuel H. Reasin	17Mar1841	E83 W84	Myers
Margaret	Benjamin Everest	12Feb1800	E17 W29	

BARR
Alexander W.	Margaret Forsyth	19Dec1840	E82 W83	Finney

BARRETT
Abner [? Burrett]	Martha Long	15Dec1821	E55 W59	
Ann [? Barrelt]	Will. Harris	m. 1778		[ret-AppA]
Elijah W.	Mary Smith	14Nov1826	E62 W65	Stephenson
[gr surname uncertain]				
Hannah	Thomas Smith	02Jun1802	E22 W32	
Rachel	John Hasson	m. 1795		[ret-AppA]

BARRON
Cornelia E.	Charles Cooley	04Jan1837	E77 W78	Furlong
Cornelia E.	George J. Johnson	15Jan1859	W109	
John	Sarah Hanson	10Dec1822	E56 W60	
Lewis H.	Sarah Parker	25May1855	H7 W102	Finney
Merrick	Emely Singleton	08Sep1828	E65 W68	Finney
William	Ann Matilda Johnson	09May1854	H5 W101	Reese

BARROW
Elizabeth	Thomas Johnson	07Dec1852	H2 W98	Robey
Harriet S.	James Bull	05Apr1842	E85 W85	Brown
James S.	Eliza W. Bull	24Jan1854	H5 W100	Cronin
John	Elizabeth Forwood	22Apr1817	E47 W53	
John H.	Margaret S. Smith	19Jan1854	H5 W100	Dumm
Martha Ann	Jacob F. Johnson	01Jan1851	W96	

BARTLEY
Elizabeth	Henry Myers	23Oct1816	E46 W52

BARTOL
Elizabeth	Joseph Sherley	22Feb1813	E40 W47	
George	Mary Baylis	05Jul1803	E23 W34	
George	Sarah Bayless	17Jun1818	E49 W55	
Harriet	John Walker	18May1825	E60 W63	Finney
Mary	Chas B. Hitchcock	18Dec1841	E84 W85	Finney
Nancy	Cornelius Chandlee	31Dec1808	E33 W41	

BARTON
Alisanna	John Lee	01Jun1837	E78 W79	Hofman
Amelia	Hugh Young	22Dec1806	E29 W38	
Caroline	Elijah Preston	11Feb1852	H1 W97	Cadden
Caroline E.	John W. Ely	12Nov1860	W112	
[repeat, same page, but issued 15Nov1860]				
Elizabeth	William Miller	11Feb1818	E48 W54	
Elizabeth	John Bell	04Feb1834	E73 W75	Finney
James	Sarah Preston	26Apr1819	E51 W56	
James	Susan Ann Stritehoof	23May1854	H5 W101	Finney

16   Harford Co. Md. Marriage Licenses, 1777-1865

BARTON, continued
Jemima	Thomas Preston	19Nov1817	E48 W54	
Joshua	Mary Amoss	18Apr1782	C6 W7	
Keziah	Elijah Heape	13Aug1822	E56 W60	
Mary	William Heaton	18Jun1809	E34 W42	
Philip A.	Elizabeth B. Norton ["B" crossed out]	03Feb1803	E23 W33	[ret-AppA]
Sarah	Thomas Allender	m. 1803		[ret-AppA]
Sarah Ann	Thomas Williams	18Nov1840	E82 W83	Finney
Susanna	John Heaton	13Nov1816	E46 W52	
Thomas	Hannah Low	18Feb1835	E75 W76	Gallion
William	Elizabeth Heaps	24Jun1819	E51 W56	

BARTONSLADE
Peen	Sarah McCulben	m. 1803	[ret-AppA]

BAT--
Sarah	Richard Butler	29Dec1792	E3 W22

BATEMAN
Elizabeth	John Nevill	09Nov1818	E50 W55	
Joseph E.	Margaret S. Prigg	20Mar1843	E85 W86	Finney
Sarah	Richard Dunn	14Jan1795	E6 W24	
Sarah E. B.	Jones Davidson	18Nov1854	H6 W101	McNally
Samuel H.	Elizabeth W. Neville	19Dec1853	H4 W100	Dumb
Thomas B.	Sarah Neville	02Jan1849	W93	
William B.	Susan J. Worthington	07Dec1813	E41 W48	
William B.	Sarah Birckhead	08Feb1822	E55 W60	

BAUER [see also BOWER]
John	Sarah Jane Claydon	08Feb1862	W115

BAUGHMAN
Margaret	George Webb	05Nov1798	E15 W27

BAXTER
Agness	Ralph Ecoff	07Aug1811	E37 W45	
Ann	James Magnes	24Dec1799	E17 W29	
Charity	William Hughes	15Feb1828	E64 W67	O'Brien
Elizabeth	Richard Ayres	10Oct1803	E24 W34	[ret-AppA]
James A.	Emely A. Hall	29May1828	E64 W67	McKay
John	Harriott A. Cord	18May1826	E61 W65	Richardson
Mary	James Tredway	23Mar1808	E31 W40	
Mary J/I.	George W. Beaver	12Oct1853	H4 W100	Lemmon
Rebecca	William Buckingham	16Mar1826	E61 W65	Richardson
Sarah	Thomas Stockdale	18Dec1797	E13 W26	John Coleman
Sarah	William Griffen	31Dec1810	E36 W44	
Sarah H. [may be 18 Dec]	Edwin T. Deaver	17Dec1854	H6 W101	Lemmon
Susanna	William Pyle, Junr	07Oct1811	E37 W45	
William	Sarah Ecoff	08Dec1813	E41 W48	
William S.	Sarah J. Knight	06Aug1855	H8 W103	Lemmon

BAY

Ann H.	Arthur Manahan	19Feb1817	E46 W53	
Charles Henry	Rebecca Jane Cairnes	27Jan1858	W108	
Daniel	Casandra Amoss	11Apr1827	E62 W66	Park
Elizth	Wm Cooley	07Jul1784	C9 W9	
George	Ann Kennady	13Jan1802	E21 W32	
George	Ann Herbert	16Nov1808	E32 W41	
Hugh	Sarah Turner	01Mar1785	C10 W10	
Hugh	Sarah Fullard	25Apr1820	E52 W57	
Hugh	Laura Louisa Ramsay	13Jan1857	H11 W105	Crafford
John	Jemima Streett	12Nov1828	E65 W68	Finney
Kennedy	Mary A. Enfield	28Mar1865	W121	
Mary Ann	Benjamin Wakeland	29Dec1821	E55 W59	
Mary Ann	George Cairnes, Jnr	05Apr1836	E76 W77	Morrison
Mary Ann	John T. Streett	24Nov1858	W109	
Mary Jane	Jacob Love	25Mar1848	W92	
Sarah	Arthur Heeps	06Nov1781	C5 W7	
Sarah Jane	Thomas R. Stewart	17Jun1846	W90	
Thomas	Asenith Ann McClure	26Mar1822	E55 W60	
William	Ruth McCandless	19Jan1808	E31 W40	
William	Sarah Foster	24Jun1823	E57 W61	
William	Elizabeth McFadden	01Mar1847	W91	
William	Laura McFadden	17Apr1865	W121	

BAYARD [see also BIARDS, BYARD]

(widow)	Thomas Davis	17Nov1860	W112

BAYLES

Elizabeth	Garshom Silvers	25Jan1803	E23 W33
Harriot	Timothy Keen	23Sep1802	E22 W33
Zephaniah	Mary Silvers	07Sep1802	E22 W32

BAYLESS [see also BAILESS, BAILISS, BALIES, BAYLES, BAYLIS]

Asael	Mary Gorrell	24Feb1820	E52 W57	
Augustin	Pamelia Brown	05Jan1784	C8 W9	
George H.	Sarah Ann Thompson	21May1859	W110	
John B.	Aurelia Botts	16Apr1814	E41 W49	
John B.	Elizabeth H. Hall	29Jul1826	E61 W65	Keech
Mary	Richard Barnes	22Feb1812	E38 W46	
Mary	Aquila Wiles	08Dec1829	E66 W69	Finney
Samuel	Mary F. Silver	27Apr1833	E72 W74	Finney
Samuel	Elizabeth Botts	08Jan1842	E84 W85	Myers
Sarah	George Bartol	17Jun1818	E49 W55	
Wm F.	Ellen Brooke	28Nov1842	E85 W85	Finney
William F.	Sarah E. Hanna	31May1853	H4 W99	Finney
William F.	Cornelia Forsythe	28Dec1858	W109	

BAYLEY

Hannah	James Hannah	--Apr1782	C5 W7

BAYLIS

Elizabeth	Lemuel Kenley	07Dec1797	E13	W26	Jno Davis
Hetebila	James McConkie	05Nov1795	E8	W24	
Mary	George Bartol	05Jul1803	E23	W34	
Sarah	Amos Gilbert	18Jan1804	E24	W34	

BAYNE

Ann	Joshua Hartlay	19Feb1798	E13	W27	Jno Allen

BEAGNAR

Anna	Adam Pratt	01Mar1847		W91
Anna	George Ricdkert	7Dec1847		W92

BEALE

Martha A.	Ezekiel Mathews	29Oct1855	H8	W103	Smith

BEAN

Elizabeth	William Bell	22Dec1804	E25	W35

BEANS

Elias H.	Susan N. Cunningham	31Mar1852	H2	W98	Bosworth

BEAR

Elizabeth	Peter Murray	26Jan1805	E26	W36

BEARD

Samuel	Lehemiah Taylor	m. 1777	[ret-AppA]

BEATTY [see also BAITY]

Ann	James Whiteford	17Mar1826	E61	W65	Ewing
Eliza	Zadock Gorrell	02Mar1826	E61	W64	Finney
Fair	Isabella Fisher	16May1785	C10	W10	
Martha	George Chalk	11Apr1850		W94	
Sarah	Joshua Glenn	21Jan1818	E48	W54	

BEATY

Arch[d]	Fra[s] Fancit	18Apr1783	C7	W8	cr-Harf
Hannah	John Kirk	29May1812	E38	W46	
James	Catharine Demos	22Apr1806	E28	W38	
Jamima	James McComas	27Dec1825	E60	W64	Ewing
Jane	James Hollis	02Jun1795	E7	W24	

BEAUMONT

Anna Eliza	Joel H. Hays	19Sep1859		W110	
Elias	Matilda Holland	30Oct1854	H6	W101	Smith
Hiram	Cecilia Norris	02May1854	H5	W101	Finney
Mifflin	Mary Lake	05Mar1821	E54	W58	

BEAUZAMY

Sophia	Peter Guichard	06Nov1805	E27	W36

BEAVER

George W.	Mary J/I. Baxter	12Oct1853	H4	W100	Lemmon

Harford Co. Md. Marriage Licenses, 1777-1865   19

BECK
John	Mary Johnson	12Sep1780	C3	W5	
Mary E.	Wilhelm Adam	15May1857	H12	W106	Monroe
Matthew	Sarah Roberts	02Dec1778	B1	W1	

BECKINGHAM
| Elizabeth B. | George Preston | 21Jun1858 | | W108 | |

BEDFORD
| Nelson | Elizabeth A. Conner | 22May1849 | | W93 | |

BEEMAN
| Susan S. | James C. Robinson | 02Oct1863 | | W118 | |
| Thomas J/I. | Mary L. Bolton | 07Apr1854 | H5 | W100 | Bolton |

BEGGS
| Jane | Samuel Baldwin, Jr. | 15Jul1857 | H12 | W106 | Smith |

BELL
Agnes	Robert McClung	20Feb1817	E46	W53	
David	Eleanor Weir	10Mar1801	E19	W30	
Elizabeth	John Gorrel	22Jun1830	E67	W70	Finney
Elizabeth	Mathias Riffle	11Jan1831	E68	W70	Stephenson
Elizabeth	Robert McClung	20Nov1847		W92	
Jane	James Amoss	20Feb1798	E13	W27	
Jane	Lyttleton Green	20Sep1845	E88	W89	
John	Grace Luckie	18Aug1800	E18	W29	
John	Elizabeth Barton	04Feb1834	E73	W75	Finney
Margaret	John Cloman	21Nov1821	E54	W59	
Mary	Alexander Massey	14Oct1818	E49	W55	
Mary	Andrew Boyd	20Dec1823	E57	W62	
Mary Ann	Henry Whittemore	20Nov1821	E54	W59	
Robert	Elizabeth Cooley	27Jul1818	E49	W55	
William	Emily Willey	06Jan1818	E48	W54	
William	Elizabeth Bean	22Dec1804	E25	W35	

BELTON
| Sophia | William H. Orchard | 29Apr1834 | E74 | W75 | Orchard |

BENJAMIN
| Margaret | Frederick Ford | 04Jun1781 | C5 | W6 | |
| William | Sarah Dunn | 31Jul1815 | E43 | W50 | |

BENNET
| Philip | Sarah Gilbert | 04Jun1795 | E7 | W24 | |
| Rachel | Harris York | 29Dec1818 | E50 | W56 | |

BENNETT
Ann	Edward York	06Feb1817	E46	W53	
Eli	Mary Taylor	16Feb1819	E50	W56	
John	Grace Cashmore	11Apr1809	E33	W42	
John E.	Eliz. J. Zimmerman	16Feb1863		W117	
Paymelia	William Brown	04Jun1817	E47	W53	
Rebecca	John Swift	30Dec1830	E68	W70	
Sarah	James McGaw	09Aug1806	E28	W38	

BENNINGTON

Jeremiah	Mary Thompson	17Sep1818	E49	W55
Sarah	Stephen Jones	29Apr1779	B2	W1
Wm	Isabella Willson	12Jan1779	B1	W1

BENSON

Benjamin	Temperance Price	28Mar1812	E38	W46
Jesse	Martha Griffith	09Nov1813	E40	W48

BENTON

Lemuel	Sarah E. Knight	28Mar1853	H3	W99	Bull

BERNARD

Harriet	Joseph Saunders	04Apr1847		W91
Henrietta	John Poplar	09Mar1858		W108

BERRY

Laura	Thomas Henry Smith	09Feb1865		W120
Mary	Moses Smith	08Jan1795	E6	W24

BESHANG

John	Elizth Rodgers	13May1783	C7	W8	cr-Harf

BESLER

Charles S. M.	Christine Seemann	06Jan1845	E87	W88	[--]

BEVARD

Charles	Amelia Chance	01Feb1798	E13	W27	
George	Mary Ann Wallis	22May1820	E52	W57	
James	Rachael Jones	m. 1778			[ret-AppA]
James	Alizanna Brannan	16Mar1832	E70	W72	Keech
Susannah	Thomas Ellett	09Oct1780	C3	W5	

BEVIN

Sarah	James Fisher	25Mar1806	E28	W37

BIARDS

Elizabeth	Thomas Wright	24Feb1824	E58	W62

BIAYS [see Sarah Biays Stump]

BIDDLE

Richard	Delilah Carroll	31Mar1801	E20	W31

BIDISON

Jeremiah	Sarah Strong	16Mar1802	E21	W32

BIGGS [see also BEGGS]

Lettice	David Swift	23Feb1796	E8	W25

BILLINGSLEA [see Billingslea Bull]

Charlton W.	Sarah A. Harryman	20May1837	E77	W79	Collins
Mary	John Williams	01Jan1806	E27	W37	
Mary Ann	Ebenezer N. Allen	02Dec1823	E57	W61	

BILLINGSLEA, continued

Mary Ann	James Wann	06Feb1832	E70	W72	Keech
Rebecca	Nathan Chamberlain	26Dec1844	E87	W88	Jones
Sarah	Thomas Ward	05Oct1863		W118	
Sarah A.	James Stephenson	03Nov1845		W89	
Sarah R.	William C. Billingslea	28Nov1853	H4	W100	Trout
Susan E.	John W. Norris	14Jan1860		W111	
Victoria	John Palmer, Jr.	16Jan1860		W111	
Walter	Frances Carr	25Apr1810	E35	W43	
William	Elizabeth Waltham	16Nov1802	E22	W33	
William	Amanda E. Taylor	26Jun1839	E81	W82	Prettyman
William C.	Sarah R. Billingslea	28Nov1853	H4	W100	Trout

BILLINGSLEY

Elizth	William Ewing	10Dec1784	C9	W10
James	Elizabeth Mathews	11Sep1797	E11	W26
Walter	Clemency Preston	26Jan1782	C5	W7

BINNS

Thomas Nelson	Amelia Durham	23Jan1795	E6	W24

BIRCKHEAD

Ann	John Massey	24Nov1798	E15	W27	
Eliza	James Reardan	06Oct1817	E47	W54	
Hannah	Elisha Osborn	30Jul1804	E25	W35	
Mathew	Charlotte E. Wetherall	18Oct1815	E43	W50	
Samuel H.	Sarah Rouse	13Jan1834	E73	W75	Dunahay
Sarah	William B. Bateman	08Feb1822	E55	W60	

BIRD

Cassandra	Rich'd. G. Smith	11Apr1865	W121

BIRMINGHAM

L. M.	Alverda Hawkins	10Jan1859		W109
Mary	John Garrison	08Jan1812	E37	W45

BIRNARD

Elizabeth	John Robinson	30Dec1844	E87	W88	Rha--

BISSELL

Lizzie R.	William S. Richardson	08Feb1864	W118

BLACK

George	Grace Brown	23Nov1779	C1	W3
Saml	Jane Johnson	03Oct1781	C5	W7

BLACKBURN

Catherine	William Andrew	26Feb1780	C1	W3	
John	Mary Kirkpatrick	m. 1778			[ret-AppA]

BLACKSTON

Isaac	Mary Harper	09Jan1816	E44	W51

BLAIR

James	Elizabeth Gibson	07Oct1806	E29	W38

BLAKE

Catharine	Isaac Whitaker	18Mar1848		W92
Catharine	George Ward	07Mar1859		W110
Ellen E.	John S. Stonebraker	10Jan1859		W109
John	Catherine Duff	19Feb1822	E55	W60
John M.	Martha Ann O'Donnell	09Feb1861		W113
Mary Ann	William Henry Judd	27Dec1849		W94
Sarah	Thomas Brooks	16Jul1798	E15	W27
Sarah	Marshall Lee	12Jan1799	E15	W27

BLANCHER

Peter	Mary Ross	04Apr1780	C1	W3

BLANEY

Ann	Moses St Clair	28Sep1809	E34	W43	
Ann	Francis S. Everist	30Dec1823	E57	W62	
Ann	John McGuigan	15Oct1838	E79	W81	Finney
Cecelia	Francis F. Upp	30Sep1850		W95	
Charles K.	Mary E. Herman	09Aug1864		W119	
Eliza Jane	Lawson Hobbs	13Nov1860		W112	
Elizabeth	Zenos Chocke	05Mar1813	E40	W47	
John	Elizabeth Tippet	29Jun1810	E35	W44	
Josias	Mary Street	07Dec1800	E19	W30	
Louisa R.	Daniel Kenly	15Feb1845	E88	W88	Billup
Mary	Thomas St Clair	03Jul1800	E18	W29	
Ruth	Abraham Weir	27Jun1807	E30	W39	
Sarah	John R. Stokes	20May1839	E81	W82	Park
William J.	Julia Ann Streett	05Apr1842	E85	W85	Wilson

BLESSING

Christian	Sarah Wilgis	07Aug1856	H10	W105 Cushing

BOARDSMAN

Ann	Elijah Mitchell	01Jun1795	E7	W24

BOARMAN

Caroline	Stansbury Gallion	20Mar1821	E54	W59	
Catherine	Henry Bussey	28Mar1837	E77	W79	Coskey
Edward A.	Charity Quinlan	12Feb1857	H11	W106	Walter
Eleanora	John Roussey	17Oct1846		W90	
Franklin	Frances E. Holland	01Jun1865		W121	
Louisa M.	Otho Scott	29Oct1823	E57	W61	
Maria L.	Edward Forward	02Sep1857	H12	W107	Brown
Mary Ann	Joseph Moore	21Apr1828	E64	W67	O'Brien
Priscilla	William Bailey	29May1849		W94	
Robert	Elizabeth Wheeler	13Oct1835	E75	W77	Crausgay
Sarah E.	John Robinson	07Jun1831	E69	W71	Wheeler

BODDEN

Catherine	John Travis	27Feb1817	E46	W53

BODNUM

Sarah	William G. Procter	02Aug1827	E63	W66

BOHMER				
Henry	Jane P. Durham	[?]02Apr1850	W94	

BOLDON				
Robert	Mary Ann Allender	16Nov1858	W109	

BOLSTER				
Thomas	Emm. Avarilla Spencer	11Dec1821	E55 W59	
William	Frances Hollis	05Jun1809	E34 W42	
William	Susan Wilson	27Jan1818	E48 W54	

BOLTON [see also BOLDON]

Hannah Bond	Isaac Thomas Murphy	20Dec1848	W93	
Mary L.	Thomas J/I. Beeman	07Apr1854	H5 W100	
Robert	Margaret B. Allen	28Jul1828	E65 W68	McGee

BONAR				
Eliza	Saml McFaddin	m. 1778		[ret-AppA]
James	Agness Baker	01Apr1784	C8 W9	cr-Harf
William	Elizabeth Grifeth	30May1780	C2 W4	

BOND [see Hannah Bond Bolton]

Abigal	Joshua Everist	03Dec1805	E27 W37	
Alesana	Ralph Lee	31Jan1805	E26 W36	
Ann	David Abbitt	04Sep1783	C7 W9	cr-Salim Co.
Ann	John A. Munnikhuysen	15Dec1829	E66 W69	Richardson
Ann Maria	William Wood	29Jan1798	E13 W27	
Benjamin R.	Susan C. Bond	22Nov1831	E70 W71	Richardson
Dennis	Polly Merryman	m. 1787		[ret-AppA]
Eliza	Robert W. Holland	21Feb1822	E55 W60	
Elizabeth	Samuel Martin	01Feb1860	W111	
Francis A.	Rachel Cassandra Webster	26Oct1859	W111	
Hannah	William Allen	12Apr1798	E13 W27	Jno. Allen
Harriott	Caleb Pue	23Apr1822	E55 W60	
Howard B.	Priscilla E. Munnikhuysen	14Jan1861	W113	
Isabella	William Nurse	03Sep1840	E82 W83	Prettiman
James	Mary Green	03Jul1832	E71 W73	Sewell
Jane	Samuel Bradford	21Jul1803	E23 W34	[ret-AppA]
John	Catharine Devin	06Sep1791	E1 W21	
John of Saml	Cynthia Richardson	18Jan1794	E5 W23	
John of W^m.	Mary Richardson	27May1802	E22 W32	[ret-AppA]
Joshua B.	Mary Ann Howard	22Feb1831	E68 W70	Richardson
Margaretta	John Hambleton	17Jun1793	E4 W22	
Martha	William Smith	24Apr1780	C2 W4	
Mary Ann	Thomas T. Bond	22Nov1821	E54 W59	
Meriken	Ann Maxwell	13Jun1807	E30 W39	
Nancy	Soloman	30May1837	E78 W79	Keech
Patience	Henry Waters	[?]17May1793	E4 W22	
Samuel L.	Elizabeth Smithson	07Jan1834	E73 W75	Porter
Susan	Edward Brinton	03Apr1811	E36 W44	
Susan C.	Benjamin R. Bond	22Nov1831	E70 W71	Richardson
Teresa	Mordecai Hammond	18Oct1815	E43 W50	
Thomas	Sarah Y. Scott	27Jan1806	E27 W37	

BOND, continued

Thomas T.	Mary Ann Bond	22Nov1821	E54	W59	
Thomas W.	Sarah Allen	01Apr1834	E74	W75	Dunahy
William B.	Charlotte H. Richardson	20Apr1837	E77	W79	Richardson
Zacheus O.	Mary Ann Lee	27Sep1804	E25	W35	
Zacheus Onion	Cassandra Lee Morgan	19Jan1797	E11	W26	
[returned by Rev. John Coleman - see AppA]					

BONER
Jas   Mary Stewart   01Mar1779 B1 W1

BONFIELD [see Bonfield Gorrell, Robert Bonfield Gorrell]

BONIS
Rose Ann   Amos Spencer   11Sep1840 E82 W83 Finney

BONNER
John   Margaret Saunders   24Sep1825 E60 W64 Tidings

BOOMER
Jane   John Middleditch   08Nov1856 H10 W105 Wilson

BOOTH
William   Fanny Paul   18Jun1856 H10 W105 Smith

BOOZER
George   Harriet Rhodes   23Jul1827 E63 W66 Richardson

BORDAN
Susan   Nicholas Smith   03Nov1838 E80 W81 Coskey

BORNEMEN
Augustus   Mary Smith   20Oct1860   W112

BOSLEY

Allesana	Robert Crawford	14Sep1802	E22 W33	
Ann	Edwd N. Tyrell	22Dec1835	E76 W77	Parks
Elizabeth	Jesse Jarrett	29Mar1804	E25 W35	
Elizabeth	William Heaton	13Jan1827	E62 W65	Rockhold
Elizabeth	John Gammill	28Sep1830	E68 W70	Parks
Ellen	John Pain	12May1834	E74 W75	Parks
Joseph C.	Ann Wiley	13Feb1847	W91	
Lucretia	Thomas P. Smithson	12Feb1849	W93	
Susannah	James St. Clair	12Jun1797	E11 W26	[ret-AppA]

BOTTS

Asael	Susan Daugherty	21Nov1853	H4 W100	Gallion
Aurelia	John B. Bayles	16Apr1814	E41 W49	
Avarilla	William Edwd Jewings	05Jan1852	H1 W97	
Clemency	Nathaniel Leithiser	31Jul1860	W112	
Elizabeth	Asael Pritchard	06Jan1825	E59 W63	Finney
Elizabeth	Samuel Bayless	08Jan1842	E84 W85	Myers
Isaac	Sarah Herring	14Jun1824	E58 W62	
Jacob	Jane Smith	21Feb1781	C4 W6	

BOTTS, continued

James	Ann Hughes	21Feb1803	E23 W33	
John	Harriett Amanda Keen	08Apr1845	E88 W88	Dulaney
John	Lizzie Morris	09Nov1864	W120	
John B.	Susan Barnard	16Nov1840	E82 W83	Finney
Mary	Joshua Wood	21May1779	B2 W2	
Sarah	Geo. Stevenson	05Oct1791	E1 W21	
Sarah	Archabald Darrah	12May1828	E64 W67	Finney
Sarah	John Smith	21Jun1859	W110	
Sarah Ann	James W. Keen	19Mar1855	H7 W102	Gallion

BOULDIN

Eliza R.	William Galloway	22Mar1848	W92	
Isabella V.	James R. Cadden	01Apr1865	W121	
Mary Amanda	Nicholas B. Holland	27Nov1854	H6 W101	Smith
Sarah Ann	Hugh Mooney	13Apr1844	E87 W87	Alexander
William	Sarah J/I. Johnson	13Oct1847	W91	
William	Harriet B. Maulsby	13Oct1852	H2 W98	Keech

BOUNCE

Rachel	Daniel Dorsey Spencer	28Aug1862	W116

BOWAN

John	Sarah Anderson	13Dec1784	C9 W10

BOWAR

Julia	John Hartman	05Mar1855	H7 W102 Cronin

BOWEN

Belinda	Samuel J. Ricketts	28Jan1858	W108	
Elisha	Cathrine Spince	10Dec1783	C8 W9	cr-Harf
Elizabeth	John Thomas Riley	20Sep1862	W116	
George	Sarah Elizth Charshe	10Dec1849	W94	
George	Elizabeth J/I. Jones	29May1857	H12 W106	Sills[?]
Henry	Mary Divers	12Jun1817	E47 W53	
James	Mary Elizabeth Hawkins	17Jun1828	E65 W67	Finney
John H.	Cordelia Ford	26Dec1854	H6 W102	Dumm
Margaret	Moses Wood	28Jan1803	E23 W33	
Mary Ann R.	Timothy Baldwin	14Aug1839	E81 W82	Gallion
Mary Rebecca	James Herman Charshe	03Jun1850	W95	
Phoebe W.	William P. Foard	29Dec1855	H9 W103	Cushing
Rebecca	William Miller	09Mar1815	E43 W49	
Robert	Elizabeth Morrison	17Oct1816	E46 W52	
Susan	Carvill T. Gilbert	10Feb1845	E88 W88	Pennell
William	Charlotte Maxwell	12Jan1819	E50 W56	
William	Rebecca A. Divers	09Oct1854	H6 W101	Dumm

BOWER [see also BAUER, BOWRE, BOWYER]

William	Elizth Thompson	20Jun1782	C6 W8

BOWERS

John	Hannah Bromwell	03Nov1793	E5 W23

BOWIE
Thomas F.   Virginia Griffith   21Jul1855 H8 W103 Crampton

BOWLER
Nancy   Henry Dearholt   11Dec1811 E37 W45
Peter   Sus Cowan   03Jan1784 C8 W9   cr-Harf

BOWMAN [see also BAUGHMAN]
Caroline   James Whitelock   02Nov1842 E85 W85 Gallion
Eliza   George Gray   07Feb1848   W92
Eliza S.   William T. Spencer   18Jun1853 H4 W99 Gallion
Henry   Priscilla Keen   28Jun1820 E52 W58
Henry C.   Mary Ann Swartz   24May1852 H2 W98 Gibson
Israel   Elizabeth Day   31Jan1801 E19 W30
John   Ann Baker   15Aug1821 E54 W59
John   Rebecca Jane Bowman   09Jun1857 H12 W106 Gallion
Rachel   James B. Gallion   30Nov1841 E84 W85 Gallion
Rebecca Jane   John Bowman   09Jun1857 H12 W106 Gallion
Robert   Mary Wheeler   01Feb1796 E8 W24
William S.   Mary Bailey   26Jan1846   W89

BOWRE
Robert   Mary A. McComas   04Dec1849   W94

BOWYER [see Bowyer Grace]
Mary   John Carter   04Jun1783 C7 W8
Thomas   Ann Calwell   04Jan1803 E23 W33

BOYCE [see Boyce Cowan]

BOYD
Alexander   Eleanor Sluby   20Aug1812 E38 W46
Andrew   Mary Bell   20Dec1823 E57 W62
Ann Eliza   J. G. Barnard   29Sep1860   W112
Cooper   Milcha Taylor   22Feb1821 E53 W58
John   Avarilla Mitchell   09Jan1797 E10 W25
John C.   Martha J. Farmer   24Mar1829 E65 W68 Keech
Louisa A.   William Edward McGaw   13Feb1862   W115
Martha   William Dinsmore   25Oct1838 E79 W81 Hoopman
Mary C.   Washington P. Chew   09Nov1840 E82 W83 Finney
Nicholas   Rachel Scarbrough   06Jan1819 E50 W56
Patrick   Susan McFeely   22Jul1851   W96
Sarah   Richard Ward, Jr.   15Jan1820 E52 W57
Stephen   Eliza C. Stump   15Feb1821 E53 W58
Thomas   Sarah Jackson   07Sep1826 E61 W65 Stephenson
William   Mary Gibson   11Feb1834 E74 W75 Higby

BOYER
Augustine   Sabina Hall   15Jan1793 E3 W22 [ret-AppA]

BOYL
Catherine   John Laughry   06Feb1826 E61 W64 O'Brian

BOYLE
Elizabeth	William Chambers	06Nov1799	E16 W28	
Patrick	Hannah Cromwell	20Jan1830	E66 W69	O'brian

BRADBERRY
John T. [before 9May]	Mary Reasin	--May1857	H12 W106	Monroe

BRADENBAUGH
Jacob	Dorcas Ayres	12Jun1811	E36 W45	
Jacob	Margaret Guyton	09Jun1837	E78 W79	Collins
Jacob	Elizabeth Ann Almony	01Jan1839	E80 W81	Finney
Thomas	Margret Ellitt	17Mar1838	E79 W80	Croft

BRADFIELD
Charlotte	Charles Baker	11Feb1856	H9 W104	Gallion
George	Martha Rebecca Shaw	19Aug1857	H12 W107	Gallion
James	Eliza Jane Courtney	27Oct1849	W94	
James	Hannah Hughes	04Feb1856	H9 W104	Reineck
John	Mary Charshee	06Dec1855	H8 W103	Smith
Mary	Richard Dever	08Apr1848	W92	
William	Mary Fox	13Aug1840	E82 W83	Dulaney

BRADFORD
Ann	Robert Bradford	20Mar1817	E46 W53	
Caroline	William Wiley	15Jun1836	E76 W78	Smith
Cecelia A.	William C. Cunningham	01Mar1831	E68 W71	Tippet
Charles H.	Frances Priscilla Drew	09Apr1833	E72 W73	Higbee
Geo.	Margt Talbott	20Apr1784	C8 W9	
George	Susanna McComas	23May1801	E20 W31	
George	Jane Mather	11Dec1804	E25 W35	
Hannah	Joshua Wood	08Jan1813	E39 W47	
Henry H.	Anna W. Sheckle	21Jun1865	W121	
John	Louisa Hutchins	19May1847	W91	
Mary	Henry Watters	31Dec1800	E19 W30	
Rebecca J.	Gabriel A. McComas	11Nov1834	E74 W76	Keech
Robert	Ann Bradford	20Mar1817	E46 W53	
Samuel	Jane Bond	21Jul1803	E23 W34	[ret-AppA]
Sarah	Nicholas Allender	26Jun1797	E11 W26	
Susannah	Nathaniel McComas	05Jun1800	E18 W29	
Wm	Margt Richardson	m. 1778		[ret-AppA]
William	Susan Drew	26Jun1811	E36 W45	
William	Eliza Fullerton	15May1817	E47 W53	

BRADICKS
Elizabeth	William Hutchins	24Feb1802	E21 W32

BRADLEE
Edward	Clare Rutledge	17Mar1784	C8 W9

BRADLEY
John	Elizabeth Gormly	01May1852	H2 W98	McNally
Mary	Patrick Kearney	24Sep1852	H2 W98	McNally
Matilda	Edward McDermody	15Sep1848	W93	

BRADLEY, continued

Michael	Bridget Kearney	24Apr1857	H11	W106	Walter
Patrick	Annestasia Quinn	28Oct1856	H10	W105	Walter
William	Rebecca Stallings	24Dec1801	E21	W31	
William	Ann Golligher	23Nov1857	H13	W107	Foley

BRADY

Francis	Maria Connelly	30Nov1850		W95	
James	Mary Curry	08Nov1837	E78	W79	Crosgay

BRAMBELL

William	Frances Saunders	21Nov1839	E81	W82	Prettyman

BRAMBLE

Ann O.	Alex. Gray	16Jan1863		W117	
Mrs. Eliza	John Glaum	03May1855	H7	W102	Cushing
John	E. Martin	02Mar1852	H2	W98	Norris
Mary	William Saunders	20Jan1836	E76	W77	Richardson
Nathan	Mary Foard	24Feb1831	E68	W70	Tippet
Rebecca	Parker Magness	17Feb1853	H3	W99	Robey
Sophia	J. Thomas Ward	12May1857	H12	W106	Cushing

BRAND

William F.	Sophia McHenry Hall	23May1843	E86	W86	Whittingham

BRANDT

Mary J/I.	Ruthen G. Maxwell	17Jan1853	H3	W99	Sanks

BRANNAN

Alizanna	James Bevard	16Mar1832	E70	W72	Keech
Biddy	Michael Christy	15Apr1854	H5	W101	McNally
Elizabeth	George Tollinger	03Feb1854	H5	W100	Gallion
Hannah	Samuel Pathre	28Mar1864		W119	
Laura	Stump Smith	15Dec1862		W116	
Matilda	Patrick McClenahan	04Jan1853	H3		McNally
[this license crossed out]					
Matilda	Solomon Robinson	29Jul1854	H6	W101	Keech
Sally Ann	Amos Miller	23Feb1865		W120	
William	Ann Coale	16Jan1822	E55	W60	

BRANNEN

Randel	Margaret Miller	16Dec1829	E66	W69	Stephenson

BRANNIAN

John	Sarah George	21Jun1791	E1	W21	

BRANNON

Ellen	William Trago	22Jan1817	E46	W52	
Jane	James Ewing	30Mar1815	E43	W50	
Margaret	John Chancy	12Jun1848		W92	
Mary	John Loftin	26Dec1803	E24	W34	
Sarah	James Sanders	07Mar1820	E52	W57	
Thomas	Jane Ford	27Dec1778	B1	W1	
Wm	Sarah Smith	23Dec1779	C1	W3	

BRASFIELD
Alice   Bennet Shay   17Jan1831   E68 W70   Tippet

BRATCHER
Nancy   George Mulhorn   11Jul1780   C2 W4

BRAZIER [see also BROSIERS]
Hannah   William Shearwood   22Mar1803   E23 W33
Harriet   Robert Knight   04Mar1824   E58 W62
Martha   John McGill   09Nov1796   E10 W25
William   Elizabeth Sanders   25Jul1805   E26 W36

BRESLOND
Dennis   Nancy Ronay   08Jul1801   E20 W31

BREWER
Isaac   Mary Hobbs   10Jan1820   E52 W57
Rachel   Samuel Carroll   24Dec1827   E64 W67   Webster
    [orig. lic. to Webster; cr-Harf]
William   Elizabeth Morris   12Sep1860   W112

BRIARLY [see also BRYARLY]
Margaret   Andrew Kirkwood   20Mar1850   W94
Mary Elizabeth   Parker H. Lee   08Jun1841   E83 W84   Keech

BRICE
Mary   Jas Webster   01Mar1780   C1 W3

BRIGHAM
Eugenia M.   Thomas E. Howard   22Dec1860   W113

BRINDLEY
Sarah   Shadrach Rutledge, Jr.   18Oct1820   E53 W58

BRINEY
Jacob   Ruth Ann Baldwin   20Aug1862   W116

BRINTON
Edward   Susan Bond   03Apr1811   E36 W44

BROADLY
Bridget   Peter McIntire   20Feb1852   H1 W97   McNally

BRODERICK
Michael   Rose Dougherty   05Oct1858   W109

BROMWELL
Hannah   John Bowers   03Nov1793   E5 W23

BROOK
James W.   Sarah Ann Lewis   01Jan1834   E73 W75   Higby

BROOKE [see Eleanor Brooke Hall]
Edward	Cassandra Prigg	20Dec1795	E8	W24	
Ellen	Wm. F. Bayless	28Nov1842	E85	W85	Finney
Mary	Isaac Wilson	16Nov1807	E30	W39	

BROOKES
William R.	Ann Walker	27May1802	E22	W32

BROOKS [see William Brooks Stokes]
Mary	Bowyer Grace	25Apr1798	E14	W27	
Minerva	Jacob Wann	09Jan1823	E56	W61	
Sarah	Charles Wann	24Nov1831	E70	W72	Sewell
Thomas	Sarah Blake	16Jul1798	E15	W27	
Thomas	Elizabeth Sprucebanks	29May1807	E30	W39	

BROOM
James	Anne Balding	04Feb1802	E21	W32

BROOMELL
Isaac	Rachel Wilkinson	19Mar1838	E79	W80	Willson

BROSIERS [see also BRAZIER]
Silas	Susan W. Smith	02Jan1865	W120

BROWN
Ann Maria	Ignatius W. Jenkins	27Jan1846		W89	
Augustus F.	Harriet S. Wheeler	30Dec1857		W107	
Benjamin F.	Catherine Baker	20Aug1835	E75	W77	Gallion
Catherine	William Adams	04Mar1811	E36	W44	
Catherine L.	Amos W. Charshee	05Dec1856	H11	W105	Smith
Ebenezer	Rebecca Mitchell	03May1832	E71	W72	Finney
Elizabeth	John Reese	23Aug1780	C3	W4	
Elizabeth	John More	11Sep1780	C3	W5	
Elizabeth	Benjamin Chancy	22Mar1791	E1	W21	
Elizabeth	William Watters	01Jul1799	E16	W28	
Elizabeth	James Walker	28Sep1826	E61	W65	Finney
Elizabeth Ann	John H. Printer	13Dec1847		W92	
Geo.	Margt Denny	08Jan1781	C4	W5	
George	Frances Cussins	22Nov1792	E3	W22	
Grace	George Black	23Nov1779	C1	W3	
Henrietta M.	Nicholas W. Luke	02Oct1820	E53	W58	
Hollyday	Edward M. Guyton	30Jan1810	E34	W43	
Jacob	Mary Brown	16Jan1809	E33	W42	
Jacob	Sarah J. Smith	30May1865		W121	
James	Hannah Hitchcock	02Dec1780	C3	W5	
Jehu	Elizabeth Parmer	29Dec1824	E59	W63	
John	Mary Mararty	m. 1777			[ret-AppA]
John	Elizabeth Morris Maulsby	24Feb1808	E31	W40	
John	Rachel Smith	23Sep1823	E57	W61	
John	Ann Simmons	01Jan1838	E78	W80	Finy
Joshua	Mary Wetherall	m. 1777			[ret-AppA]
Juliann	William Smith	16Aug1830	E67	W70	Tippit
Lydia E.	George T. R. Howe	16Jul1864		W119	
Margaret F.	William H. Dobson	14Jun1858		W108	

BROWN, continued

Maria Ann	James Manahan	07Nov1822	E56	W60	
Mary	Edward Day	09Jan1801	E19	W30	
Mary	Jacob Brown	16Jan1809	E33	W42	
Mary	Charles Harwood	26Nov1812	E39	W47	
Mary	William Hassit[?]	11May1816	E45	W51	
Mary	Ephriam H. Murphy	29Jan1842	E84	W85	Cunningham
Mary	William Jones	14Aug1848		W92	
Mary A. M.	Matthew J. Cammeron	03Nov1847		W91	
Mary Ann	Stephen Watters	31Mar1802	E21	W32	
Mary E.	George J. McAtee	02Mar1835	E75	W76	Crosgy
Pamelia	Augustin Bayless	05Jan1784	C8	W9	
Peragrine	Ann Proctor	28Jul1780	C2	W4	
Rebecca	William Everit	10Jun1807	E36	W39	
Sarah	Henry Johns	22Feb1785	C10	W10	
Sarah	Thomas Swift	18Dec1852	H2	W98	Finney
Simon	Sarah Jones	15Aug1809	E34	W42	
Simon	Susannah Swift	29Aug1855	H8	W103	Lemmon
Solomon	Alisannah Foster	05Apr1780	C1	W3	
Susan	John Luster Webster	19Dec1839	E81	W82	Finney
Susanna	Edward Judd	08Dec1818	E50	W55	
Susannah	Jesse Manhone	06Nov1802	E22	W33	
Tho.	Mary Clark	m. 1778			[ret-AppA]
Thomas	Eleanor Gorden	17Feb1794	E5	W23	
Thomas	Clemency G. Mitchell	01Jul1820	E52	W58	
William	Caroline Webster	11Nov1815	E44	W50	
William	Paymelia Bennett	04Jun1817	E47	W53	
William	Hannah Hopkins	13May1833	E72	W74	Gallion
William	Eveline Whitelock	25Dec1850		W95	
William	Charlotte A. Cullum	10Oct1864		W119	
William H.	Sarah Stritehoof	11Jun1853	H4	W99	Keech

BROWNING

Martha	Thomas Hill	05Jun1801	E20	W31

BROWNLEY

Ann	David McClaskey	21Nov1805	E27	W37
Sarah	James Ewing	09Oct1805	E27	W36

BRUCEBANKS

Benjamin	Mary Daugherty	m. 1789	[ret-AppA]

BRUFF

Laura	George Hanson Garrettson	06Mar1837	E77	W79	Richardson

BRUNER

Benjamin	Sarah Sutton	27Sep1819	E51	W57

BRYAN

Margt*	Benjamin Gibson	29Jan1801	E19	W30

[*Sarah crossed out]

BRYARLY [see also BRIARLY]
James	Mary Moores	08Dec1817	E48 W54	

[marginal note: "Mr. Clendinen payd"]
Nansey	John Smith	13Jun1801	E20 W31	
Wakeman	Priscilla Elizabeth Lee	30Jan1816	E44 W51	
William	Delia Clark	07Nov1805	E27 W36	

BRYERLY
Henneritta	Johnston Campbell	01Nov1784	C9 W10	
Marg^t	John Carr	15Jul1779	B3 W2	
Robert	Sarah Moore	30Dec1782	C7 W8	cr-Harf

BRYON
Sarah	Luke West	27May1779	B2 W2

BUCKINGHAM
Ann	Jonas Schaeffer	07Dec1812	E39 W47	
Laura A.	Charles Treusch	16Sep1850	W95	
William	Rebecca Baxter	16Mar1826	E61 W65	Richardson

BUCKLEY
John W.	Isabella Kee	21Jul1849	W94

BUDD [see William Budd Gould]
Sally	Daniel Moores	03Dec1792	E3 W22

[may be 03Jan1793]

BULL
Belenda	Isaac Garrett	06Apr1838	E80 W82 Rockwell
Billingslea	Catharine Ashton	17May1808	E31 W40
Edmund	Margaret Gay	02Jun1832	E71 W73 Finney
Eliza W.	James S. Barrow	24Jan1854	H5 W100 Cronin
Elizibeth	George Young	31Jul1781	C5 W7
Esther	Jacob Bull	17Jun1780	C2 W4
Hannah	James White	05Jun1798	E15 W27
Henry Ja^s	Elizabeth Ann Watters	22May1855	H7 W102 Cushing
Isaac	Sarah Love	01Mar1779	B1 W1
Jacob	Esther Bull	17Jun1780	C2 W4
James	Harriet S. Barrow	05Apr1842	E85 W85 Brown
James L.	Cassandra Duff	26May1851	W96
John	Delia Standiford	08Dec1782	C6 W8
John E.	Mary Bull	31Oct1833	E73 W74 Keech
Martha	Thomas Tredway	31Oct1850	W95
Mary	Nathaniel Smithson	24Jan1779	B1 W1
Mary	John E. Bull	31Oct1833	E73 W74 Keech
Noah R.	Ann Grafton	16Dec1851	H1 W97 Robey
Priscilla	Merryman Streett	06Jan1844	E86 W87 Keech
Rachel	William James	15Aug1780	C2 W4
Rachel	Jacob Rush	04Feb1806	E27 W37
Rachel C.	John S. Baldwin	03Dec1842	E85 W85 Keech
Ruth	Lloyd Lee	12Aug1811	E37 W45
Sarah	Thomas Inloes	28Mar1818	E49 W55
Sarah A.	Thomas H. Streett	25Oct1853	H4 W100 Keech
Susan Jane	James H. Delevet	09Jan1861	W113

BULL, continued
William	Avarillah Hanson	26Aug1780	C3 W4	
Wm	Mary Bussey	02Jun1784	C8 W9	[ret-AppA]
William	Polly Hicks	m. 1803		[ret-AppA]
William	Elizabeth Ruff	13Apr1809	E33 W42	
William E.	Elizabeth Smithson	25May1847	W91	
William H.	Harriet Duff	10Jun1851	W96	

BULLICK
Margaretta   Theodore Gorrell   05Oct1844   E87 W87   Parnell

BULLOCK
Lydia   Otho W. Magness   23Aug1827   E63 W66   Keech

BUNCE
Jacob   Margaret A/H. McCommons   18Aug1864   W119

BUNTS
Louisa F.   James W. Hamby   08Jun1857   H12 W106 Monroe

BURGOIN
John   Hannah Reed   25May1808   E31 W40

BURK
William G.   Elizabeth Wareham   19Feb1827   E62 W66   Reynolds

BURKE
John   Susanna Templeton   28Dec1796   E10 W25

BURKHEAD
Ann   John Massey   09Dec1802   E22 W33

BURKIN
Charles   Eleanor Parker   m. 1778   [ret-AppA]

BURKINS
Charles A.	Sallie J. Slade	08May1864	W119
James	Margaret Ann Mowbray	26Dec1861	W115
John	Mary E. Logan	15Nov1864	W120
Margaret	John H. Troutner	24Oct1861	W114

BURNES
Susan   John McKenney   11Mar1818   E48 W54

BURNETT [see also BARNETT]
Hannah	Isaac Atkinson	29Mar1809	E33 W42
Harriett	George E. Pearce	22Feb1864	W118

BURNS
Caroline   Florence Mahoney   27Nov1843   E86 W81   Reid

BURNSIDE
Catherine   John Hogg   18Jan1819   E50 W56

BURT [see Burt Whitson]

BURTON
Ann	Charles Barnett	24Mar1795	E7	W24

BUSH
Catharine	Fred. Hanrick	12Sep1864		W119	
Martha F.	John F. Myers	06Sep1852	H2	W98	Robey
Mary F.	William J. Carpenter	24Dec1849		W94	
William	Annie Webley	16Jun1862		W116	

BUSSEY [see James Bussey Amoss]
Alice	Francis C. Smith	14Jan1856	H9	W104	McManus
Benedict T.	Martha E. O'Donnell	17Aug1857	H12	W106	Walter
Edward B.	Sarah Howard	m. 1803			[ret-AppA]
Edward F.	Juliana Wheeler	23Aug1811	E37	W45	
Elizabeth M.	Thomas Fortune	14Jan1851		W96	
Harriet	Henry Treadwell	08Jan1849		W93	
Henry	Catherine Boarman	28Mar1837	E77	W79	Coskey
Henry G.	Elizabeth Susanna Harris	05Oct1807	E30	W39	
Martha	Abraham White	03Jun1797	E10	W26	
Mary	Wm Bull	02Jun1784	C8	W9	

BUTLER
Anna (cold.)	Jarrett Hollis (cold.)	25Sep1862		W116	
Clement	Isabella Streett	05Feb1821	E53	W58	
Elizabeth	Samuel Whiteford	02Mar1799	E15	W28	
Elizabeth	Nathaniel Glenn	24Jan1814	E41	W48	
Henrietta [month uncertain]	Thomas Sutton	25Nov1844	E87	W88	Reid
Jane	Silvester Macatee	23Feb1829	E65	W68	O'Brian
John	Ann Ragan	16Nov1829	E66	W69	Poisel
Maria	Ignatius G. McAtee	11Feb1824	E58	W62	
Mary Ann	William Montgomery	08Feb1820	E52	W57	
Mary F.	William G. Roberts	01Jan1859		W109	
Richard	Sarah Bat--	29Dec1792	E3	W22	
William	Sarah Touchstone	01Apr1818	E49	W55	

BUXSTER
Rebecca	Daniel Noggle	24Mar1839	E80 W81	Dulaney

BYARD
Cassandra	John Hamilton	21Jan1835	E75	W76	Richardson
Ephraim	Elizabeth Gorrell	13Dec1803	E24	W34	
Louis	Rachel Chandley	21Sep1807	E30	W39	

CABTIL
Wm	Mary Rigdon	29Feb1780	C1	W3

CADDEN
James R.	Isabella V. Bouldin	01Apr1865	W121

CAFEE
Ellen	Redman Kane	07Sep1846	W90

CAHILL
Henry	Mary Ryan	14Apr1858	W108	
Mary	John Lynch	29Jan1855	H7 W102	Walter

CAIN [see also KAIN, KANE, KEAN]
Ellen	John Mansfield	14Sep1859	W110	
James M.	Elizabeth Kean	09Jan1855	H6 W102	Walter
Jane	Benjamin Guyton	13Feb1817	E46 W53	
John	Jane Holmes	28May1816	E45 W51	
John	Ann Kelly	23Feb1850	W94	
Mary	Henry Lilley	19Nov1805	E27 W37	
Rachael	James Carroll	09May1854	H5 W101	McNally
Richard	Mary Sheredine	02Jan1823	E56 W61	
Sarah	Arthur Curry	26Mar1805	E26 W36	

CAIRNES [see also CAREINS, CARINS, CARNES]
George, Jnr.	Mary Ann Bay	05Apr1836	E76 W77	Morrison
Hannah E.	Alexander McComas	04Jan1864	W118	
Isabel R.	George C. Kirkwood	28Feb1859	W110	
Mary Ann	Henry G. Wheeler	01May1854	H5 W101	Carter
Mary Ann	James Hope	12Dec1855	H8 W103	Carter
Mary V.	William B. Jarrett	05Jan1857	H11 W105	McCartny
Rebecca Jane	Charles Henry Bay	27Jan1858	W108	
Sallie S.	Henry Stauffer	27Sep1858	W109	

CAIRNS
William	Elizabeth Vance	13Jan1830	E66 W69	Morrison

CALARY
Peter F.	Elizabeth B. Barber	31Jan1862	W115

CALDER [see also COLDER]
Agness	James Smith	26Mar1845	E88 W88	Reid
Neoma	Joseph Renshaw	07Jul1808	E32 W41	
Sarah	James Turner	22Apr1811	E36 W45	

CALDWELL
John W.	Hannah Sadler	09Apr1859	W110

CALHOUN
Benjamin	Elizabeth A. Weeks	18Mar1846	W90

CALISLE [see Calisle Francis]

CALLAHAN
Catharine	Michael Farrell	15May1861	W114

CALVERT
Wm H.	Caroline R. McComas	14Jan1828	E64 W67	Finney

CALWELL
Ann	Thomas Bowyer	04Jan1803	E23 W33	
Ann	Augustus Webster	22Mar1828	E64 W67	Richardson
Caroline S.	John C. Norris	26Nov1827	E63 W66	Breckenridge
Laura A.	David Lee Norris	12Oct1857	H12 W107	Myers
Thomas	Sally Gallion	14Feb1793	E4 W22	
Thomas J.	Ann Amelia Watters	01Dec1834	E74 W76	Webster
William	Eleanor Grindall	20Nov1800	E18 W30	
William	Mary Amoss	01Dec1813	E41 W48	

CAMEL
Rosa	James Carroll	18Apr1860	W112

CAMERON
Elizabeth	Robert* Moore	23Nov1855	H8	W103 Smith
[* George crossed out]				
Francis Alexander	Mary Ann Hopkins	11Mar1861		W113
Mary Jane	John Lafayette Johnson	08Jun1854	H5	W101 Smith

CAMMERON
Matthew J.	Mary A. M. Brown	03Nov1847	W91

CAMPBEL
Nelson B.	Martha E. Turner	11Oct1864	W119

CAMPBELL [see also CAMEL]
Anne E.	Thomas R. Silk	30Oct1861		W114
Cathrine	Patrick McLaughlin	28Sep1784	C9	W9
Jacob W.	Margaret Lynch	25Dec1861		W115
Johnston	Henneritta Bryerly	01Nov1784	C9	W10
M--	Thos Riley	05Jan1780	C1	W3
Mary Ann	Samuel Lynch	14May1861		W114

CANNEN
Amelia	John Dutton	24Jun1800	E18 W29 br-A. A.

CANNON
Artregue	Noble Rider	28Dec1808	E33 W41	
Caroline	William McGaw	19Apr1804	E25 W35	
Elizabeth	Mordecai Dawes	11Apr1812	E38 W46	
John	Rebecca Yokely	15Jun1814	E42 W49	
John W.	Mary Ann Cole	23Aug1838	E79 W80	Goldsborough
Martha M.	Thomas F. Gallup	11Jul1859	W110	
Mary	James Taylor	07Apr1814	E41 W49	
Noble	Semelia O. Cole	20Sep1834	E74 W75	Donahay
Rachel	Micajah All	04Dec1802	E22 W33	
Rachel	Richard Deaver	15Feb1817	E46 W53	
Thomas	Anna J/I. Wiggers	27Aug1853	H4 W99	Trout
William	Mary Kimberly	28May1810	E35 W43	

CANON
Susie	B. H. Hanson, Jr.	21Jan1862	W115

CANTLER
Benjamin F.	Elizabeth Ann Cantler	29May1856	H10 W105	Gallion
David R.	Susanna L. Harrowwood	04May1853	H3 W99	Gallion
Elizabeth Ann	Benjamin F. Cantler	29May1856	H10 W105	Gallion
John	Mary Hogs	26Aug1833	E73 W74	Stephenson

CARDIFF [see Cardiff D. Norris]

CAREINS
Robert　　　　Mary Ann Street　　　　28Sep1840　E82 W83　Cross

CARINS
William　　　Mary St. Clair　　　　18Aug1808　E32 W41

CARLEN
Thomas　　　Mary Watt　　　　27Nov1816　E46 W52

CARLILE
John W.　　　Ann Knight　　　　18Feb1826　E61 W64
　[minister - Isaac Webster; orig. lic. to Webster; cr-Harf]
Lancelot　　　Ann Taylor　　　　22Jul1781　C5　W6
Marg^t　　　　Richard Dallam　　　30Dec1792　E3　W22

CARLON
Mary　　　　John Toy　　　　11Feb1793　E4　W22

CARMACK
David　　　　Eliza Morgan　　　30May1810 E35 W43

CARMAN
Amos	Jane Marshall	23Feb1818	E48 W54	
And^w	Mary Davis	27Aug1781	C5 W7	
Ann	Robert Chappall	04Dec1826	E62 W65	Poteet
Hester	John Kennedy	31May1821	E54 W59	
John	Mary Marshell	08Feb1809	E33 W42	
Mary	William Miskimon	08Aug1814	E42 W49	
Nathan	Ann Ellen Rockhold	19Jun1824	E58 W62	
Samuel	Mary Deaver	13Jun1842	E85 W85	Wilson

CARNACLE
Ann　　　　George Crissel　　　31Jan1816　E44 W51
George　　　Ann Mcfaden　　　10Oct1809　E34 W43

CARNAY
Eliz^th　　　Daniel Carroll　　　13May1856　H10 W104 Walter

CARNES
Margaret　　Joseph Huggins　　　30Jan1781　C4　W6

CARPENTER
Mary F.　　　James A. Woods　　　31Jan1859　　　W109
William J.　　Mary F. Bush　　　24Dec1849　　　W94

CARR [see also Kerr]

Ann J.	David M. Dixon	05Jun1865	W121	
Frances	Walter Billingslea	25Apr1810	E35 W43	
James H.	Elizth H. Proctor	04Feb1862	W115	
John	Marg^t Bryerly	15Jul1779	B3 W2	
John D.	Susanna Jones	05Feb1812	E37 W45	
Jesse	Lidia A. Forwood	25May1840	E82 W83	Prettyman
Mary	Henry Rowland	21Nov1778	B1 W1	
Mary	Robt Reeds	13Mar1781	C4 W6	
[br surname and month uncertain]				
Mary A.	Andrew J. Famous	19May1860	W112	
Richard	Rebecca Grafton	14Nov1837	E78 W79	Collins
Richard H.	Anna Mary Osborn	19Jan1850	W94	
Sarah L.	Thomas J. Walker	20Apr1864	W119	
William	Sarah Murray	05Feb1803	E23 W33	[ret-AppA]
Wm Amoss	Mary Virginia Lancaster	27Oct1852	H2 W98	

CARROL

James, Esq.	Sophia Gough	m. 1787		[ret-AppA]
Mary Ann	William Hawkins	22Mar1841	E83 W84	Gallion

CARROLL

Adrianus D.	Sarah E. Hawkins	08Mar1856	H9 W104	Riniek
Ann	John McGahen	29Jul1794	E5 W23	
Ann B.	Abraham B. Swarts	02Jul1816	E45 W51	
Aquila	Rachel Whitaker	11Jan1815	E42 W49	
Benjamin F.	Clara R. Martin	06Nov1840	E82 W83	Finney
Bridget	Michael Whalen	14Aug1854	H6 W101	McNally
Charity	Elisha Galloway	23Mar1811	E36 W44	
Daniel	Elizth Carnay	13May1856	H10 W104	Walter
Delia	Nathan Horner	30Apr1799	E16 W28	
Delilah	Richard Biddle	31Mar1801	E20 W31	
Elizabeth	Abraham Gorrell	29Mar1806	E28 W37	
Ellen	James Davlin	01Mar1859	W110	
Ellen E.	Thomas West	29May1833	E72 W74	Richardson
Emely P.	John Poll	08Apr1835	E75 W76	Keech
Hannah	William Stiles	24Dec1821	E55 W59	
James	Susannah Lisby	04Apr1802	E22 W32	
James	Mary Richardson	18Dec1823	E57 W62	
James	Rebecca W. Yarnel	01Nov1830	E68 W70	Tippet
James	Rachael Cain	09May1854	H5 W101	McNally
James	Elizabeth H. Galloway	24Sep1859	W110	
James	Rosa Camel	18Apr1860	W112	
John	Isabella Cowan	16Jan1779	B2 W2	
John	Jane Ewing	02Feb1808	E31 W40	
John	Nancy Martin	10May1859	W110	
Margaret	John Ewing	01Jan1814	E41 W48	
Margaret	John Hawkins	11Oct1831	E69 W71	Sewell
Margaret Jane	Amos Tredaway	17Jun1847	W91	
Mary	Edward Pursel	17Jul1781	C5 W7	
[follows later July entries]				
Mary	William Fox	15Aug1797	E12 W26	
[ret'd by John Allen]				

CARROLL, continued

Mary	Christopher Smith	21May1817	E47	W53	
Mary	Aquila Donahoe	27Dec1826	E62	W65	Stephenson
Mary	Hugh Conothen	29Sep1855	H8	W103	Walter
Patrick	Kate Allen	13Feb1857	H11	W106	Walter
Permelia Ann	Herman Tutchtone	14Dec1846		W90	
Samuel	Rachel Brewer	24Dec1827	E64	W67	Webster

  [orig. lic. to Webster; cr-Harf]

Sarah	John Standiford	08Jan1813	E39	W47	
Wm	Marg^t Tuchstone	14Nov1782	C6	W8	
William	Effy Garrell	23Feb1819	E50	W56	
William	Priscilla Clines	11Feb1832	E70	W72	Finney

CARSIN

Martha	James Johnson	25Feb1851		W96
Sarah Ann	Elias Green Richardson	29Nov1849		W94

CARSINS

Elizabeth	Nicholas Baker	02Nov1837	E78	W79	Colls
Mary	Amos Gilbert	16Jan1845	E88	W88	Wysong
William	Martha Maxwell	28Dec1847		W92	

CARSON

John	Ann* Cowen	21Oct1818	E49	W55

  [*Nancy crossed out]

CARSONS [?]

Martha	Saml Foresith	03Apr1780	C1	W3

CARTER

Asabel	John Stephonson	20May1819	E51	W56	
Benjamen	Catharine Sturgen	m. 1777			[ret-AppA]
Hannah	Saml Sreark	16Mar1779	B1	W1	
Hannah	Samuel Stump	28Mar1822	E55	W60	
John	Mary Bowyer	04Jun1783	C7	W8	
John W.	Sarah Jane Waulstrum	25Sep1852	H2	W98	Lemon
Martha	Thomas Nichols	16Jun1796	E8	W25	

CARTHAIN

Alexander	Elizth Ellen Welch	28Aug1845	E88	W89

CARTY

Eliza	Nicholas Spencer	12Aug1822	E56	W60	
Hannah	Jno Gold Howard	m. 1778			[ret-AppA]
Hannah	Joseph Thomas	27Oct1799	E16	W28	
James Wm.	Martha Agnes Zears	24Jan1860		W111	
John	Statia York	18Jun1823	E57	W61	
Mary Magdalen	Daniel Sweeney	24Dec1802	E22	W33	
Thomas	Martha Swift	09Apr1816	E45	W51	
William	Maria Wilson	16Mar1841	E83	W84	Cullum

CARVEEL [see Carveel Mathews]

CARVER [see also KERVER]
Aaron	Mary Trisler	17Mar1812	E38 W46	
Elizabeth	George W. Demby	23Dec1839	E81 W82	Goldsborough
George W.	Sarah A. Peters	09May1853	H3 W99	Bull
Joseph C.	Mottelenor Peterman	07Nov1820	E53 W58	

CARVILL [see Carvill Hall Prigg]

CASHMAN
Elizabeth S.	Joshua Stricklen	03May1814	E42 W49	
Grace	William Galley	m. 1788[?]		[ret-AppA]

CASHMORE
Grace	John Bennett	11Apr1809	E33 W42

CASKEY
John	Hannah Hickey	13Jan1819	E50 W56

CASMONS
Mary	William Greenland	17Feb1816	E44 W51

CASSE
Mary	Dennis Londreagrin	25Dec1780	C4 W5

CASSIDINE [?]
Alasanna	William Evans	14Jan1783	C7 W8	cr-Harf

CASSIDY
John	Bridget Henry	09Feb1858	W108

CATHCART
Ellen	David Wiley	10Oct1845	W89	
Hannah A.	Robt. R. McClung	27Dec1864	W120	
Jemima	Thomas Johnson	16Dec1861	W115	
Joseph	Ruth Tredway	15Nov1836	E77 W78	Jordan[?]
Mary	Benjamin N. Payne	16Jan1829	E65 W68	Park
Mary Ann	John Folkner	06Mar1851	W96	
Thomas M.	Mary Ann Slade	08Feb1848	W92	
William N.	Jane Phillips	20Oct1863	W118	Webstr

CATON
Nich!	Mary Hackett	22Mar1779	B1 W1

CATOR
Joseph B.	Elizabeth Jane Dove	30May1836	E76 W78	Dulany

CATTIGAN [see COTTIGAN]

CAUGHRAN
Barbara	Charles Holland	21Jun1838	E79 W80	Richardson

CAULFOR
Martin	Catharine Elizth Tranar	16Jun1858	W108

CAVE
Ellen				William Priestly			28Jan1843	E85 W86	Alexander

CAVENDER
John				Hannah E. Scarborough		30Jan1857	H11 W105 Cushing

CETHERWOOD
Jane				John Thomas			28Dec1807	E31 W40

CHAPMAN
Francis				Lydia A. Nelson			11Nov1852	H2 W98	Smith

CHALK [see also CHOCKE]
Elizabeth			John Irvin			20Mar1852	H2 W98	Park
George				Martha Beatty			11Apr1850	W94
John Hendon			Esther Ann Kennedy		28Oct1847	W91
Mary Virginia			Isaac Vanhorn			30Dec1861	W115 ALJ1-34,223
Naasson				Elizabeth Hughes		13Jan1816	E44 W51
William L.			Mary L. Trainor			21Dec1861	W115

CHAMBERLAIN [see Henrietta Maria Chamberlain Hughes]
Elizabeth			John J. Hunt			09Nov1859	W111
Mary Ann			William Durham			11Nov1807	E30 W39
Nathan				Rebecca Billingslea		26Dec1844	E87 W88	Jones
Rebecca J.			Samuel Wesley Forwood		26Jun1860	W112
Samuel				Ann Jenkins			22Jun1798	E15 W27

CHAMBERLAND
Chas T.				Pamelia H. Archer		21Nov1843	E86	W87 Finney

CHAMBERLIN
Elizabeth			James Holland			22Dec1810	E36 W44

CHAMBERS
Elizabeth			Hutchings William Layton	28Jun1803	E23 W34
William				Elizabeth Boyle			06Nov1799	E16 W28
William				Sarah Strong			15Dec1801	E21 W31

CHANCE
Amelia				Charles Bevard			01Feb1798	E13 W27

CHANCEY [see also CHAUNCEY]
George, Junr.			Frances Rebecca Dorsey		14Nov1796	E10 W25
Sarah				James Weatherall		19Feb1783	C7 W8

CHANCY
Benjamin			Elizabeth Brown			22Mar1791	E1 W21
John				Margaret Brannon		12Jun1848	W92

CHANDLEE
Cornelius			Nancy Bartol			31Dec1808	E33 W41
Elizabeth			Jesse Ergood			15Dec1837	E79 W79	Goldsborough
Maria J.			Robert Culley			21Jan1835	E75 W76	Goldsborough
William				Panetta Gore			14Nov1820	E53 W58

CHANDLER
Drosilla	John Levi	25Aug1812	E38 W46	

CHANDLEY
James S.[or J?]	Ann Haney	01Apr1819	E50 W56	
Rachel	Louis Byard	21Sep1807	E30 W39	
Rebecca	John Raburgh	15Jul1807	E30 W39	
Susan	Thomas Dempsey	18Aug1819	E51 W56	

CHANSEY
Catharin	George Lytle	m. 1778		[ret-AppA]

CHANEY
Absalom	Rebecca Lancaster	30Sep1807	E30 W39

CHAPMAN
Annie E.	Walter Harwood	03Jan1854	H4 W100	Cronin
William H.	Cornelia B. Hall	28Oct1851	W97	

CHAPPALL
Robert	Ann Carman	04Dec1826	E62 W65	Poteet

CHAPPELL
George W.	Eliza J. Keene	22Jan1863	W117

CHARLTON
James	Harriet Shrader	18Nov1824	E59 W63	McElhiney

CHARSHA
James	Ann Fletcher	05Sep1816	E45 W52

CHARSHE
Bennet	Harriet Cook	09Jan1849	W93	
James Herman	Mary Rebecca Bowen	03Jun1850	W95	
Sarah Elizth	George Bowen	10Dec1849	W94	
Septimus F.	Rebecca J/I. Fisher	05Aug1853	H4 W99	Finney

CHARSHEE
Amos W.	Catherine L. Brown	05Dec1856	H11 W105	Smith
Mary	John Bradfield	06Dec1855	H8 W103	Smith

CHAUNCEY [see also CHANCE, CHANCEY, CHANCY, CHANSEY]
Ann	John Daugherty	01Apr1800	E17 W29	
Benjn	Sarah Rebecca Wood	31May1843	E86 W86	Aggey
Cordelia	Henry Vansickle	01Feb1804	E24 W34	
Elizabeth	Ebenezer N. Allen	13Feb1816	E44 W51	
Garret	Elizabeth G. Vansickle	24Jan1809	E33 W42	
John	Cordelia Vansickel	30Jan1816	E44 W51	
John H.	Mary A. Henderson	05May1835	E75 W76	Goldsboro
Martha	Joseph Webster	30May1792	E2 W21	[ret-AppA]
Mary	Toppan Webster	14Apr1817	E47 W53	
Sarah	Boyce Cowin	05Apr1802	E22 W32	
Susan	Samuel Sutton	26Mar1832	E70 W72	Hiby
Susanna	Bennett Vansickle	02Feb1807	E29 W38	

CHENOWETH [see Chenoweth Tredway; see also CHINOWORTH]
John P.   Mary Ann Snyder   22Mar1856   H9 W104 Hoopman

CHENWORTH
Sarah E.   Jones Major   07Apr1857   H11 W106 Cushing

CHERRY
William   Charlotte Henderson   05Jun1827   E63 W66 Keech

CHESNEY
Ann   William Wood   28Mar1812   E38 W46
Ann   William Wiles, Jnr.   24Feb1832   E70 W72 Sewall
Benjamin   Ann Everist   10Feb1826   E61 W64 Tidings
Benjamin   Frances A. Thompson   08Jan1853   H3 W98 Finney
Cordelia A.   James L. Gorrell   27Dec1847   W92
Daniel B.   Martha Rebecca Osborn   11Feb1845   E88 W88 Rohr
John   Ann Mitchell   27Nov1815   E44 W50
John   Eleanor Keen   18Apr1818   E49 W55
Kent M.   Hannah Jane Price   01Dec1830   E68 W70 Tippit
Lidia Rebecca   Henry Foster   01Dec1840   E82 W83 Prettyman
Mary   Ezra Quimby   08Nov1821   E54 W59
Mary E.   Isaach Fletcher   01Oct1838   E79 W81 Chesney
Susanna   Ezekiel Everist   20Feb1826   E61 W64 Stephenson
Thomas   Hannah Mitchell   18Feb1806   E28 W37
William   Mary Hughes   10Jun1817   E47 W53
William   Elizabeth Gilbert   05Apr1831   E69 W71 Finney
William T.   Elizabeth S. Jackson   06Nov1855   H8 W103 Reese

CHEW
Edward M.   Margaret M. Hopkins   14Feb1832   E70 W72 Poisall
Edward M.   Caroline F. Hall   09Nov1863   W118
Elizabeth M.   John Hopkins   30Apr1833   E72 W74 Keech
Nathaniel   Margaret Rogers   m. 1793   [ret-AppA]
Sarah   William Jolly   28May1793   E4 W22 [ret-AppA]
Sarah   Samuel Worthington   11Apr1809   E33 W42
Susa   Jo: Miller   05Sep1779   B3 W2
Washington P.   Mary Hall   03Jan1831   E68 W70 Tippet
Washington P.   Mary C. Boyd   09Nov1840   E82 W83 Finney
William M.   Anne W. Richardson   16Feb1814   E41 W48

CHILLITTE
Sarah Rebecca   Benjamin Wann   04Jul1855   H8 W103 Brand

CHINOWORTH
Mary Ellen   William B. Hitchcock   16Feb1861   W113
Washington   Sidney Almira Noonan   04Dec1845   W89

CHINWORTH [see also CHENOWETH]
Norris   Rebecca Pierce   20Feb1822   E55 W60
Sidney   Thomas Curry   02Aug1819   E51 W56

CHIPMAN
Daniel   Mary McCann   26Nov1817   E48 W54

CHISHOLM
John	Mary Taylor	05Dec1808	E32 W41	
John	Elizabeth Price	08Apr1841	E83 W84	Cullum
Mary	Robert Saunders	29May1823	E57 W61	
Thomas	Comfort Rigdon	25Jan1796	E8 W24	

CHOCK
Cordelia	Henry Lindimore	06Jul1807	E30 W39

CHOCKE [see also CHALK]
Eudosia	Joseph Withers	[25Mar]1843	E85 W86	
Hendon	Ann Maria Hughes	26Feb1834	E74 W75	Richardson
Sarah	John Deaver	21Sep1819	E51 W56	
Zenos	Elizabeth Blaney	05Mar1813	E40 W47	

CHOKE
Israel	Heziah Hitchcock	16Dec1816	E46 W52

CHRISTIE
Delia	Alexander Rodgers	13Oct1801	E20 W31	
Francina	George Stephenson	22Oct1836	E77 W78	McGrady
Gabrial	Prisilla Hall	15[?]Nov1779	C1 W3	
James	Ann Whiteford	10Jul1834	E74 W75	Finney
John	Delia Ferrell	19Feb1816	E44 W51	
Margaret	Henry S. J. McCay	28Aug1854	H6 W101	Crampton

CHRISTY
Michael	Biddy Brannan	15Apr1854	H5 W101	McNally

CHURCHMAN
Enoch	Martha Norris	01[?]Feb1792	E2 W21

CLAGETT
Eli	Mary Grant	20Jan1816	E44 W51

CLARK
Ann	John Tardy	04Apr1781	C4	
Ann	Michael Gilbert	07Aug1784	C9 W9	
Ann	Thomas Mahan	18Dec1851	H1 W97	McNulty
Barnet J.	Elizabeth Rigdon	12Jan1836	E76 W77	Richardson
Barnett	Catharine A. Starr	04Feb1860	W111	
Delia	William Bryarly	07Nov1805	E27 W36	
Elizabeth	Luther Hitchcock	01Apr1865	W121	
Geo.	Lydia Garrett	10Aug1784	C9 W9	
Hannah	James Curry	20Aug1818	E49 W55	
Jane	Wiley Jones	30Jun1784	C9 W9	
John	Rebecca Smith	01Mar1815	E42 W49	
Julia Ann	George N. Wiles	27Feb1856	H9 W104	Lemmon
Margaret Ann	William K. Lytle	25Jan1860	W111	
Mary	Tho. Brown	m. 1778		[ret-AppA]
Mary	John McKenny	12Jul1847	W91	
Mary	John Gourmly	10Feb1857	H11 W106	Walter
Matthew	Temperance Glenn	26Mar1816	E45 W51	
Nathan	Ann Ashmead	28Apr1803	E23 W33	
Patrick	Margaret A. Kerr	12Feb1851	W96	

CLARK, continued

Ralph	Eliza C. Monks	19Nov1821	E54 W59
Sarah	Isaac Hitchcock	30Nov1809	E34 W43
Mrs. Sarah Ann	Bennett Green	04Feb1850	W94
Sarah Frances	Luther Hitchcock	13Jun1859	W110
Thomas	Hannah Evans	18Feb1812	E38 W46
Thomas	Sarah Ann Johnson	24Mar1838	E79 E80 Keech
Thomas	Grace Ann Downfield	13May1842	E85 W85 Reid
William	Margaret Johnson	17Jun1818	E49 W55

CLARKE

Martha — William Commiger — 05Jul1796 E8 W25

CLAY

Joseph M. — Louisa Wilson — [27?]Jun1855 H8 W103 Crampton

CLAYDON

Sarah Jane — John Bauer — 08Feb1862 W115

CLEAVELAND

Anthony B. — Rachel S. Harlan — 03Aug1833 E73 W74 Porter

CLEMMONS

William — Mary James — [17?]Dec1780 C3 W5

CLENDENEN

John — Eliz^th Glasgow — 27May1793 E4 W22

CLENDENING

Jane — Robert Alexander — 04Sep1800 E18 W30

CLENDINEN [see James Bryarly entry]

Mary	James Alexander	05May1801	E20 W31
Mary	Henry G. Watters	04Feb1823	E56 W61

CLINDENING

Mary — James Gladen — 22Feb1785 C10 W10

CLINES

Martha	Samuel Jay	08Aug1826	E61 W65 Stephenson
Priscilla	William Carroll	11Feb1832	E70 W72 Finney

CLINGING

William — Jane Gilmore — 08Mar1783 C7 W8

CLION

Henry — Catharine Cramer — 05Mar1842 E84 W85 Herron

CLOAK

George — Sarah Smith — 07Apr1857 H11 W106 Monroe

CLOEMAN

Charlotte — James Linch — 11Jul1844 E87 W87 Reid

CLOMAN
Edward	Elizabeth Sampson	10Nov1838	E80	W81	Gallion
John	Margaret Bell	21Nov1821	E54	W59	

CLOSE
George	Elizabeth Fowl	21Feb1781	C4	W6	

CLOWMAN [see also CLOEMAN, CLOMAN]
Harriot	Aquila Greenland	10May1810	E35	W43	
Mary	David Norris	05Nov1829	E66	W69	Finney
Phebe Rebecca Ann	David Lee Anderson	29Dec1851	H1	W97	Robey

COALBY
Ann	Leonard Howard	21Apr1819	E51	W97	Robey

COALE [see also COLE]
Ann	James Fisher	14Sep1803	E23	W34	
Ann	John Courci	04Nov1803	E24	W34	
Ann	William Brannan	16Jan1822	E55	W60	
Avarilla	Thomas Everist	26Jan1803	E23	W33	
Clarissa C.	John L. James	04Mar1861		W113	
Cornelia A.	Christian H. Walker	22Jun1857	H12	W106	Littleton
Elizabeth	Job Guest	14Nov1810	E36	W44	
Elizbeth [sic]	Tho. C. Everist	23Jan1828	E64	W67	Finney
[orig. lic. to Finney; cr-Harf; br Elizabeth; gr Thomas]					
Emely	Jesse Huff	28Dec1836	E77	W78	Furlong
Frances	John Dixon	05Feb1812	E38	W46	
Hiram	Elizabeth Taylor	12Aug1830	E67	W70	Webster
[orig. lic. to Webster; cr-Harf]					
Jane J.	John Smith Hamby	03Jan1828	E64	W67	Keech
Jesse	Mary Millar	03Apr1817	E47	W53	
Jesse E.	Mary Ann Johnson	03Jan1859		W109	
John	Cassandra Course	31Oct1832	E71	W73	Finney
Jonas	Martha C. Nevill	06Feb1844	E87	W87	Thomas
Mary	George Lytle	18Feb1807	E29	W39	
Mary	Edward Miller	10May1817	E47	W53	
Margaret Elgar	John Yellott Worthington	03May1832	E71	W73	Magraw
Philip	Margaret Thompson	13Jan1836	E76	W77	Keech
Sarah	Joseph Ford	25Jan1804	E24	W34	
Sarah	James C. Daddrell	06Sep1809	E34	W42	
Thomas	Elizabeth Thompson	24Nov1807	E30	W40	
William	Mary Ann Wells	23Dec1834	E74	W76	Dunaha
William J. H.	Sarah J. Pike	13Sep1832	E71	W73	Sewell
William S.	Mary Agnes Keitly	12Oct1860		W112	

COALEMAN
Jas	Alisannah Pendergast	27Dec1780	C4	W5	
Mary	Wm Hollowell	28Aug1783	C7	W8	cr-Harf

COARD
Ashberry	Sarah Daws	04Mar1783	C7	W8	
Athur	Bathias Swain	28Jul1783	C7	W8	
Susannah	Jacob Potts	31Oct1781	C5	W7	

COATES
Sarah Ann   Matthew Day   01Oct1855   H8   W103 Smith

COBURN
Catharine L.   William Horner   28Oct1861   W114
Kate J/I.   William W. Horner   04Aug1862   W116

COCHRAN [see also CAUGHRAN]
Catharine   John Gibson   10Nov1813   E41 W48
Dennis   Rosa Daugherty   02Oct1863   W118
James   Pleasance Lucas   05Dec1811   E37 W45
Rebecca   Henry Woolsey   08Jun1803   E23 W33
Robert A.   Mary L. Rouse   19Sep1837   E78 W79   Keech

CODE
Peter   Hester Baker   02Sep1854   H6   W101 Gallion

CODES
Peter   Harriett Willey   14Sep1859   W110

COEN [see also COHEN, COWAN, COWEN, COWIN]
Elizabeth   John Maxwell   03Nov1817   E48 W54
Elizabeth   Parker Gilbert   09Jun1840   E82 W83   Goldsborough
Henry C.   Mary J/I. Ewing   02Feb1863   W117
John   Elizabeth Bailey   07Oct1817   E47 W54
John   Nancy Bailey   04Aug1825   E60 W64   Finney

COFMAN
Icabird   Jacob Stallions   25Jun1807   E30 W39

COHEN
Martha   Aquila Bailey   07Jan1834   E73 W75   Higby

COLDER [see also CALDER]
Martin   Nancy Slade   12Jul1838   E79 W80   Keech
Sarah J.   John T. Ayres   08Dec1862   W116

COLDHAM
Cathrine   John Wright   20Dec1780   C4   W5

COLE [see Elizabeth Cole Herbert; see also COALE]
Abraham   Sarah E. Nelson   07Jun1847   W91
Alanson   Margaret Numbers   02Jun1847   W91
Ann   George Mahan   11Feb1817   E46 W53
Benjamin   Elizabeth Arnold   14Feb1815   E42 W49
Cassander   Robt McCoy   09Jan1797   E10 W25
Charity   George Henderson   17Jun1800   E18 W29
Charity A.   Paca Mitchell   01Jan1844   E86 W87
Cornelius   Martha Osborn   09Jun1808   E31 W41
Eliza   William R. Hill   19Dec1826   E62 W65   Richardson
Elizabeth   Nicholas Baker   06Jan1801   E19 W30
Elizabeth   William H. Wells   22Jan1849   W93
Elizabeth L.   Elijah J. B. Moore   11Mar1856   H9   W104 Alexander
Ezekiel   Sarah Courtney   05Aug1793   E4   W22   [ret-AppA]

COLE, continued

Hanson	Susan A. Proctor	22Nov1859	W111	
Henry M.	Charlotte Hughes	13Jan1845	E88 W88	Finney
Isaac W.	Martha Davis	25May1846	W90	
James	Catharine Hollis	31Mar1797	E10 W26	
James	Elizabeth Gilbert	03Dec1823	E57 W61	
John	Priscilla Drew	30Apr1796	E8 W25	
John T.	Frenetta M. Mahan	20Apr1861	W114	
Louise	John Wareham	03Aug1844	E87 W87	Finney
Maria J.	Charles H. James	26Mar1855	H7 W102	Finney
Mary Ann	John W. Cannon	23Aug1838	E79 W80	Goldsborough
Mary Sophia	John Traverse	28Jul1845	E88 W89	
Michael	Elizabeth Martin	21Dec1819	E51 W57	
Sarah	Jarrett B. Moore	23Jan1865	W120	
Semelia O.	Noble Cannon	20Sep1834	E74 W75	Donahay
Sophia	Jervis Gilbert	27Nov1798	E15 W27	
Susan D.	Lewis G. Martin	07Nov1864	W120	
Susanna	George Walker, Junr	01Nov1837	E78 W79	Finney
Taylor	Sarah Louisa Kimble	14Jun1854	H6 W101	Reese

COLEMAN [see also COALEMAN]

Rebecca Ridgely	John Yellott	01May1806	E28 W38

COLLINGS

Sarah	John Hatton	m. 1803	[ret-AppA]

COLLINS

Ann	Isaac Tolson	26Oct1780	C3 W5
[additional entry for 20Nov1780 on C3]			
Cassy	Edward Collins	29Feb1796	E8 W25
Catherine	Mich¹ Fitzpatrick	03Jun1779	B2 W2
Charlotte	Elias Nowland	26Oct1809	E34 W43
Edward	Cassy Collins	29Feb1796	E8 W25
Elizth	James Milburn	23Sep1782	C6 W8
[possibly October, not September]			
Ephraham	Charity Combess	04Oct1780	C3 W5
Henry	Mary Irons	29Oct1784	C9 W10
Jacob	Hannah Mecarty	25Jun1780	C2 W4
Mahlon	Mary Greenlee	10Apr1805	E26 W36
Maynard	Sarah Jones	07Jan1779	B1 W1
Patience	John Morris	10Apr1781	C4 W6
Permelia	Joseph Thomas	14Aug1805	E26 W36
William T.	Sophia T. Richardson	13Oct1837	E78 W79 Finney

COLLISON

John	Elizabeth Finney	22Aug1845	E88 W89

COLYER

John E.	Rebecca Jane Dorney	14Sep1832	E71 W73 Sewell

COMBESS

Charity	Ephraham Collins	04Oct1780	C3 W5
Charlotte	Samuel J. Riley	08Apr1823	E54 W61
Susan	James Strong	06Jun1810	E35 W44

COMBEST
Mary — Moses Crabston — 25Aug1817 E47 W53

COMMIGER
William — Martha Clarke — 05Jul1796 E8 W25

COMMONS [see also McCommons]
Zebulon — Nancy Gallion — 14Aug1824 E58 W62

CONDRUM
William — Elinor Stuard — 08May1780 C2 W4

CONLEN
John — Lucy Linghan — 13Dec1850 W95

CONLEY
Elizabeth Jane — Henry S. Whiteford — 01Jun1841 E83 W84 Myers
Henry — Rachel H. Bagley — 13Dec1825 E60 W64 Finney
John D. — Sarah Thompson — 22Nov1810 E36 W44
Sarah — Aquila Deaver — 21Jan1811 E36 W44
Susanna — James Wilgis — 07Feb1839 E80 W81 Collis

CONN
Ann — Jesse Matthews — 30Jun1792 E2 W21
Esther — Arnold Rush — 21Jun1813 E40 W48
Margaret — Benjamin Amoss — 05Nov1800 E18 W30

CONNALLY
Catharine — Elisha Cooper — 31Dec1811 E37 W45
Eleanor — John Cook — 18Jan1781 C4 W5
John — Ellen Meany — 06Oct1848 W93

CONNARD
John — Susannah West — 13Oct1783 C8 W9 cr-Harf

CONNELLY
Elizabeth — Arthur Curry — 23Apr1829 E66 W68 O'Brian
Maria — Francis Brady — 30Nov1850 W95

CONNER
Catharine — Patrick Gugart — 21Jun1865 W121
Charlotte — James B. Wells — 15Dec1851 H1 W97 Huntington
Elizabeth A. — Nelson Bedford — 22May1849 W93
Judah [br] — Francis Deacon [gr] — m. 1778 [ret-AppA]
Mary Ann — John Hicks — 15Jan1861 W113

CONNICK [?]
Mary Ann — John Griffin — 27Sep1779 B3 W2

CONNOLLY
Elizabeth — John Watson — 07Mar1859 W110

CONOLLY
John — Jemima Wilgis — 08Apr1841 E83 W84 Cullum

CONOTHEN
Hugh	Mary Carroll	29Sep1855	H8	W103	Walter

CONSTABLE
Albert	Hannah S. Archer	21Dec1829	E66	W69	Finney

COOK
Harriet	Bennet Charshe	09Jan1849		W93	
James	Ann Catharine Haeston	19Dec1860		W113	
Jane	William Holmes	05Dec1796	E10	W25	
John	Eleanor Connally	18Jan1781	C4	W5	

COOLEY
Charles	Cornelia E. Barron	04Jan1837	E77	W78	Furlong
Corbin	Mary Stephenson	08Jan1833	E72	E73	Stephenson
Daniel M.	Hariet Wiles	28Sep1839	E81	W82	Finney
Elizabeth	Robert Bell	27Jul1818	E49	W55	
James	Elizabeth Smith	26Oct1808	E32	W41	
John	Sarah Gilbert	08Dec1779	C1	W3	
Lawson	Amanda C. Jarrett	16Feb1832	E70	W72	Stephenson
Wm	Elizth Bay	07Jul1784	C9	W9	

COOMS
Amelia	Philip Ruley	10Aug1792	E3	W21

COONROD
Jacob	Amelia M. Naimier	21Mar1851	W96

COOPER [see Cooper Boyd]
Bazel	Belinda Rutledge	18Jan1826	E60	W64	Poteitt
Eleanor	James Greenfield	12Dec1807	E30	W40	
Elisha	Catharine Connally	31Dec1811	E37	W45	
Hannah	Abraham Hays	06May1807	E29	W39	
Henry C.	Martha A. Ayres	18Dec1862		W116	
Margaret	William Ingle	28Nov1853	H4	W100	Trout
Nancy	Francis Lenlan	05Dec1803	E24	W34	
Philip	Sarah Green	13Feb1797	E10	W25	
Susanna	James Quinlin	07Apr1798	E13	W27	

COPELAND [see Wm. Copeland Goldsmith]
Frances	Greenbury Dorsey	m. 1787			[ret-AppA]
John	Margaret Cowan	28Aug1794	E6	W23	
Sarah	Nathaniel Moreton[?]	23Feb1798	E13	W27	Jno Allen

CORBIN [see Corbin Amoss, Corbin Cooley, Corbin L. Mitchell, Corbin Lee Onion]
Delia	Thomas Turner	24Oct1797	E11	W26	
Eleanor*	William Price	08Nov1802	E22	W33	
[*Susanna crossed out]					
Margaret	John Price	04Apr1829	E65	W68	Richardson
Mary Barbara	Henry S. Shinn	17Jan1853	H3	W99	Brand
Nathan	Sophia Enloes	07Apr1800	E17	W29	

CORD [see also COARD]
Amos	Elizabeth Swaine	22Jan1798	E13	W27	Jno Allen
Amos	Sarah Howard	08Apr1806	E28	W38	
Amos	Catharine Weeks	27Jul1822	E56	W60	
Asberry	Ann Rigdon	21Nov1806	E29	W38	
Elizabeth Sarah	Ford Deaver	15Feb1836	E76	W77	Smith
Harriott A.	John Baxter	18May1826	E61	W65	Richardson
John	Rebecah Wilson	13Feb1797	E10	W25	
John	Ellean Deaver	09Mar1857	H11	W106	Crampton
Mary Ann	George Deaver	04Jan1832	E70	W72	Sewall
Neomia	Isaac Tolson	01Jul1780	C2	W4	
Sarah	James Olliver	m. 1778			[ret-AppA]
Thomas	Louisa Jane Hopkins	05Feb1840	E81	W82	Prettiman
Zacheus	Susanna Watkins	06Apr1801	E20	W31	

CORHAM
William Henry	Margaret Lindamore	07Apr1858		W108

CORKENY
William	Ellen Fitzimmons	10Jun1852	H2	W98	McNally

CORKERY
Dennis	Margaret Flavin	10Feb1854	H5	W100	McNally

CORKORAN
Morris	Bridget Kelly	02Sep1853	H4	W99	McNally

CORNWELL
Cristian	William Shanbargar	28Aug1857	H12	W107	Wilson

CORRIGAN
James	Catharine C. Lochary	10Jan1851		W96

CORSE [see also COURCI, COURSE]
Elizabeth	Joseph James	15Aug1853	H4	W99	Finney

COSLEY
Thos	Jane Timmons	20Sep1779	B3	W2

COTT
John	Hannah Ealey	19Jan1781	C4	W6

COTTIGAN [or Cattigan]
Sarah	James McAdaw	01May1794	E5	W23	[ret-AppA]

COTTY
Edward	Mary Yoakly	12May1780	C2	W4

COULSON
Joseph C.	Martha Ann Love	05Nov1850		W95	
Mary	John Williams	23Nov1783	C8	W9	cr-Harf

COULTON
Margaret	John W. Lanpher	11Apr1846		W90

COURCI
John	Ann Coale	04Nov1803	E24 W34	

COURSE
Cassandra	John Coale	31Oct1832	E71 W73	Finney

COURTNAY
Eleanor	Richard Taylor	19Dec1800	E19 W30	
John	Clemency Mitchell	17Mar1801	E19 W30	
Matilda	John Hynson	31Jan1801	E19 W30	

COURTNEY
Adaline	Richard Loflin	03Jan1843	E85 W86	Finney
Avarilla A.	William B. Michael	19Dec1847	W92	
Benjamin S.	Mary Ann Maxwell	24Dec1832	E72 W73	Finney
Cornelia F.	Henry C. Michael	17Jan1854	H5 W100	Cronin
Cyrus	Avarilla Bailey	22Dec1812	E39 W47	
Edward	Cassandra Hawkins	09Apr1811	E36 W44	
Effa	Henry E. Michael	22May1826	E61 W65	Finney
Elen Jane	George Sheilds	23Jan1838	E78 W80	Finny
Eliza Jane	James Bradfield	27Oct1849	W94	
Elizabeth	Benjamin Hanson	30Jun1812	E38 W46	
Elizabeth M.	Henry A. Zollinger	19Apr1843	E86 W86	Happerset
Emily	William A. Courtney	07Feb1846	W89	
George W., Jr.	Ellen Baker	28Apr1841	E83 W84	Myers
George Washington	Phoebe Silver	11Feb1806	E28 W37	
Georgianna	Samuel Acres	29Oct1862	W116	
Hanson	Harriott Arnold	24Dec1816	E46 W52	
Harriet	John Wells	10Aug1832	E71 E73	---
Hollis	Eleoner Everest	18Mar1791	E1 W21	
Hollis	Sarah Ann Baker	25Aug1819	E51 W56	
John	Sarah Deaver	09May1803	E23 W33	
Julian	Benjamin F. Gallion	21Jun1851	W96	
Mary	Robert F. McGaw	28Nov1837	E78 W79	Finney
Mary	William Slee	[21?]Mar1843	E85 W86	Finney
Mary E.	James L. Richardson	10Jan1859	W109	
Matilda	William Maxwell	05Mar1827	E62 W66	Finney
Milkah	John Dunn	03Nov1802	E22 W33	
Sarah	Ezekiel Cole	05Aug1793	E4 W22	[ret-AppA]
Sarah Ann	Alvin C. Herbert	19Dec1842	E85 E86	Habborset[?]
Sarah Elizabeth	Benjamin F. Cronin	04Mar1846	W90	
Semelia	James Michael	m. 1778		[ret-AppA]
William A.	Emily Courtney	07Feb1846	W89	

COUSINS
George	Elizth White	10Sep1794	E6 W23	
John	Elizabeth Jackson	05Feb1799	E15 W28	

COVEY
Eliza.	Danl Donnavin	m. 1778		[ret-AppA]

COWAN [see also COEN]

Benjn	Martha Knight	06Feb1782	C5	W7	
Isabella	John Carroll	16Jun1779	B2	W2	
Margaret	John Copeland	28Aug1794	E6	W23	
Mary	Robert Porter	20Oct1803	E24	W34	
Sarah	George Henderson	15Nov1820	E53	W58	
Sus	Peter Bowler	03Jan1784	C8	W9	cr-Harf
Susanna	William Hamby	13Aug1800	E18	W29	
Thomas	Mary Richardson	19Feb1785	C10	W10	
Thomas	Sarah Barnes	m. 1790			[ret-AppA]

COWEN

Ann*	John Carson	21Oct1818	E49	W55	
[*Nancy crossed out]					
John	Priscilla A. Henderson	14Jan1840	E81	W82	Goldsborough
Mary	Samuel Fletcher	26Jan1836	E76	W77	Goldsborough

COWFIELD

William	Elizabeth A. Dutton	18Dec1833	E73	W74	Finney

COWIN

Boyce	Sarah Chauncey	05Apr1802	E22	W32

COWNOVER

Easther	Timothy Kain	08Apr1783	C7	W8	cr-Harf

COX

Ann	Hugh Malone	07Jun1779	B2	W2	
Elizabeth	Henry Fullard	19Jul1821	E54	W59	
Ephraim	Elizabeth Wilson	30Nov1802	E22	W33	
Guley Ann	Charles G. Stansbury	26Aug1802	E22	W32	
Hannah	John Hallard	31Mar1779	B1	W1	
John	Martha Gallion	28Mar1793	E4	W22	
Joseph	Elizabeth Shields	26Jun1798	E15	W27	
Maria	William Alexander	27Jan1851		W96	
Mary	Joseph Prigg	03Feb1801	E19	W30	
Mercy	John S. Williamson	24Sep1832	E71	W73	Park
Nicholas	Ann Weeks	12Aug1820	E53	W58	
Sarah	William Street	15Dec1799	E17	W28	
Sarah	James Griffith	08Aug1803	E23	W34	
Sarah	William Stansbury	05Dec1808	E32	W41	
Sarah	Joseph Hopkins	26Nov1811	E37	W45	
Sarah Ann	Edward T. Prigg	15Mar1836	E76	W77	Stevenson

CRABSON

Sarah	Benj. Harbert	15Aug1795	E7	W24

CRABSTON

John	Rebecca Hill	18Jul1836	E76	W78	Dulany
Moses	Mary Combest	25Aug1817	E47	W53	

CRAIG

John	Lucretia F. Mitchell	12Jan1861	W113

CRAIL
John	Ann Moore Baker	04Mar1812	E38 W46

CRAMER
Catharine	Henry Clion	05Mar1842	E84 E85	Herron

CRAMPTON
Jane	Thomas Lynch	18Jul1816	E45 W52
Savington W.	Isabella Perryman	28Jan1858	W108

CRANE
David, Junr.	Susanna Osborn	17Mar1795	E7 W24
Lida L.	Joel Pusey	04Aug1863	W117
Susanna	Jacob Michael	28Dec1808	E33 W41

CRANGAN [?]
Bartis[?]	Elizabeth Hultz[?]	23Dec1799	E17 W29

CRAPSON
Alice	Daniel Pogue	16Oct1805	E27 W36

CRAWFORD [see Crawford Gorrell]
Cassandra	John Reese	14Oct1823	E57 W61	
J. Taylor	Sally A. Healy	30Aug1860	W112	
John	Francis McLaughlin	16May1782	C6 W8	
John	Rebecca Rodgers	26Apr1809	E33 W42	
John	Mary J/I. McCann	21Jul1854	H6 W101	Trout
Margaret	Benjamin Wilmer	28May1800	E18 W29	
Robert	Peggy Ward	04Jul1784	C9 W9	
Robert	Allesanna Bosley	14Sep1802	E22 W33	
Ruth	Robt Orr	09Aug1794	E5 W23	[ret-AppA]

CREAL
Margaret	John Watkins	30Oct1817	E47 W54

CREAMER
Hannah	Michael Whitteman	05Jun1846	W90

CREIGH
Matilda	Nicholas McComas	29Oct1818	E49 W55

CRESWELL
George	Margaret Dolan	22Aug1863	W117	
Martha	Robert Elliott	23Feb1820	E52 W57	
Robert	Jane Meek	m. 1795		[ret-AppA]

CREVENSTEN
Martha C.	William Richardson	09Jan1862	W115

CREVENSTIN
George A.	Sarah J. Welsh	29Jun1858	W108

CREVISTEN
George	Mary Ann Everist	21May1817	E47 W53
George	Martha Greenfield	20Apr1818	E49 W55

CREW
Jefferson	Mary J. Singleton	30Jan1857	H11 W105 McCartney
Jonas	Cordelia Powell	18May1824	E58 W62

CRISPIN [see Crispin Cunningham]

CRISSEL
George	Ann Carnacle	31Jan1816	E44 W51

CRISSOL
James	Temperance Gorden	27Oct1812	E39 W46

CRISWELL
Charles	Catharine Baker	01Jul1844	E87 W87 Norris
Elizabeth	Mathews Dyer	11Jun1860	W112
Isabella	Thomas Whitson	02Apr1812	E38 W46
John	Elizabeth Mahan	18Mar1808	E31 W40
John L.	Mary Ann Wells	26Dec1854	H6 W102 Herron
Mary Jane	John Isen	04Sep1855	H8 W103 Cushing
Sarah R.	Thomas J/I. Peterson	05Apr1853	H3 W99 Keeck
William	Margaret Baker	16Mar1843	E85 W86 Wilson

CROGHAN
Catharine	James Sullivan	10Jul1857	H12 W106 Walter

CROMWELL
Deborah	Edward Ward	18Oct1808	E32 W41
Frances	Reason Dorsey	09Aug1797	E11 W26
Hannah	Patrick Boyle	20Jan1830	E66 W69 O'Brian
Jesse	Margaret Paca	16Nov1799	E17 W28
Joseph M.	Sophia Fullerton	04Mar1833	E72 E73 Sewell
Ruth	William McCubbin	m. 1803	[ret-AppA]

CRONAN
William	Margaret Whitaker	23Apr1806	E28 W38

CRONIN
Benjamin F.	Sarah Elizabeth Courtney	04Mar1846	W90
Mary	John Armstrong	12Jan1865	W120
Wm T.	Elizth Hoopman	05Jan1857	H11 W105 Cushing

CROOKS
Thos	Jane Cussin	31Jan1780	C1 W3

CROSEN
Catharine	Danl Bailey	27Mar1781	C4 W6
Rebeca	Robert Landrum	18Oct1781	C5 W7

CROSMORE
Phoebe	Hugh Ely	31Dec1805	E27 W37

CROSS
Elizabeth	Frederick Parks	30Jul1817	E47 W53	
Letitia	Joseph Johnson	10Jul1779	B3 W2	
Robert	Margaret Kenny	08Jan1863	W117	

CROW
Julian	Thomas H. Gray	23May1806	E28 W38	
Mary	John Murphy	26May1853	H4 W99	McNally
Stephen	Bridget Welch	31Oct1864	W119	

CRUISE
Ellen	Richard O'Brien	03Sep1850	W95	

CRUMLISH
James	Lizzie Donahoo	17Oct1857	H13 W107	Walter

CULHAM
Jesse	Susanna Jones	25Jun1801	E20 W31	

CULLEY
Robert	Maria J. Chandlee	21Jan1835	E75 W76	Goldsborough

CULLUM [see John Cullum Frazier; see also CULHAM]
Ann E.	David G. Elliott	23Aug1864	W119	
Ann Eliza	Wm Greenland	20Jun1864	W119	
Ann Jane	James Thompson	04May1853	H3 W99	Finney
Charlotte A.	William Brown	10Oct1854	W119	
George	Ann Hammond	04Jun1808	E31 W41	
Harriett	John T. Moffitt	26Mar1859	W110	
Jesse	Elizabeth Grindall	27Apr1835	E75 W76	Finney
Jesse	Eliza Preston	24Dec1838	E80 W81	Rese
Jesse	Jemima Ackers	10Jan1861	W113	
Martha J.	William T. Cullum	08Feb1865	W120	
Mary Catharine	James Michael Keitley	20Dec1858	W109	
Richard	Elizabeth England	01Apr1802	E21 W32	
Richard R.	Naomi P. Taylor	24Mar1825	E59 W63	Morrison
Susan	James Mallick	01Jan1862	W115	
Sutton	Ruth Gordon	14Dec1807	E30 W40	
William	Jane Greenland	20Dec1836	E77 W78	Reese
William H.	Editha H. Williams	15Aug1864	W119	
William T.	Martha J. Cullum	08Feb1865	W120	

CUMMINS
Ann M.	Isaac E. Willey	26Feb1856	H9 W104	Reineck
Cassandra	Isaac Pennington	17Mar1802	E21 W32	
Maria	William Mahan	25Jun1827	E63 W66	Webster
[orig. lic. to Webster; cr-Harf; bn-Cummings]				

CUNNINGHAM [see Cunningham S. Ramsay]
Ann	Bazill Smith	01May1781	C4 W6	
Bell S.	George W. Deaver	26Dec1863	W118	
Chrispian	Elizabeth Horner	m. 1789		[ret-AppA]
Crispin	Charity Fullerton	29Sep1825	E60 W64	Tidings
Daniel	Ann Amoss	16Oct1797	E11 W26	[ret-AppA]

CUNNINGHAM, continued

Daniel	Susan Norris	08Feb1815	E42 W49	
Edward L.	Elizabeth Hollingsworth	05Sep1838	E79 W80	Williams
Elizabeth	Edward A. Richardson	28Apr1836	E76 W77	Richardson
Elizabeth	Silas Norris	28Feb1861	W113	
George	Ann Gilbert	30Sep1800	E18 W30	
Henry	Frances Sprucebanks	25May1796	E8 W25	
James F.	Elizabeth Stearns	23Dec1862	W117	
John Worthy	Elizabeth Young	09Jan1846	W89	
Kezia Araminta	Henry McComas	07May1840	E82 W83	Prettyman
Lloyd	Elizabeth Jones	06Feb1817	E46 W53	
Mary	Andrew Thompson	26Dec1804	E25 W35	
Mary	James Denison	11Oct1814	E42 W49	
Mary C.	David Deckman	05Oct1864	W119	
Mortimer	Martha E. Dorney	29Oct1827	E63 W66	Poole
Rhesa N.	Elizabeth L. Davison	17Nov1847	W92	
Sarah Ann	James Jervis	28Jan1829	E65 W68	Richardson
Susan N.	Elias H. Beans	31Mar1852	H2 W98	Bosworth
Walter	Cassandra Turk	21Jun1804	E25 W35	
Walter	Jane Turk	29Dec1814	E42 W49	
Walter	Eliza Troutner	15Dec1847	W92	
William C.	Cecelia A. Bradford	01Mar1831	E68 W71	Tippet

CURLEY

Mary	Gideon Herbert	19Mar1802	E21 W32	
Patrick	Agnes Tarbet	14Mar1814	E41 W49	

CURREY

Amos	Hannah Price	26Jul1820	E53 W58	
Hannah Ann	John W. Flinn	24Dec1839	E81 W82	Finney

CURRIER

Barney	Martha Thomas	22Aug1780	C2 W4	

CURRY

Andrew J.	Martha J/I. Touchtone	17Aug1863	W117	
Ann	Archibald Holland	05Jun1813	E40 W47	
Ann C.	Joseph Wallace	16Jul1855	H8 W103	Beatty
Arthur	Sarah Cain	26Mar1805	E26 W36	
Arthur	Elizabeth Connelly	23Apr1829	E66 W68	O'Brian
Eliza E.	Silas Kennedy	11Jan1845	E87 W88	
George	Eleanor Sturgeon	19Oct1780	C3 W5	
Israel	Jane Vernay[?]	27Dec1825	E60 W64	Richardson
Jas	Kerzias Kidd	04Dec1780	C4 W5	
[after 19 & 3 December]				
James	Hannah Clark	20Aug1818	E49 W55	
John B.	Elizabeth Hitchcock	18Dec1824	E59 W63	Richardson
Mary	James Brady	08Nov1837	E78 W79	Crosgay
Mary	Henry Tenly	13Nov1847	W92	
Mary Jane	George Dollenger	07Dec1861	W115	
Mina	Lysias Rockhold	14Mar1865	W121	
Thomas	Sidney Chinworth	02Aug1819	E51 W56	
William[?]	Ann Smith	03Aug1780	C2 W4	

CURRY, continued
William   Hannah Ann Maddon   02Oct1827   E63 W66 Finney
  [orig. lic. to Finney; cr-Harf]
William T.   Hannah C. Moore   11Dec1857   W107

CURTIS
Alvin   Mary Turk   07Apr1817   E47 W53
Elizabeth   Hugh Haughy   30Jan1849   W93
Mary   John Jones   29Jan1827   E62 W65 Pool
Mary   John Harward   27Nov1848   W93
Rebecca   Joseph Strobridge   02May1832   E71 W72 Sewell

CURTUS
Ira   Elizabeth Miles   21Dec1826   E62 W65 Rockhold

CUSICK
Mary   Tho. Sorah   m. 1778   [ret-AppA]

CUSSIN
Jane   Thos Crooks   31Jan1780   C1 W3

CUSSINS
Frances   George Brown   22Nov1792   E3 W22

CYLE
Amos   Betsey Herbert   22Jun1844   E87 W87 Alexander

DADDRELL
James C.   Sarah Coale   06Sep1809   E34 W42

DAGG
Mary E.   Henry W. Hopkins   17Jul1839   E81 W82 Finney

DAGGS
Thomas   Margarett R. Dever   30Mar1821   E54 W59

DAILEY
Ann Elizabeth   Andrew J. Dunn   13Oct1862   W116
Bernard   Ruth Sweney   10Feb1843   E85 W86 Reid

DAILY
Andrew   Ellen McAdow   02Mar1839   E80 W81 Finney

DALBY [see Helen Dalby Bailey]

DALE
Ann   Thomas Nailor   16Aug1814   E42 W49

DALLAM
Amanda	James Lee Hopkins	23Nov1841	E84	W84	Brown
Cassandra	Winston Smith	26Oct1796	E9	W25	
Cassandra	Aquila Lockwood	14Sep1815	E43	W50	
Elizth	Parker Hall Lee	10Apr1781	C4	W6	
Elizth	Harman Stump	19Jun1793	E4	W22	
Elizth	John Jolly	19Apr1796	E9	W25	
Frances	Isaac Toy	18Mar1793	E4	W22	
Francis	martha Smith [sic]	24Apr1780	C2	W4	
Francis J.	Sarah P. Phillips	02Mar1815	E42	W49	
John	Mary Willson	13May1780	C2	W4	
John S.	Amanda M. Prigg	17Jun1845	E88	W88	
Joseph	Mary Worthington	22Sep1803	E23	W34	
Joseph W.	Octavia A. Gough	30Jan1855	H7	W102	Trout
Margaret W.	Samuel Wallis	27May1833	E72	W74	Donohay
Mary	Stacy West	09Feb1832	E70	W72	Keech
Richard	Marg^t Carlile	30Dec1792	E3	W22	
Richard	Sarah Wallace	14Oct1815	E43	W50	
Richard B.	Priscilla Paca	25Mar1799	E15	W28	
Sarah Winston	John Paca	13Sep1804	E25	W35	
Susan R.	Lyttleton F. Morgan	25Mar1840	E82	W83	Morgan
Susanna	John Wallis Hopkins	09Oct1800	E18	W30	
William	Josephine Webster	24Apr1843	E86	W86	Finney
William H.	Mary C. Maulsby	22Jan1852	H1	W97	Keech
William M.	Frances Smith	31Aug1808	E32	W41	

DALY
Ruth	Thomas Hutchins	23Jul1816	E45	W52

DANA
John	Catharine Martin	17Feb1848	W92

DANCE
Jesse G.	Caroline Richardson	19Oct1859	W110

DANIEL [?]
Sarah	Nathan^l Baker	07May1781	C4	W6

DARLIN
John	Mary Riley	24Jan1835	E75	W76	Donahay

DARRAH
Archabald	Sarah Botts	12May1828	E64	W67	Finney

DAUGERTY
Letty	George[?] York	03Apr1781	C4	W6

DAUGHERDAY
Thomas	Jemima German	01May1832	E71	W72	Frey

DAUGHERTY
Ann	Bennett Green	22Jan1838	E78	W80	Crosgay
Catharine Ann	George Langley	12Nov1839	E81	W82	Finny
James	Polly Quanland	21Nov1803	E24	W34	

DAUGHERTY, continued

Jane	Wm Smith	17Feb1779	B1	W1
Jane	Robert F. Gallion	02Sep1848		W93
John	Ann Chauncey	01Apr1800	E17	W29
Margaret	John Little	24Jun1800	E18	W29
Margaret Jane	Wm C. Knight	05Sep1857	H12	W107 Monroe
Mary	Benjamin Brucebanks	m. 1789		[ret-AppA]
Mary	George Kanney	29Jul1801	E20	W31
Rosa	Dennis Cochran	02Oct1863		W118
Saml	Hannah Ealey	17Jan1781	C4	W5
Susan	Asael Botts	21Nov1853	H4	W100 Gallion

DAVENPORT

Frances A.	Joseph G. Mitchell	28Oct1863		W118
Persis R.	Thomas Marsh	24Dec1859		W111

DAVIDSON

Jones	Sarah E. B. Bateman	18Nov1854	H6	W101 McNally

DAVIS [see Davis Norris]

Aquilla H.	Elizabeth A. Jones	21Feb1865		W120
Blanch W.	William Wiles, Jr.	26Jul1836	E76	W78 Smith
Cassandra	William Nevill	18Jan1809	E33	W42
Cassandra	John W. Harry	20Oct1846		W90
David	Pelitha Williams	19Mar1822	E55	W60
Elijah	Mary G. Garretson	m. 1788		[ret-AppA]
Elijah	Elizabeth Griffith	12Feb1817	E46	W53
Eliza	Bernard Smith	28Jun1838	E79	W80 Coskrey
Elizth	Wm Nash	12May1782	C6	W7
Elizth	Francis Gibson	10Mar1783	C7	W8
Elizabeth J.	Jonas John Potts	24Dec1845		W89
Fannie A.	Arian M. Hancock	22Feb1862		W115
George	Ann Grant	28Sep1780	C3	W5
George	Elizabeth Scott	13Aug1795	E7	W24
George A.	Harriet Keen	28Dec1844	E87	W88 Davis
George C.	Jane Kirk	12Feb1835	E75	W76 Finney
George T.	Sarah A. McCausland	15Mar1849		W93
Hannah	John Mitchell	15Jan1806	E27	W37
Harriet	Richard Holloway	15Apr1846		W90
James S.	Sarah Snograss	26Oct1854	H6	W101 Trout
Jesse	Mary Sowers	31Mar1806	E28	W37
Jesse	Ann Smith	05Nov1817	E48	W54
John	Peggy Watt	24Mar1804	E25	W35
John	Phebe Webster	26Dec1822	E56	W60
John C.	Jane Hazlett	20Jun1857	H12	W106 Finney
John P.	Eliza J/I. Jeffries	07Jul1852	H2	W98 Finney
Joseph	Harriot Welch	11Dec1810	E36	W44
Joshua	Margaret Miskimon	14Jan1822	E55	W59
Mrs. Lyle	Dr. D. G. Rush	24Dec1864		W120
Martha	Isaac W. Cole	25May1846		W90
Mary	Andw Carman	27Aug1781	C5	W7
Mary	William Moore	08Nov1810	E36	W43
Mary	Richard Kenly	19May1821	E54	W59
Mary G. E.	John Jay	31[?]Oct1844	E87	W88 Finney
Reese	Sarah Lee	27Feb1810	E35	W43

Harford Co. Md. Marriage Licenses, 1777-1865

DAVIS, continued
Reuben H.	Mary A. Hays	20Feb1821	E53 W58	
Sallie A.	William A. Neeper	07Jan1863	W117	
Sarah	Greenberry Presbury	18Jun1803	E23 W34	[ret-AppA]
Thomas	Widow Bayard	17Nov1860	W112	
Virginia P.	Edward Quarles	23Feb1853	H3 W99	Waugh
William J.	Melissa A. Watkins	21Jan1853	H3 W99	Wilson

DAVISON
Elizabeth L.	Rhesa N. Cunningham	17Nov1847	W92	
John	Hannah Taylor	m. 1793		[ret-AppA]

DAVLIN
James	Ellen Carroll	01Mar1859	W110

DAWES
Ann	Francis E. Monks	05Feb1825	E59 W63	O'Brien
Martha	Nathan Grafton	18Nov1810	E36 W44	
Milcah	Barnet Harper	18Jul1804	E25 W35	
Mordecai	Elizabeth Cannon	11Apr1812	E38 W46	

DAWNEY
Elizabeth	Samuel Webb	07Jul1814	E42 W49
Henry	Martha Hill	10Sep1799	E16 W28
Sarah	Joshua Day	11Nov1812	E39 W46

DAWS
Binjamin	Rachel Magniss	06Apr1783	C7 W8
Edward	Ann Grunden	27Dec1793	E5 W23
Mary	Richard Thrift	02Oct1801	E20 W31
Mordica	Elizth Goddard	16Feb1781	C4 W6
Sarah	Ashberry Coard	04Mar1783	C7 W8

DAWSON [see William Dawson Wilson]
Mary	Richard Hill	04Oct1795	E7	
[above license crossed out]				
Mary	David Small	05Sep1805	E26 W36	
Sarah Ann	Sylvester Mitchell	23Oct1839	E81 W82	Goldsborough

DAY [see Lloyd Day Onion]
Amos G.	Mary A. Richardson	07Jan1862	W115	
Augusta M.	John C. Lyon	13Apr1833	E72 W74	Hamilton
Charlotte	John Saunders	11Jul1796	E8 W25	[or 16Jul?]
Charlotte E.	Henry Weatheral	27Apr1797	E10 W26	[ret-AppA]
Edward	Mary Brown	09Jan1801	E19 W30	
Edward of John	Hannah Wilmer	01Aug1801	E20 W31	
Elizabeth	Israel Bowman	31Jan1801	E19 W30	
Frances	Andrew Thompson	04Mar1805	E26 W36	
Grafton	Sarah E. Johnson	12May1856	H10 W104	McKinsey
Hannah	John Dorsey	29Apr1780	C2 W4	
Israel	Mary Baker	22Feb1821	E53 W58	
Israel	Ellen M. Lawrence	13Jun1861	W114	
James H.	Emily J. McFadden	31Jan1861	W113	
James M.	Sarah Hollis	01Sep1810	E35 W44	
James Maxwell	Rebecca Nabb	03Dec1804	E25 W35	

DAY, continued

John	Mary Ann Weatherell	24Jan1783	C7	W8	
John	Sarah Allender	m. 1788[?]			[ret-AppA]
John W.	Sarah Ruff	15Apr1830	E67	W69	Richardson
Joshua	Sarah Hanson	29Dec1784	C9	W10	
Joshua	Sarah Dawney	11Nov1812	E39	W46	
Letitia	James J. Wilmer	m. 1803			[ret-AppA]
Mary Ann	William W. Dorney	26May1828	E64	W67	Richardson
Mary G.	Christopher C. Rouse	14Apr1834	E74	W75	Donahay
Matthew	Sarah Ann Coates	01Oct1855	H8	W103	Smith
Priscilla Presbury	Henry Augustus Inloes	26Jun1837	E78	W79	Lyons
Sarah	Wm Groves	26Feb1794	E5	W23	[or 27Feb?]
Sarah E.	John Macomber	27May1862		W116	

DEACON

Francis [gr]	Judah Conner [br]	m. 1778		[ret-AppA]

DEAKINS

Joseph M.	Catherine Ann Hollis	23Jun1831	E69	W71	Sewall

DEAN

Lydia	Jehue Otley	22Mar1796	E8	W25	
Nathan	Ann Jarvis	28Nov1805	E27	W37	
Nathan	Rachel L. Robinson	02Jan1854	H4	W100	Trout

DEANE

Eliza	John Forward	m. 1778		[ret-AppA]

DEARHOLT

Eliza	Robert Deaver	04Dec1811	E37	W45
Henry	Nancy Bowler	11Dec1811	E37	W45
Henry	Elizabeth Saunders	04Sep1824	E58	W62

DEAVER

Aquila	Rebecca Osborn	17Dec1805	E27	W37	
Edwin T. [poss. 18Dec]	Sarah H. Baxter	17Dec1854	H6	W101	Lemmon
Eliza	William Holloway	19Jan1835	E75	W76	Porter
Elizth	Isaac Jones	09Jul1779	B3	W2	
Ellean	John Cord	09Mar1857	H11	W106	Crampton
Ford	Elizabeth Sarah Cord	15Feb1836	E76	W77	Smith
Fra^s	Isaac Jones	27Feb1781	C4	W6	
Frances R.	James Deaver	05Aug1851		W96	
George	Mary Ann Cord	04Jan1832	E70	W72	Sewall
George	Priscilla Jones	02Jan1838	E78	W80	Park
George W.	Bell S. Cunningham	26Dec1863		W118	
Hannah	John York	m. 1777			[ret-AppA]
Hugh	Marg^t Smith	12Apr1782	C6	W7	cr-Harf
James	Frances R. Deaver	05Aug1851		W96	
Jefferson	Martha Forwood	31Dec1832	E72	W73	Sewell
John	Jane Smith	26Nov1812	E39	W47	
John	Sarah Chocke	21Sep1819	E51	W56	
John	Sarah Baldwin	14Nov1864		W120	
John W.	Mary Jane Hanby	10Oct1850		W95	
Joshua	Martha Kimble	21Aug1807	E30	W39	

DEAVER, continued

Mary	Bennet Taylor	13May1806	E28 W38	
Mary	Samuel Carman	13Jun1842	E85 W85	Wilson
Micajah	Dianna Ellis	03Apr1792	E2 W21	
Nancy	Henry W. Shane	03Oct1815	E43 W50	
Richard	Rachel Cannon	15Feb1817	E46 W53	
Robert	Eliza Dearholt	04Dec1811	E37 W45	
Samuel	Ann Vandegrift	04Jan1809	E33 W42	
Sarah	John Courtney	09May1803	E23 W33	
Sarah A.	Robert G. Taylor	16Aug1862	W116	
William	Elizabeth Standley	03Jan1785	C10 W10	
William	Angelina Hopkins	01Apr1847	W91	

DEAVERS

Aquila	Sarah Conley	21Jan1811	E36 W44

DEAVOUR

John	Mary Fowler	12May1780	C2 W4

DEBRULA

William G.	Martha Tunis Hill	25Mar1829	E65 W68	Richardson

DEBRULAR

Cajah Greenfield	Hannah T. Hill	06Jul1815	E43 W50
Fras	Danl McLaughlin	10Feb1779	B1 W1

DEBRULER

Anthony	Sarah Philison	m. 1778		[ret-AppA]
Delia	Elijah Waskey	25May1819	E51 W56	
Elizabeth Greenfield	Theodore J. Webster Middleton	26Jan1836	E76 W77	Dulaney
Frances	James Hathhorn	21Jan1806	E27 W37	
George	Aramenta Nutterville	11Jul1791	E1 W21	
Greenberry	Rachel Healy	23May1799	E16 W28	
Jno	Mary Pierce	m. 1778		[ret-AppA]
Micajah	Sarah York Howard	31Jan1801	E19 W30	
Sarah Elizth	Nicholas Wilson	02Apr1846	W90	
Thomas Wm	Mary Jane Wilson	29Mar1855	H7 W102	Reese

DECKMAN

David	Mary C. Cunningham	05Oct1864	W119
Evans	Jane Ann Morrison	21Sep1864	W119
James R.	Mary E. Thompson	28Apr1865	W121

DEETS

Catharine	William Tipton	25Apr1849	W93

DELANEY

Joshua	Lydea Hughs	31Oct1791	E1 W21

DELEVET

James H.	Susan Jane Bull	09Jan1861	W113

DELMAS

Elizabeth V.	Grove U. Hotchkiss	26Oct1842	E85 W85	Reid

DELMOS
Francis   Mary Watters   01Apr1806   E28 W38

DEMATT
Sarah   William Fizzee   m. 1777   [ret-AppA]

DEMBY
George W.   Elizabeth Carver   23Dec1839   E81 W82   Goldsborough

DEMOS
Aquila   Ann Henderson   22Feb1814   E41 W48
Catharine   James Beaty   22Apr1806   E28 W38
Mary   Taylor Hughes   05Jan1818   E48 W54

DEMOSS
Amanda F. M.   Albert R. Magness   31Dec1860   W113
Eleanor   Edward Guyton   14Mar1815   E43 W49
James   Minerva Robinson   01May1863   W117
John   Hannah Meads   13Nov1816   E46 W52
Mary   James G. Bankhead   18Dec1826   E62 W65
Mary Susan   James M. Magness   01Dec1858   W109
Sarah Ann   John D. Meads   15Nov1848   W93

DEMPSEY
Thomas   Susan Chandley   18Aug1819   E51 W56

DEMPSTER
Luke   Sarah Scott   m. 1788   [ret-AppA]

DENBOW
Clemency   Joseph Kannaday   10Jun1800   E18 W29
John, Junr Elizabeth Street   18Jan1808   E31 W40
John   Martha Sharp   09Mar1819   E50 W56
Martha   Benjamin Towland   06Dec1814   E42 W49
Sarah   John Street   16Dec1839   E81 W82   Poteet
Thomas   Catharine Stritehoof   01Mar1852   H1 W98   Robey

DENISON
Eliza   John D. Henley   26Mar1816   E45 W51
James   Mary Cunningham   11Oct1814   E42 W49
Jane   William Arnold   03Oct1835   E75 W77   Dulany
Matthew   Sarah Shearwood   12Aug1798   E15 W27
Thomas H.   Mary Rumsey[?] Diven[?] 14May1812 E38 W46   [or Divers]

DENNISON
Minerva   Comd^r John Rodgers 21Oct1806   E29 W38

DENNY
Margaret   Grafton White   03Jan1781   C4 W5   "Wheat"
Marg^t Geo. Brown   08Jan1781   C4 W5

DENOVIN
Jacob   Sus^a Gilbert   m. 1778   [ret-AppA]

Harford Co. Md. Marriage Licenses, 1777-1865

DEVEE
Fras	Harmon Hill	10Dec1779	C1 W3	

DEVER
George	Margaret Forsythe	24Feb1840	E82 W83	Anderson
George	Mary E. Arnold	08Jan1864	W118	
Hannah E.	Caleb Emlin	01Dec1848	W93	
Hugh Jefferson	Susan Arnold	02Sep1862	W116	
Jefferson	Jane Forsythe	09Apr1844	E87 W87	Edgy
Margarett R.	Thomas Daggs	30Mar1821	E54 W59	
Mary	Bonfield Gorrell	30Nov1836	E77 W78	Finney
Richard	Mary Bradfield	08Apr1848	W92	

DEVERAUX [see Deveraux Jarrett]

DEVEREUX
Alexander	Eliza Hays[?]	17Aug1857	H12 W106	Walter

DEVIN
Catharine	John Bond	06Sep1791	E1 W21
Michael	Elizabeth Rice	09Jan1781	C4 W5

DEVOE
Ann	Caleb P. Way	25Jun1849	W94	
Annie E.	Daniel Gallup	27Apr1864	W119	
James	Mary Streett	22Jan1834	E73 W75	Finney
John	Sarah Grafton	31Dec1827	E64 W67	Keech
John	Alice Jones	15Aug1861	W114	
Joseph	Clarisa Green	10Feb1830	E67 W69	O'Brian
Mary J.	Caleb P. Way	04Mar1845	E88 W88	Wilson
Mollie M.	William Holland Divers	17Oct1861	W114	
Sarah	Abel Durham	23Apr1817	E47 W53	
Sarah Ann	John Heaton	10Dec1858	W109	
Thomas B.	Mary O. Lytle	15Feb1842	E84 E85	Keech

DeWILTON [see DeWilton Haines]

DICK
David	Mary Wilson	17Dec1780	C3 W5	
James	Mary Allender	05Sep1830	E67 W70	Tippit
Mary Eliza	John G. West	29Mar1858	W108	
Robert W.	Harriet Bailey	24Oct1859	W111	

DICKERSON
Julian	Robert T. P. Allen	07Jul1834	E74 W75	Dunahay

DICKEY
Dr. Robert	Laura Jane Watters	19Dec1862	W116

DICKINSON
Jacob T.	Martha M. Allen	22Jul1837	E78 W79	Collins
Martha	Ebenezer N. Allen	28May1827	E63 W66	Allen

DICKS
Elizabeth	George Hirnar	23Oct1860	W112

DICKSON
Rachel	Michael Johnson	17May1820	E52	W57
Samuel M.	Harriet A. Wilson	14Jun1865		W121

DILLION
Edwd	Ann Tasker	29Jun1792	E2	W21	[ret-AppA]

DILLMAN
George	Lizzie Oram	26Jan1865	W120

DILWORTH
Rachel	Joshua Tracy	06Oct1817	E47	W53

DINAN
Bridget	John Keating	09Feb1855	H7	W102	Walter
Juda	Martin Kelly	13Jan1855	H6	W102	Walter
Patrick	Loucinda McCausland	24Aug1847		W91	

DINSMORE
Ann [Dinsmore?]	Evan Stollinger	10Feb1835	E75	W76	Hoopman
John	Jane Herbert	04Oct1808	E32	W41	
William	Martha Boyd	25Oct1838	E79	W81	Hoopman
William	Mary Elizabeth Tollinger	09Aug1845	E88	W89	

DITTO
Abraham	Ann Amoss	23May1796	E8	W25
Lovey	Reubin Jones	30Dec1812	E39	W47

DIVEN [poss. Divers]
Mary Rumsey[?]	Thomas H. Denison	14May1812	E38	W46

DIVER
Thomas	Martha Holloway	20Nov1850	W95

DIVERS
Ananias	Mary Ann Jones	02Jan1854	H4	W100	Hawk[?]
Annanias	Elizabeth Amos	19Feb1828	E64	W67	Keech
Charity	Josiah S. McComas	22May1808	E31	W40	
Charlotte S.	George H. Gorrell	12Aug1857	H12	W106	Smith
Elizabeth Ann	Joshua James	12Jul1831	E69	W71	Finney
Harriet S.	Seth W. Herrick	16Jan1862		W115	
Henry	Rachel Yearly	17May1815	E43	W50	
John	Charity Onion	03Jan1804	E24	W34	[ret-AppA]
John	Elizabeth Pyle	20Dec1850		W95	
Joseph	Mary Matilda McClaskey	09Feb1836	E76	W77	Morrison
Mary	Henry Bowen	12Jun1817	E47	W53	
Mary E.	James R. Andrew	20Nov1850		W95	
Rebecca A.	William Bowen	09Oct1854	H6	W101	Dumm
Sarah H.	James R. Lilly	28Dec1854	H6	W102	Finny
William	Elizabeth Hanna	12Apr1803	E23	W33	
William	Sarah Wilson	09Jun1829	E66	W68	McGee
William H.	Elizabeth Osborn	29Nov1827	E63	W67	Webster
William Holland	Mollie M. Devoe	17Oct1861		W114	

Harford Co. Md. Marriage Licenses, 1777-1865

DIVES
Wm	Rebecca Kain	16Dec1779	C1 W3	

DIXON [see Dixon Slade]
Benjn	Ann McAdoo	27Apr1779	B2 W1	
Cina	Henry Lowman	17Sep1829	E66 W69	Richardson
David M.	Ann J. Carr	05Jun1865	W121	
Druy Elizabeth	John Henry Simon	15Jan1840	E81 W82	Prettyman
John	Frances Coale	05Feb1812	E38 W46	
John	Lucy Ann Ford	28May1816	E45 W51	
Margaret	George McLaughlin	18Oct1817	E47 W54	
Rachel	Harvey D. Spears	30Dec1834	E74 W76	Dulany
Sarah	Andrew J. Whitelock	02Nov1863	W118	
Susan	Isaac Webster	05Aug1813	E40 W48	
Susa	Wm Jones	m. 1778		[ret-AppA]

DOBBINS
John	Elizabeth Ammons	23Dec1818	E50 W56

DOBSON
Henrietta	Thomas P. Barnard	09Feb1846	W90
William H.	Margaret F. Brown	14Jun1858	W108

DODDRIDGE [see Doddridge Whiteford]

DOLAN
Margaret	George Creswell	22Aug1863	W117

DOLLENGER
George	Mary Jane Curry	07Dec1861	W115

DONAHAE
Danl	Mary Treadaway	14Jun1779	B2 W2

DONAHOE
Aquila	Mary Carroll	27Dec1826	E62 W65	Stephenson
Daniel	Sarah Wood	18Jan1785	C10 W10	

DONAHOO
Bridget	Francis Kearney	18Nov1857	H13 W107	Walter
John	Elizabeth Wood	18Feb1812	E38 W46	
John C.	Ann Eliza Jewens	02Jun1864	W119	
Lizzie	James Crumlish	17Oct1857	H13 W107	Walter

DONAVAN
John	Rosa Miskimmons	31May1845	E88 W88

DONAVIN
John	Francis Gilbert	06Nov1779	C1 W3

DONCLAN
Patrick	Margaret Gallagher	06Dec1849	W94

DONN
George S.	Marian A. Donohoo	16May1859	W110

DONNAVIN
Dan¹ Eliza. Covey m. 1778 [ret-AppA]

DONNELY
Sarah A. James Gorrell 03Apr1852 H2 W98 Finney

DONNOND
Elizabeth William McCubbin 07Mar1801 E19 W30

DONOHOO
James L. Mary Elizth Osborn 27Jan1862 W115
Marian A. George S. Donn 16May1859 W110
Mary Barney O'Neill 30Nov1860 W112

DONOVAN [see also DONAVAN, DONAVIN, DONNAVIN]
Thos Rachel Greenard 28May1780 C2 W4

DOOLEY
Edward Mary Smith 28Aug1781 C5 W7
Elizth Bazil Smith 14Aug1782 C6 W8
John Cathrine Poteet[?] 23Jul1781 C5 W7

DORAN
Ann John Shipley 06Feb1830 E67 W69 O'Brian
Catherine Joshua Shipley 01Feb1820 E52 W57
Edward Mary Allman 12Sep1801 E20 W31
Mary Ann Nicholas Sutton 05Jan1827 E62 W65 O'Brian

DORMAN
Julia Cristoff Kindsley 19Mar1855 H7 W102 Forbes

DORNEY
George W. Mary Ann Dove 14Jan1839 E80 W81 Reese
Henry, Junr Harriott Woolen 06Mar1827 E62 W66 Richardson
Martha E. Mortimer Cunningham 29Oct1827 E63 W66 Poole
Rebecca Jane John E. Colver 14Sep1832 E71 W73 Sewell
Sarah Jane Joseph Henry Miller 22Aug1859 W110
Thomas Mary Taylor 07Nov1808 E32 W41
William W. Mary Ann Day 26May1828 E64 W67 Richardson

DORSET
Cyrena Thomas Pilkington 16Nov1812 E39 W47
Jonathan Martha Mitchell 23Jul1807 E30 W39
Martha Benjamin Ward 16Apr1807 E29 W39

DORSEY [see Daniel Dorsey Spencer, Dorsey H. Whitaker]
Algernon S. Mary A. Webster 03Jun1851 W96
Archibald Sarah McComas 10Oct1820 E53 W58
Charlotte Richard Graves 29May1798 E15 W27
Frances Rebecca George Chancey, Junr. 14Nov1796 E10 W25
Greenbury Frances Copeland m. 1787 [ret-AppA]
Henry of Edwd Eliz. Smithson 05Feb1795 E6 W24
Jane L. Philip Littig 22Aug1843 E86 W86 Thomas
John Hannah Day 29Apr1780 C2 W4

DORSEY, continued

Mary	Hollis Hanson	30Apr1781	C4	W6
Mary E.	Walter Farnandis	20Jun1816	E45	W51
Milcah	Joseph Gallop	28Sep1792	E3	W22
Reason	Frances Cromwell	09Aug1797	E11	W26
Sarah	Stephen Waters	24Feb1794	E5	W23

DOUGHERTY

Rose   Michael Broderick   05Oct1858   W109

DOVE

Elizabeth Jane	Joseph B. Cator	30May1836	E76 W78	Dulany
Mary Ann	George W. Dorney	14Jan1839	E80 W81	Reese
William G.	Martha Paul	16Jan1816	E44 W51	

DOWLING

James   Georgiana Starr   23Jun1856   H10 W105 Cushing

DOWNER

Frances L. J. D.   Alonzo G. W. Barnes   12Oct1836   E77 W78 Crosgrey

DOWNFIELD

Grace Ann   Thomas Clark   13May1842   E85 W85 Reid

DOWNING

Johana	James Sullivan	03Jul1858		W108
Joseph	Elizabeth Webster	23Apr1799	E16	W28
Richard [after 22Jul]	Margaret Webb	16Jul1780	C2	W4
Samuel	Prissilla Webb	15Jul1784	C9	W9

DOWNS

Elizabeth   John Smith   09Sep1794   E6 W23

DOXEN

Elizabeth	Joseph Lee	15Mar1860	W111
Sarah Jane	William H. Starr	14Feb1860	W111
William W.	Martha Gordon	15Mar1860	W111

DOXON

Catharine	John Markley	03Feb1853	H3 W99	Robey
Sarah Ann	John Milwake	24Nov1852	H2 W98	Robey

DOYLE

Andrew	Elizabeth Fields	m. 1789	[ret-AppA]
John	Adaline Minnick	01Mar1856	H9 W104 Cushing

DRAGHORN

John   Elizabeth Luckey   12May1853   H4 W99 Foobs

DRENNEN

Sarah   George Arel   19Jan1785   C10 W10

DREW

Aquila	Martha Nelson	21Jan1812	E37 W45	
Frances Priscilla	Charles H. Bradford	09Apr1833	E72 W73	Higbee
Henry	Sarah Henderson	18[?]Jun1783	C7 W8	
Priscilla	John Cole	30Apr1796	E8 W25	
Sarah	David Thompson	01Apr1779	B2 W1	
Susan	William Bradford	26Jun1811	E36 W45	

DRUMMOND

John W.	Cordelia E. Standiford	20Nov1851	W97	

DUBRE

Joseph	Mary Kiser	20Nov1794	E6 W23	B. Bond

DUER

Charles	Elizabeth Ann Norris	31Jan1826	E60 W64	Keeck
John	Susanna Norris	13Sep1811	E37 W45	

DUFF

Ailizanna	Edward Lingan	27May1830	E67 W69	O'Brian
Cassandra	James L. Bull	26May1851	W96	
Catherine	John Blake	19Feb1822	E55 W60	
Harriet	William H. Bull	10Jun1851	W96	

DUKE

Philip	Ellen Early	28Jan1845	E88 W88	Reid

DULANEY

Charlotte	James Taylor of Stephn.	03May1809	E33 W42	
Mary	Lawrence Harps	29Aug1796	E9 W25	

DULANY

Aquila	Susan Ann Taylor	19Dec1827	E64 W67	Finey
[orig. lic. to Finney; cr-Harf]				
Joseph	Mary Ann Mitchell	30Dec1820	E53 W58	
Joshua H.	Naomi Taylor	25Jan1821	E53 W58	

DULEY

Elizabeth	Clement Thomas	31Jul1805	E26 W36
Priscilla	John Roberts	31Jul1813	E40 W48
Robert	Rebecca Scarbrough	26Jun1816	E45 W51
William	Elizabeth Kitely	20Jun1798	E15 W27

DULL

Susan	Edward H. Fredericks	27Jun1861	W114

DUNCAN

Benjamin W.	Martha Smith	01Feb1830	E67 W69	Stevenson
Sampson S.[?]	Hannah Hughes	28Jan1845	E88 W88	Park
William	Hannah Wiley	29Dec1852	H3 W98	Smith

Harford Co. Md. Marriage Licenses, 1777-1865

DUNN
Andrew J.	Ann Elizabeth Dailey	13Oct1862		W116
Anne M.	John D. Alderson	27Nov1860		W112
John	Milkah Courtney	03Nov1802	E22	W33
Mary	Thomas Annis [or Onins?]	02Sep1797	E11	W26
Michael	Mary Tracey	25Nov1808	E32	W41
Richard	Sarah Bateman	14Jan1795	E6	W24
Sarah	William Benjamin	31Jul1815	E43	W50

DUNSHEATH
Elizth	Charles Gelaspy	20Nov1778	B1	W1
Mary	Jonas Stephenson	16Jul1800	E18	W29

DUNSTONE
Jane	John Thornton	10Apr1779	B2	W1

DURBIN [see Drucilla Durbin Nicols]
Ann	John H. Hughes	05Nov1784	C9	W10
Cassandra	Richard Sappington	02Oct1784	C9	W9
Eliza	John Anderson	24Oct1808	E32	W41
Mary	Richard Jones	15Sep1796	E9	W25
Thos	Clemence Litten	05Oct1779	B3	W2

DURHAM
Abel	Sarah Devoe	23Apr1817	E47	W53	
Abraham	Martha Prine	23Sep1813	E40	W48	
Abraham	Susannah Durham	15Sep1847		W91	
Amelia	Thomas Nelson Binns	23Jan1795	E6	W24	
Charlotte	Thomas Whitaker	22Feb1800	E17	W29	
David	Mary A. Harker	01Apr1864		W119	
Elizabeth	Joseph Hunter	m. 1777			[ret-AppA]
Elizabeth D.	Andrew J. Huff	19Mar1839	E80	W81	Keech
Elizth Frances	Abraham Gladden	25Aug1851		W96	
Jane P.	Henry Bohmer	[02?]Apr1850		W94	
Marietta	Abraham Gladden	30Sep1857	H12	W107	Trott
Martha Ellen	George Smith	01Dec1851	H1	W97	Wilson
Mary	Francis Jinkins	13Oct1780	C3	W5	
Nathaniel	Jane Montgomery	15May1854	H5	W101	Wilson
Sarah Ann	Humphy Wilson	10Feb1844	E87	W87	Keech
Susanna	Alexander Hellen[?]	16May1799	E16	W28	
Susannah	Abraham Durham	15Sep1847		W91	
Thomas of David	Rachel Smithson	11Apr1807	E29	W39	
William	Mary Ann Chamberlain	11Nov1807	E30	W39	
William A.	Rachel A. Gladden	30Nov1857	H13	W107	Keech
Zachariah	Frances Wilson	01Jan1817	E46	W52	

DUTTON
Elizabeth	Ford Barnes	22Dec1806	E29	W38	
Elizabeth A.	William Cowfield	18Dec1833	E73	W74	Finney
John	Amelia Cannen	24Jun1800	E18	W29	br-A.A.
Mary	Aquila Norris	22Dec1804	E25	W35	
Mary F.	Cardiff D. Norris	28Jun1834	E74	W75	Richardson
Robert	Mary Waltham	22Mar1784	C8	W9	
Susan	Reese Norris	29Oct1804	E25	W35	[ret-AppA]

DUVALL
Felima Jane	Isaiah J/I. Spicer	09Jun1830	E67 W69	Richardson
R. Ellen	DeWilton Haines	04Jun1851	W96	
Susan H.	John R. Barnes	25Nov1839	E81 W82	Hunt[?]

DUZAN
Peter	Keziah A--	m. 1777		[ret-AppA]

DYER
Mathew	Ann Elizth Stockdale	06Oct1863	W118
Mathews	Elizabeth Criswell	11Jun1860	W112

EAGON
Mary	Thomas James	11Nov1780	C3 W5
["4 Dollars Hard Money"]			

EALEY
Hannah	Samuel Daugherty	17Jan1781	C4 W5
Hannah	John Cott	19Jan1781	C4 W6

EARLE
Mark A.	Caroline H. McCormick	24Jun1845	E88 W89

EARLY
Ellen	Philip Duke	28Jan1845	E88 W88	Reid

EASTER
Wm Thomas	Euphemia Silver	11May1853	H4 W99	Hamilton

EATON
Elizabeth	Benj. Richardson	02Feb1797	E11 W25
[return by Parson Luckie]			

EBAUGH
Benjamin F.	Sophia C. Norris	14May1831	E69 W71	Finney
R. Caroline	Thomas Miller	28Dec1859	W111	

ECK
Miny [br]	Christian Mies [gr]	09Nov1861	W114

ECOFF
David	Hannah Thomas	10Feb1813	E39 W47	
Gertrude	James H. Monks	25Jul1857	H12 W106	Keech
Hannah	Elisha R. Tucker	16Oct1854	H6 W101	Wilson
Ralph	Agness Baxter	07Aug1811	E37 W45	
Samuel	Susanna Wann	25Nov1830	E68 W70	Keeck
Sarah	William Baxter	08Dec1813	E41 W48	

EDEN
Jeremiah	Mary Summers	02May1791	E1 W21

EDIE
David A.	Mary E. Payne	25Feb1856	H9 W104	Smith

EDWARDS
Ann	Stephen Fell	21Feb1779	B1 W1	
Elizabeth	John* Armstrong	14Aug1791	E1 W21	
[*Solomon crossed out]				
Mary	Benjamin Rogers	02Mar1826	E61 W64	
William P.	Ann Morris	12Jun1861	W114	

EGGLESTON
George W.	Mary Elizabeth Warner	18Oct1851	W97

EICHELBERGER
Wm	Henrietta M. Luke	01May1827	E63 W66	O'Brian

EISENBREY
Peter	Catherine Proctor	20Sep1837	E78 W79	Goldsborough

ELGAR [see Margaret Elgar Coale]

ELGIN
George L.	Elizabeth A. Alderson	13Oct1849	W94

ELLETT
Thomas	Susannah Bevard	09Oct1780	C3 W5

ELLIOTT
David G.	Ann E. Cullum	23Jul1864	W119	
Harriett M.	Jas T. Sullivan	21Jan1835	E75 W76	Goldsborough
John	Elizabeth Hawkins Morgan	11Jun1810	E35 W44	
Keziah	Benjamin Williams	26Feb1847	W91	
Laura H.	George F. Walker	25Nov1862	W116	
Robert	Martha Creswell	23Feb1820	E52 W57	
Sarah	James Lee	08Apr1779	O2 W1	
William	Catherine Ann Barnes	10Dec1836	E77 W78	Furlong

ELLIS
Dianna	Micajah Deaver	03Apr1792	E2 W21
John	Jemima Baldwin	06May1802	E22 W32
Mary	Matthew A. Thompson	24Mar1806	E28 W37
Permelia	Thomas Griffin	19Dec1816	E46 W52

ELLITT
Margret	Thomas Bradenbaugh	17Mar1838	E79 W80	Croft

ELY
Amos	Ann Jones	27Oct1808	E32 W41	
Ann	Ire Southwick	24Feb1820	E52 W57	
Ann	James Holland	25Sep1845	E88 W89	
Eliza Jane	Mark Atkinson	28Oct1851	W97	
Ellen S.[?]	Elisha Barnes	10Feb1842	E84 W85	Keech
Hugh	Phoebe Crosmore	31Dec1805	E27 W37	
Isaac J.	Sarah Rogers	04Nov1828	E65 W68	Stephenson
John	Jane Meeks	24Dec1792	E3 W22	[ret-AppA]
John	Margaret Williams	21May1817	E47 W53	

ELY, continued

John W.	Caroline E. Barton	12Nov1860	W112	
[same, repeated 15 November 1860]				
Mary Ann	John Patton	19Oct1857	H13 W107	Kithcart
Mary J.	Henry C. Fowler	15Mar1864	W119	
Matilda	Joseph Sanders	11Jun1822	E55 W60	
Rachel	John Rogers	07Jan1818	E48 W54	
Sarah	Squire Scotten	24Aug1816	E45 W52	
Sarah Ann	Samuel T. Prigg	21Dec1847	W92	
Thomas	Ann Maria Lancaster	18Oct1814	E42 W49	
Thomas	Mary Ann Lee	04Oct1827	E63 W66	Finney
Thomas	Sarah Ann Forsythe	23Mar1840	E82 W83	Anderson
Thomas J.	Hannah Way	17May1836	E76 W77	Richardson

EMLIN

Caleb	Hannah E. Dever	01Dec1848	W93	

EMORY

George	Catharine Shaffer	28Oct1863	W118	
Thomas L.	Graselda Holmes	25Oct1864	W119	

EMRICK

Jacob	Maria Baehr	14Sep1859	W110	
John	Catharine Hess	17Mar1864	W119	

ENFIELD

Eliza S.	Charles Moore	26Jan1858	W108	
Jacob	Nancy Howlett	20Oct1835	E75 W77	Park
Jacob	Ruth Smith	14May1861	W114	
Mary A.	Kennedy Bay	28Mar1865	W121	
William	Tacy Ann Weeks	26Nov1862	W116	

ENGLAND

Elisha	Margaret Rutledge	30Mar1829	E65 W68	Richardson
Elizabeth	Richard Cullum	01Apr1802	E21 W32	
Elizabeth	Andrew Gordon	09Mar1829	E65 W68	Finney
Elizabeth D.	Isaiah Watkins	09May1842	E85 W85	Keech
James	Hannahretta Holland	24Jan1863	W117	
Rachel	Andrew Gordon	09May1855	H7 W102	Wilson
Sarah	Deveraux Jarrett	09Apr1839	E80 W82	Barton

ENLOES

Sophia	Nathan Corbin	07Apr1800	E17 W29	

ENLOWS

Abraham	Mariah Galoway	10Apr1809	E33 W42	
Jemima	James Kennedy	26Dec1805	E27 W37	
John	Jane Jervis	03Apr1824	E58 W62	
Nacky	Edward Allender	21Dec1802	E22 W33	[ret-AppA]
Rebecca G.	John W. McCleary	17Mar1831	E68 W71	Keech

ERGOOD

Jacob	Ann Suter	19Dec1821	E55 W59	
Jesse	Elizabeth Chandlee	15Dec1837	E78 W79	Goldsborough

Harford Co. Md. Marriage Licenses, 1777-1865

ERWIN					
Isaac	Margaret Jane Stull	25Apr1862		W116	
Jacob	Elizabeth Arthur	07Sep1861		W114	
John	Rachel Killcreas	19Apr1808	E31	W40	
ESHELMAN					
Martin	Mary Elizabeth Jones	03Jan1853	H3	W98	Lemmon
ESLEY					
Robert	Frances S. Harward	27Dec1847		W92	
ETHERINGTON					
Rebecca	Leonard Howard	04Sep1793	E5	W23	
EVA					
William T.	Anna Mary Rogers	04Mar1847		W91	
EVANS [see Evans Deckman]					
Amos	Ann Saunders	16Dec1823	E57	W62	
Edward	Rebecca Barnes	03Nov1818	E49	W55	
Elizth	John Watkins	16Aug1779	B3	W2	
Elizabeth	Vincent Rickets	14Jan1815	E42	W49	
Evan	Elizabeth Madden	17Dec1817	E48	W54	
Frances	James Wilson	06May1826	E61	W65	Finney
Hannah	Thomas Clark	18Feb1812	E38	W46	
Hannah Jane	Henry O. Harlan	23Feb1865		W120	
Jacob	Elizabeth Lynch	23May1811	E36	W45	
John	Jane Madden	23Jan1812	E37	W45	
John	Mary Wakeland	02Nov1822	E56	W60	
John	Rebecca N. Sappington	05Jun1854	H5	W101	Finney
John T.	Ellen R. Watson	05Dec1842	E85	W86	Brown
Kitty	Thomas Huggins	29Dec1807	E31	W40	
Martha	Aquila Bailey	08Nov1810	E36	W44	
Mary Elizabeth	John J. Roberts	24Mar1838	E79	W80	
Rebecca	James Worthington	05Oct1850		W95	
Robert	Anna E. Wareham	20Jun1855	H7	W103	
Sarah	John Hopkins	12May1840	E82	W83	Finney
Will.	Sarah Reese	m. 1778			[ret-AppA]
Wm	Alasanna Cassidine[?]	14Jan1783	C7	W8	cr-Harf
William	Caroline Greenland	23Aug1858		W108	
William F.	Elen Barns	22Jan1838	E78	W80	Finny
EVATT					
Ann	Charles Yokum	03Jan1798	E13	W27	
Elizabeth	Andrew Martin	23Jul1799	E16	W28	
William	Elizabeth Wiley	m. 1794			[ret-AppA]
EVEREST					
Benjamin	Margaret Barns	12Feb1800	E17	W29	
Eleoner	Hollis Courtney	18Mar1791	E1	W21	

EVERETT [see Everett G. Hughes]
Benjn	Rachael Mitchell	01Apr1780	C1	W3
Elizth	Danl Grafton	01Mar1781	C4	W6
Frances F.	James W. Livezey	08Dec1863		W118
James	Mary Barnes	26Oct1782	C6	W8
James	Margret Walker	09Feb1793	E4	W22
John D.	Caroline E. Klinesmith	17Jan1865		W120
Joseph	Clare Wheeler	21Nov1795	E8	W24

EVERIST
Ann	Joshua Thompson	02Feb1825	E59	W63	Stephenson
Ann	Benjamin Chesney	10Feb1826	E61	W64	Tidings
Benjamin	Sarah Ann Singleton	22Feb1832	E70	W72	Webster
Charity	Nathan Everist	23Feb1798	E13	W27	

[minister - Caleb Johnson]
Clarissa	Thomas Shay	28Feb1810	E35	W43	
Emeline	Levi Robb	27May1837	E78	W79	Hoffman
Ezekiel	Mary Weeks	13Mar1823	E56	W61	
Ezekiel	Susanna Chesney	20Feb1826	E61	W64	Stephenson
Francis S.	Ann Blaney	30Dec1823	E57	W62	
George T.	Elizabeth Baker	11Apr1859		W110	
James	Ellen Jones	19Sep1831	E69	W71	Finney
James	Sarah Spence	21Oct1835	E76	W77	Reese
Job	Skiss Michael	12Mar1808	E31	W40	
Job	Isabella Armstrong	11Jun1816	E45	W51	
Joshua	Abigal Bond	03Dec1805	E27	W37	
Margaret	Isaac Whitaker	09Feb1798	E13	W27	Jno Allen
Margaret	Andrew J. Gorrell, Sr.	22Oct1862		W116	
Margaretta	Christian Baker	23Jul1822	E56	W60	
Martha	Amos Singleton	06Jan1848		W92	
Mary Ann	Bennett Vansickel	21May1817	E47	W53	
Mary Ann	George Crevisten	21May1817	E47	W53	

[immediately follows prior entry above]
Nathan	Charity Everist	23Feb1798	E13	W27

[minister - Caleb Johnson]
Richard	Sarah Michael	10Aug1804	E25	W35	
Sarah	William Simmons	29Dec1808	E33	W41	
Sarah Ann	William Taylor	03Nov1846		W90	
Sarah Ann	Asa William Taylor	26Nov1846		W90	
Thomas	Avarilla Coale	26Jan1802	E23	W33	
Thomas	Anna Weeks	16Feb1813	E40	W47	
Tho. C.	Elizbeth [sic] Coale	23Jan1828	E64	W67	Finney

[orig. lic. to Finney; gn-Thomas C.; bn-Elizabeth; cr-Harf]

EVERISTT
Elizabeth	Jacob Greenfield	26Sep1791	E1	W21

EVERIT [see Everit Gairy]
Cloe	Andrew Pearse	15May1799	E16	W28
Elizabeth	Henderson Laughard	27Nov1815	E44	W50
Joseph	Ruth McCulloh	30Nov1812	E39	W47
Samuel	Mary Rigdon	19Oct1805	E27	W36
William	Rebecca Brown	10Jun1807	E30	W39

EVERITT [see Everitt Gilbert Hughes]

Casander E.	John H. Middendorf	09Aug1859		W110	
Eadeth	Joseph Swift	15Jan1835	E75	W76	Sheppard
Richard	Cynthia Martin	27Nov1806	E29	W38	
Sophia	John Harvey	09Mar1826	E61	W65	Richardson
William	Mary Warrick	29Apr1820	E52	W57	

EVETT

And^w	Eleanor Porter	13Apr1780	C1	W4	

EVORETT

Ann	James Norris	19Apr1782	C6	W7	cr-Harf

EWEING

Charles	Teressa Ireland	15Feb1820	E52	W57	

EWEN

Jane	William Gilbert	02Dec1794	E6	W23	[ret-AppA]
John	Sarah Gorrell	01Mar1815	E42	W49	

EWIN

James	Caroline Gilbert	09Jan1840	E81	W82	Finney

EWING

Edwin	Harriet Osborne	12Jul1843	E86	W86	Finney
Elizabeth	Joseph Riley	29Apr1836	E76	W77	Dulany
Ellen	Andrew Jackson Gorrell	03Apr1837	E77	W79	Gallion
George	Jane Harris[?]	20Jun1781	C5	W6	
Harriet	William Ewing	16Aug1842	E85	W85	Finney
James	Mary Kean	14Apr1783	C7	W8	cr-Harf
James	Sarah Brownley	09Oct1805	E27	W36	
James	Jane Brannon	30Mar1815	E43	W50	
James W.	Eliza Gorrell	18Jul1850		W95	
Jane	John Carroll	02Feb1808	E31	W40	
John	Margaret Carroll	01Jan1814	E41	W48	
John	Caroline Simmons	26Jun1846		W90	
Joseph	Mary Gorrell	13Apr1793	E4	W22	
Joseph	Mary Kenley	14Mar1801	E19	W30	
Margaret	George Knight	19Dec1838	E80	W81	Dulaney
Martha Matilda	Samuel H. Bagely	20Jun1862		W116	ALJ1-21,34
Mary Ann	Thomas J. Ives	02Jun1836	E76	W78	Hoopman
Mary J/I.	Henry C. Coen	02Feb1863		W117	
Maskell C.	Cornelia Lansdale	18Feb1840	E82	W83	Goldsborough
Nancy	Ephraim G. Hopkins	12Oct1805	E27	W36	
William	Elizth Billingsley	10Dec1784	C9	W10	
William	Elizabeth Russell	19Sep1821	E54	W59	
William	Harriet Ewing	16Aug1842	E85	W85	Finney
Wm H.	Rachel Elizth Mitchell	04Aug1863		W117	
William Jacob	Eliza Ann Pretzman	04Nov1862		W116	

EXTON

John	Julia M. Smith	17May1826	E61	W65	Reynolds

FAIR [see Fair Beatty]

FAIRBANK
James	Mary Williams	24Jan1844	E86	W87
Robert E.	Eliza R. Williams	06Dec1849		W94

FALLS
Mary	Jesse Hitchcock	09May1792	E2	W21

FAMOUS
Andrew J.	Mary A. Carr	19May1860	W112
Ellen	Stewart Homburger	18Oct1860	W112
Samuel C.	Mary E. Hornburger	24Aug1861	W114

FANCIT
Fras	Arch^d Beaty	18Apr1783	C7	W8	cr-Harf

FARDWELL
Sophia	Richard Jones	09Feb1813	E39	W47

FARLEY
Alice	Thomas McDermot	18Feb1853	H3	W99	McNally
Alice	Robert Young	23Sep1854	H6	W101	McNally

FARMER
Ann	Reuben Smith	04Feb1824	E57	W62	
Martha J.	John C. Boyd	24Mar1829	E65	W68	Keech
Mary	William Wallis	26Nov1817	E48	W54	

FARNANDIS
Walter	Mary E. Dorsey	20Jun1816	E45	W51

FARRALL
Michael	Mary Millway	04Dec1837	E78	W79	Crosgay

FARRELL
James	Bridget Hopkins	14Jan1840	E81	W82	Reid
Michael	Ellen Tobin	08May1856	H10	W104	Walter
Michael	Catharine Callahan	15May1861		W114	

FAVOR [see Jean Favor Umshead]

FAWCET
Elizabeth	William Lester	15Nov1799	E17	W28

FAYERWEATHER
Randsome	Frances Lander	18Mar1830	E67	W69	Higby

FEELY
Rose	Patrick McCabe	29Feb1860	W111

FELL [see Mary Louisa Fell Allen]
Stephen	Ann Edwards	21Feb1779	B1	W1

FENDALL
Alice L.	Jer. Y. Maynadier	18Apr1865	W121

FENELL [see FERRELL]

FERGURSON
Rich᷃ T.   Mernerva A. McClaskey   17May1841 E83 W84 Goldsbor.

FERGUSON
Ann   William W. Wilson   06May1853 H3 W99 McMullin

FERNALD
Samuel   Sarah C. Sanks   04Aug1852 H2 W98 Sanks

FERRALL
William   Elizabeth Ann Ghisholm   15Nov1836 E77 W78 Dulany

FERREL
Benjamin   Sarah A. Maxwell   30Nov1857 H13 W107 Monroe

FERRELL
Delia   John Christie   19Feb1816 E44 W51
John   Sarah Phrisby   05Sep1792 E3 W22
   [ret-AppA; name may be Fenell or Fevrel]

FERRY
Annie   John McDermitt   03Oct1862   W116

FEVREL [see FERRELL]

FEW
Geo. T.   Anna Arthur   23Dec1864   W120

FIE
Baltice   Artreque Rider   01Feb1825 E59 W63
Baltice   Catharine Streighthoof   10Jun1825 E60 W63 Webster
   [orig. lic. to Webster; cr-Harf]
Paltus   Mary White   08Dec1782 C6 W8

FIELDS
Elizabeth   Andrew Doyle   m. 1789   [ret-AppA]
Susanah   James Wood   24Jan1792 E2 W21

FINCH
Joseph   Elizabeth Spence   21Jan1808 E31 W40

FINECUM
Benjamin   Elizabeth Scantling   02Jul1801 E20 W31

FINK
Anna Femelia   Robert H. Howard   11Dec1858   W109
Louisa   Josias Morgan   08Apr1847   W91
William H. H.   Sarah M. Knight   15Jan1861   W113

FINLEY
George	Sarah R. Perryman	21May1821	E54	W59
Rebecca	Ralph H. Thomas	31Dec1857		W107
Sarah	John Laird	15Jul1779	B3	W2

FINNAGAN
H. Patrick	Areanea Slemaker	25Apr1792	E2	W21

FINNEY [see Wm. Finney Hanna]
Elizabeth	John Collison	22Aug1845	E88	W89

FISHER
Amanda	William Jones	27Mar1862		W116	
Edna	John P. Shure	24Dec1861		W115	
Isabella	Fair Beatty	16May1785	C10	W10	
James	Ann Coale	14Sep1803	E23	W34	
James	Sarah Bevin	25Mar1806	E28	W37	
James	Elizabeth Swift	18Jan1807	E29	W38	
Margaret	James Barclay	29Nov1803	E24	W34	
Mary	Jeremiah Heaton	07Jan1799	E15	W27	
Rebecca J/I.	Septimus F. Charshe	05Aug1853	H4	W99	Finney
Sarah	George Forsythe	13Sep1825	E60	W64	Webster
  [orig. lic. to Webster; cr-Harf]

FITZGERALD
Rich^d	Judith Suter	25Jul1780	C2	W4

FITZHUGH
George D.	Elizabeth Worthington	01May1832	E71	W72	Wyatt

FITZIMMONS
Ellen	William Corkeny	10Jun1852	H2	W98	McNally

FITZPATRICK
John	Angeline Tompkins	08Apr1856	H10	W104	Smith
Mich^l	Catherine Collins	03Jun1779	B2	W2	

FIZZEE
William	Sarah Dematt	m. 1777	[ret-AppA]

FLAHARTY
John	Atheliah Hudson	27Jan1817	E46	W52

FLANAGAN
Elizabeth	Zenas Wells	04Sep1799	E16	W28
Elizabeth	Samuel Magness	08Apr1805	E26	W36

FLANNAGAN
Elizabeth	Owen McCarty	07Apr1779	B2	W1

FLAVIN
Margaret	Dennis Corkery	10Feb1854	H5	W100	McNally

Harford Co. Md. Marriage Licenses, 1777-1865

FLEHARTY
Mary   William Johnson   24Mar1803   E23 W33

FLETCHER
Ann   James Charsha   05Sep1816   E45 W52
Bennet   Rachel Miller   16Oct1841   E84 W84   Myers
George W.   Mary E. Osmond   13Mar1865   W121
Isaach   Mary E. Chesney   01Oct1838   E79 W81   Chesney
John   Martha Michael   24Mar1823   E56 W61
Mary   James Noble   24Jan1823   E56 W61
Samuel   Mary Cowen   26Jan1836   E76 W77   Goldsborough
Spencer D.   Roberta C. Lee   18Oct1855   H8   W103 Keech
Thomas C.   Elizabeth Barnes   17Jan1837   E77 W78   Finney
William   Phoebe Gallion   11Oct1813   E40 W48
William   Matilda Michael   24Mar1830   E67 W69   Finney
William   Mary Matilda Irvin   06Feb1855   H7   W102 Collins

FLINN
John W.   Hannah Ann Currey   24Dec1839   E81 W82   Finney

FLOWERS
Ann   William Paca   13Sep1838   E79 W80   Richardson
David   Rhoda Watters   01Jan1803   E23 W33
David   Elizabeth Watters   02Nov1844   E87 W88   Keech
James T.   Charlotte M. Kelly   03Jul1855   H8   W103 Cushing
Mary Elizabeth   Charles Price   11Nov1840   E82 W83   Prettyman
Ruth   William Judd   31Jul1839   E81 W82   Richardson

FOARD [see Foard Barnes]
Ann   William Walters   02Oct1817   E47 W53
Elizabeth   John G. Hill   26Apr1831   E69 W71   Sewell
George   Caroline Keath   01Jan1851   W96
George   Louisa Shay   12Jun1865   W121
Hannah A.   George G. Jeffery   11Jan1849   W93
Hannah E.   Samuel Hamilton   31Mar1857   H11 W106 Daugherty
Harriott   Joseph Gray   19Aug1819   E51 W56
James   Mary Timmons   28Apr1838   E79 W80   Richardson
Mary   Abraham Taylor   m. 1777   [ret-AppA]
Mary   Nathan Bramble   24Feb1831   E68 W70   Tippet
Mary Louisa   William W. Stritehoof   19Dec1857   W107
Nancy   John Kimble   28Nov1808   E32 W41
Rebecca   Aaron Hill   12Feb1810   E35 W43
William   Harriot Pennington   25Mar1817   E47 W53
William   Elizabeth Timmons   02Jun1827   E63 W66   McVey
William P.   Phoebe W. Bowen   29Dec1855   H9   W103 Cushing

FOLEY
Patrick   Bridget O'Toole   22Sep1853   H4   W100 McNally

FOLK
Rachel M.   James T. Trundle   03Jul1850   W95

FOLKNER
John   Mary Ann Cathcart   06Mar1851   W96

FORCE
Joseph   Ann Holland   10Dec1851 H1 W97 Robey

FORCYTHE
Joseph   Rachel Jones   12Jul1831 E69 W71 Finney

FORD [see Ford Barnes]

Alex.	Rachel Barnes	m. 1789			[ret-AppA]
Amelia B.	William Ross	16Jan1833	E72	W73	Sewell
Benjⁿ	Mary Anderson	01Sep1781	C5	W7	
Benjamin	Mary Ann Pike	27Apr1825	E59	W63	Tidings
Cordelia	John H. Bowen	26Dec1854	H6	W102	Dumm
Frederick	Margaret Benjamin	04Jun1781	C5	W6	
James H.	Cassandra Greenland	18Nov1847		W92	
Jane	Thomas Brannon	27Dec1778	B1	W1	
Joseph	Sarah Coale	25Jan1804	E24	W34	
Joseph	Dorothy Hudson	28Jul1804	E25	W35	
Lucy Ann	John Dixon	28May1816	E45	W51	
Martha N.	John F. Hill	15Feb1859		W109	
Mary E.	Jacob G. Gallion	09Feb1825	E59	W63	Webster

 [orig. lic. to Webster 9 Nov 1825; cr-Harf]

Rachel	John Huse	01May1780	C2	W4	
Sarah Elizabeth	John Webster Johnson	19Dec1836	E77	W78	Furlong
William	Mary Sillin	10Apr1785	C10	W10	
William	Rachel Woollen	04Feb1806	E27	W37	
William H.	Harriet E. Stockham	01Apr1856	H9	W104	Smith

FORESITH
Saml   Martha Carsons[?]   03Apr1780 C1 W3

FORSYTH
Margaret   Alexander W. Barr   19Dec1840 E82 W83 Finney
Samuel   Amelia Gorrell   05Jan1811 E36 W44

FORSYTHE [see also FORCYTHE]

Cornelia	William F. Bayless	28Dec1858		W109	
Elizabeth	William A. Bair	13Apr1858		W108	
George	Sarah Fisher	13Sep1825	E60	W64	Webster

 [orig. lic. to Webster; cr-Harf]

Henrietta	William Forsythe, Junr	08Jan1852	H1	W97	Finney
Jane	James Silver	19Dec1822	E56	W60	
Jane	Jefferson Dever	09Apr1844	E87	W87	Eagy
Margaret	George Dever	24Feb1840	E82	W83	Anderson
Martha J.	Elijah Thompson	25Sep1840	E82	W83	Finny
Mary	Edward D. Markland	10Mar1856	H9	W104	Finney
Rachel	James Howe	26Feb1838	E79	W80	Gallion
Sarah Ann	Thomas Ely	23Mar1840	E82	W83	Anderson
William, Junr	Henrietta Forsythe	08Jan1852	H1	W97	Finney
William Andrew	Rachel D. Saunders	12Feb1863		W117	

FORT
Sarah   James Barnes   22Mar1780 C1 W3

FORTUNE
Thomas	Elizabeth M. Bussey	14Jan1851	W96

FORWARD
Edward	Maria L. Boarman	02Sep1857	H12 W107	Brown
John	Eliza Deane	m. 1778		[ret-AppA]

FORWOOD
Constant	Roger Mathews	09Oct1800	E18 W30	
Elizabeth	Barnet Johnson of Jno.	19Jan1805	E26 W36	
Elizabeth	Richard Ward	15Feb1814	E41 W48	
Elizabeth	John Barrow	22Apr1817	E47 W53	
Elizabeth	Joshua Anderson	06Jan1831	E68 W70	Reese
Hannah	David Konklin	03Dec1781	C5 W7	
Hannah	John Smith	07Jun1837	E78 W79	Parks
Hannah E.	Alexander C. Ramsay	26Oct1846	W90	
Hannah J.	Franklin Hanway	24Mar1863	W117	
Jacob	Elizabeth Warriner	07[?]May1781	C5 W6	
Jacob	Elizabeth Richardson	14Jul1818	E49 W55	
Jacob	Mary Scarborough	02Feb1848	W92	
Jane	Josiah Mathews	16Jan1792	E2 W21	[ret-AppA]
John the 3d	Mary Loney	06Dec1803	E24 W34	
John C.	Hannah Warner	22Dec1828	E65 W68	Keeck
Lidia A.	Jesse Carr	25May1840	E82 W83	Prettyman
Martha	Jefferson Deaver	31Dec1832	E72 W73	Sewell
Martha	Joseph Ward	22Jun1841	E83 W84	Wilson
Mary E.	William Loney Forwood	02Mar1826	E61 W65	Parke
Parker	Harriott Moore	04Oct1821	E54 W59	
Parker Lee	Julia Ann Smithson	03Oct1863	W118	
Samuel	Mary Murray	28Oct1794	E6 W23	
Samuel	Ann Perkins	13Jun1795	E7 W24	
Samuel of Jno	Rachel C. Stump	04Apr1828	E64 W67	Stephenson
Samuel Wesley	Rebecca J. Chamberlain	26Jun1860	W112	
Sarah	John Murry	20Jan1782	C5 W7	
Sarah	Francis Herbert	11Jun1812	E38 W46	
W. Smithson	Rebecca Glenn	29Dec1860	W113	
William	Elizabeth Jane Stewart	05Feb1844	E86 W87	Finney
William Loney	Mary E. Forwood	02Mar1826	E61 W65	Parke
William Warner	Sarah Taylor Gilbert	26Feb1816	E44 W51	

FOSTER
Alisannah	Solomon Brown	05Apr1780	C1 W3	
Charles	Cassandra Jackson	08Aug1859	W110	
Daniel	Ann Wheeler	05Aug1824	E58 W62	
Elizabeth	Henry Baker	24Sep1838	E79 W80	Collins
Faithful	Daniel Mcfadden	15Jan1814	E41 W48	
Henry	Lidia Rebecca Chesney	01Dec1840	E82 W83	Prettyman
Mary	William Allender	27Jan1810	E34 W43	
Mary	Samuel Parker Hopkins	23Dec1845	W89	
Mary Ann	Thomas Streett (of Thos)	27Mar1832	E70 W72	Finney
Mary Ann	Jonathan Orr	15Jan1841	E83 W84	Goldsborough
Robert	Jane Riley	m. 1787		[ret-AppA]
Sarah	William Bay	24Jun1823	E57 W61	
William	Rachel Kerver[?]	11Feb1812	E38 W46	[or Kerwen?]

FOWL
Elizabeth	George Close	21Feb1781	C4	W6

FOWLER
Henry C.	Mary J. Ely	15Mar1864		W119
Mary	John Deavour	12May1780	C2	W4
Rachel	William Lauder	03Jan1792	E2	W21
Wm	Cathrine Garland	08Oct1784	C9	W10

FOX
Barbary	Michael Yeit	10Aug1855	H8	W103	Alexander
Charlotte	James Froney	07Sep1848		W93	
Eliza E.	Henry Kimble	03Nov1845		W89	
Mary	William Bradfield	13Aug1840	E82	W83	Dulaney
William	Mary Carroll	15Aug1797	E12	W26	
[ret'd by Jno Allen]					
Wm	Jane Greenland	01Nov1854	H6	W101	Boulton

FOY
Henry	Harriott Rockhold	01Jul1820	E52	W58
John	Sarah Ann Michael	03Apr1854	H5	W100 Wells

FRANCES
Martha M.	James W. Tipton	21May1857	H12	W106 Cushing

FRANCIS
Calisle [gr]	Julian Shultz [br]	26Jul1834	E74	W75 Keech

FRAZIER
John Cullum	Elizabeth Holland	04Aug1859		W110
Joseph	Elizabeth Talbot	26Apr1823	E57	W61

FREDERICK
Henry	Catharine Mary Weaver	25Nov1852	H2	McNally

FREDERICKS
Edward H.	Susan Dull	27Jun1861		W114

FREDRICK
John D.	Elizabeth Gallion	15Apr1841	E83	W84 Gallion

FREEBORN [see Freeborn Garretson]

FREEHEART
Matilda	Benjamin Hudson	28Aug1816	E45	W52

FRIEZE
J. Thompson	Elizabeth Green	15Oct1858		W109

FRISBY
Mary	Wm Loney	24Dec1782	C7	W8	cr-Harf
Susan	Joshua Wood	02Mar1816	E44	W51	
Thomas P.	Susanna Mahon	28Aug1811	E37	W45	

FRONEY
James   Charlotte Fox   07Sep1848   W93

FROST
William   Sarah Stollcup   10Aug1802   E22 W32

FRY
Eve   John Smith   07Dec1857   W107

FULFORD
Eleanor	George Torrance	30Jun1829	E66 W68 Keech
Mary	Nathaniel W. S. Hays	28Jan1834	E73 W75 Finney
William	Mary Frances Patterson	18Jun1804	E25 W35

FULLARD
Elizabeth	John A. Barnett	01Feb1834	E73 W75 Parke
Henry	Elizabeth Cox	19Jul1821	E54 W59
Sarah	Hugh Bay	25Apr1820	E52 W57

FULLERD
Hannah   Robert Hambleton   04Apr1829   E65 W68 Richardson

FULLERTON
Ann Jane	John M. Nelson	27Oct1825	E60 W64 Tidings
Charity	Crispin Cunningham	29Sep1825	E60 W64 Tidings
Eliza	William Bradford	15May1817	E47 W53
Mary C.	William S. Gaskins	01Aug1833	E73 W74 Porter
Sophia	Joseph M. Cromwell	04Mar1833	E72 W73 Sewell

FULLUM
John   Mary McMahon   15Jun1861   W114

FULMER
Charlott W.   John G. Hopfer   24Mar1856   H9 W104 Keech

FULTON
Avarilla	John Barnes	04Feb1847	W91
James	Susanna Trago	13Aug1803	E23 W34
James	Hannah Amoss	01Feb1809	E33 W42
James	Elizabeth Hanna	18Dec1817	E48 W54
John	Lydia Mitchell	10Dec1799	E17 W28
John C.	Eliza Jane Hogg	04Feb1834	E73 W75 Finney
John J.	Sallie A. Heaps	22Dec1860	W113
Mary Ann	Stephen B. Hanna	20Apr1824	E58 W62
Mensal W.	Harriet C. Osborn	18Apr1850	W95
Philip	Sarah Hanna	30Mar1801	E20 W31
Rachel	John Jordan	14Dec1813	E41 W48
Susan R.	James M. Anderson	30Nov1859	W111
Susanna	John Ashton	03May1800	E18 W29

GAFFORD
Aley	John Hambleton	24Jan1797	E10 W25	[ret-AppA]
Ann Statia	Aquila Hughes	21Apr1804	E25 W35	
Joseph	Mary Ann Watkins	15Feb1813	E39 W47	
Mary	Charles Norris	26May1810	E35 W43	

GAILY
R. E.	Thomas S. Gemmill	08May1860	W112	

GAIMES
Ann	Benjamin Prewit	25Apr1821	E54 W59	

GAIRY
Everit	Mary Hall	10Mar1812	E38 W46	

GALBREATH
Ann	David H. Silver	28Nov1842	E85 W85	Park
Hannah Jane	Henry A. Silver	16Nov1849	W94	
James	Martha Maria Wilson	17Jun1845	E88 W88	
Matthew C.	Margaret L. Heaps	18Dec1861	W115	
Nancy	Richard B. McCoy	16Feb1849	W93	

GALE
William H.	Anna J. Walker	28Sep1858	W109	

GALION
Aquilla	Rhody McCommons	25Jun1839	E81 W82	Galion

GALLAGHER
Margaret	Patrick Donclan	06Dec1849	W94	

GALLAHER
Margaret	James Husbands	25Jul1804	E25 W35	[ret-AppA]

GALLEY
William	Grace Cashman	m. 1788[?]		[ret-AppA]

GALLIAN
Joseph P.	Mary Spence	03Dec1838	E80 W81	Gallian

GALLION
Alexr	Mary Spencer	14Jan1800	E17 W29	
Alexander	Nancy L. Spence	09Aug1858	W108	
Alice B.	James Maxwell	28Dec1824	E59 W63	Webster
[orig. lic. to Webster; cr-Harf]				
Ann R.	Edward McCommons	26Jan1857	H11 W105	Gallion
Avarilla	Jacob Norris	30Mar1784	C8 W9	
Benjamin F.	Julian Courtney	21Jun1851	W96	
Caleb	Ann Troutner	12Jun1823	E57 W61	
Charity	Joseph Page	20Dec1861	W115	
Elizabeth	Joseph Gallion	19Mar1832	E70 W72	Gallion
Elizabeth	John D. Fredrick	15Apr1841	E83 W84	Gallion
Greenberry	Mary Shareswood	23Feb1809	E33 W42	
Gregory	Ann Antley	16Oct1784	C9 W10	

Harford Co. Md. Marriage Licenses, 1777-1865   87

GALLION, continued

Jacob G.	Mary E. Ford	09Feb1825	E59 W63	Webster
James	Ann Keen	11Jul1805	E26 W36	
James B.	Rachel Bowman	30Nov1841	E84 W85	Gallion
John	Sarah Garretson	14Dec1796	E10	
[above lic. crossed out]				
John W.	Martha J. Miller	28May1839	E81 W82	Gallion
Joseph	Elizabeth Gallion	19Mar1832	E70 W72	Gallion
Mahala	Asbury Sheredine	27Dec1853	H4 W100	Gallion
Martha	John Cox	28Mar1793	E4 W22	
Mary	Ruthan Garrison	20Nov1797	E13 W26	John Coleman
Mary	William McMorris	11Nov1830	E68 W70	Tippet
Nancy	Zebulon Commons	14Aug1824	E58 W62	
Phoebe	William Fletcher	11Oct1813	E40 W48	
Priscilla	Aquila Gilbert	09Jan1779	B1 W1	
Rachel	Joshua Wyle	30Nov1815	E44 W50	
Richard S.	Lucy Ann Middleditch	28Sep1832	E71 W73	Park
Robert F.	Jane Daugherty	02Sep1848	W93	
Sally	Thomas Calwell	14Feb1793	E4 W22	
Sarah	Luke Amoss	26Nov1794	E6 W23	
Sarah	Robert Trager	31Jan1809	E33 W42	
Sarah	Benjamin Mahan[?]	03Oct1827	E63 W66	Finney
Stansbury	Caroline Boarman	20Mar1821	E54 W59	
Zaney	Levi Howard	20Dec1808	E32 W41	

GALLOP

Joseph	Milcah Dorsey	28Sep1792	E3 W22
Joseph	Sarah Spencer	20Oct1810	E35 W44
Thomas	Phebie Smith	01Feb1792	E2 W21

GALLOWAY

Absalom, Jur.	Rennis B. Smithson	13Jun1833	E73 W74	Keech
Absolum	Mary Merrett	04May1799	E16 W28	
Avarilla	Thomas Sunderland	01Jan1856	H9 W104	Reineck
Bathia	Jonas Watters	05Jan1813	E39 W47	
Elisha	Charity Carroll	23Mar1811	E36 W44	
Elizabeth	Elijah Stokes	11Sep1807	E30 W39	
Elizabeth H.	James Carroll	24Sep1859	W110	
John	Eliza Osborn	06Apr1831	E69 W71	Finney
John	Catharine James	24Apr1844	E87 W87	Keech
Peter	Ellen Gillespie	16Jul1847	W91	
Samuel	Sarah M. J. Hays	14May1833	E72 W74	Keech
Sarah	Dorsey H. Whitaker	26Oct1826	E62 W65	Keech
William	Averilla Griffith	22Jul1843	E86 W86	Maddox
William	Eliza R. Bouldin	22Mar1848	W92	
William K.	Lydia J/I. Ricketts	02Mar1858	W108	

GALLUP [see also GALLOP]

Daniel	Annie E. Devoe	27Apr1864	W119	
Elizabeth	George A. Nelson	31Dec1860	W113	
Margaret	Charles Holloway	13Jan1846	W89	
Oliver	Permelia Ann Holleway	13Feb1821	E53 W58	
Oliver	Catharine Martin	14Jan1828	E64 W67	Finney
Thomas	Isabella Michael	07Mar1809	E33 W42	
Thomas F.	Martha M. Cannon	11Jul1859	W110	

GALOWAY
Mariah   Abraham Enlows   10Apr1809 E33 W42

GAMMEL
James   Mary Ann Norris   19Dec1837 E78 W80 Park

GAMMELL[?]
Jane   Benjamin Almony   12Apr1854 H5 W100 Smith

GAMMILL
John   Elizabeth Bosley   28Sep1830 E68 W70 Parks

GARDNER
Sarah   Isaac Acres   19Oct1857 H13 W107 Hoopman
Susan   John J. Allender   07Feb1853 H3 W99 Finney

GARDNOR
Margaret   Charles Tracy   27Sep1816 E45 W52

GARLAND
Cathrine   Wm Fowler   08Oct1784 C9 W10

GARNER
Catharine   Edmond Standiford   05Nov1803 E24 W34
Joseph   Levitha Ayres   01Nov1802 E22 W33

GARRATT [see Garratt Thompson]

GARRELL
Effy   William Carroll   23Feb1819 E50 W56

GARRET [see Garret Chauncey]
Eleanor   Daniel Haney   14Dec1807 E30 W40

GARRETSON
Freeborn   Eliza Richardson   28Dec1811 E37 W45
Martha   Josias Hall   m. 1787   [ret-AppA]
Martha   John Scarff   15Jun1815 E43 W50
Mary   Hosea Barnes   23Mar1812 E38 W46
Mary G.   Elijah Davis   m. 1788   [ret-AppA]
Sarah   John Gallion   14Dec1796 E10
  [above lic. crossed out]

GARRETT
Ann   Thomas Haney   04Mar1808 E31 W40
Augusta   David Heaps   27Jan1865   W120
Elizabeth   William Simmons   26Jan1818 E48 W54
Isaac   Belenda Bull   06Apr1839 E80 W82 Rockwell
Lydia   Geo. Clark   10Aug1784 C9 W9
Martha   Michael McKarnan   06Jul1802 E22 W32
Mary   James Harkness   16Feb1818 E48 W54
Milcah   Bendct Edwd Hall   02Mar1781 C1 W3
Rozetta   Ephraim Hargrove   30May1811 E36 W45

GARRETTSON

Elizabeth	Benjamin Osborn	22Apr1780	C2	--	
Eliz^th	Samuel Griffith	21Dec1791	E2	W21	
Enoch C.	Lydia Matilda Groscup	19Mar1863		W117	
Garrett	Susannah Olliver	18Sep1784	C9	W9	
George Hanson	Laura Bruff	06Mar1837	E77	W79	Richardson
Laura	Joseph B. Whitson	28Dec1860		W113	
Martha	Benjamin Hanson	12Oct1779	B3	W2	
Rebecca Matilda	George M. Johnson	30Apr1832	E70	W72	Richardson

GARRISON

Alexander	Mary Greenfield	16Dec1785[?]	C10	W10	
Alfred S.	Mary A. Hutchins	11Feb1854	H5	W100	Carter
Ann	Thomas Miles	19Jun1805	E26	W36	
Ann	Henry Slofer	06Jan1829	E65	W68	Richardson
Ann Maria	German McClure	25Oct1836	E77	W78	Dulany
Eliz^th	Benjn Osborn	08Apr1780	C1	W3	
Hannah	Henry Scarff	17Oct1815	E43	W50	
James	Martha Osborn	05Jan1780	C1	W3	
James	Susanna Amos	26Jan1825	E59	W63	Richardson
John	Rebecca Wiggers	26Nov1833	E73	W74	Keech
John	Mary Birmingham	08Jan1812	E37	W45	
John	Rebecca Speaden	02May1864		W119	
Rebecca	Edward Rutledge	24Sep1850		W95	
Ruthan	Mary Gallion	20Nov1797	E13	W26	John Coleman
Samuel Jefferson	Ann Spencer	07Aug1823	E57	W61	

GASKINS

William S.	Mary C. Fullerton	01Aug1833	E73	W74	Porter

GASSAWAY

Ann	John Nowland	28Jan1802	E21	W32

GAVIN

Maria	Thomas Holmes	28Dec1850	W96

GAY

Henry	Mary Lanagan	30Mar1802	E21	W32	
Margaret	Edmund Bull	02Jun1832	E71	W73	Finney
William	Julia Sullivan	03May1861		W114	

GEBE

Anne	John Mohrlin	06Oct1854	H6	W101 Smith

GELASPY

Charles	Eliz^th Dunsheath	20Nov1778	B1	W1

GEMMEL

John	Sarah Mathews	12Nov1849	W94

GEMMILL

James	Hannah Streett	17Feb1825	E59	W63	Poteet
Thomas S.	R. E. Gaily	08May1860		W112	

GEORGE
Mary	Samuel Jeffery	27May1840	E82 W83	Emory
Sarah	John Brannian	21Jun1791	E1 W21	

GERMAN [see German McClure]
Jemima	Thomas Daugherday	01May1832	E71 W72	Frey

GEST
John	Rebecca Hall	13Nov1792	E3 W22	[ret-AppA]

  [ret has John Guest of Phila.]

GHERGATY
Patrick	Mary McDermott	17Jan1858	W108	

CHISHOLM
Elizabeth Ann	William Ferrall	15Nov1836	E77 W78	Dulany

GIBSON
Benjamin	Marg^t * Bryan	29Jan1801	E19	W30

  [* Sarah crossed out]
Elizabeth	James Blair	07Oct1806	E29 W38	
Ellen	James Waters	14Sep1816	E45 W52	
Francis	Elizth Davis	10Mar1783	C7 W8	
Ignatius	Mary Sutton	04Apr1815	E43 W50	
Jacob	Margaret Gibson	03Feb1835	E75 W76	Parks
James F.	Araminta Saunders	18Jan1841	E83 W84	Dulaney
John	Catharine Cochran	10Nov1813	E41 W48	
John	Sarah Gibson	20Nov1833	E73 W74	Park
Margarett	Jacob Gibson	03Feb1835	E75 W76	Parks
Mary	William Boyd	11Feb1834	E74 W75	Higbee
Mary Ann	Alexander Sangster	12Dec1815	E44 W50	
Sarah	John Gibson	20Nov1833	E73 W74	Park

GIFFORD
John	Mary Sangsture	03Nov1781	C5 W7	

GILBERT [see Everett Gilbert Hughes, Jarvis Gilbert James,
            Waldon Gilbert Middleton]
Amos	Sarah Baylis	18Jan1804	E24 W34	
Amos	Clemency Hopkins	24Aug1819	E51 W56	
Amos	Mary Carsins	16Jan1845	E88 W88	Wysong
Ann	George Cunningham	30Sep1800	E18 W30	
Ann	Amos Anderson	09Apr1821	E54 W59	
Ann	Caleb Wright	22Dec1828	E65 W68	Finney
Ann Martha	John Mitchell	04Dec1821	E55 W59	
Aquila	Priscilla Gallion	09Jan1779	B1 W1	
Avarilla	Robert A. Barnes	28May1846	W90	
Bennett	Martha S. McComas	03Jun1834	E74 W75	Finney
Caroline	James Ewin	09Jan1840	E81 W82	Finney
Carvill T.	Susan Bowen	10Feb1845	E88 W88	Pennell
Cassandra	Michael Gilbert	16Dec1817	E48 W54	
Cassandra	John W. Paca	06Dec1858	W109	
Charles	Mary Horner	m. 1794		[ret-AppA]
Charles B.	Susan M. Morris	26Sep1859	W110	

GILBERT, continued

Charles L.	Rose F. Kerr	13Feb1847	W91	
Christina Ann	Corbin L. Mitchell	12Feb1839	E80 W81	Finney
Clemency Hughes	Isaac Webster	27Apr1809	E33 W42	
Ebenezer	Anna Anderson	26Feb1807	E29 W39	
Eliza	Elisha Mitchell	22Mar1832	E70 W72	Finney
Eliz^th	W^m. McComass	11Jun1784	C8 W9	
Elizabeth	Isaac Wilson	m. 1792		[ret-AppA]
Elizabeth	Bennet Love	22Apr1809	E33 W42	
Elizabeth	James Cole	03Dec1823	E57 W61	
Elizabeth	Caleb Wright	24Feb1825	E59 W63	Rockhold
Elizabeth	George Moore	15Oct1829	E66 W69	Finney
Elizabeth	William Chesney	05Apr1831	E69 W71	Finney
Elizabeth	James Noble	27Sep1837	E78 W79	Finney
Elizabeth	James Gilbert	23May1839	E81 W82	Finney
Elizabeth F.	James Thompson	11Apr1845	E88 W88	Gallion
Emily J.	Amos A. Mitchell	21Mar1862	W115	
Ephraim	Ann Loflin	15Mar1823	E56 W61	
Frances Eliz^th	William H. Patton	26Apr1862	W116	
Francis	John Donavin	06Nov1779	C1 W3	
Frenetter	William Mahan	04Mar1834	E74 W75	Dunahay
George	Ellen McComas	16Oct1839	E81 W82	Finney
George T.	Sarah Louisa T. Wilson	16Jul1835	E75 W76	Finney
Gideon	Clemency Mitchell	09Apr1856	H10 W104	Rankin
Gideon	Rachel A. Gilbert	27Feb1865	W120	
Hannah	James Hughes	14Dec1801	E21 W31	
Hannah S.	J. Rich Grier	03Oct1864	W119	
Henry	Sarah Amoss	25Jul1816	E45 W52	
Henry	Elizabeth Miller	23Jun1819	E51 W56	
Henry Ruff	Margaret Barnes	29Dec1814	E42 W49	
Jacob	Ann Horton	28Oct1807	E30 W39	
James	Mary Johnson	12Jan1782	C5 W7	
James	Elizabeth Gilbert	23May1839	E81 W82	Finney
Jervis	Sophia Cole	27Nov1798	E15 W27	
Joel	Rachel Gilbert	19Jan1841	E83 W84	Goldsborough
Johanna	Adam Johnson	17Aug1797	E12 W26	
[ret'd by John Allen]				
John N.	Sarah Mitchell	20Feb1839	E80 W81	Finney
Julian	Thomas Treadway	08Jan1806	E27 W37	
Mahala	Thomas Keithley	21Apr1831	E69 W71	Webster
[orig. lic. to Webster; cr-Harf]				
Margaret	Cornelius O'Brien	26Feb1835	E75 W76	Hoopman
Martha	Aaron McComas, Jun.	19Feb1798	E13 W27	Jno Allen
Martha	Michael Gilbert	01Apr1844	E87 W87	Gallion
Martha	Everett G. Hughes	13Feb1864	W118	
Martin	Clemency Hughes	26Jul1864	W119	
Martin T.	Elizabeth Tredway	02Apr1805	E26 W36	
Mary	Ford Barnes	m. 1788		[ret-AppA]
Mary	Charles McComas	14Jun1800	E18 W29	
Mary	John Weeks	05Nov1816	E46 W52	
Mary	George Ruff	03Oct1837	E78 W79	Collins
Mary G.	Scott Hughes	23Jun1804	E25 W35	
Mary Jane	William Hugg	27Sep1854	H6 W101	Gallion
Matilda Eliz^th	George Baldwin	12Nov1850	W95	
Micha.	Mary J. Highfield	22May1865	W121	

GILBERT, continued

Michael	Elizth Presbury	18Nov1782	C6	W8	
Michael	Ann Clark	07Aug1784	C9	W9	
Michael	Betsy Stiles	30Apr1794	E5	W23	[ret-AppA]
Michael	Mary Gilmore	31Dec1804	E25	W35	
Michael	Cassandra Gilbert	16Dec1817	E48	W54	
Michael	Martha Gilbert	01Apr1844	E87	W87	Gallion
Naomi	Daniel Michael	13Jan1820	E52	W57	
Nicholas B.	Kate Wills	27Mar1854	H5	W100	Reese
Parker	Martha McComas	19Sep1797	E11	W26	[ret-AppA]
Parker, Junr	Martha Hughes	01Oct1800	E18	W30	
Parker	Elizabeth Henderson	14Dec1803	E24	W34	
Parker	Elizabeth Coen	09Jun1840	E82	W83	Goldsborough
Phebe	John McGaw	02Jul1801	E20	W31	
Phillip	Sarah Ruff	09Feb1782	C5	W7	
Priscilla	Richard Mitchell	12Feb1798	E13	W27	Jno Allen
Rachel	Joel Gilbert	19Jan1841	E83	W84	Goldsborough
Rachel A.	Gideon Gilbert	27Feb1865		W120	
Sarah	John Cooley	08Dec1779	C1	W3	
Sarah	Philip Bennet	04Jun1795	E7	W24	
Sarah	Jacob James	02Mar1825	E59	W63	Finney
Sarah	Hosea Barnes	14Dec1840	E82	W83	Finny
Sarah Ann	Gerrard Mitchell	28Dec1841	E84	W85	Finney
Sarah Catharine	George Sidney Armstrong	09Jan1850		W94	
Sarah Taylor	William Warner Forwood	26Feb1816	E44	W51	
Sophia H.	William Jewins	22Dec1830	E68	W70	Tippit
Susan	William Hamby	14May1833	E72	W74	Hoopman
Susan S.	Daniel Anderson	23Mar1847		W91	
Sus^a	Jacob Denovin	m. 1778			[ret-AppA]
Talitha E.	Thomas Henry Strong	29Jan1862		W115	
Taylor	Sophia Baker	12Feb1823	E56	W61	
William	Jane Ewen	02Dec1794	E6	W23	[ret-AppA]
William H.	Mary Ann Michael	29Jan1839	E80	W81	Finney

GILDEA

Rebecca Jane	David Parrott	12Oct1824	E58	W63

GILES [see Giles T. Green, Giles Kimble]

Jacob Edward	Cordelia Phillips	23Dec1808	E32	W41
Jacob W.	Ann Bacon	14May1817	E47	W53
Jacob Washington	Martha Phillips	15Nov1802	E22	W33
William	Martha E. Scotten	10Sep1849		W94

GILL

Owen Augustus	Eliza Adams Gillet	01May1832	E71	W72	Millgram

GILLALAND

David	Sarah Pearce	19Dec1834	E74	W76	Richardson

GILLEN

Francis	Charlotte A. Greenland	04May1853	H3	W99	Sanks

GILLESPIE

Ellen	Peter Galloway	16Jul1847	W91

GILLET
Eliza Adams   Owen Augustus Gill   01May1832   E71 W72   Millgram

GILLISPIE
Elihu H.   Mary Ella Porter   01Feb1842   E84 W85   Reid

GILLUM
Ann   John Andrews   14Feb1811   E36 W44
Luke   Ann Harrod   31Dec1812   E39 W47
Temperance   William Gordon   02Jan1806   E27 W37

GILMORE
Ann   Foard Barnes   30Nov1792   E3 W22
Jane   Wm Clinging   08Mar1783   C7 W8
Mary   Michael Gilbert   31Dec1804   E25 W35

GILPIN
William   Margaret Ann Price   19Apr1833   E72 W74   Stephenson

GINET
Mary   Elijah Tayson   02Nov1820   E53 W58

GITTINGS [see Elizabeth Gittings Gover]
Archibald   Martha Rumsey[?]   30May1815   E43 W50
John R.   Mary Watters   17Oct1849   W94

GIVINS
Sarah   John Armitage   03Mar1799   E15 W28

GLACKIN
John   Mary Ann Welsh   22Dec1862   W116

GLADDEN
Abraham   Elizth Frances Durham   25Aug1851   W96
Abraham   Marietta Durham   30Sep1857   H12 W107 Trott
Elizabeth   Robert Street   08Aug1826   E61 W65   Keech
Jacob   Jane Wilson   07Apr1830   E67 W69   Parke
Rachel A.   William A. Durham   30Nov1857   H13 W107 Keech
Sarah   James Thompson   04Nov1815   E43 W50
William   Elizabeth M. Wetherill   26Nov1858   W109

GLADEN
James   Mary Clindening   22Feb1785   C10 W10

GLANVILLE
Claracy   Josiah Smith   23Feb1808   E31 W40
James W.   Ann Maria Allen   23Oct1830   E68 W70   Tippet

GLASGOW
Deliverance H.   James C. Lee   18Jun1844   E87 W87   Finney
Eliza M.   James O. Ramsay   08Jan1863   W117
Elizth   John Clendenen   27May1793   E4 W22

GLASGOW, continued
James	Helen Theresa Gough	26Jan1852	H1	W97	Davis
Susanna P.	Thomas Archer	16Nov1841	E84	W84	Finney
William C.	Rebecca J. Proctor	24Dec1864		W120	

GLAUM
John   Mrs. Eliza Bramble   03May1855   H7   W102 Cushing

GLEASON
Andrew   Catharine Maagher   26Jan1861   W113

GLEEM
Mary Jane   John M. Amoss   04Mar1848   W92

GLEESON
Patrick   Mary Lingum   05Nov1853   H4   W100 McNally

GLENN
Isabella	Amos McComas	20Jun1807	E30	W39	
Joshua	Sarah Beatty	21Jan1818	E48	W54	
Joshua	Martha Amoss	03Apr1845	E88	W88	Park
Nathaniel	Elizabeth Butler	24Jan1814	E41	W48	
Rebecca	Hugh Ross	23Jun1829	E66	W68	Morrison
Rebecca	W. Smithson Forwood	29Dec1860		W113	
Robert	Orpah Ellen Montgomery	11Nov1818	E50	W55	
Temperance	Matthew Clark	26Mar1816	E45	W51	
William, Junr	Sarah Nelson	29Nov1824	E59	W63	Morrison
William M.	Sarah L. Ashton	25Jan1858		W108	

GODDARD
Elizth   Mordica Daws   16Feb1781   C4   W6

GODMAN [see GODWIN]

GODWIN
Thomas	Amanda M. Swift	09Apr1860		W112
W^m	Delilah White	15Jul1797	E11	W26

    [see AppA for return under name Godman]

GOLD [see John Gold Howard]

GOLDEN
Mary   John Kellay   21Apr1854   H5   W101 McNally

GOLDSBOROUGH
Howes   Mary Rodgers   12Oct1812   E39   W46

GOLDSMITH
Wm. Copeland   Sarah Weatherall   m. 1778   [ret-AppA]

GOLLAHER
Mary   James McClure[?]   m. 1789   [ret-AppA]

GOLLIGHER				
Ann	William Bradley	23Nov1857	H13 W107	Foley
GOLWAY				
Mary	Francis Hare	25Jun1794	E5 W23	
GOODING				
Ann	James Wood	07May1781	C4 W6	
GOODWIN				
Elizabeth	Jacob Herrington	10Jun1803	E23 W34	
GORDAN				
Alexander	Martha McClentan	16May1780	C2 W4	
Mary	Silas Baldwin	11Feb1852	H1 W97	Robey
GORDEN				
Eleanor	Thomas Brown	17Feb1794	E5 W23	
John	Elizabeth Stansberry	22Nov1803	E24 W34	
Nathan	Delia Stevenson	01Nov1797	E13 W26	Jno Allen
Temperance	James Crissol	27Oct1812	E39 W46	
GORDIN				
Christian	Tho. Lancaster	m. 1777		[ret-AppA]
GORDON				
Agness	John Wright, Junr	24Jan1820	E52 W57	
Andrew	Elizabeth England	09Mar1829	E65 W68	Finney
Andrew	Rachel England	09May1855	H7 W102	Wilson
Elizabeth	Leonard Ady	24Feb1838	E79 W80	Cosgray
James	Mary Riddle	30Jul1782	C6 W8	
John W.	Delia McKenny	23Aug1832	E71 W73	Finney
M.[?] Easter	David Hampton	28Aug1782	C6 W8	
Martha	William W. Doxen	15Mar1860	W111	
Philip	Delia White	14Jul1797	E11 W26	
Ruth	Sutton Cullum	14Dec1807	E30 W40	
William	Temperance Gillum	02Jan1806	E27 W37	
GORE				
Nicholas	Preshoshy Price	m. 1804		[ret-AppA]
Panetta	William Chandlee	14Nov1820	E53 W58	
GORMLY				
Elizabeth	John Bradley	01May1852	H2 W98	McNally
GORREL				
John	Elizabeth Bell	22Jun1830	E67 W70	Finny
GORRELL				
Abraham	Elizabeth Carroll	29Mar1806	E28 W37	
Amelia	Samuel Forsyth	05Jan1811	E36 W44	
Andrew J., Sr.	Margaret Everist	22Oct1862	W116	
Andrew Jackson	Ellen Ewing	03Apr1837	E77 W79	Gallion
Ann	Joshua Smith	29Mar1813	E40 W47	

GORRELL, continued

Bonfield	Mary Dever	30Nov1836	E77	W78	Finney
Catharine	Charles C. Smith	26Dec1861		W115	
Crawford	Frances Judd	29Dec1819	E51	W57	
Eliza	James W. Ewing	18Jul1850		W95	
Elizabeth	Ephraim Byard	13Dec1803	E24	W34	
Garsham	Rachel Spence	02Jan1821	E53	W58	
George H.	Charlotte S. Divers	12Aug1857	H12	W106	Smith
George W.	Sarah Jones	05Nov1859		W111	
Henrietta	William Jones	16Apr1847		W91	
James	Ann Pritchard	20Jan1806	E27	W37	
James	Sarah Johnson	22Jan1849		W93	
James	Sarah A. Donnely	03Apr1852	H2	W98	Finny
James L.	Cordelia A. Chesney	27Dec1847		W92	
Jane	John Whitelock	12Jan1839	E80	W81	Reese
John	Avarila Griffeth	21Aug1780	C2	W4	
Joseph	Sarah Hopkins	16Aug1821	E54	W59	
Joseph	Sarah J/I. Ward	20Dec1855	H8	W103	McCartney
Martha	Richard Mitchell	26Feb1833	E72	W73	Finney
Martha Jane	Charles H. Thompson	12Jun1850		W95	
Mary	Joseph Ewing	13Apr1793	E4	W22	
Mary	Asael Bayless	24Feb1820	E52	W57	
Reason	Martha West	18Nov1819	E51	W57	
Rezen	Susanna M. Jones	24Oct1836	E77	W78	Finey
Rezin	Martha Tredway	19Dec1831	E70	W72	Finney
Robert Bonfield	Mary E. Work	30Dec1857		W107	
Sarah	John Ewen	01Mar1815	E42	W49	
Skipwith C.	Priscilla Hopkins	17Jan1842	E84	W85	Gallion
Theodore	Margaretta Bullick	05Oct1844	E87	W87	Parnell
Wm	Ann Kelly	29Nov1779	C1	W3	
William G.	Anna Mitchell	27Aug1840	E82	W83	Finney
Zadock	Eliza Beatty	02Mar1826	E61	W64	Finney

GORSUCH

Eleanor	Thomas Walker	03Feb1852	H1	W97	Reed
Jesse	Jane Poteet	11Nov1815	E44	W50	
Joshua[?]	Prissila Standaford	m. 1804			[ret-AppA]
Luther M.	Sarah Ellen Henderson	27Dec1841	E84	W85	Brown
Mary E.	James W. Reed	18Feb1858		W108	
Sarah	Thomas Rutledge	m. 1804			[ret-AppA]
Susannah	Archibald Henderson	11Jan1842	E84	W85	Brown
Thomas J.	Ellen Wells	17Nov1859		W111	
Westley	Susan Jane Rogers	28May1835	E75	W76	Reese

GORTHROP

Elizth	James Sheradine	04Dec1794	E6	W23
John	Sarah Sheradine	30Jan1794	E5	W23

GORTHRUP

Deborah S.	Jarvis Gilbert James	16Nov1859		W111

GOUGH

Hannah Eliza	Preston McComas	19Oct1809	E34	W43	
Harry, Esq.	Patty Onion	m. 1788[?]			[ret-AppA]
Harry D.	Mary H. O'Brien	31Dec1822	E56	W60	

GOUGH, continued
Helen Theresa	James Glasgow	26Jan1852	H1	W97	Davis
Martha	John Hilton	07Feb1810	E35	W43	
Octavia A.	Joseph W. Dallam	30Jan1855	H7	W102	Trout
Sophia	James Carrol, Esq.	m. 1787			[ret-AppA]
William	Hannah Price	26Dec1833	E73	W74	Finney

GOULD
Frances	William P. Patterson	19Feb1810	E35	W43	
Wm B.	Martha Mitchell	26Oct1792	E3	W22	[ret-AppA]

GOURMLY
Ann	Jeremiah Lynch	31Jan1853	H3	W99	McNally
John	Mary Clark	10Feb1857	H11	W106	Walter

GOVER [see Gover Hopkins, S. Gover McNutt]
Cassandra L.	Samuel M. Lee	24Dec1844	E87	W88	Jones
Elizabeth Gittings	Richard Nun Allen	17Feb1819	E50	W56	
Isabella A.	George H. Perryman	11Dec1832	E71	W73	Higby
Mary	Saml W. Lee	02Feb1795	E6	W24	
Philip	Sallie R. Moores	23Feb1854	H5	W100	Keech
Priscilla	Saml Wilson	08Dec1794	E6	W23	
Robert	Cassandra Lee	04Nov1800	E18	W30	

GRACE
Bowyer	Mary Brooks	25Apr1798	E14	W27	
Peter B.	Prisilla Mercer	04Apr1792	E2	W21	
Rebecca	Thomas Ashley	02Feb1783	C7	W8	cr-Harf

GRAFTON [see Grafton Day, Grafton White]
Alexander	Mary Elizabeth Turner	21Apr1852	H2	W98	Davis
Ann	Thomas Thompson of Josa	16Jan1805	E26	W36	
Ann	Stevenson Harkins	16Nov1836	E77	W78	Wilson
Ann	Noah R. Bull	16Dec1851	H1	W97	Robey
Aqa	Margt Perine	08Aug1779	B3	W2	
Basil	Ann Elizabeth Hines	15Dec1827		W107	
Danl	Elizth Everett	01Mar1781	C4	W6	
Delila	Joshua S. Patterson	17Oct1816	E45	W52	
Elizabeth Ann	Robert L. Martin	23Nov1861		W115	
Hester	Thomas Wann	07Dec1826	E62	W65	Keech
James	Rachel Streett	04Jun1807	E30	W39	
Jesse	Mary Ann Norrington	26Aug1829	E66	W69	Richardson
John	Elizabeth Hanna	27Mar1802	E21	W32	
John	Hester Ann Harkins	20Dec1836	E77	W78	Reese
John D.	Ellender Thompson	03Apr1862		W116	
John H.	Ann Standiford	31Mar1846		W90	
Joseph	Sarah R. Saunders	28Sep1857	H12	W107	Gallion
Martha	Benjamin Streett	14Sep1807	E30	W39	
Martin	Hannah Lee	30Sep1816	E45	W52	
Mary	Thomas Martin	21Dec1820	E53	W58	
Nathan	Martha Dawes	18Nov1810	E36	W44	
Phoebe J/I.	John W. McCommons	14Feb1856	H9	W104	Cushing
Rebecca	Richard Carr	14Nov1837	E78	W79	Collins

GRAFTON, continued
Sarah	John Devoe	31Dec1827	E64	W67	Keech
Sarah Jane	David Gray	03Nov1858		W109	
William	Patty Stockdale	26Aug1807	E30	W39	
William	Eleaner Guyton	02Jun1813	E40	W47	

GRAINGER
William	Margaret Scarff	03May1812	E38	W46	

GRANGER
George W.	Mary Hammon	24Feb1832	E70	W72	Richardson

GRANT
Ann	George Davis	28Sep1780	C3	W5	
Catharine	George E. Banar	04Oct1852	H2	W98	McNally
Mary	Eli Clagett	20Jan1816	E44	W51	
William	Ann Maria Harward	18Oct1859		W110	
William M.	Catherine W. Rogers	21Dec1839	E81	W82	Hunt

GRAVES
Richard	Charlotte Dorsey	29May1798	E15	W27	

GRAY
Alex.	Ann O. Bramble	16Jan1863		W117	
Andrew	Rebecca Rodgers	23Feb1802	E21	W32	
Anna Mary	John Tyson	01Feb1848		W92	
David	Sarah Jane Grafton	03Nov1858		W109	
George	Susan Pritchard	30Jul1825	E60	W64	Tidings
George	Eliza Bowman	07Feb1848		W92	
James	Eliza Hooper	02Jul1829	E66	W68	Richardson
John	Martha Kimbly	26Feb1816	E44	W51	
(Jno Henderson to pay)					
Joseph	Harriott Ford	19Aug1819	E51	W56	
Thomas H.	Julian Crow	23May1806	E28	W38	

GREEN [see Elias Green Richardson]
Ann	Thomas Wright	16Mar1791	E1	W21	
Ann Maria	Edward O'Donnell	08Feb1836	E76	W77	Crosgay
Bennett	Ann Daugherty	22Jan1838	E78	W80	Crosgay
Bennett	Mrs. Sarah Ann Clark	04Feb1850		W94	
Clarisa	Joseph Devoe	10Feb1830	E67	W69	O'Brian
Constance C.	Hannah Wiles	29Aug1855	H8	W103	Wiles
Elizth	Benjn Wheeler	04Feb1793	E4	W22	
Elizabeth	Samuel Mcatee	05Jul1814	E42	W49	
Elizabeth	James Shields	25Jul1836	E76	W78	Crosgry
Elizabeth	J. Thompson Frieze	15Oct1858		W109	
George	Elizabeth Touchstone	05Jan1839	E80	W81	Reese
Giles T.	Deborah Kirkwood	30May1825	E60	W63	O'Brien
Henrietta	Joseph A. Wheeler	13Apr1820	E52	W57	
Joshua	Elizabeth Myers	10Oct1805	E27	W36	

GREEN, continued
Louisa	Derias W. Wells	09Jun1838	E79	W80	Burrows
Lyttleton	Jane Bell	20Sep1845	E88	W89	
Mary	James Bond	03Jul1832	E71	W73	Sewell
Patty	Benjamin Quinlin	06Dec1800	E19	W30	
Sarah	Philip Cooper	13Feb1797	E10	W25	
Susan	James McComas	19Oct1816	E46	W52	
Susanna	John Love	08Nov1791	E1	W21	
Susannah	Robert Owens	06Jan1800	E17	W29	
Thomas	Rebecca Kirkwood	03Feb1852	H1	W97	Yerkes

GREENARD
Rachel	Thos Donovan	28May1780	C2	W4

GREENBERRY [see Greenberry Debruler, Greenberry Gallion, Greenberry Presbury]

GREENE
Mary W.	John H. O'Neill	24May1849	W94

GREENFIELD [see Cajah Greenfield Debrular, Elizabeth Greenfield Debruler]
Ann	John Pogue	23Jan1802	E21	W32	
Eleanor	William Poteet	16Feb1819	E50	W56	
Elizabeth	Edward B. Thompson	04Jan1825	E59	W63	Guest
Henry Austin	Mary Ann Vansickel	14May1821	E54	W59	
Jacob	Elizabeth Everistt	26Sep1791	E1	W21	
James	Eleanor Cooper	12Dec1807	E30	W40	
Martha	George Crevisten	20Apr1818	E49	W55	
Mary	Alexander Garrison	16Dec1785[?]	C10	W10	
Mary	Daniel Michael	03Jul1841	E83	W84	Finny
Patty	Thomas Waltham	21May1795	E7	W24	
Saml K. Jenning	Mary Elizabeth Saunders	22Nov1856	H10	W105	Cushing

GREENLAND
Amanda E.	William P. Wakeland	29Jan1850		W94	
Aquila	Harriot Clowman	10May1810	E35	W43	
Caroline	William Evans	23Aug1858		W108	
Cassandra	James H. Ford	18Nov1847		W92	
Cassandra	William R. Greenland	08Oct1851		W97	
Charlotte A.	Francis Gillen	04May1853	H3	W99	Sanks
Elisha	Ann Osborn	23Feb1826	E61	W64	Stephenson
Elizabeth	George Baker	26Feb1838	E79	W80	Collins
Jane	William Cullum	20Dec1836	E77	W78	Reese
Jane	Wm Fox	01Nov1854	H6	W101	Boulton
John	Elizth Wilkerson	23Feb1848		W92	
John A.	Ruth C. Andrews	20Feb1855	H7	W102	Dumm
Martha A.	William T. Thompson	15Jan1853	H3	W99	Chapman
Mary B.	Nicholas Baker	03Mar1856	H9	W104	Reese
Mary Susan	James Wakeland	17Mar1856	H9	W104	Finney
Nicholas B.	Sarah Elizth Williams	08Sep1863		W118	
Richd	Jane Hearn	m. 1778			[ret-AppA]
William	Mary Casmons	17Feb1816	E44	W51	
Wm	Ann Eliza Cullum	20Jun1864		W119	
William R.	Cassandra Greenland	08Oct1851		W97	

GREENLEE
James	Mary Redman	08Apr1800	E17 W29	
Mary	Mahlon Collins	10Apr1805	E26 W36	
Rachel	Basil Moxley	05Oct1808	E32 W41	

GREENLEY[?]
Martha	Norris Lester	16Apr1841	E83 W84	Dulaney

GREENLY
Thomas	Mary Howard	25Apr1800	E17 W29

GREENWAY
Clarence E.	Sarah B. Hoke	13Jun1856	H10 W105	Binade
Sarah B.	Joseph Henriques	17Oct1863	W118	gr-of N.Y.
William W. S.	Mary Williams	05Jun1843	E86 W86	Billup

GREME
Laura Julian	Samuel Smith	04Feb1823	E56 W61

GRIER
Catharine	John Thomas	20Jan1846	W89	
J. Rich.	Hannah S. Gilbert	03Oct1864	W119	
Mary Jane	Joseph Arther	19Dec1843	E86 W87	Keech
Thomas	Eliza Monks	13Jan1854	H4 W100	Keech

[groom's surname not certain]

GRIFFETH
Elizabeth	William Bonar	30May1780	C2 W4

GRIFFEE
Susannah	Roland Hughes	08Oct1780	C3 W5

GRIFFEN
John	Harriott Turk	09Nov1809	E34 W43
William	Sarah Baxter	31Dec1810	E36 W44

GRIFFETH
Avarila	John Gorrell	21Aug1780	C2 W4

GRIFFEY
James	Elizabeth Loflin	24Feb1840	E82 W83	Finny

GRIFFIN
Emeline	William Numbers	05Aug1844	E87 W87	Eggy
James	Sarah Ann Singleton	23May1855	H7 W102	Gallion
John	Mary Ann Connick[?]	27Sep1779	B3 W2	
Joseph	Sarah Ann Andrews	05Mar1860	W111	
Joshua	Zena Numbers	22Jul1846	W90	
Mary	James Numbers	23Dec1817	E48 W54	
Thomas	Permelia Ellis	19Dec1816	E46 W52	
Thomas B.	Mary Ann Quigley	24Oct1859	W110	
William	Amelia Magness	07Oct1812	E38 W46	
William	Ann Stolinger	06Jun1833	E73 W74	Finney
William W.	Catharine Shirren	28Oct1861	W114	

GRIFFITH
Averilla	William Galloway	22Jul1843	E86 W86	
Edward	Cordelia Hall	10Jan1805	E26 W36	
Edward	Hannah E. Stump	15Feb1817	E46 W53	
Elizabeth	Elijah Davis	12Feb1817	E46 W53	
Francis	John Smith	m. 1787		[ret-AppA]
George	Emily Perryman	16Nov1813	E41 W48	
James	Sarah Cox	08Aug1803	E23 W34	
John L.	Priscilla Stump	26Jun1837	E78 W79	Goldsborough
Luke	Rebcca [sic] Hayward	25Oct1825	E60 W64	Finny
Martha	Alexander Lawson Smith	28Aug1792	E3 W22	[ret-AppA]
Martha	Jesse Benson	09Nov1813	E40 W48	
Mary	William Perry	13Aug1799	E16 W28	
Samuel	Martha Presbury	19Nov1778	B1 W1	
Samuel	Elizth Garrettson	21Dec1791	E2 W21	[ret-AppA]
Sarah	Samuel Jay	06Apr1810	E35 W43	
Sarah	Henry Michael	10Oct1816	E45 W52	
Scott	Elizabeth Noble	21May1812	E38 W46	
Virginia	Thomas F. Bowie	21Jul1855	H8 W103	Crampton

GRIFFY
Mary	Isaac Wattle	04Nov1834	E74 W76	Hoopman

GRINDALL
Eleanor	William Calwell	20Nov1800	E18 W30	
Elizabeth	Jesse Cullum	27Apr1835	E75 W76	Finney
John G.	Eleanor Wheeler	17Nov1807	E30 W39	

GROENLEE
Martha	John Murphy	24Sep1806	E28 W38

GROOM
George T.	Margaret Silver	05Aug1851	W96

GROOME
George T.	Mary F. Pritchard	04Dec1858	W109

GROSCUP
Lydia Matilda	Enoch C. Garrettson	19Mar1863	W117

GROSS
John	Mary Walter	28Jul1864	W119	
Julian	Adam Reirec[?]	03Mar1856	H9 W104	Young
Margaret	Henry Hess	12Apr1842	E85 W85	Keech

GROVE [see Grove U. Hotchkiss]

GROVEL
Ann Maria	William M. McKinnie	16Sep1834	E74 W75	Finney

GROVER
Eleanor	William Prater	04Jul1812	E38 W46

GROVES
Eleanor	Giles Kimble	19Mar1779	B1	W1	
Martha	Thomas Welch	21May1793	E4	W22	
Sarah	Oliver York	09Nov1779	C1	W3	
William	Jane Hughstone	13Jan1781	C4	W5	
William	Elizabeth Meads	m. 1778			[ret-AppA]
Wm	Sarah Day	26Feb1794	E5	W23	[or 27Feb?]

GRUNDEN
Ann	Edward Daws	27Dec1793	E5	W23

GRUPY
Jacob	Eliza B. Amos	18Feb1823	E56	W61
William H.	Lotte V. Henderson	20Mar1858		W108

GUBBIN
Mary	Robert Price	15May1810	E35	W43

GUEST
Job	Elizabeth Coale	14Nov1810	E36	W44	
John	Rebecca Hall	m. 1792			[ret-AppA]
[see also under Gest]					

GUGART
Patrick	Catharine Conner	21Jun1865	W121

GUICHARD
Peter	Sophia Beauzamy	06Nov1805	E27	W36

GUYTON [see William Hunter entry]
Archibald M.	Hannah E. Scarff	02May1856	H10	W104	Myers
Benjamin	Jane Cain	13Feb1817	E46	W53	
Benjamin	Elizabeth Laren	06Apr1864		W119	
Benjamin S.	Eleanora Spicer	18Jun1842	E85	W85	John Reese
Darcas Ann	William Johnson	15Apr1852	H2	W98	Yerkes
Edward	Eleanor Demoss	14May1815	E43	W49	
Edward M.	Hollyday Brown	30Jan1810	E34	W43	
Eleaner	William Grafton	02Jun1813	E40	W47	
Elisha	Catharine Shultz	21Dec1812	E39	W47	
Elizth	George McComas	17Dec1827	E64	W67	Keech
James	Rachel Robinson	30Jun1813	E40	W48	
John	Salley Slater	06Feb1809	E33	W42	
John	Mary Ann Johnson	31Jan1832	E70	W72	Keech
John H.	Mary E. Sappington	31Jul1856	H10	W105	Keech
Joshua	Sarah Mitchell	12Jan1781	C4	W5	
Joshua, Jr.	Eliza McClaskey	26Dec1822	E56	W60	
Margaret	James Murray	18Aug1800	E18	W29	
Margaret	Jacob Bradenbaugh	09Jun1837	E78	W79	Collins
Robert	Eliza Holland	20Dec1823	E57	W62	
William A.	Cecelia Sherman	17Apr1860		W112	

HABURN
William	Sarah Scarborough	01Oct1823	E57	W61

Harford Co. Md. Marriage Licenses, 1777-1865   103

HACKETT
James H.   Jane E. McGilton   12Oct1826   E62 W65   Pool
Mary   Nichl Caton   22Mar1779   B1 W1

HAESTON
Ann Catharine   James Cook   19Dec1860   W113

HAGERTY
Danl   Elizabeth Jones   14Mar1796   E8 W25

HAINES
Charles Y.   Sarah Elizabeth Allen   12Oct1833   E73 W74   D. Bond
Claudius R.   Cordelia G. Hall   02Oct1858   W109
DeWilton   R. Ellen Duvall   04Jun1851   W96
Samuel   Mary Ann Rockhold   11Jul1833   E73 W74   Donohay

HAIR[?]
James   Mary All   07Jan1786   C10 W10

HAITHHORN
Jane   Morris Baker   20Aug1781   C5 W7
Martha   Thomas Synott   12Mar1794   E5 W23
Polly   Mathew Kennard   29Jul1794   E5 W23

HALE
John W.   Susan Slade   19Dec1837   E78 W79   Cross

HALEY
Sarah   James Smith   20Sep1797   E11 W26   [ret-AppA]

HALL [see Blanch Hall Lee, Parker Hall Lee, Carvill Hall Prigg]
Andrew   Martha P. Hall   02Nov1857   H13 W107   Crampton
Ann   John O'Connor   17Jun1813   E40 W47
Aquila   Catharine Amos   05Nov1822   E56 W60
Avarilla   John Patterson   08Feb1780   C1 W3
Bendct Edwd   Milcah Garrett   02Mar1780   C1 W3
Caroline F.   Edward M. Chew   09Nov1863   W118
Charlotte White Walter Tolley Hall   05Jan1801   E19 W30
Cordelia   Edward Griffith   10Jan1805   E26 W36
Cordelia G.   Claudius R. Haines   02Oct1858   W109
Cornelia B.   William H. Chapman   28Oct1851   W97
Delia M.   Thomas Penniman   05May1829   E66 W68   Keech
Edward C.   Frances M. Lee   30Nov1815   E44 W50
Eleanor Brooke   William White Ramsay   04Mar1816   E44 W51
Elizabeth H.   John B. Bayless   29Jul1826   E61 W65   Keech
Emely A.   James A. Baxter   29May1828   E64 W67   McKay
George W.   Sophia W. Lewis   07Feb1816   E44 W51
Jacob   Mary Wilmot   20May1784   C8 W9
Jane   Israel D. Maulsby   08Feb1806   E28 W37
John Beedle   Sarah Hall   m. 1778   [ret-AppA]
John T.   Elizth Rogers   12May1828   E64 W67   Finney
Josias   Martha Garretson   m. 1787   [ret-AppA]
Martha Matilda   Andrew H. Lemon   16Dec1823   E57 W61
Martha P.   Andrew Hall   02Nov1857   H13 W107   Crampton

HALL, continued

Mary	Everit Gairy	10Mar1812	E38 W46	
Mary	Washington P. Chew	03Jan1831	E68 W70	Tippet
Mary Moore	Robert H. Smith	05Dec1861	W115	
Prisilla	Gabrial Christie	15[?]Nov1779	C1 W3	
Rebecca	John Gest	13Nov1792	E3 W22	[ret-AppA]
Robert Lyon	Blanch Hall Lee	27Oct1808	E32 W41	
Sabina	Augustine Boyer	15Jan1793	E3 W22	[ret-AppA]
Sarah	John Beedle Hall	m. 1778		[ret-AppA]
Sarah	John Proser	09Feb1798	E13 W27	Jno Allen
Sophia McHenry	William F. Brand	23May1843	E86 W86	Whittingham
Sophia White	John D. Lewis	04Nov1806	E29 W38	
Thos	Isabella Presbury	19Mar1793	E4 W22	[ret-AppA]
William	Sophia Presbury	m. 1788		[ret-AppA]
William W. R.	Sarah Amanda Pritchard	29Oct1860	W112	

HALLARD

John	Hannah Cox	31Mar1779	B1 W1	

HAMBLETON [see John Hambleton Jones]

Ann	John Hynes	23Apr1805	E26 W36	
Edward, Junr	Priscilla Johnson	27Mar1806	E28 W37	
James L.	Hannah E. Maulsby	20May1843	E86 W86	Keech
John	Margaretta Bond	17Jun1793	E4 W22	
John	Aley Gafford	24Jan1797	E10 W25	[ret-AppA]
John	Elizabeth Lego	17Apr1809	E33 W42	
Robert	Hannah Fullerd	04Apr1829	E65 W68	Richardson

HAMBY

James	Ann Williams	13Jan1800	E17 W29	
James W.	Louisa F. Bunts	08Jun1857	H12 W106	Monroe
John Smith	Jane J. Coale	03Jan1828	E64 W67	Keech
John W.	Mary Jane Mitchell	25Jan1856	H9 W104	McDaniel
Martha	Hugh Reed	26Feb1780	C1 W3	
Rebecca	Joseph Horton	04May1861	W114	
Scott	Miram Webster	29Dec1829	E66 W69	McGee
William	Susanna Cowan	13Aug1800	E18 W29	
William	Susan Gilbert	14May1833	E72 W74	Hoopman

HAMILTON [see Hamilton Lefevre; see also HAMBLETON]

Alex.	Eliza M. McFadden	11Feb1863	W117	
George	Sarah Scarff	06Jul1818	E49 W55	
John	Cassandra Byard	21Jan1835	E75 W76	Richardson
Samuel	Hannah E. Foard	31Mar1857	H11 W106	Daugherty
Samuel	Emily E. Harvey	16Dec1863	W118	
William	Charlotte Knight	26Oct1816	E46 W52	

HAMMER

James	Mary Johnson	30Aug1831	E69 W71	Dorsey

HAMMERSMITH

John	Jane Hanna	10Feb1842	E84 W85	Finney

HAMMON

Mary	George W. Granger	24Feb1832	E70 W72	Richardson

HAMMOND
Ann	George Cullum	04Jun1808	E31 W41	
James	Fra⁸ Patterson	23Apr1781	C4 W6	
Mordecai	Teresa Bond	18Oct1815	E43 W50	

HAMPTON
David	M.[?] Easter Gordon	28Aug1782	C6 W8	

HANAWAY
Rebecca	Enos West	18Dec1800	E19 W30	

HANAY
Ann	Joseph R. Impire	02Jul1850	W95	

HANBY
Mary	Isaac Sanders	06Jun1827	E63 W66	Finney
Mary Jane	John W. Deaver	10Oct1850	W95	

HANCOCK
Arian M.	Fannie A. Davis	22Feb1862	W115	
Zachariah	Elizabth Hipkins	08Jan1824	E57 W62	

HANDLY
Alice	Patrick Riley	14Jun1859	W110	

HANEY
Ann	James S.[or J?] Chandley	01Apr1819	E50 W56	
Daniel	Eleanor Garret	14Dec1807	E30 W40	
Patrick	Mary Kearney	21Jun1847	W91	
Thomas	Ann Garrett	04Mar1808	E31 W40	

HANNA
Eliza Ann	Richard Smith	06Dec1849	W94	
Elizabeth	John Grafton	27Mar1802	E21 W32	
Elizabeth	William Divers	12Apr1803	E23 W33	
Elizabeth	James Fulton	18Dec1817	E48 W54	
Hannah E. [possibly 9 March]	Armintus T. Patterson	11[?]Mar1857	H11 W106	Finney
James A.	Melissa J/I. Hanson	19Mar1855	H7 W102	Finney
Jane	Henry Watters	09Mar1815	E43 W49	
Jane	John Hammersmith	10Feb1842	E84 W85	Finney
John	Ann Rogers	22Mar1796	E8 W25	
John Calvin	Lucretia G. Mechem	22Dec1859	W111	
Magy	Thomas Rogers	01Jan1795	E6 W24	
Mary	John McKenney[?]	23Aug1793	E4 W23	
Mary	William Rodgers	20Mar1800	E17 W29	
Robert	Elizabeth Jarvis	30Jul1812	E38 W46	
Robert	Rebecca Silvers	25Jan1837	E77 W78	Finney
Sarah	Philip Fulton	30Mar1801	E20 W31	
Sarah E.	William F. Bayless	31May1853	H4 W99	Finney
Stephen B.	Mary Ann Fulton	20Apr1824	E58 W62	
William	Jane McGaw	26Mar1818	E49 W55	
William	Mary Ann Watson	13Aug1828	E65 W68	Finney
Wm. Finney	Martha Barnes	29Dec1863	W118	

HANNAH
Hugh	Rebecca Vance	04Feb1781	C4 W6	
James	Rebecca Hanson	m. 1778		[ret-AppA]
James	Hannah Bayley	--Apr1782	C5 W7	
Jane	John Harkins	25Mar1807	E29 W39	
Robert	Mary Thomas	25Jan1779	B1 W1	

HANRICK
Fred.	Catharine Bush	12Sep1864	W119

HANSON [see George Hanson Garrettson, Hanson Cole, Hanson Courtney]
A. B. [gr]	A. E. Middelton [br]	29Nov1864	W120	
Avarillah	William Bull	26Aug1780	C3 W4	
Benedict	Ann Mathews	27Dec1807	E31 W40	
Benedict	Lydia Barnes	24Sep1829	E66 W69	McGee
Benjamin	Martha Garrettson	12Oct1779	B3 W2	
Benjamin	Elizabeth Courtney	30Jun1812	E38 W46	
B. H., Jr.,	Susie Canon	21Jan1862	W115	
Elizth	Edwd Thompson	08Feb1780	C1 W3	
Elizabeth	Samuel Jackson	m. 1790		[ret-AppA]
Elizabeth	Henry P. Ruff	08Feb1816	E44 W51	
Elizabeth	Robert McGaw	16Dec1833	E73 W74	Finney
Hollis	Avarilla Hollingsworth	m. 1777		[ret-AppA]
Hollis	Mary Dorsey	30Apr1781	C4 W6	
Jacob	Ann Nowers	02Sep[?]1793	E5 W23	
John	Averilla Hollis	04Dec1781	C5 W7	
M. Annie	Frederick Hinkson	09Jan1861	W113	
Mary	Abraham Andrews	17Mar1779	B1 W1	
Melissa J/I.	James A. Hanna	19Mar1855	H7 W102	Finney
Rebecca	James Hannah	m. 1778		[ret-AppA]
Sarah	Joshua Day	29Dec1784	C9 W10	
Sarah	John Barron	10Dec1822	E56 W60	
W^m	Mary Mathews	04Nov1781	C5 W7	

HANWAY
David	Mary Ann Warner	27Jan1836	E76 W77	Keech
Eliza	Silas Silver	16Jul1929	E66 W68	Keech
Franklin	Hannah J. Forwood	24Mar1863	W117	
J. B.	Sarah L. Rouse	21Nov1864	W120	
Joseph	Martha R. Amos	18Feb1851	W96	
Thomas	Sarah Ann Keen	28Nov1835	E76 W77	Smith

HARBERT
Benj.	Sarah Crabson	15Aug1795	E7 W24

HARCUM
Emaline	Robert Haynie	03Jul1854	H6 W101 Collins

HARDEN
John	Mary Sessions	13May1779	B2 W2

HARDY
Martha M.	James A. McFadden	03Oct1864	W119

HARE
Francis	Mary Golway	25Jun1794	E5 W23	
Jehu	Margaret McAdow	07May1835	E75 W76	Finney

HARGROVE
Ephraim	Rozetta Garrett	30May1811	E36 W45
Ruth	Isaac Montgomery	01Oct1798	E15 W27

HARKER
Mary A.	David Durham	01Apr1864	W119

HARKINS
Aaron	Sarah Lewin	20Mar1833	E72 W73	Keech
Ann	Samuel Morton	10Nov1849	W94	
Ann Eliza	Elisha Johnson	05Feb1862	W115	
Hannah	John Ward	09Jun1829	E66 W68	McGee[?]
[minister may be McVey]				
Hannah H.	Samuel Holland	29Oct1829	E66 W69	McGee
Hester Ann	John Grafton	20Dec1836	E77 W78	Reese
John	Jane Hannah	25Mar1807	E29 W39	
Priscilla	Franklin Rigdon	11Dec1848	W93	
Sarah Jane	Herman Pyle	03Jan1846	W89	
Stephen	Sarah Jones	27Oct1819	E51 W57	
Stephen W.	Sarah Elizth Michael	22Dec1859	W111	
Stevenson	Ann Grafton	16Nov1836	E77 W78	Wilson

HARKNESS
James	Mary Garrett	16Feb1818	E48 W54

HARLAN
Alice	Philip W. Silver	18Dec1832	E72 E73	Finney
David	Margaret R. Herbert	02Mar1846	W90	
Elizabeth	Robert A. Watters	21Feb1846	W90	
Henry O.	Hannah Jane Evans	23Feb1865	W120	
Rachel S.	Anthony B. Cleaveland	03Aug1833	E73 W74	Porter

HARLON
Jeremiah	Esther Stump	08Sep1800	E18 W30

HARMAN
Margaret A.	John C. Zimmerman	03Nov1864	W120
Mary	Theo. Walder	10Mar1865	W121
Sarah Jane	Joseph R. Walker	20Dec1861	W115

HARMER
Joseph M.	Catharine A. McNabb	27May1856	H10 W104	Lemmon

HARONEINA
Mary	Joseph Barber	02Aug1851	W96

HARPER
Anna	Francis Hopkins	06Jun1863	W117
Barnet	Milcah Dawes	18Jul1804	E25 W35
Elizabeth	Abraham Rutledge	05Feb1823	E56 W61

HARPER, continued
Mary	Isaac Blackston	09Jan1816	E44 W51	
Samuel	Hannah Watson	03Apr1833	E72 W73	Finney
Sarah	William Stroble	05Jul1816	E45 W52	

HARPLEY
Nathaniel	Ann McGuire	01Jul1801	E20 W31

HARPS
Lawrence	Mary Dulaney	29Aug1796	E9 W25

HARRIMAN
Hezekiah	Sarah Watters	28Jan1806	E27 W37

HARRIS [see Harris York]
Elizabeth	Bennet Nelson	13Jan1845	E88 W88	Wysong
Elizabeth Susanna	Henry G. Bussey	05Oct1807	E30 W39	
George	Mary Hopkins	17Feb1845	E88 W88	Ego
James	Ann McNiece	24Sep1803	E23 W34	
Jane	George Ewing	20Jun1781	C5 W6	
[br surname uncertain]				
Will.	Ann Barrett[or Barrelt?] m. 1778			[ret-AppA]

HARRISON [see Mary Harrison Sewell, Harrison Laver, Harrison Shaw]
Henry	Mary Ann Kennedy	02Mar1863	W117

HARROD
Ann	Luke Gillum	31Dec1812	E39 W47

HARROWWOOD
Susanna L.	David R. Cantler	04May1853	H3 W99	Gallion

HARRY
Ann	Job Way	03Sep1806	E28 W38
David	Maria Jane Warner	05Feb1861	W113
John W.	Cassandra Davis	20Oct1846	W90

HARRYMAN
Elizabeth	Ringold Smith	29Aug1836	E76 W78	Smith
Sarah A.	Charlton W. Billingslea	20May1837	E77 W79	Collins

HART
William J.	Sarah Jane Saunders	30Sep1843	E86 W86	Switzer[?]

HARTLAY
Joshua	Ann Bayne	19Feb1798	E13 W27	Jno Allen

HARTLEY
Martha	Thomas Kelly	15Jul1799	E16 W28

HARTMAN
Christopher	Sarah McComas	12Sep1843	E86 W86	Maddox
John	Julia Bowar	05Mar1855	H7 W102	Cronin

HARTMANN
Mary	Henry Stinereader	13Dec1848	W93	

HARTSHORN
Sarah	Robert Leech	28Oct1834	E74 W75	Hoopman

HARVEY [see Harvey S. Jones]
Alexander	Eleanor McDaniel	m. 1777		[ret-AppA]
Emily E.	Samuel Hamilton	16Dec1863	W118	
James	Elizabeth A. Starr[?]	26Dec1850	W95	
John	Sophia Everitt	09Mar1826	E61 W65	Richardson
John	Maggie A. Mitchell	30Jun1864	W119	
Margaret	Samuel D. Moser	19Nov1859	W111	
Rachel	Joseph Jones	11Jul1825	E60 W64	Richardson

HARWARD
Ann Maria	William Grant	18Oct1859	W110	
Frances S.	Robert Esley	27Dec1847	W92	
James C.	Catharine Hile	28Jan1853	H3 W99	McNally
John	Mary Curtis	27Nov1848	W93	
Susan[surname?]	Hugh Hinghay	11Aug1800	E18 W29	
Walter	Leaven Lusby	08Dec1837	E78 W79	Collins
Walter	Annie E. Chapman	03Jan1854	H4 W100	Cronin
Wesley	Harriet V. James	17Nov1856	H10 W105	Cushing
William H.	Catharine F. Welch	18Jan1842	E84 W85	Reid

HARWOOD
Charles	Mary Brown	26Nov1812	E39 W47	
James	Susanna Mann	05Sep1811	E37 W45	

HASLAM
Robert H.	Rosena Scotten	11Apr1833	E72 W74	Damphoux

HASSIT[?]
William	Mary Brown	11May1816	E45 W51	

HASSON
John	Rachael Barrett	m. 1795		[ret-AppA]

HASTINGS
Benjamin S.	Frances Ellen Oliver	12Jun1860	W112	

HATHHORN
James	Frances Debruler	21Jan1806	E27 W37	

HATTON
Elizabeth P.	Benjamin Standiford	19Dec1831	E70 W72	Sewall
John	Sarah Collings	m. 1803		[ret-AppA]
Ruth	Isaac Holland	m. 1804		[ret-AppA]

HAU[?]
Chrisdan	Rosa Anna Jamison	02Dec1862	W116	

HAUGHY
Hugh	Elizabeth Curtis	30Jan1849	W93	

HAUY
John	Hannah Johnson	03Mar1799	E15 W28	

HAVELIN
Margaret	Michael Kehoe	31Dec1857	W107	
Sirce	Michael Linch	25Jul1830	E67 W70	O'Brian

HAVLIN
Mary	Sylvester Kelly	14May1855	H7 W102	Walter
Rosanna	William O. Kaafa	19Aug1846	W90	

HAWKINS [see Elizabeth Hawkins Morgan]
Alverda	L. M. Birmingham	10Jan1859	W109	
Ann	George Smith	27Jan1802	E21 W32	
Avarilla	Robert Mitchell	27Jun1831	E69 W71	Webster
Caroline P.	William Wilson	15Jan1846	W89	
Cassandra	Edward Courtney	09Apr1811	E36 W44	
Charles	Mary Ann Legue	26Jan1824	E57 W62	
Elizabeth	Thomas Stake	06Jan1818	E48 W54	
Elizabeth	David Silver	15Jan1818	E48 W54	
Elizabeth B.	George Williams	30May1815	E43 W50	
George	Christeen Tredway	29Jan1838	E79 W80	Finy
John	Mary Vandegrift	06Jan1807	E29 W38	
John	Susan Thompson	02Mar1826	E61 W64	Richardson
John	Margaret Carroll	11Oct1831	E69 W71	Sewall
John	Mary Hawkins	29Oct1838	E80 W81	Finney
John W.	Matilda Russell	06Oct1860	W112	
Joshua	Elizabeth Hopkins	08Feb1820	E52 W57	
Lydia	George Vandegrift	15May1807	E29 W39	
Mary	Michael Sennoth	17Jun1828	E65 W67	O'Brien
Mary	William Mahan	21Dec1829	E66 W69	Webster
Mary	John Hawkins	29Oct1838	E80 W81	Finney
Mary E.	George W. Wood	31Aug1850	W95	
Mary Elizabeth	James Bowen	17Jun1828	E65 W67	Finney
Mary Jane	Francis Mitchell	25May1850	W95	
Mathew	Martha Perryman	27Jul1815	E43 W50	
Philip G.	Lizzie E. James	11Feb1862	W115	
Richard	Julian Touchstone	11Dec1813	E41 W48	
Robert	Ann Mitchell	20Jul1797	E12 W26	
Samuel	Hannah Standiford	04Feb1784	C8 W9	cr-Harf
Sarah E.	Adrianus D. Carroll	08Mar1856	H9 W104	Rinick
Susanna	George Osborn	08Feb1827	E62 W66	Stephens
William	Mary Ann Carrol	22Mar1841	E83 W84	Gallion
William	Rachel Miller	04Feb1852	H1 W97	Cadden

HAYCOCK
Cornelia	Samuel Lewis	16Oct1819	E51 W57	

HAYES
George	Margaret D. Silver	06Sep1828	E65 W68	Finney
Julia Ann	Patrick O'Brian	15Aug1856	H10 W105	Walter
Michael	Anna Bannon	25Jul1859	W110	

HAYGHE
Mary Jane	Thomas Johnson	21Nov1862	W116 ALJ1-94,106	

HAYNES
Mary A.	James C. Wheat	23Oct1838	E79 W81	Reese

HAYNIE
Robert	Emaline Harcum	03Jul1854	H6 W101	Collins

HAYS
Abraham	Hannah Cooper	06May1807	E29 W39	
Archibald	Hannah Smith	23Feb1780	C1 W3	
Eliza [Hay?]	Alexander Devereux	17Aug1857	I112 W106	Walter
Elizabeth S.	Abraham Jarrett, Junior	16Oct1817	E47 W54	
Harriet H.	Robert W. Whaland	10Nov1835	E76 W77	Finney
Isaac	Elizabeth McComas	17Aug1801	E20 W31	
Joel H.	Anna Eliza Beaumont	19Sep1859	W110	
John	Elizabeth Sampson	20Sep1808	E32 W41	
Mary A.	Reuben H. Davis	20Feb1821	E53 W58	
Nathaniel W. S.	Mary Fulford	28Jan1834	E73 W75	Finney
Pamelia B.	Stevenson Archer	20Jan1811	E36 W44	
Sarah M. J.	Samuel Galloway	14May1833	E72 W74	Keech
Thomas	Ann Hollis	04Jun1822	E55 W60	
Thomas A.	Elizabeth Jones	08Apr1802	E22 W32	
Wm	Cynthia Thompson	11Feb1796	E8 W25	

HAYTHORN
Samuel	Ann Rockhold	29Jun1800	E18 W29	

HAYWARD
Mary	John Johnson	02Jan1812	E37 W45	
Mary B.	Stephen J. Thompson	10Oct1826	E62 W65	Keech
Rebcca [sic]	Luke Griffith	25Oct1825	E60 W64	Finney

HAZELETT
Henry	Mary Ward	22Aug1857	H12 W107	Finney

HAZLET
Franklin	Elizabeth Norris	30Dec1857	W107	

HAZLETT
Jane	John C. Davis	20Jun1857	H12 W106	Finney

HEALY
Rachel	Greenberry Debruler	23May1799	E16 W28	
Sally A.	J. Taylor Crawford	30Aug1860	W112	

HEAPE
Elijah	Keziah Barton	13Aug1822	E56 W60	
Mary A.	William Wallace	28May1859	W110	
Sarah C.	John Allen	24Dec1858	W109	

HEAPES
William	Rebecca Wiley	13Jan1834	E73 W75	Parke

HEAPS
David	Augusta Garrett	27Jan1865	W120	
Elizabeth	William Barton	24Jun1819	E51 W56	
Margaret L.	Matthew C. Galbreath	18Dec1861	W115	
Mary Martha	R. N. Ramsay	12May1860	W112	
Nancy J.	George H. Shane	28Apr1863	W117	
Sallie A.	John J. Fulton	22Dec1860	W113	
Sarah	Richard King	20May1802	E22 W32	
Sarah Jane	Archibald Wallace	30Dec1828	E65 W68	Park

HEARN
Jane	Richd Greenland	m. 1778		[ret-AppA]

HEATHCOTE
James	Mary Elizabeth Whitaker	10Jul1843	E86 W86	Reid

HEATON
Elizabeth A.	John McClung	27Jan1857	H11 W105	Durm
Jeremiah	Mary Fisher	07Jan1799	E15 W27	
John	Susanna Barton	13Nov1816	E46 W52	
John	Sarah Ann Devoe	10Dec1858	W109	
William	Mary Barton	18Jun1809	E34 W42	
William	Elizabeth Bosley	13Jan1827	E62 W65	Rockhold
William	Sarina C. Almony	31Mar1857	H11 W106	Durm

HEBNER
Catharine	John Christian Sturts	21Nov1858	W109	
Elijah	Mary Jane McComas	31Dec1859	W111	

HECK
Charles L.	Catharine Morgan	08Apr1857	H11 W106	Crawford

HEDERICK
John	Rebecca Miller	15Dec1835	E76 W77	Richardson

HEDRIC
William	Mary Andrews	28Oct1819	E51 W57

HEEPS
Arthur	Sarah Bay	06Nov1781	C5 W7
Robert	Martha James	21Aug1781	C5 W7

HEINLEIN
Anna	Kilian Kub	01Mar1862	W115
Conrad	Susanna Sibold	09Jun1863	W117
Mary	Frederick Keiferte	05Nov1860	W112

Harford Co. Md. Marriage Licenses, 1777-1865   113

HEIR
Christian   Susannah Young   05Aug1851   W96

HEIRS
Susannah   William Munk   23Mar1781 C4 W6

HELLEN[?]
Alexander   Susanna Durham   16May1799 E16 W28

HEMP
Louisa   Henry Lueding   27Aug1860   W112

HEMPHILL
Wm   Margt Ashmore   10Nov1778 B1 W1

HENDERSON [see Henderson Laughard]
Abigal   Jas Rathers   20Sep1781 C5 W7
Ann   Aquila Demos   22Feb1814 E41 W48
Archibald   Susannah Gorsuch   11Jan1842 E84 W85 Brown
Charlotte   William Cherry   05Jun1827 E63 W66 Keech
Elizabeth   Parker Gilbert   14Dec1803 E24 W34
Elizabeth   James McCormick   19Oct1813 E40 W48
Ellen   William Wright   28Sep1815 E43 W50
George   Charity Cole   17Jun1800 E18 W29
George   Sarah Cowan   15Nov1820 E53 W58
Lotte V.   William H. Grupy   20Mar1858   W108
Mary   James Thomas   03Apr1817 E47 W53
Mary A.   John H. Chauncey   05May1835 E75 W76 Goldsboro
Mary Jane   William McAdow   01Feb1837 E77 W79 Dulany
Nathaniel   Elizabeth Perryman   12Sep1792 E3 W22 [ret-AppA]
Priscilla A.   John Cowen   14Jan1840 E81 W82 Goldsborough
Sarah   Henry Drew   18[?]Jun1783 C7 W8
Sarah E.   Andrew J. McAdow   11Apr1843 E86 W86 Finney
Sarah Ellen   Luther M. Gorsuch   27Dec1841 E84 W85 Brown

HENDON [see John Hendon Chalk, Hendon Chocke]
Benjamin   Eliza Ann Treadwell   03Jan1839 E80 W81 Crosgey
Mary   Lloyd Standiford   17Nov1812 E39 W47
Thomas   Mary Amanda Hollis   01May1832 E71 W72 Sewall

HENDRICK
Sally   John Yokely   21Dec1795 E8 W24 [ret-AppA]

HENLEY
John D.   Eliza Denison   26Mar1816 E45 W51

HENNING
Anna M.   Christian Linlop   09Jul1850   W95

HENRIGUES
Joseph   Sarah B. Greenway   17Oct1863   W118 gr-of N.Y.

HENRY

Bridget	John Cassidy	09Feb1858	W108	
Elizabeth	Robert Whiteford	14Apr1818	E49 W55	
Elizabeth	Sedgwick James, Junr	27Jan1820	E52 W57	
Robert	Susan Waltham	22Sep1849	W94	
Samuel	Margaret Reese	21Aug1823	E57 W61	

HERBERT

Alvin C.	Sarah Ann Courtney	19Dec1842	E85 W86	Habborset[?]
Ann	George Bay	16Nov1808	E32 W41	
Ann E.	George W. Pritchard	10Mar1828	E64 W67	Keech
Benedict	Harriot Johnson	12Mar1816	E45 W51	
Betsey	Amos Cyle	22Jun1844	E87 W87	Alexander
Catherine	Charles Whitelock	18Jun1839	E81 W82	Goldsborough
Eliza	John Walker	15Nov1848	W93	
Elizabeth Cole	Jarrett Spencer	02Sep1844	E87 W87	Gallion
Francis	Sarah Forwood	11Jun1812	E38 W46	
Francis J.	Charles L. Willey	19Dec1848	W93	
George	Lavina Kennedy	17Jan1809	E33 W42	
George	Jane Kennedy	07Mar1816	E45 W51	
Gideon	Mary Curley	19Mar1802	E21 W32	
Irah	Maria Layer[?]	10Aug1835	E75 W76	Dulany
Jane	John Dinsmore	04Oct1808	E32 W41	
Jane	Samuel W. Pennington	25Jan1815	E42 W49	
Jera[?]	Mary S. Willey	08Oct1856	H10 W105	Gallion
John	Ann Nalor	29Jun1822	E56 W60	
Joseph	Aesha Ward	09Mar1815	E43 W49	
Margaret R.	David Harlan	02Mar1846	W90	
Mary	Richard Johnson	22Oct1799	E16 W28	
Mary	Charles White	07Sep1809	E34 W43	
Mary	James McGaw	02Mar1831	E68 W71	Finney
Mary Ann	Henry Smith	17Oct1831	E70 W71	Finney
Richard	Mary Lear	24Jan1806	E27 W37	
Thomas	Elizabeth Mitchell	16Feb1807	E29 W39	

HERMAN

Mary E.	Charles K. Blaney	09Aug1864	W119	
William O.	Hannah E. Holland	19Sep1860	W112	
William S.	Margaret A. Wollen	13Jan1857	H11 W105	Cushing

HERRICK

Seth W.	Harriet S. Divers	16Jan1862	W115

HERRING

Mary	Isaac Allen	23Dec1800	E19 W30
Sarah	Isaac Botts	14Jun1824	E58 W62

HERRINGTON

Jacob	Elizabeth Goodwin	10Jun1803	E23 W34

HERRON

Charles	Charlotte Luster	02Feb1820	E52 W57
James	Elizth Reynolds	03Jun1863	W117

HESS
Catharine   John Emrick   17Mar1864   W119
Henry   Margaret Gross   12Apr1842   E85 W85 Keech

HEVERINE
Sarah Jane   George W. Barnes   04Sep1848   W93

HEWETT
Rebecca M.   Allen Wilson   20Jan1851   W96

HICKEY
Hannah   John Caskey   13Jan1819   E50 W56

HICKMAN
Elizabeth   Thomas Wilson   11Sep1797   E11 W26

HICKS
James, Junr   Rebecca Trapnall   18Jan1806   E27 W37
John   Mary Ann Conner   15Jan1861   W113
Polly   William Bull   m. 1803   [ret-AppA]

HIGBEE
Edward Y.   Mary Sophia Stump Thomas 14Oct1835   E75 W77 Goldsborough

HIGHFIELD
George H.   Mary J. Sherren   31Aug1859   W110
Mary J.   Micha. Gilbert   22May1865   W121

HIGINBOTHAM
Ralph   Isabella Presbury   23Feb1799   E15 W28

HILD
Henry   Mary Ellen Spedden   20Dec1847   W92

HILDT
John W.   Sarah Vanhorn   19Oct1863   W118

HILE
Catharine   James C. Harward   28Jan1853   H3 W99 McNally

HILL
Aaron   Rebecca Foard   12Feb1810   E35 W43
Ann   William Vanzandt   12Feb1822   E55 W60
Benedict   Blanch York   13Jul1811   E36 W45
Benjamin   Sarah Roberts   02Mar1803   E23 W33
Elizabeth   John Barnet   m. 1797   [ret-AppA]
Elizabeth   James Wilson   11Feb1834   E74 W75 Dulaney
Elizabeth J.   Michael W. Johnson   25Jun1835   E75 W76 Dulany
Hannah   Jarrett Hipkins   08Jan1824   E57 W62
Hannah T.   Cajah Greenfield Debrular 06Jul1815   E43 W50
Harmon   Fras Devee   10Dec1779   C1 W3
John F.   Martha N. Ford   15Feb1859   W109
John G.   Elizabeth Foard   26Apr1831   E69 W71 Sewell
Martha   Henry Dawney   10Sep1799   E16 W28

HILL, continued
Martha	Samuel Hudson	27Apr1814	E41 W49	
Martha	John E. Hughes	03Mar1846	W90	
Martha Tunis	William G. Debrula	25Mar1829	E65 W68	Richardson
Mary	Spencer Lego	08Jun1810	E35 W44	
Mary Ann	Jacob Stall	06Jan1841	E83 W84	Wilson
Milkey	Samuel Taylor	14Nov1825	E60 W64	Tidings
Moses	Patty Thomas	14Oct1823	E57 W61	
Rebecca	John Crabston	18Jul1836	E76 W78	Dulany
Richard	Mary Dawson	04Oct1795	E7	
[above lic. crossed out]				
Sarah	Jas Anderson	03Apr1780	C1 W3	
Sarah	Thomas Simmons	m. 1787		[ret-AppA]
Susan	James H. Wetherall	29Aug1833	E73 W74	Donahay
Thomas	Martha Browning	05Jun1801	E20 W31	
Thomas J.	Sarah Ann Strong	24Nov1834	E74 W76	Dulany
William	Mary York	10Feb1806	E28 W37	
William R.	Eliza Cole	19Dec1826	E62 W65	Richardson

HILT
Adam   Caroline Amos   20Oct1851   W97

HILTON
John   Martha Gough   07Feb1810 E35 W43

HINDLEY [see Hindley Wilson]

HINES
Ann Elizabeth   Basil Grafton   15Dec1857   W107
Jane   Peter Jones   m. 1778   [ret-AppA]

HINGHAY
Hugh   Susan Harward[?]   11Aug1800 E18 W29

HINKSON
Frederick   M. Annie Hanson   09Jan1861   W113

HINSEY
Emma   Andrew J. Tason   23Aug1853 H4 W99 Wilson

HIPKINS
Elizabeth   Zachariah Hancock   08Jan1824 E57 W62
Hannah   William Johnson   12Dec1833 E73 W74 Donahay
Jarrett   Hannah Hill   08Jan1824 E57 W62

HIRNAR
George   Elizabeth Dicks   23Oct1860   W112

HITCHCOCK
Chas B.   Mary Bartol   18Dec1841 E84 W85 Finney
Delia   Cladius Standiford   17Dec1805 E27 W37
Elizabeth   John B. Curry   18Dec1824 E59 W63 Richardson
Hannah   James Brown   02Dec1780 C3 W5
Heziah   Israel Choke   16Dec1816 E46 W52
Isaac   Sarah Clark   30Nov1809 E34 W43

HITCHCOCK, continued

Israel	Delia Anderson	10Mar1812	E38 W46	
Jamima	Isaac Low	26Sep1791	E1 W21	
Jason	Elizabeth Hollingsheade	22Mar1854	H5 W100	Gaily
Jesse	Mary Falls	09May1792	E2 W21	
Lucinda	John Strite	16Feb1857	H11 W106	McCartny
Luther	Sarah Frances Clark	13Jun1859	W110	
Luther	Elizabeth Clark	01Apr1865	W121	
Martha Rebecca	Charles T. Scarff	30Jan1855	H7 W102	Trout
Mary	Isaac Trulap	19Jan1781	C4 W5	
Mary	Joseph Watt	07Sep1817	E47 W53	
Mary Amanda	George Robinson	03Apr1860	W111	
Rachel	Elijah Rockhold	08Nov1815	E43 W50	
Sarah	Caleb Adams	07Dec1819	E51 W57	
William B.	Mary Ellen Chinoworth	16Feb1861	W113	

HITHCOCK

Caroline M.	Erastus Miriam	24May1853	H4 W99	Smith

HOBBARD

Mary	Nehemiah Baily	m. 1777	[ret-AppA]

HOBBS

Benjamin	Rachel Thompson	01Dec1801	E21 W31
Lawson	Eliza Jane Blaney	13Nov1860	W112
Mary	Isaac Brewer	10Jan1820	E52 W57
William	Mary Ward	29Nov1811	E37 W45

HODGE

James	Julia Timmons	06Feb1839	E80 W81 Collins

HOEY

George	Mary Mitchell	20Apr1833	E72 W74 Donahay

HOGG

Eliza Jane	John C. Fulton	04Feb1834	E73 W75 Finney
John	Catherine Burnside	18Jan1819	E50 W56

HOGS

Mary	John Cantler	26Aug1833	E73 W74 Stephenson

HOHN

John Casper	Amanda A. C. Pepoo	14May1861	W114

HOKE

Sarah B.	Clarence E. Greenway	13Jun1856	H10 W105 Binade

HOLLAND [see John Holland Barney, William Holland Divers]

Aaron	Rebecca Robinson	04Apr1811	E36 W44	
Amanda Jane	Corbin Amoss	04Sep1861	W114	
Ann	Joseph Force	10Dec1851	H1 W97	Robey
Archibald	Ann Curry	05Jun1813	E40 W47	
Charles	Barbara Caughran	21Jun1838	E79 W80	Richardson
Charles	Hesther A. Wilson	25Dec1850	W95	
Eliza	Robert Guyton	20Dec1823	E57 W62	

HOLLAND, continued

Elizabeth	John Cullum Frazier	04Aug1859	W110	
Elizabeth	John Wood	03Jan1861	W113	
Elizabeth Ann	Benjamin Wann	21Dec1841	E84 W85	Keech
Frances E.	Franklin Boarman	01Jun1865	W121	
Hannah E.	William O. Herman	19Sep1860	W112	
Hannahretta	James England	24Jan1863	W117	
Isaac	Ruth Hatton	m. 1804		[ret-AppA]
James	Elizabeth Chamberlin	20Dec1810	E36 W44	
James	Ann Ely	25Sep1845	E88 W89	
James C.	Rebecca Wann	24Feb1831	E68 W70	Tippet
John	Jane Wilson	11Dec1850	W95	
Louisa A.	Harrison Laver	18Mar1863	W117	
Mary Jane	James Morgan	12Mar1856	H9 W104	Keech
Matilda	Elias Beaumont	30Oct1854	H6 W101	Smith
Nicholas B.	Mary Amanda Bouldin	27Nov1854	H6 W101	Smith
Robert W.	Eliza Bond	21Feb1822	E55 W60	
Samuel	Hannah H. Harkins	29Oct1829	E66 W69	McGee
Sarah	John H. Rummel	05Jun1855	H7 W102	Cushing

HOLLAWAY

Lydia	Robert Wilson	07Jan1828	E64 W67	Finney

HOLLEWAY

Permelia Ann	Oliver Gallup	13Feb1821	E53 W58	

HOLLEY

John	Amanda Parsons	20Apr1846	W90

HOLLINGSHEAD

John Smith	Hannah Shane	30Nov1822	E56 W60

HOLLINGSHEADE

Elizabeth	Jason Hitchcock	22Mar1854	H5 W100	Gaily

HOLLINGSWORTH

Elizabeth	Edward L. Cunningham	05Sep1838	E79 W80	Williams
Francis	Mary Yelliott	24Dec1801	E21 W31	
James	Mary McCrackin	m. 1777		[ret-AppA]
Jesse	Guli Emla Maria Spicer	01Oct1821	E54 W59	

HOLLIS [see Hollis Courtney, Hollis Hanson]

Alonzo	Frances L. Mathews	18Jun1828	E65 W67	Pool
Amos	Frances Osborn	22Mar1823	E56 W61	
Ann	Thomas Hays	04Jun1822	E55 W60	
Avarilla	Benjamin N. Wells	31Dec1831	E70 W72	Sewall
Avarilla	John Hanson	04Dec1782	C5 W7	
Ben	Eliz^th Lusby	30Oct1783	C8 W9	cr-Harf
Benjamin O.	Mary Matthews	13Oct1825	E60 W64	
[minister - Isaac Webster; orig. lic. to Isaac Webster; cr-Harf]				
Catharine	James Cole	31Mar1797	E10 W26	
Catharine	Jacob F. Matthews	15May1830	E67 W69	Tippit
Catherine Ann	Joseph M. Deakins	23Jun1831	E69 W71	Sewall
Clark	Amelia Lancaster	12Jan1803	E23 W33	
Frances	William Bolster	05Jun1809	E34 W42	

Harford Co. Md. Marriage Licenses, 1777-1865

HOLLIS, continued

James	Jane Beaty	02Jun1795	E7 W24	
Jarrett (cold.)	Anna Butler (cold.)	25Sep1862	W116	
Maria Jane	Henry E. Michael	28Sep1840	E82 W83	Prettyman
Martha	James Reason Rockhold	25Nov1813	E41 W48	
Martha	John Irvin	05Nov1818	E49 W55	
Martha	John C. Matthews	02Aug1831	E69 W71	Sewell
Mary	William Webster	29Feb1804	E24 W35	
Mary	Luther Augustus Norris	22Jul1819	E51 W56	
Mary Amanda	Thomas Hendon	01May1832	E71 W72	Sewall
Richard F.	Catherine T. Norris	21Oct1813	E40 W48	
Sarah	James M. Day	01Sep1810	E35 W44	
Semelia	James Wells	25Feb1839	E80 W81	Dulaney
Susanna	John H. Martin	06Feb1839	E80 W81	Collis
W.	Elizabeth Howard	15Nov1784	C9 W10	
Wm. J.	Elizabeth Wells	05Mar1845	E88 W88	Dulaney

HOLLIWAY

Lydea Ann	Nathaniel Smith	29Jan1845	E88 W88	Eage

HOLLOWAY

Charles	Jane Lytle	23Mar1826	E61 W65	Webster
[orig. lic. to Webster; cr-Harf]				
Charles	Margaret Gallup	13Jan1846	W89	
Elizth	Benjamin H. Pritchard	07Apr1854	H5 W100	Finney
Gilbert	Rebecca Nevill	31Jan1812	E37 W45	
Hugh S.	Hester Ann Stump	13Feb1843	E85 W86	Hoopman
James E.	Maria S. Keen	14Jan1862	W115	
Martha	Thomas Diver	20Nov1850	W95	
Richard	Elizabeth Smith	27Nov1810	E36 W44	
Richard	Harriet Davis	15Apr1846	W90	
William	Marjary Roberts	04Mar1818	E48 W54	
William	Eliza Deaver	19Jan1835	E75 W76	Porter
William	Sarah A. Hopkins	11Jan1864	W118	
William L.	Mary M. Hoopman	19Jun1857	H12 W106	Lyttleton

HOLLOWELL

Wm	Mary Coaleman	28Aug1783	C7 W8	cr-Harf

HOLLY

Elizabeth	Nathan Howard	21Jan1817	E46 W52	
Mary	John Singleton	10Aug1840	E82 W83	Finney
Susan	Henry Mitchell	27Sep1851	W97	

HOLLYDAY [see Hollyday Brown]

HOLMES

Daniel	Hanora O'Brien	07Jan1851	W96	
Graselda	Thomas L. Emory	25Oct1864	W119	
Jane	John Cain	28May1816	E45 W51	
Thomas	Maria Gavin	28Dec1850	W96	
William	Jane Cook	05Dec1796	E10 W25	

HOMBURGER

Stewart	Ellen Famous	18Oct1860	W112

HOOFMAN
Allen	Minerva J. Taylor	06Jun1865		W121	
Peter	Mary Stump	01Aug1825	E60	W64	Stephenson
Wm	Cathrine Smith	30Aug1783	C7	W9	

HOOKER
Edward G.	Elizabeth E. Horney	08Mar1859		W110

HOOPER
Eliza	James Gray	02Jul1829	E66	W68	Richardson
Michael	Elizabeth Shultz	08Jun1818	E49	W55	
Sarah	John Paul	22Jun1822	E55	W60	

HOOPMAN
Catharine	Robert Walker	04Dec1821	E55	W59	
Elizth	Wm T. Cronin	05Jan1857	H11	W105	Cushing
Isaac	Lucinda Ann Rogers	04Dec1823	E57	W61	
Jacob	Margaret Wareham	16Dec1818	E50	W56	
Jacob	Sarah Kenley	26Jan1839	E80	W81	Stier
Mary Eliza	Jeremiah P. Silver	31Dec1851	H1	W97	Finney
Mary M.	William L. Holloway	19Jun1857	H12	W106	Lyttleton

HOPE
Ann	William Johnson	23Feb1797	E11	W25	
[returned by Parson Luckie]					
Elizabeth	John Rusk Streett	16Dec1845		W89	
Ellen	Joshua Nelson	20Jan1845	E88	W88	Cross
Hannah Ann	Nicholas H. Hutchins	12Jan1836	E76	W77	Morrison
James	Sarah Nelson	24Feb1836	E76	W77	Morrison
James	Mary Ann Cairnes	12Dec1855	H8	W103	Carter
Naomi	Robert Kearns	14Dec1807	E30	W40	
Thomas M.	Elizabeth Amos	12Dec1837	E78	W79	Cross

HOPFER
John G.	Charlott W. Fulmer	24Mar1856	H9	W104	Keech

HOPKINS
Angelina	William Deaver	01Apr1847		W91	
Ann E.	Thomas Knight	26Feb1838	E79	W80	Collins
Annie P.	Charles D. Alderson	28Sep1863		W118	
Bennet	Elizabeth Morris	27Mar1848		W92	
Bridget	James Farrell	14Jan1840	E81	W82	Reed
Caroline	Nathaniel Smith	16Nov1836	E77	W78	Stephenson?
Caroline E.	Samuel Hopkins	29Dec1845		W89	
Cassandra	William Rowland	03Feb1836	E76	W77	Stephenson
Cassandra W.	James Stephenson	23Apr1850		W95	
Charles	Nancy Jenkins	22Jul1793	E4	W22	
Charlotter	James Stephenson	26Jul1831	E69	W71	Stephenson
Clemency	Amos Gilbert	24Aug1819	E51	W56	
Eliza	Charles Willey	12Jan1821	E53	W58	
Elizabeth	Robert Allen	17Dec1813	E41	W48	
Elizabeth	Joshua Hawkins	08Feb1820	E52	W57	
Elizabeth	James Small	17Aug1841	E83	W84	Gallion
Elizabeth	Charles W. Wells	06Jan1858		W107	

HOPKINS, continued

Ephraim	Mary Morgan	19Oct1802	E22 W33	
Ephraim G.	Nancy Ewing	12Oct1805	E27 W36	
Ephraim G.	Sarah Ann Wills	21Dec1855	H9 W103	Reese
Frances (E. Guyton to pay)	William Hunter	14Jun1825	E60 W64	Stephenson
Francis	Anna Harper	06Jun1863	W117	
George W.	Sophia Spencer	21Feb1842	E84 W85	Gallion
Gover	Sarah Hughes	02Feb1836	E76 W77	Finney
Hannah	William Brown	13May1833	E72 W74	Gallion
Henry	Ann Hughes	22Dec1830	E68 W70	Stephenson
Henry W.	Mary E. Dagg	17Jul1839	E81 W82	Finney
James Lee	Amanda Dallam	23Nov1841	E84 W84	Brown
John	Eleanor Morgan	15Apr1798	E13 W27	
John	Sarah Wilson	29May1809	E34 W42	
John	Elizabeth M. Chew	30Apr1833	E72 W74	Keech
John	Sarah Evans	12May1840	E82 W83	Finney
John	Margaret Ann Singleton	02May1849	W93	
John	Elizabeth Irvin	31Dec1850	W96	
John M.	Phoeby Ann Huff	25Nov1841	E84 W84	Finney
John Wallis	Susanna Dallam	09Oct1800	E18 W30	
Joseph	Sarah Morgan	12Apr1799	E16 W28	
Joseph	Clemency Mitchell	19Dec1803	E24 W34	
Joseph	Sarah Cox	26Nov1811	E37 W45	
Joseph	Leatty Miller	07Oct1817	E47 W54	
Joseph R.	Maria McCausland	31Dec1864	W120	
Louisa Jane	Thomas Cord	05Feb1840	E81 W82	Prettyman
Margaret	Robert Miller	12Jan1813	E39 W47	
Margaret	Thomas Smith	14Apr1838	E79 W80	Gallion
Margaret Ann	Richard M. Taylor	16May1861	W114	
Margaret M.	Edward M. Chew	14Feb1832	E70 W72	Poisall
Mary	George Harris	17Feb1845	E88 W88	Ego
Mary Ann	Daniel Tollenger	12Apr1827	E63 W66	Stephenson
Mary Ann	Francis Alexander Cameron	11Mar1861	W113	
Nancy	William Wiles	25Mar1834	E74 W75	Gallion
Priscilla	James Stephenson	30Jul1799	E16 W28	
Priscilla	Daniel Martin	13May1833	E72 W74	Finney
Priscilla	Skipwith C. Gorrell	17Jan1842	E84 W85	Gallion
Rachel	James Lytle	10May1831	E69 W71	Sewall
Richard	Frances Smith	06Jun1816	E45 W51	
Richard	Mary Ann Taylor	21Jul1832	E71 W73	Finney
Samuel	Mary Mitchell	24Nov1801	E21 W31	
Samuel	Caroline E. Hopkins	29Dec1845	W89	
Samuel Parker	Mary Foster	23Dec1845	W89	
Sarah	Joseph Gorrell	16Aug1821	E54 W59	
Sarah A.	William Holloway	11Jan1864	W118	
Sarah Ann	John M. Taylor	21Jul1835	E75 W76	Furlong
Sarah Ann	John W. Ware [Ward?]	21Dec1853	H4 W100	Dumm
Thos C.	Priscilla W. Worthington	28May1834	E74 W75	Finney
Wakeman B.	Hannah R. Worthington	20Oct1829	E66 W69	Stephenson
William	Elizabeth Spence	16Nov1836	E77 W78	Hoopman
William	Ellen Morris	07Jan1852	H1 W97	Reed

HOPPER

James	Sallie E. Barnes	28Jan1861	W113	

HORN
Charity	John Hues [Hull?]	10Feb1807	E29	W38
Rich^d	Martha Tunis	27Jul1779	B3	W2

HORNBURGER [see also Homburger]
Mary E.	Samuel C. Famous	24Aug1861	W114

HORNER
Cassandra	John Perryman	17Oct1791	E1	W21	[re-AppA]
Elizabeth	Chrispian Cunningham	m. 1789			[re-AppA]
John W.	Maria M. Lansdale	13Oct1835	E75	W77	Higby
Martha	Daniel Michael	15Apr1807	E29	W39	
Mary	Charles Gilbert	m. 1794			[re-AppA]
Nathan	Sarah Wheeler	09Dec1794	E6	W23	
Nathan	Delia Carroll	30Apr1799	E16	W28	
William	Catharine L. Coburn	28Oct1861		W114	
William W.	Kate J/I. Coburn	04Aug1862		W116	

HORNEY
Elizabeth E.	Edward G. Hooker	08Mar1859	W110

HORTON
Ann	Jacob Gilbert	28Oct1807	E30	W39
Elizth	Wm Welch	29Jul1794	E5	W23
Joseph	Rebecca Hamby	04May1861		W114

HOTCHKISS
Grove U.	Elizabeth V. Delmas	26Oct1842	E85	W85	Reid

HOUSTON
John	Sarah Ann Almony	02Mar1846	W90

HOUZE
Ann	George Stine	22Apr1828	E64	W67	Keech

HOW
Mary E.	James Thompson	15Apr1861	W114

HOWARD
Ann	Benjamin Smithson	24Dec1792	E3	W22	
Betsy	John Hambleton Jones	01Sep1783	C7	W9	
Caroline B.	Charles H. Rumsey	18Dec1820	E53	W58	
Charles W.	Amanda Z. Slade	22Sep1834	E74	W75	Keech
Edward Aquila	Charlotte Rumsey	10Dec1798	E15	W27	
Elizabeth	W. Hollis	15Nov1784	C9	W10	
Elizabeth[*]	Benjamin Richards	14Jun1795	E7	W24	
[* surname written over another]					
Francis	Mary Amoss	21Mar1805	E26	W36	
John	Mary Harrison Sewell	06Apr1802	E22	W32	[re-AppA]
J^{no} Gold	Hannah York	m. 1778			[re-AppA]
J^{no} Gold	Hannah Carty	m. 1778			[re-AppA]
John P.	Mary E. Strong	07Sep1845	E88	W89	
Leonard	Rebecca Etherington	04Sep1793	E5	W23	
Leonard	Ann Coalby	21Apr1819	E51	W56	

HOWARD, continued

Levi	Zaney Gallion	20Dec1808	E32 W41	
Margaret	Francis A. Richardson	10Jan1861	W113	
Mary	Thomas Greenly	25Apr1800	E17 W29	
Mary Ann	Joshua B. Bond	22Feb1831	E68 W70	Richardson
Nathan	Elizabeth Holly	21Jan1817	E46 W52	
Robert H.	Anna Femelia Fink	11Dec1858	W109	
Sarah	James McComas	27May1794	E5 W23	
Sarah	Edward B. Bussey	m. 1803		[re-AppA]
Sarah	Amos Cord	08Apr1806	E28 W38	
Sarah Ann	Sampson Tutchton	07Jan1840	E81 W82	Prettyman
Sarah York	Micajah Debruler	31Jan1801	E19 W30	
Thomas E.	Eugenia M. Brigham	22Dec1860	W113	
Thomas G.	Margaret M. Maulsby	20Nov1823	E57 W61	

HOWE

George T. R.	Lydia E. Brown	16Jul1864	W119	
James	Rachel Forsythe	26Feb1838	E79 W80	Gallion

HOWES [see Howes Goldsborough]

HOWEL

Samuel	Rebeca Price	11Jul1780	C2 W4

HOWLET

Andrew	Mary Elizabeth Scarbrough	11Dec1843	E86 W87	Thomas
John	Betsy Smith	21Jun1804	E25 W35	
Mary	Nicholas Suter	03Nov1840	E82 W83	Goldsbrough
Mathew	Eliza Mitchell	30Dec1814	E42 W49	

HOWLETT

Caroline	William A. Adams	16Feb1855	H7 W102	Collins
Eliza	Joseph S. Robinson	30[?]Mar1843	E85 W86	Car--
[page damaged]				
Eliza A.	William P. Walker	07Jan1851	W96	
Julia Ann	John W. Scarborough	16Dec1846	W90	
Mary H.	Daniel S. Morrison	08Nov1824	E59 W63	Sark
Nancy	Jacob Enfield	20Oct1835	E75 W77	Park
Richard T.	Annie Milligan	05Jan1858	W107	
William	Hannah Turner	03Feb1838	E79 W80	Collins
William	Elizabeth U.[?] Jeanny	22Nov1849	W94	

HOWLMAN

Abrm.	Margaret Lampre	07Oct1783	C8 W9	cr-Harf

HUDSON [see Hudson Wood]

Atheliah	John Flaharty	27Jan1817	E46 W52
Benjamin	Matilda Freeheart	28Aug1816	E45 W52
Dorothy	Joseph Ford	28Jul1804	E25 W35
Samuel	Martha Hill	27Apr1814	E41 W49

HUES

John	Charity Horn	10Feb1807	E29 W38
[name may be Hull]			

HUFF

Abraham	Gulielma P. Scarborough	23Mar1847	W91	
Andrew J.	Elizabeth D. Durham	19Mar1839	E80 W81	Keech
George	Hannah H. Robinson	26Nov1849	W94	
Jesse	Emely Coale	28Dec1836	E77 W78	Furlong
John S.	Elizabeth Robinson	08Dec1845	W89	
Lydia L.	John Lewin	26Nov1839	E81 W82	Finney
Michael	Rachel Scarbrough	31Dec1803	E24 W34	
Phoeby Ann	John M. Hopkins	25Nov1841	E84 W84	Finney
Zachariah	Hannah Smith	01Nov1804	E25 W35	

HUGG

William	Mary Jane Gilbert	27Sep1854	H6 W101	Gallion

HUGGINS

James	Sally Barett	m. 1803		[re-AppA]
Joseph	Margaret Carnes	30Jan1781	C4 W6	
Thomas	Kitty Evans	29Dec1807	E31 W40	

HUGHES [see Clemency Hughes Gilbert]

Aaron	Martha Sprucebanks	09Feb1808	E31 W40	
Amos H.	Hannah C. Adams	23Feb1841	E83 W84	Wiggins
Ann	James Botts	21Feb1803	E23 W33	
Ann	Henry Hopkins	22Dec1830	E68 W70	Stephenson
Ann Maria	Hendon Chocke	26Feb1834	E74 W75	Richardson
Aquila	Ann Statia Gafford	21Apr1804	E25 W35	
Catharine	Elijah Pocock	25Jul1808	E32 W41	
Charlotte	Heny M. Cole	13Jan1845	E88 W88	Finney
Clemency	Martin Gilbert	26Jul1864	W119	
Eliza P.	Richard C. Stockton	09May1814	E42 W49	
Elizabeth	Naasson Chalk	13Jan1816	E44 W51	
Elizabeth	Soloman McComas	06Feb1837	E77 W79	Finney
Emily Jane	James B. Meads	07Jan1863	W117	
Esrom	Elizabeth Whiteford	01Apr1800	E17 W29	
Everett G.	Martha Gilbert	13Feb1864	W118	
Everitt Gilbert	Ann E. Mitchell	20Dec1831	E70 W72	Sewall
Hannah	William St. Clair	20Jan1803	E23 W33	
Hannah	Sampson S.[?] Duncan	28Jan1845	E88 W88	Park
Hannah	Joseph G. Robinson	30Dec1847	W92	
Hannah	James Bradfield	04Feb1856	H9 W104	Reineck
Henrietta Maria Chamberlain	William Brooks Stokes	27Jun1808	E31 W41	
Isakah	Lydia Amos	16Aug1815	E43 W50	
James	Hannah Gilbert	14Dec1801	E21 W31	
James C.	Maria Lee	14Dec1813	E41 W48	
Jemmima	Thomas Turner	31Mar1801	E20 W31	
Jesse	Anna B. Arnutt	02May1859	W110	
John E.	Martha Hill	03Mar1846	W90	
John H.	Ann Durbin	05Nov1784	C9 W10	
Martha	Parker Gilbert, Junr	01Oct1800	E18 W30	
Mary	Edward york [sic]	29Dec1781	C5 W7	
Mary	William Smith	27Dec1803	E24 W34	
Mary	William Chesney	10Jun1817	E47 W53	
Nathan	Elizabeth Maclain	22Sep1807	E30 W39	
Nathan	Frances Taylor	06Jan1813	E39 W47	

HUGHES, continued
Rachel	Jonah Stephenson	10May1799	E16 W28	
Roland	Susannah Griffee	08Oct1780	C3 W5	
Samuel	Elizabeth Wadsworth	23Apr1821	E54 W59	
Sarah	Richard Allen	29Dec1812	E39 W47	
Sarah	Gover Hopkins	02Feb1836	E76 W77	Finney
Sarah Ann	George Price	07Jan1852	H1 W97	Gallion
Scott	Mary G. Gilbert	23Jun1804	E25 W35	
Susan	Benjamin F. Anderson	30Nov1855	H8 W103	Smith
Taylor	Mary Demos	05Jan1818	E48 W54	
Wm	Lydya Jones	16Sep1782	C6 W8	
William	Charity Baxter	15Feb1828	E64 W67	O'Brien
William	Sarah Hutchins	11Jan1841	E83 W84	Cross

HUGHS
Frances	Daniel Norris	18Aug1792	E3 W21
Lydea	Joshua Delaney	31Oct1791	E1 W21

HUGHSTONE
Jane	William Groves	13Jan1781	C4 W5

HUGSTON
Joseph	Hanah Pummel[?]	27Aug1780	C3 W4

HULTZ[?]
Elizabeth	Bartis[?] Crangan[?]	23Dec1799	E17 W29

HUMPHREY
Andrew	Agnes Anderson	16Aug1779	O3 W2

HUNT
John J.	Elizabeth Chamberlain	09Nov1859	W111

HUNTER
Ann	John C. McComas	07Apr1835	E75 W76	Dulany
Elizabeth	Jacob Morrison	03Jan1839	E80 W81	Finney
Frances	Joshua W. Knight	30Jan1845	E88 W88	Eage
Geo. W.	Mary Elizabeth Norris	26Oct1843	E86 W86	Mattox
Joseph	Elizabeth Durham	m. 1777		[ret-AppA]
Mary	William H. Williams	18Jan1827	E62 W66	Poole
Sophia E.	Daniel McComas	24Jun1861	W114	ALJ1-94,142
Susan	Martin Mahan	09Apr1849	W93	
William	Frances Hopkins	14Jun1825	E60 W64	Stephenson
(E. Guyton to pay)				

HURST
Sarah E.	Edmund Scarborough	25Sep1855	H8 W103	Smith

HUSBAND
Hannah	John O. Bageley	05Jun1833	E72 W74	Finney
Rachel	Isaac Weaver	25Dec1811	E37 W45	

Harford Co. Md. Marriage Licenses, 1777-1865

HUSBANDS
Elizth	Geo. Young	18Mar1780	C1	W3	
Elizabeth	John Quarles	13May1797	E10	W26	[re-AppA]
James	Margaret Gallaher	25Jul1804	E25	W35	[re-AppA]
Mary	James Kelley	01Jan1802	E21	W32	

HUSE
Clemency G.	Walter Jarvis	26Dec1837	E78	W80	Finy
John	Rachel Ford	01May1780	C2	W4	

HUTCHENSON
John	Elizabeth Myers	16Jun1802	E22	W32

HUTCHINS
Amanda Z.	Josias Payne	09Mar1837	E77	W79	Parks
Ann	Harrison Shaw	03Mar1835	E75	W76	Morrison
Louisa	John Bradford	19May1847		W91	
Mary	William C. Vance	07May1832	E71	W73	Morison
Mary A.	Alfred S. Garrison	11Feb1854	H5	W100	Carter
Nicholas	Martha E. Nelson	29Nov1847		W92	
Nicholas H.	Hannah Ann Hope	12Jan1836	E76	W77	Morrison
Sarah	William Hughes	11Jan1841	E83	W84	Cross
Thos	Catherine Mitchell	03Oct1779	B3	W2	
Thomas	Ruth Daly	23Jul1816	E45	W52	
W^m	Elanor Miles	07Mar1781	C4	W6	

[Eleanora crossed out; may be 11 Mar]
William	Elizabeth Bradicks	24Feb1802	E21	W32

HUTCHINGS [see Hutchings William Layton]

HUTCHISON
Ann	Samuel Townsley	05Apr1858	W108

HUTSON [see Hutson Wood]

HUTTON
Jesse M.	Eliza T. Stricklen	16Mar1841	E83	W84	Alexander
Lydia Ann	John Benjamin Stricklen	18Mar1841	E83	W84	Cullum

HYNES
John	Ann Hambleton	23Apr1805	E26	W36

HYNSON
John	Matilda Courtnay	31Jan1801	E19	W30

ILEY
Jacob	Lucinda Warner	05Dec1859		W111
John	Elizabeth Rutledge	03Dec1818	E50	W55

IMPIRE
Joseph R.	Ann Hanay	02Jul1850	W95

INGHAM
Robert	Lydia Yorke	18Apr1800	E17	W29

INGLE
William   Margaret Cooper   28Nov1853 H4 W100 Trout

INGLEHART
Ann   James London   01Oct1855 H8 W103 Lemon

INGRAM
James   Sarah Anderson   01Nov1828 E65 W68 Richardson

INLOES
Ann   John Tudar   29Mar1780 C1 W3
Henry Augustus   Priscilla Presbury Day   26Jun1837 E78 W79 Lyons
Thomas   Sarah Bull   28Mar1818 E49 W55

IRELAND
Teressa   Charles Eweing   15Feb1820 E52 W57

IRONS
Mary   Henry Collins   29Oct1784 C9 W10

IRVIN
Elizabeth   John Hopkins   31Dec1850   W96
Frances   John Wilson   27Jan1817 E46 W52
John   Martha Hollis   05Nov1818 E49 W55
John   Elizabeth Chalk   20Mar1852 H2 W98 Park
Martha J/I.   John Wright   15Dec1855 H8 W103 Smith
Mary Matilda   William Fletcher   06Feb1855 H7 W102 Collins

ISEN
John   Mary Jane Criswell   04Sep1855 H8 W103 Cushing

ISREAL
Esther   Andrew McCleary   01Dec1800 E19 W30

IVANS
Samuel B.   Sarah Ary   18Oct1859   W110

IVES
Thomas J.   Mary Ann Ewing   02Jun1836 E76 W78 Hoopman

JACK
Eliza   Andrew Moscow   21Mar1818 E49 W55

JACKSON
Cassandra   Charles Foster   08Aug1859   W110
Edward   Sophia Arnold   04Feb1824 E57 W62
Elizabeth   Elijah Kimble   22Jun1795 E7 W24
Elizabeth   John Cousins   05Feb1799 E15 W28
Elizabeth   Thomas Thompson   08Feb1809 E33 W42
Elizabeth S.   William T. Chesney   06Nov1855 H8 W103 Reese
Harriet M.   Bennet Osborn   22Apr1858   W108
Margarett   Andrew Lynch   22Jul1819 E51 W56
Mary A.   Lee M. Whistler   09Jan1865   W120
Mary J/I.   John C. Smith   08Jan1856 H9 W104 Reese

JACKSON, continued

Richard I.	Kezia C. Stump	30Apr1833	E72 W74	Finney
Robert	Rebecca Lee	16Oct1824	E58 W62	
[orig. lic. to Finney; cr-Harf]				
Samuel	Elizabeth Hanson	m. 1790		[ret-AppA]
Samuel	Cassandra Price	01Dec1837	E78 W79	Richardson
Sarah	Thomas Boyd	07Sep1826	E61 W65	Stephenson
Susan	Edwd Frederick Krelis	27Oct1836	E77 W78	Richardson

JACOBS

Charles Watters	Hester S. Parker	02May1833	E72 W74	Hinkle

JACSON

Thomas Wm.	Hester Touchstone	15Jun1814	E42 W49	

JAMES

Aaron	Catharine Judd	04Feb1834	E73 W75	Todrig
Anna E.	James E. Scott	10May1859	W110	
Blanche	Thomas Mottson	14Nov1861	W114	
Catharine	John Galloway	24Apr1844	E87 W87	Keech
Charles H.	Maria J. Cole	26Mar1855	H7 W102	Finney
Elizabeth	Aquila Keen	13Jan1813	E39 W47	
George B.	Sarah Elizth Keithley	10Jan1861	W113	
Harriet V.	Wesley Harward	17Nov1856	H10 W105	Cushing
Jacob	Mary Bailey	12Dec1821	E55 W59	
Jacob	Sarah Gilbert	02Mar1825	E59 W63	Finney
Jarvis Gilbert	Deborah S. Gorthrup	16Nov1859	W111	
John	Sarah Jane Knight	03Apr1851	W96	
John L.	Clarissa C. Coale	04Mar1861	W113	
Joseph	Elizabeth Corse	15Aug1853	H4 W99	Finney
Joshua	Elizabeth Ann Divers	12Jul1831	E69 W71	Finney
Lizzie E.	Philip G. Hawkins	11Feb1862	W115	
Martha	Robert Heeps	21Aug1781	C5 W7	
Mary	William Clemmons	17[?]Dec1780	C3 W5	
Mary	James Roberts	13Feb1802	E21 W32	
Mary Ann	James H. Mitchell	07Jun1856	H10 W105	Cushing
Rachel	Abel Watkins	13Feb1810	E35 W43	
Samuel	Ann York	29Dec1824	E59 W63	Richardson
Samuel W.	Annie Reese	08Oct1861	W114	
Sedgwick, Junr	Elizabeth Henry	27Jan1820	E52 W57	
Susanna	Euclidus Scarborough	12Apr1809	E33 W42	
Thomas	Mary Eagon	11Nov1780	C3 W5	
["4 Dollars Hard Money"]				
Thomas M.	Elizabeth Pyle	09Mar1846	W90	
William	Rachel Bull	15Aug1780	C2 W4	
William	Mary Mitchell	17Jan1796	E60 W64	Finney
William J/I.	Mary Ann Lilly	19Jan1850	W94	

JAMISON

Margt	Joseph Jarvis	28Sep1779	B3 W2	
Rachel	Thomas Wright	03Feb1805	E26 W36	
Rosa Anna	Chrisdan Hau[?]	02Dec1862	W116	
Sally	William Yackett	27Mar1806	E28 W37	

JANNEY
Francis H.   Emily C. Templer   13Apr1853 H3 W99 [min --]

JARRETT [see Elizabeth Jarrett Thomas, Jarrett Spencer, Jarrett Ward]
Abraham   Elizabeth Stump   13Nov1804 E25 W35
Abraham, Junior   Elizabeth S. Hays   16Oct1817 E47 W54
Abraham L.   Mary Ann E. Jones   03Nov1836 E77 W78 Keech
Amanda C.   Lawson Cooley   16Feb1832 E70 W72 Stephenson
Ann Eliza   Thomas W. Reed   30Dec1851 H1   W97 Reid
Deveraux   Sarah England   09Apr1839 E80 W82 Barton
Elizabeth   John Amos   20Feb1804 E24 W35
Jesse   Elizabeth Bosley   29Mar1804 E25 W35
Luther M.   Juliann Scarff   02Mar1830 E67 W69 McGee
Sarah E.   James B. Nelson   23Jan1860   W111
William B.   Mary V. Cairnes   05Jan1857 H11 W105 McCartney

JARVIS [see Jarvis Gilbert James]
Ann   Nathan Dean   28Nov1805 E27 W37
Elizabeth   Robert Hanna   30Jul1812 E38 W46
Joseph   Marg^t Jamison   28Sep1779 B3   W2
Margaret   Joseph Thompson   01Aug1805 E26 W36
Rebecca   Ja^s Rigdon   30Dec1779 C1   W3
Walter   Ann Frances Allen   13Sep1830 E67 W70 Stephenson
Walter   Clemency G. Huse   26Dec1837 E78 W80 Finy

JARVOS
William   Margaret Thompson   24Aug1780 C3   W4

JAY
Ann   Enoch Pearson, Junr   22Jan1819 E50 W56
Hannah Y.   James Thompson   m. 1788   [ret-AppA]
John   Mary G. E. Davis   31[?]Oct1844 E87 W88 Finney
Samuel   Sarah Griffith   06Apr1810 E35 W43
Samuel   Martha Smith   07Feb1812 E38 W46
Samuel   Martha Clines   08Aug1826 E61 W65 Stephenson

JEANNY
Elizabeth U.[?]   William Howlett   22Nov1849   W94

JEFFERS
Benjamin   Sarah Ann Stapleford   21Sep1855 H8 W103 Reese
Mary Elizabeth   John Sweeting   06Dec1847   W92

JEFFERSON [see Hugh Jefferson Dever, Samuel Jefferson Garrison, Jefferson Crew, Jefferson Deaver, Jefferson Dever]

JEFFERY
Alexander   Adelia Barns   07Apr1802 E22 W32
Eliza Jane   John B. Yarnall   02Jan1826 E60 W64 Webster
  [orig. lic. to Webster; cr-Harf; month not stated]
George G.   Hannah A. Foard   11Jan1849   W93
James   Jane A. Anderson   13Sep1830 E67 W70 Finney

JEFFERY, continued
Mary	William Williams	03Jan1817	E46 W52	
Samuel	Mary George	27May1840	E82 W83	Emory
Telitha	John H. Mitchell	29Jan1827	E62 W66	Finney

JEFFRIES
Eliza J/I.	John P. Davis	07Jul1852	H2 W98	Finney

JEMEISON
Rebeccah	Elijah Small	21Feb1799	E15 W28

JEMISON
Ann	Richard Wood	10Jun1802	E22 W32

JENKINS
Ann	Samuel Chamberlain	22Jun1798	E15 W27
E. Morris	Sallie A. Johnson	04Feb1858	W108
Ignatius W.	Ann Maria Brown	27Jan1846	W89
James	Hannah Watkins	29May1820	E52 W58
Nancy	Charles Hopkins	22Jul1793	E4 W22

JENNING [see Samuel K. Jenning Greenfield]

JENNINGS
Robert	Sarah M. Mepham	07Apr1856	H10 W104	Carter

JENNIS
James Henry	Hannah Jane Wilkinson	26May1839	E81 W82	Wilson
Levi S.	Mary E. White	25Dec1850	W95	

JERVIS [see Jervis Gilbert]
James	Sarah Ann Cunningham	28Jan1829	E65 W68	Richardson
Jane	John Enlows	03Apr1824	E58 W62	

JESSUP
George	Elizabeth Ashton	18May1840	E82 W83	Keech

JEWEL
George	Sarah Whitson	02Apr1803	E23 W33

JEWELL
W^m	Mary M. Thomas	29Jun1784	C8 W9

JEWENS
Ann Eliza	John C. Donahoo	02Jun1864	W119

JEWINS
Harriet E.	James Smith	14Feb1857	H11 W106	Finney
William	Sophia H. Gilbert	22Dec1830	E68 W70	Tippit

JEWINGS
William Edwd	Avarilla Botts	05Jan1852	H1 W97	Finney

JINKINS
Francis | Mary Durham | 13Oct1780 | C3 W5

JINNEY
Thomas | Sarah Wilson | 03Nov1799 | E16 W28

JOHNS
Ann	William Barnes	12Mar1813	E40 W47
Drucilla A.	John Streett	02Jan1854	H4 W100 Smith
Edward F.	Jane R. Spicer	09Jul1845	E88 W89
Henry	Sarah Brown	22Feb1785	C10 W10
Henry	Eliza Prigg	02Feb1814	E41 W48
Martha	Robert Amoss	31Mar1808	E31 W40
Mary	Robert E. Morgan	03Jan1857	H11 W105 Crawford
Polly	Philip Rodgers	17Mar1804	E25 W35
Sarah	David Stokes	09May1800	E18 W29

JOHNSON
Adam	Johanna Gilbert	17Aug1797	E12 W26
[Ret'd by John Allen]			
Ann	Alexander Rigdon	11Dec1780	C3 W5
Ann	Charles Kinzil	08Feb1798	E13 W27 Jno Coleman
Ann	William Pyle	01Dec1804	E25 W35
Ann	Edward Prigg	12Feb1816	E44 W51
Ann Matilda	William Barron	09May1854	H5 W101 Reese
Arch^d	Elizth Voshall	23Sep1783	C7 W9
Archibald	Charlotte Lear	31Mar1823	E56 W61
Archibald	Louisa Lytle	25Oct1841	E84 W84 Dulaney
Barnet	Jane Thomas	27Apr1791	E1 W21
Barnet of Jno.	Elizabeth Forwood	19Jan1805	E26 W36
Barnet	Ann Michael	04Feb1819	E50 W56
Catherine	William Whiteford	11Dec1854	H6 W101 Crawford
Charles	Mary Sunderland	25Jan1823	E56 W61
Charles D. W.	Eliza McConkey	11May1822	E55 W60
Christopher	Sephronia Ann Price	24Jun1841	E83 W84 Wilson
Darcus	Nathan^l Lancaster	09Dec1815	E44 W50
Elisha	Cassandra Rogers	09Apr1821	E54 W59
Elisha	Sarah Thompson	27Jan1858	W108
Elisha	Ann Eliza Harkins	05Feb1862	W115
Elisha	Rosa Ward	20May1864	W119
Elizth	Roger McKenly	03Sep1780	C3 W4
Elizabeth	Edward Reynolds	22Feb1842	E84 W85 Keech
Elizabeth	Jacob Osborn	30Jun1847	W91
George J.	Cornelia E. Barron	15Jan1859	W109
George M.	Rebecca Matilda Garrettson	30Apr1832	E70 W72 Richardson
Hannah	John Hauy	03Mar1799	E15 W28
Hannah	Amos Spicer	19Jan1831	E68 W70 Richardson
Harriot	Benedict Herbert	12Mar1816	E45 W51
Henry C.	Mary Matilda Ozman	11Feb1862	W115
Hugh	Joanna Barnett	08Jun1822	E55 W60
Jacob F.	Martha Ann Barrow	01Jan1851	W96
James	Martha Carsin	25Feb1851	W96

JOHNSON, continued

Jane	Alex^r. Turner	10May1780	C2	W4	
Jane	Saml Black	03Oct1781	C5	W7	
John	Cathrine Turner	14Nov1780	C3	W5	
John	Elizabeth Magnes	02Jan1800	E17	W29	
John	Frances Renshaw	22Jun1809	E34	W42	
John	Mary Hayward	02Jan1812	E37	W45	
John	Charlotte Michael	12Feb1816	E44	W51	
John	Sophia Norris	08Jan1827	E62	W65	Richardson
John Lafayette	Mary Jane Cameron	08Jun1854	H5	W101	Smith
John Webster	Sarah Elizabeth Ford	19Dec1836	E77	W78	Furlong
Joseph	Letitia Cross	10Jul1779	B3	W2	
Joseph	Rebekah Ashley	30Dec1795	E8	W24	
Joseph	Jane Shannon	05Jan1835	E75	W76	Dunahay
Joseph T.	Mary Jane Wallis	20Feb1856	H9	W104	Finney
Josias	Peggy Morgan	10Jan1792	E2	W21	
Lucinda	James H. Sewell	02Jan1811	E36	W44	
Margaret	Thomas Turner	05Mar1816	E44	W51	
Margaret	William Clark	17Jun1818	E49	W55	
Margaret	Ignatius McAtee	11Apr1836	E76	W77	Crosgay
Martha	Danl McComas	17Oct1781	C5	W7	
Martha	James Robinson	05Mar1804	E24	W35	
Mary	John Beck	12Sep1780	C3	W5	
Mary	James Gilbert	12Jan1782	C5	W7	
Mary	Joseph Worthington	30May1793	E4	W22	
Mary	Arthur Manahon	12Aug1819	E51	W56	
Mary	James Hammer	30Aug1831	E69	W71	Dorsey
Mary Ann	John Guyton	31Jan1832	E70	W72	Keech
Mary Ann	Jesse E. Coale	03Jan1859		W109	
Mathew	Jane Jordan	06Jan1820	E52	W57	
Michael	Rachel Dickson	17May1820	E52	W57	
Michael W.	Elizabeth J. Hill	25Jun1835	E75	W76	Dulaney
Priscilla	Edward Hambleton, Junr.	27Mar1806	E28	W37	
Rachel	John Whitacare	06Sep1780	C3	W4	
Richard	Mary Herbert	22Oct1799	E16	W28	
Sallie A.	E. Morris Jenkins	04Feb1858		W108	
Sarah	Robt Nelson	20May1781	C5	W6	
Sarah	Robert Nelson	20Jun1781	C5	W6	
Sarah	Joseph Woolsey	28Nov1784	C9	W10	
Sarah	David Thomas	08Jun1800	E18	W29	
Sarah	William Michael	31Mar1815	E43	W50	
Sarah	James Gorrell	22Jan1849		W93	
Sarah Ann	Thomas Clark	24Mar1838	E79	W80	Keech
Sarah E.	Grafton Day	12May1856	H10	W104	McKinsey
Sarah J/I.	William Bouldin	13Oct1847		W91	
Sarah Lettie	John Richardson	07Jul1864		W119	
Thos	Ann Love	29May1793	E4	W22	
Thomas [ret-AppA]	Elizabeth Taylor	12Nov1796	E10	W25	John Coleman
Thomas	Elizabeth Barrow	07Dec1852	H2	W98	Robey
Thomas	Jemima Cathcart	16Dec1861		W115	
Thomas	Mary Jane Hayghe	21Nov1862		W116	ALJ1-94,106
William [Returned by Parson Luckie]	Ann Hope	23Feb1797	E11	W25	

Harford Co. Md. Marriage Licenses, 1777-1865   133

JOHNSON, continued

William	Mary Fleharty	24Mar1803	E23 W33	
William	Ann Standiford	02Feb1807	E29 W38	
William	Hannah McCaskey	25Oct1816	E46 W52	
William	Hannah Hipkins	12Dec1833	E73 W74	Donohay
William	Darcas Ann Guyton	15Apr1852	H2 W98	Yerkes

JOHNSTON [see Johnston Campbell]

JOLLEY

Edward	Frances Smith	17May1810	E35 W43
Louisa C.	John Wallace	27Jun1815	E43 W50

JOLLY

John	Elizth Dallam	19Apr1796	E9 W25
William	Sarah Chew	28May1793	E4 W22 [ret-AppA]

JONES [see Jones Major, James Jones Willmore]

Agnes	William Mahan	25Nov1800	E18 W30	
Alice	John Devoe	15Aug1861	W114	
Ann	John Loveit	13Apr1782	C6 W7	cr-Harf
Ann	Amos Ely	27Oct1808	E32 W41	
Annie A.	George W. Sutor	13Jun1861	W114	
Benj.	Charity Taylor	13Sep1791	E1 W21	
Benjamin	Rachel Ann Wright	17Mar1862	W115	
Cassandra Adelin	Frederick T. Amos	19Jan1837	E77 W78	Reese
Cathrine	James Townsen	12Sep1780	C3 W5	
Daniel	Rebecca Scarbrough	16Jan1813	E39 W47	
Elizabeth	Danl Hagerty	14Mar1796	E8 W25	
Elizabeth	Thomas A. Hays	08Apr1802	E22 W32	
Elizabeth	John Miller	21Dec1808	E32 W41	
Elizabeth	Lloyd Cunningham	06Feb1817	E46 W53	
Elizabeth A.	Aquilla H. Davis	21Feb1865	W120	
Elizabeth J/I.	George Bowen	29May1857	H12 W106	Sills[?]
Ellen	James Everist	19Sep1831	E69 W71	Finney
Hannah	John Streett of Thos	04Jul1804	E25 W35	
Hannah	Edward M. Richardson	04Aug1819	E51 W56	
Harvey S.	Sarah R. Rodgers	01Jan1853	H3 W98	Robey
Isaac	Elizth Deaver	09Jul1779	B3 W2	
James	Mary Stockdale	29May1795	E7 W24	
James	Sarah Mason	16Mar1802	E21 W32	
James O.	Rebecca Jane Morris	13Apr1861	W114	
Jane	David Troutner	03Jul1861	W114	
John	Mary Curtis	29Jan1827	E62 W66	Pool
John Hambleton	Betsy Howard	01Sep1783	C7 W9	
Joseph	Rachel Harvey	11Jul1825	E60 W64	Richardson
Lydya	Wm Hughes	16Sep1782	C6 W8	
Margaret C.	James A. Richardson	27Oct1860	W112	
Mary	William Monjar	09Jan1793	E3 W22	[ret-AppA]
Mary	William H. Thompson	25Feb1830	E67 W69	Keech
Mary Ann	Ananias Divers	02Jan1854	H4 W100	Hawk[?]
Mary Ann E.	Abraham L. Jarrett	03Nov1836	E77 W78	Keech
Mary Elizabeth	Martin Eshelman	03Jan1853	H3 W98	Lemmon
Mary M.	S. Gover McNutt	16Jun1847	W91	
Mathias	Annie Lorris	28Aug1856	H10 W105	Gamble

JONES, continued

Morgan	* Baker	25Jan1798	E13 W27	
[*given name not stated]				
Peter	Jane Hines	m. 1778		[ret-AppA]
Priscilla	George Deaver	02Jan1838	E78 W80	Park
Rachael	James Bevard	m. 1778		[ret-AppA]
Rachel	Joseph Forcythe	12Jul1831	E69 W71	Finney
Rebecca A.	Josiah J/I. Shure	03Jun1858	W108	
Reubin	Lovey Ditto	30Dec1812	E39 W47	
Richard	Mary Durbin	15Sep1796	E9 W25	
Richard	Sophia Fardwell	09Feb1813	E39 W47	
Samuel	Mary Molton	22Jan1822	E55 W60	
Samuel	Rebecca Riley	29Jun1837	E78 W79	Finy
Sarah	Maynard Collins	07Jan1779	B1 W1	
Sarah	John Parker	26Aug1779	B3 W2	
Sarah	Simon Brown	15Aug1809	E34 W42	
Sarah	William D. Rezin	20Feb1813	E40 W47	
Sarah	Stephen Harkins	27Oct1819	E51 W57	
Sarah	George W. Gorrell	05Oct1859	W111	
Sarah A.	William H. Tucker	28Mar1848	W92	
Sarah Priscilla	Richard Mechem	30Apr1831	E69 W71	Keech
Stephen	Sarah Bennington	29Apr1779	B2 W1	
Stephen	Mary Taylor	24Nov1808	E32 W41	
Susanna	Jesse Culham	25Jun1801	E20 W31	
Susanna	John D. Carr	05Feb1812	E37 W45	
Susanna M.	Rezen Gorrell	24Oct1836	E77 W78	Finney
Susannah	Ephraim Swarts	25Nov1806	E29 W38	
Walter T.	Willamina Jones	23Dec1819	E51 W57	
Wiley	Jane Clark	30Jun1784	C9 W9	
Willamina	Walter T. Jones	23Dec1819	E51 W57	
Wm	Susa Dixon	m. 1778		[ret-AppA]
William	Sarah Rebecca Richards	08Aug1842	E85 W85	Briscoll
William	Henrietta Gorrell	16Aug1847	W91	
William	Mary Brown	14Aug1848	W92	
William	Valeria J. Bageley	06Mar1855	H7 W102	Lemmon
William	Amanda Fisher	27Mar1862	W116	

JORDAN

Elizabeth	Isaac Norris	27Apr1807	E29 W39	
Jane	Mathew Johnson	06Jan1820	E52 W57	
John	Rachel Fulton	14Dec1813	E41 W48	
John	Henrietta Prigg	02Feb1841	E83 W84	Reid

JORDON

Catharine	John Ashmead	14Jul1800	E18 W29

JUDD

Ann	William Michael	08Jul1797	E11 W26	
Catharine	Aaron James	04Feb1834	E73 W75	Todrig
Edward	Susanna Brown	08Dec1818	E50 W55	
Frances	Crawford Gorrell	29Dec1819	E51 W57	
John	Ann McCleary	03Mar1824	E58 W62	
Margaret Priscilla	John C. Stonebraker	02Dec1858	W109	
Rennis	James Peterson	06Mar1861	W113	

JUDD, continued

William	Ruth Flowers	31Jul1839	E81	W82	Richardson
William H.	Amanda M. Stearns	03Nov1853	H4	W100	Wilson
William Henry	Mary Ann Blake	27Dec1849		W94	

JURY

Richard	Ann Stallians	22Nov1780	C3	W5

KAAFA

William O.	Rosanna Havlin	19Aug1846	W90

KAIN

Rebecca	Wm Dives	16Dec1779	C1	W3	
Timothy	Easther Crownover	08Apr1783	C7	W8	cr-Harf

KAISER

Catharine	John P. Orth	19Sep1856	H10	W105	Alexander

KANE

Redman	Ellen Caffee	07Sep1846	W90

KANNADAY

Joseph	Clemency Denbow	10Jun1800	E18	W29

KANNEY

George	Mary Daugherty	29Jul1801	E20	W31

KAUFMAN

Margarett	Samuel Baldwin	25Oct1821	E54	W59

KEAN

Ann	Andrew Kearney	26Aug1844	E87	W87	Reed
Bridget	Alexander Keenan	04May1853	H3	W99	McNally
Cassandra	Samuel M. Ady	02Jun1862		W116	
Elizabeth	James M. Cain	09Jan1855	H6	W102	Walter
James	Cassandra A. Wilson	03Feb1829	E65	W68	O'Brian
John, Jur.	Precilla Thompson	12Oct1801	E20	W31	
John	Elizabeth Kennedy	14Apr1818	E49	W55	
John, Junr	Clarissa Wilson	27Dec1831	E70	W72	O'Brien
John	Martha H. Whitaker	18Aug1834	E74	W75	Todrick
John	Chloe Ady	18Jan1841	E83	W84	Reid
Mary	James Ewing	14Apr1783	C7	W8	cr-Harf
Nancy	John Price	26Sep1811	E37	W45	

KEARNEY

Andrew	Ann Kean	26Aug1844	E87	W87	Reed
Andrew	Bridget McCluskey	18Jul1862		W116	
Bridget	Michael Bradley	24Apr1857	H11	W106	Walter
Francis	Bridget Donahoo	18Nov1857	H13	W107	Walter
Mary	Patrick Haney	21Jun1847		W91	
Matilda	Michael Kelly	22Jul1846		W90	
Patrick	Mary Bradley	24Sep1852	H2	W98	McNally

KEARNS
Robert   Naomi Hope   14Dec1807 E30 W40

KEATH
Caroline   George Foard   01Jan1851   W96

KEATING
John   Bridget Dinan   09Feb1855 H7   W102 Walter
Thomas J.   Sarah F. Webster   11Jun1862   W116

KEE
Isabella   John W. Buckley   21Jul1849   W94

KEECH
Aaron   Elizabeth Wiley   29Aug1850   W95

KEEN
Alisann   Jarrett T. Baldwin   24Jan1846   W89
Ann   James Gallion   11Jul1805 E26 W36
Aquila   Elizabeth James   13Jan1813 E39 W47
Aquila D.   Sarah Ann Walker   22Apr1833 E72 W74 Finney
Benedict H.   Mary E. Wareham   01Dec1852 H2   W98 Smith
Cassandra   James Price   11Feb1833 E72 W73 Sewall
Eleanor   John Chesney   18Apr1818 E49 W55
Elizabeth   James Walker   17Jan1831 E68 W70 Tippet
Harriet   George A. Davis   28Dec1844 E87 W88 Davis
Harriett Amanda   John Botts   08Apr1845 E88 W88 Dulaney
James W.   Sarah Ann Botts   19Mar1855 H7   W102 Gallion
Lizzie   James Michael   10Feb1863   W117
Maria S.   James E. Holloway   14Jan1862   W115
Mary Ann   John W. Andrews   14Mar1843 E85 W86 Thomas
Mary B.   John McGaw   25Nov1828 E65 W68 Finney
Mary D.   George W. Murphy   31Dec1855 H9   W103 Crampton
Mary E.   George Anderson   22Jan1852 H1   W97 Chapman
Priscilla   Henry Bowman   28Jun1820 E52 W58
Rebecca   John W. Spencer   21Jul1817 E47 W53
Sally   Tyler Baldwin   20Mar1806 E28 W37
Samuel   Kesiah Knight   01Jan1856 H9   W104 McCartney
Sarah Ann   Thomas Hanway   28Nov1835 E76 W77 Smith
Sophia   Asael Bailess   23Feb1809 E33 W42
Susan E.   John T. Wareham   05Jul1853 H4   W99 Smith
Timothy   Harriot Bayles   23Sep1802 E22 W33
Timothy L.   Amanda M. Sutton   16Dec1850   W95
William Henry   Sarah Ann Baldwin   10Jan1849   W93
William J.   Sarah E. Mitchell   21May1864   W119

KEENAN
Alexander   Bridget Kean   04May1853 H3   W99 McNally

KEENE
Eliza J.   George W. Chappell   22Jan1863   W117

KEENER
Susan R.   Martin Russell   06Apr1864   W119

KEETH
Martha — William Vance — 23Feb1781 C4 W6

KEETS
Ann — John Wright — 08Feb1808 E31 W40

KEHOE
Michael — Margaret Havelin — 31Dec1857 W107

KEIFERTE
Frederick — Mary Heinlein — 05Nov1860 W112

KEITH
Rebecca A. — Edward T. Mask — 26Feb1855 H7 W102 Anderson

KEITHLEY
John — Helen Taylor — 11May1846 W90
Sarah Elizth — George B. James — 10Jan1861 W113
Thomas — Mahala Gilbert — 21Apr1831 E69 W71 Webster
  [orig. lic. to Webster; cr-Harf]

KEITLEY
James Michael — Mary Catharine Cullum — 20Dec1858 W109

KEITLY
Mary Agnes — William S. Coale — 12Oct1860 W112

KELLAY
John — Mary Golden — 21Apr1854 H5 W101 McNally

KELLER
Jacob A. — Margaret Ann Towson — 24Dec1863 W118

KELLEY
James — Mary Husbands — 01Jan1802 E21 W32
James — Elizabeth Lyons — 30Oct1809 E34 W43
Mary Ann — Thomas Arnett — 26May1830 E67 W69 O'Brian

KELLY
Ann — Wm Gorrell — 29Nov1779 C1 W3
Ann — John Cain — 23Feb1850 W94
Bridget — Morris Corkoran — 02Sep1853 H4 W99 McNally
Charlotte M. — James T. Flowers — 03Jul1855 H8 W103 Cushing
Isaac — Drucilla Durbin Nicols — 02Apr1801 E20 W31
Martin — Juda Dinan — 13Jan1855 H6 W102 Walter
Michael — Matilda Kearney — 22Jul1846 W90
Rosanna — Patrick McDermott — 23Sep1851 W97
Sarah Ann — Jesse Price — 06Mar1855 H7 W102 Gallion
Sylvester — Mary Havlin — 14May1855 H7 W102 Walter
Thomas — Martha Hartley — 15Jul1799 E16 W28

KEMBLE
Nancy — John Riley — 31Dec1839 E81 W82 Hoopman

KENLEY
Eliza	Henry Barnes	09Sep1841	E84 W84	Wilson
Lemuel	Elizabeth Baylis	07Dec1797	E13 W26	Jno Davis
Letitia	John Willson	27Aug1779	B3 W2	
Letitia	James Townley	26Jul1845	E88 W89	
Mary	Joseph Ewing	14Mar1801	E19 W30	
Richard	Avis Ward	25Mar1781	C4 W6	
Saml	Jane Willson	05Sep1779	B3 W2	
Sarah	Jacob Hoopman	26Jan1839	E80 W81	Stier

KENLY
Daniel	Louisa R. Blaney	15Feb1845	E88 W88	Billup
Richard	Mary Davis	19May1821	E54 W59	

KENNADAY
Sarah	Thomas Street	29May1800	E18 W29

KENNADY
Ann	George Bay	13Jan1802	E21 W32

KENNARD
Eliza	Caleb Pue	08Feb1831	E68 W70	Tippet
George	Mary E. Pue	24Sep1838	E79 W80	Collins
Mary	Walter Watters	06Jun1822	E55 W60	
Mathew	Polly Haithhorn	29Jul1794	E5 W23	

KENNEDY [see Kennedy Bay]
Caroline A.	James Montgomery, M.D.	06Apr1831	E69 W71	Park
Elizabeth	John Kean	14Apr1818	E49 W55	
Esther Ann	John Hendon Chalk	28Oct1847	W91	
James	Jemima Enlows	26Dec1805	E27 W37	
James	Catherine Latimore	16Oct1852	H2 W98	Gallion
Jane	George Herbert	07Mar1816	E45 W51	
John	Hester Carman	31May1821	E54 W59	
John	Elizabeth Wann	12Apr1832	E70 W72	Keech
Lavina	George Herbert	17Jan1809	E33 W42	
Mary Ann	Richard M. Tracy	03Feb1858	W108	
Mary Ann	Henry Harrison	02Mar1863	W117	
Minerva Jane	John J/I. Martin	30Jan1860	W111	
Silas	Eliza E. Curry	11Jan1845	E87 W88	

KENNY
Margaret	Robert Cross	08Jan1863	W117	
Mary	Wm Strond	m. 1778		[ret-AppA]

KENT [see Kent M. Chesney, Kent Mitchell]

KERMAN
Nancy	Robert Whiteford	02Feb1796	E11 W26

KERNAN
Margaret	Richard H. Kirkwood	16Oct1826	E62 W65	Poteet

KERR [see also CARR]
Edward	Lucinda McGriger	19Dec1810	E36 W44	
Elizabeth G.	Thomas Maxwell	22May1841	E83 W84	Parke
Jane	Amos Scarbrough	17Dec1825	E60 W64	Park
Margaret A.	Patrick Clark	12Feb1851	W96	
Robert, Junior	Ann Whiteford	01Mar1819	E50 W56	
Rose F.	Charles L. Gilbert	13Feb1847	W91	

KERVER [or Kerwen?; see CARVER]
Rachel	William Foster	11Feb1812	E38 W46

KESLER
Wm F. A.	Martha Reed	10May1855	H7 W102	Hersey[?]

KIDD
Elizth	John Ware	20Mar1779	B1 W1
Elizabeth	Alexander Thompson of Danl	27Nov1807	E30 W40
John	Sarah Rieston	15Mar1779	B1 W1
Kerzias	Ja^s Curry	04Dec1780	C4 W5
[after 19 & 3 December]			
Sarah	Richard Barnes	17Dec1782	C6 W8
Sarah	Henry Scarff	10Dec1806	E29 W38

KIDHEY[?]
Honer	Jacob Wood	22Mar1779	B1 W1

KILCREAS
Rachel	John Erwin	19Apr1808	E31 W40

KILGOR
Robt	Mary Wilson	12Dec1843	E86 W87	Park

KILGORE
John N.	Eliza Wiley	01Feb1851	W96

KILGOUR
Jane D.	John Shartle	18Mar1854	H5 W100	Herron

KILIAN [see Kilian Kub]

KILLOUGH
Eleanor	Elijah T. Tomlinson	21Jun1840	E82 W83	Finney

KIMBALL
William	Frances Shareswood	06Nov1834	E74 W76	Dunahay

KIMBERLY
Mary	William Cannon	28May1810	E35 W43

KIMBLE
Catharine	Isaiah Taylor	01Jan1805	E26 W36	
Elijah	Elizabeth Jackson	22Jun1795	E7 W24	
Elijah	Polly Stephenson	02Dec1795	E8 W24	
Florilla	George Taylor	24Jan1806	E27 W37	
Giles	Eleanor Groves	19Mar1779	B1 W1	
Hannah	Asa Taylor	m. 1777		[ret-AppA]
Hannah	Robert Armstrong	28Oct1809	E34 W43	
Henry	Eliza E. Fox	03Nov1845	W89	
Jemimah	Amasa Taylor	01Jan1780	C1 W3	
John	Nancy Foard	28Nov1808	E32 W41	
Martha	Joshua Deaver	21Aug1807	E30 W39	
Naomi	Perrgrine Nowland	02Jul1816	E45 W51	
Nelly*	William Kimble	08Sep1792	E3 W22	[ret-AppA]

  [*Mary crossed out]

Sarah	John Atkinson	19Jan1825	E59 W63	Richardson

  [orig. lic. to Benjn Richardson; cr-Harf]

Sarah Jane	Albert Vanhorn	24Nov1862	W116	
Sarah Louisa	Taylor Cole	14Jun1854	H6 W101	Reese
Stephen	Hannah Taylor	11Feb1793	E4 W22	[ret-AppA]
Susan	George Pritchard	18Dec1832	E71 W73	Han--[?]
Susannah	James Taylor	06Feb1804	E24 W34	
William	Nelly* Kimble	08Sep1792	E3 W22	[ret-AppA]

  [*Mary crossed out]

William	Sarah Pritchard	21Oct1809	E34 W43	
William	Jemima Stephenson	28Feb1821	E54 W58	

KIMBLY
Martha	John Gray	26Feb1816	E44 W51

  (Jno Henderson to pay)

KINDSLEY
Cristoff	Julia Dorman	19Mar1855	H7 W102	Forbes

KING
Elizabeth Ann	Oliver H. Amos	16Mar1829	E65 W68	Keech
John R.	Elizabeth B. Robinson	27May1858	W108	
Richard	Sarah Heaps	20May1802	E22 W32	

KINGSTON
Elizth	Ely Shipley	16Feb1781	C4 W6

KINSEY
Rev. Edward	Martha Wells	27Oct1860	W112

KINSLEY
Margaret	William Russell	17Jun1806	E28 W38

KINZIL
Charles	Ann Johnson	08Feb1798	E13 W27	Jno Coleman

Harford Co. Md. Marriage Licenses, 1777-1865   141

KIRK
Elijah	Elizabeth A. Sherdan	20Feb1865	W120	
George W.	Balinda P. Amos	23Aug1841	E83 W84	Keech
Jacob	Frances Whitaker	23Jan1838	E79 W80	Keech
James	Jane Wilie	31Dec1799	E17 W29	
James	Isabella Wiley	23Dec1804	E25 W35	
Jane	George C. Davis	12Feb1835	E75 W76	Finney
John	Hannah Beaty	29May1812	E38 W46	
John P.	Sarah M. Baldwin	03Jan1865	W120	
Margaret A.	Wm. H. Smith	02Jun1863	W117	
Susannah	Henry Silver	17Mar1863	W117	

KIRKPATRICK
Mary	John Blackburn	m. 1778	[ret-AppA]

KIRKWOOD
Abel	Elizth Jane Miskimmon	12Jun1843	E86 W86	Cross
Andrew	Margaret Briarly	20Mar1850	W94	
Deborah	Giles T. Green	30May1825	E60 W63	O'Brien
George C.	Isabel R. Cairnes	28Feb1859	W110	
Jane	William Robinson	23May1832	E71 W73	Morison
John A.	Mary G. Alexander	06Mar1832	E70 W72	Sewall
John H.	Ruth Ann Miskimmon	25Nov1843	E86 W87	Cross
Rebecca	Thomas Green	03Feb1852	H1 W97	Yerkes
Richard H.	Margaret Kernan	16Oct1826	E62 W65	Poteet
Sarah Ann	John W. Anderson	29Oct1859	W111	
William C.	Jane Thompson	30Jun1824	E58 W62	

KISER
Mary	Joseph Dubre	20Nov1794	E6 W23	B. Bond

KITELY
Elizabeth	William Duley	20Jun1798	E15 W27

KLINESMITH
Caroline E.	John D. Everett	17Jan1865	W120

KNIGHT
Abraham	Rachel Robinson	16Oct1827	E63 W66	Finey
Ann	John W. Carlile	18Feb1826	E61 W64	
[minister - Isaac Webster; orig. lic. to Webster; cr-Harf]				
Cassandra	Charles Standiford	20Feb1865	W120	
Charlotte	William Hamilton	26Oct1816	E46 W52	
Eleanor	William Norris	13Jun1826	E61 W65	Stephenson
Elizabeth Ann	Edward McCommons	29Jan1848	W92	
George	Margaret Ewing	19Dec1838	E80 W81	Dulaney
George	Cassandra Price	11Jun1846	W90	
Jane	John Wilson	20Mar1843	E85 W86	Dulany
John	Jane Swift	08May1833	E72 W74	Donahay
John	Elizabeth Miller	23Apr1839	E80 W82	Galien
John	Solivia Scheckle	09Dec1845	W89	
Joshua W.	Frances Hunter	30Jan1845	E88 W88	Eage
Kesiah	Samuel Keen	01Jan1856	H9 W104	McCartney
Martha	Benjn Cowan	06Feb1782	C5 W7	

KNIGHT, continued
Mary Ann	Burt Whitson	10Apr1824	E58 W62	
Mary Ann	William Russell	29Apr1838	E79 W80	Greenbanks
R. C. [br]	B. B. Snyder [gr]	27Sep1837	E78 W79	Roberts
Rebecca	Joseph E. Taylor	18Oct1830	E68 W70	Tippit
Robert	Harriet Brazier	04Mar1824	E58 W62	
Samuel R.	Margaret J. Sheridine	22Nov1859	W111	
Sarah	Wm Perkins	09Jan1779	B1 W1	
Sarah E.	Lemuel Benton	28Mar1853	H3 W99	Bull
Sarah Elizth	Evan W. Thompson	19Aug1859	W110	
Sarah J.	William S. Baxter	06Aug1855	H8 W103	Lemmon
Sarah Jane	John James	03Apr1851	W96	
Sarah Jane	William C. Standiford	19Nov1860	W112	
Sarah M.	William H. H. Fink	15Jan1861	W113	
Thomas	Sarah Barnes	20Jan1804	E24 W34	
Thomas of Wm.	Serene Spence	13Jul1830	E67 W70	Stephenson
Thomas	Elizabeth Rhodenhesen	13Aug1831	E69 W71	Sewell
Thomas	Ann E. Hopkins	26Feb1838	E79 W80	Collins
Thomas Charles	Emeline Miller	12Jan1832	E70 W72	Sewall
[orig. lic. to Sewall; cr-Harf]				
William	Mary Sutten	22Jul1780	C2 W4	
[surname given as "knight", not capitalized]				
William	Sarah Robinson	29Sep1797	E12 W26	
[Ret'd by John Allen]				
William	Sarah Martin	29Jan1812	E37 W45	
William	Jane Scott	17Oct1851	W97	
William	Caroline J. Tayson	26Jan1859	W109	
Wm C.	Margaret Jane Daugherty	05Sep1857	H12 W107	Monroe
William Henry	Eliza Ann Price	19Mar1839	E80 W81	Finney

KONKLIN
David	Hannah Forwood	03Dec1781	C5 W7	

KRELIS
Edwd Frederick	Susan Jackson	27Oct1836	E77 W78	Richardson

KUB
Kilian	Anna Heinlein	01Mar1862	W115

KURTZ
Sabastian	Martha Elizth McIntire	17Aug1847	W91

KYLE [see CYLE]

LAIN
Daniel	Elizth Morris	3Sep1779	B3 W2

LAIRD
John	Sarah Finley	15Jul1779	B3 W2

LAKE
Mary	Mifflin Beaumont	05Mar1821	E54 W58

LAMBERT [see Lambert Pennington]

Harford Co. Md. Marriage Licenses, 1777-1865 143

LAMBERTH
Job. W.   Martha C. Thompson   20Mar1848   W92

LAMPRE
Margaret   Abrm. Howlman   07Oct1783 C8 W9   cr-Harf

LANAGAN
Mary   Henry Gay   30Mar1802 E21 W32

LANCASTER
Aaron   Hannah Ady   28Mar1815 E43 W49
Amelia   Clark Hollis   12Jan1803 E23 W33
Ann Maria   Thomas Ely   18Oct1814 E42 W49
Christian   Thomas McKinney   11Apr1785 C10 W10
Esther   Israel Atkinson   21Apr1829 E66 W68 Richardson
Mary Virginia   Wm Amoss Carr 27Oct1852 H2 W98 Robey
Nathan¹   Darcus Johnson   09Dec1815 E44 W50
Rebecca   Absalom Chaney   30Sep1807 E30 W39
Tho.   Christian Gordin   m. 1777   [ret-AppA]

LAND
Mary   William Anderson   22Dec1845   W89

LANDER
Frances   Randsome Fayerweather   18Mar1830 E67 W69 Higby

LANDRUM
Elizabeth B.   Abraham Larue   04Jan1817 E46 W52
Rebecca   John Taylor   01Jul1795 E7 W24
Robert   Rebeca Crosen   18Oct1781 C5 W7

LANG
Luke   Eliza Rhodes   20Aug1810 E35 W44

LANGLEY
George   Catharine Ann Daugherty   12Nov1839 E81 W82 Finney

LANPHER
John W.   Margaret Coulton   11Apr1846   W90

LANSDALE
Cornelia   Maskell C. Ewing   18Feb1840 E82 W83 Goldsborough
Maria M.   John W. Horner   13Oct1835 E75 W77 Higby

LARBOURD[?]
Catharine   Henry Mitchell   11Dec1827 E64 W67 Keech

LAREN
Elizabeth   Benjamin Guyton   06Apr1864   W119
James   Sarah Maynes   03Sep1863   W118

LARKIN
Cathrine   Francis Picket   13May1780   C2 W4

LARREW
George — Catharine C. Shay — 05Jun1865 — W121

LARUE
Abraham — Elizabeth B. Landrum — 04Jan1817 — E46 W52

LASTAKER
Gabriel — Julian Waskey — 04Feb1806 — E27 W37

LATIMORE
Catherine — James Kennedy — 16Oct1852 — H2 W98 Gallion

LAUDER
Charlotte — William Michael — 29Nov1831 — E70 W72 Sewell
Samuel — Eliza Miller — 27Feb1833 — E72 W73 Finney
William — Rachel Fowler — 03Jan1792 — E2 W21

LAUGHARD
Henderson — Elizabeth Everit — 27Nov1815 — E44 W50

LAUGHRY
John — Catherine Boyl — 06Feb1826 — E61 W64 O'Brian

LAURANCE
George — Barbara Webb — 19Aug1812 — E38 W46

LAURENCE
William — Jemima Touchstone — 06Sep1830 — E67 W70 Webster

LAVER
Harrison — Louisa A. Holland — 18Mar1863 — W117

LAWDER
Samuel — Caroline Miller — 10Aug1847 — W91

LAWRANCE
James — Ann Taff — 01May1782 — C6 W7 cr-Harf

LAWRENCE
Ellen M. — Israel Day — 13Jun1861 — W114
John — Mary Thomas — 16May1854 — H5 W101 Trout

LAWSON [see Lawson Cooley, Lawson Hobbs, Lawson W. Rodgers, Alexander Lawson Smith]
James — Elizabeth Middle — 06Feb1796 — E8 W25

LAYER[?]
Maria — Irah Herbert — 10Aug1835 — E75 W76 Dulany

LAYTON
Hutchings William — Elizabeth Chambers — 28Jun1803 — E23 W34

LEAR
Charlotte — Archibald Johnson — 31Mar1823 — E56 W61
Mary — Richard Herbert — 24Jan1806 — E27 W37

LEATOR
Eliza J.   William O'Neil   22Nov1843   E86 W87   Billup

LEATTOR
Mary C.   Henry P. Sutor   15Aug1843   E86 W86   Billup

LEDLEY
Charity   Samuel Oram   m. 1803   [ret-AppA]

LEE [see David Lee Anderson, Parker Lee Forwood, James Lee Hopkins,
    James Lee Morgan, Cassandra Lee Morgan, David Lee Norris,
    Corbin Lee Onion, Lee Tipton, Lee M. Whistler]

Alice	James H. Parker	25Jun1861	W114	
Archer	Rachel Wilson	06Apr1807	E29 W39	
Blanch H.	James C. Worthington	08Apr1846	W90	
Blanch Hall	Robert Lyon Hall	27Oct1808	E32 W41	
Cassandra	Robert Gover	04Nov1800	E18 W30	
Charles	Martha Wilson	16Jan1792	E2 W21	
Elizabeth	James Lee	24Feb1800	E17 W29	
Elizabeth	John Timmons	11Feb1817	E46 W53	
Elizabeth	William Smithson	11Mar1818	E49 W55	
Frances M.	Edward C. Hall	30Nov1815	E44 W50	
Hannah	Martin Grafton	30Sep1816	E45 W52	
James	Sarah Elliott	08Apr1779	B2 W1	
James	Elizabeth Lee	24Feb1800	E17 W29	
James	Delia Poteet	08Jan1807	E29 W38	
James C.	Deliverance H. Glasgow	18Jun1844	E87 W87	Finney
John	Rebecca McGregury	29Dec1783	C8 W9	cr-Harf
John	Mary Walstrum	22Feb1832	E70 W72	Gallion
John	Alisanna Barton	01Jun1837	E78 W79	Hofman
John T.	Rebecca H. Temple	25Feb1864	W118	
Joseph	Rosanna Towson	16Jan1851	W96	
Joseph	Elizabeth Doxen	15Mar1860	W111	
Josiah	Catharine E. Sewell	02Jun1831	E69 W71	Higby
Julian B.	James T. McCormick	13Jan1853	H3 W99	Cornelius
Lloyd	Ruth Bull	12Aug1811	E37 W45	
Margaret	William Smithson	05Sep1805	E26 W36	
Margaretta	James Ryley	22Jun1826	E61 W65	Webster
[orig. lic. to Webster; cr-Harf]				
Maria	James C. Hughes	14Dec1813	E41 W48	
Marshall	Sarah Blake	12Jan1799	E15 W27	
Marshall	Anne Bailey	10Apr1817	E47 W53	
Mary	Morris Malsby	16Mar1802	E21 W32	
Mary	Thomas Magness	15Oct1811	E37 W45	
Mary	Jesse Miller	17Jun1832	E71 W73	Sewall
Mary Ann	Zacheus O. Bond	27Sep1804	E25 W35	
Mary Ann	Thomas Ely	04Oct1827	E63 W66	Finney
Parker H.	Mary Elizabeth Briarly	08Jun1841	E83 W84	Keech
Parker Hall	Elizth Dallam	10Apr1781	C4 W6	
Priscilla Elizabeth	Wakeman Bryarly	30Jan1816	E44 W51	
Ralph	Alesana Bond	31Jan1805	E26 W36	
Ralph	Elizabeth Smithson	15Jan1812	E37 W45	
Rebecca	Edward Norris	14Dec1799	E17 W28	
Rebecca	Joshua Wilson	20Apr1824	E58 W62	

LEE, continued
Rebecca	Robert Jackson	16Oct1824	E58 W62	

[orig. lic. to Finney; cr-Harf]

Roberta C.	Spencer D. Fletcher	18Oct1855	H8 W103	Keech
Samuel M.	Cassandra L. Gover	24Dec1844	E87 W88	Jones
Saml W.	Mary Gover	02Feb1795	E6 W24	
Sarah	William Wilson	28Feb1798	E13 W27	Jno Coleman
Sarah	Reese Davis	27Feb1810	E35 W43	
Sarah	John Oatman	19May1825	E60 W63	Webster

[orig. lic. to Webster; cr-Harf]

Thomas	Fanny Andrews	19Dec1805	E27 W37
William D.	Ann Wilson	14Feb1810	E35 W43

LEECH
Robert	Sarah Hartshorn	28Oct1834	E74 W75	Hoopman

LEEDOM [see Leedom B. Moore]

LEFEVRE
Hamilton	Sarah Jane Streett	09Oct1837	E78 W79	Holmeads

LEGO
Benjamin	Elizabeth York	02Apr1806	E28 W38	
Benjamin	Maria Watts	27Nov1843	E86 W87	Lurtzer
Elizabeth	John Hambleton	17Apr1809	E33 W42	
Spencer	Mary Hill	08Jun1810	E35 W44	

LEGOE
Salathiel	Ellen Roberts	28Dec1838	E80 W81	Richardson

LEGUE
Mary Ann	Charles Hawkins	26Jan1824	E57 W62

LEIGH
Reubin	Nancy Williams	21May1806	E28 W38

LEITHISER
Nathaniel	Clemency Botts	31Jul1860	W112

LEMMON
Elizabeth	William Anderson	27Feb1849	W93	
Letitia	Leedom B. Moore	13Sep1853	H4 W100	Lemmon
Sarah C.	John Thomas Mumma	20Oct1852	H2 W98	Yerkes

LEMON
Andrew H.	Martha Matilda Hall	16Dec1823	E57 W61

LENIGAN
Anna	Clemence Francis Weber	15Jul1850	W95

LENLAN
Francis	Nancy Cooper	05Dec1803	E24 W34

LENNOX
William A.	Mary Louisa Fell Allen	13Apr1835	E75 W76	D. Bond

LENOX
Mary Louisa F.   Saml Wilson Raymond   01Nov1842 E85 W85   Reid

LESTER
Alice   Philip Trager   08Mar1826 E61 W65   Webster
  [orig. lic. to Webster; cr-Harf]
Caroline Elizth   Charles Reed   04Aug1858   W108
Elizabeth   Hosea Barnes   06Jan1809 E33 W42
Norris   Martha Greenley[?]   16Apr1841 E83 W84   Dulaney
William   Elizabeth Fawcet   15Nov1799 E17 W28

LEVI
John   Drosilla Chandler   25Aug1812 E38 W46
John   Sarah Molton   20Dec1836 E77 W78

LEVY [see also LIEVY]
Frances   Thomas Sutor   11May1833 E72 W74   Higby

LEWIN [see William Lewin Bailey]
John   Lydia L. Huff   26Nov1839 E81 W82   Finney
Rachel Frances   John Barclay Scarborough   18Dec1860   W113
Sarah   Aaron Harkins   20Mar1833 E72 W73   Keech

LEWIS
John D.   Sophia White Hall   04Nov1806 E29 W38
Nicholas   Mary Mackie   23Dec1800 E19 W30
Rebecca   William H. Sewell   15Feb1803 E23 W33   [ret-AppA]
Samuel   Cornelia Haycock   16Oct1819 E51 W57
Sarah Ann   James W. Brook   01Jan1834 E73 W75   Higby
Sarah R.   John Monks   25Feb1805 E26 W36
Sophia W.   George W. Hall   07Feb1816 E44 W51
William A.   Susannah G. Amos   08Mar1842 E84 W85   Keech
William T.   Mary Minerva Marks   18Oct1834 E74 W75

LIEVY
William   Ann Myers   22Dec1812 E39 W47

LILBOURN [see Lilbourn B. Rogers]

LILLEY
Henry   Mary Cain   19Nov1805 E27 W37
John   Hannah C. Stump   13Jun1826 E61 W65   O'Brian

LILLY
James R.   Sarah H. Divers   28Dec1854 H6 W102 Finney
John   Avarilla Mitchell   10Apr1834 E74 W75   Todrig
Mary Ann   William J/I. James   19Dec1850   W94
Thomas   Juliann Wakeland   02Feb1828 E64 W67   Keech
  [orig. lic. to Keech; cr-Harf]

LINAM
William   Sarah Pinix   05Dec1797 E13 W26   John Coleman

LINCH
Cassandra	Roger McNial	25Jan1802	E21 W32	
James	Charlotte Cloeman	11Jul1844	E87 W87	Reid
Michael	Sirce Havelin	25Jul1830	E67 W70	O'Brian

LINDAMORE
Margaret	William Henry Corham	07Apr1858	W108

LINDEMORE
William	Elizabeth Banks	20Feb1864	W118

LINDIMORE
Henry	Cordelia Chock	06Jul1807	E30 W39

LINDSEY
Issabella	Joshua Shaw	01Nov1831	E70 W71	Sewall

LINGAN
Edward	Ailizanna Duff	27May1830	E67 W69	O'Brian
Edward	Mary Jane Wright	29Jan1861	W113	
John F.	Miss Lizzie Wann	11May1859	W110	
Lucy	John Conlen	13Dec1850	W95	
Martha	James Tobin	17Nov1857	H13 W107	Walter

LINGUM
Mary	Patrick Gleeson	05Nov1853	H4 W100	McNally

LINLOP
Christian	Anna M. Henning	09Jul1850	W95

LINTON
Francis Alexander	Susan Reed	22Dec1849	W94

LISBY
Susannah	James Carroll	04Apr1802	E22 W32

LITTIG
Laura M.	John H. Maynadier	13Dec1855	H8 W103	Poisell
Philip	Jane L. Dorsey	22Aug1843	E86 W86	Thomas

LITTLE
James, Jr.	Mary McMath	17Aug1829	E66 W68	Keech
John	Margaret Daugherty	24Jun1800	E18 W29	

LITTON
Clemence	Thos Durbin	05Oct1779	B3 W2

LIVERES
Mary A.	Henry F. Ruth	17Nov1849	W94

LIVEZEY
Edith W.	Joseph R. Terry	10Sep1857	H12 W107	Cushing
James W.	Frances F. Everett	08Dec1863	W118	

LOCHARY
Ann	Joseph B. Treadwell	17Feb1857	H11 W106	Walter
Catharine C.	James Corrigan	10Jan1851	W96	
Catharine C.	Benjamin A. Slade	03Apr1851	W96	
Michael	Julia Slade	08Sep1841	E84 W84	Reid

LOCKWOOD
Aquila	Cassandra Dallam	14Sep1815	E43 W50

LOCUST [see SOCUST]

LOFFLIN
William	Emely Bailey	21Apr1831	E69 W71	Finney

LOFLIN
Ann	Ephraim Gilbert	15Mar1823	E56 W61	
Anne	Robert Lumsden	20May1851	W96	
Daniel	Chloe A. Preston	10Nov1839	E81 W82	Finny
Daniel A.	Mary Loflin	23Feb1853	H3 W99	Finney
Elizabeth	James Griffey	24Feb1840	E82 W83	Finney
Frances	Samuel Baldwin	10Sep1838	E79 W80	Hoopman
John S.	Ellen Bailey	23Mar1844	E87 W87	Finney
Mary	Daniel A. Loflin	23Feb1853	H3 W99	Finney
Richard	Adaline Courtney	03Jan1843	E85 W86	Finney
Thomas	Matilda Smith	03Sep1808	E32 W41	

LOFTIN
Hannah	Thomas Shannon	28Mar1831	E69 W71	Tippit
John	Mary Brannon	26Dec1803	E24 W34	

LOFTON
Thomas	Sarah Wilson	22Feb1802	E21 W32
William	Rachel Anderson	31Jan1804	E24 W34

LOGAN
Mary E.	John Burkins	15Nov1864	W120	
Patrick	Jane McClurg	25Mar1840	E82 W83	Finney

LOGRAN
Annie	Robert Miller	13May1856	H10 W104	Littleton

LOGUE
Catharine	Eli Mantel	20Apr1824	E58 W62	
James	Elizabeth Amos	02Mar1830	E67 W69	Poteet

LOMAN
Lucy Ann	Thomas S. Proctor	05May1832	E71 W73	Richardson

LONDON
James	Ann Inglehart	01Oct1855	H8 W103	Lemmon

LONDREAGRIN
Dennis	Mary Casse	25Dec1780	C4 W5

LONEY [see William Loney Forwood]
Annaballa	Wm Young	16Jan1783	C7	W8	cr-Harf
Mary	John Forwood the 3d	06Dec1803	E24	W34	
Wm	Mary Frisby	24Dec1782	C7	W8	cr-Harf

LONG
Daniel	Eliza Shewell	19Mar1821	E54	W58	
Hannah	Daniel Thompson of Alexr	30Jun1808	E32	W41	
Henry	Ruth West	13Dec1831	E70	W72	Sewell
John	Ann Scott	21Feb1779	B1	W1	
Martha	Abner Barrett	15Dec1821	E55	W59	[Burrett?]
Mary Martha	John J. McComas	12Dec1861		W115	
Nancy	William Smith	23Jul1817	E47	W53	

LORRIS
Annie	Mathias Jones	28Aug1856	H10	W105	Gumble

LOUGE
Elizabeth	Conrod Shineflue	27Jun1797	E11	W26

LOVE
Ann	Thos Johnson	29May1793	E4	W22
Bennet	Elizabeth Gilbert	22Apr1809	E33	W42
Jacob	Mary Jane Bay	25Mar1848		W92
John	Susanna Green	08Nov1791	E1	W21
Martha Ann	Joseph C. Coulson	05Nov1850		W95
Ruth	Richard Ashton	10Nov1807	E30	W39
Sarah	Isaac Bull	01Mar1779	B1	W1

LOVEIT
John	Ann Jones	13Apr1782	C6	W7	cr-Harf

LOVETT
Ann Eliza	John Mitchell	28Oct1850	W95

LOW
Eunice	John Watters	04Apr1853	H3	W99	Gailey
Hannah	Thomas Barton	18Feb1835	E75	W76	Gallion
Isaac	Jamima Hitchcock	26Sep1791	E1	W21	

LOWE
Alice R.	Sam'l J. Ankram	29Dec1863		W118	
Obed	Mary J/I. Almony	20Feb1854	H5	W100	Smith

LOWMAN
Henry	Cina Dixon	17Sep1829	E66	W69	Richardson

LUCAS
Mary	David Swarts	12Apr1809	E33	W42	
Pleasance	James Cochran	05Dec1811	E37	W45	
Thos	Sarah Lynch	m. 1788[?]			[ret-AppA]

LUCKEY
Elizabeth	John Draghorn	12May1853	H4	W99	Foobs
Susannah	Jno Thompson	05[?]Jul1781	C5	W6	

[above entry after 17Jul]

LUCKIE
Grace	John Bell	18Aug1800	E18	W29
Rebecca	Patterson Bane	20Aug1800	E18	W30

LUEDING
Henry	Louisa Hemp	27Aug1860	W112

LUFBOROUGH
Nathan	May Webster	23Apr1795	E7	W24

[ret-AppA has *Mary* Webster]

LUKE
Henrietta M.	Wm Eichelberger	01May1827	E63	W66	O'Brian
Nicholas W.	Henrietta M. Brown	02Oct1820	E53	W58	

LUKINS
Ann	David Way	11Dec1801	E21	W31

LUMSDEN
Robert	Anne Loflin	20May1851	W96

LUSBY
Elizth	Ben Hollis	30Oct1783	C8	W9	cr-Harf
Leaven	Walter Harward	08Dec1837	E78	W79	Collins

LUSTATER
Jacob	Tamer Parr	31Jul1795	E7	W24

LUSTER [see Joseph Luster {Lester} Webster]
Charlotte	Charles Herron	02Feb1820	E52	W57

LYLE [see Mrs. Lyle Davis]

LYNCH
Andrew	Margarett Jackson	22Jul1819	E51	W56	
Elizabeth	Jacob Evans	23May1811	E36	W45	
Hannah	Joseph Wooley	10May1816	E45	W51	
Jeremiah	Ann Gourmly	31Jan1853	H3	W99	McNally
John	Mary Cahill	29Jan1855	H7	W102	Walter
Margaret	Jacob W. Campbell	25Dec1861		W115	
Mary	George Sims	m. 1778			[ret-AppA]
Matthias	Elizabeth Saunders	20Dec1779	C1	W3	
Saml	Mary Seager[?]	24Mar1784	C8	W9	
Samuel	Mary Ann Campbell	14May1861		W114	
Sarah	Thos Lucas	m. 1788[?]			[ret-AppA]
Thomas	Jane Crampton	18Jul1816	E45	W52	

LYON [see Robert Lyon Hall]
John C.	Augusta M. Day	13Apr1833	E72	W74	Hamilton

LYONS
Elizabeth	James Kelley	30Oct1809	E34	W43	
Martha	Nicholas Allender	06Oct1823	E57	W61	

LYTLE
Ann	Wm Osborn	16Dec1780	C3	W5	"Wheat"
Betsy	Geo. Presbury	06Nov1793	E5	W23	
George	Catharin Chansey	m. 1778			[ret-AppA]
George	Mary Coale	18Feb1807	E29	W39	
James	Rachel Hopkins	10May1831	E69	W71	Sewall
James S.	Mary Ann Michael	22Dec1859		W111	
Jane	Charles Holloway	23Mar1826	E61	W65	Webster
[orig. lic. to Webster; cr-Harf]					
Louisa	Archibald Johnson	25Oct1841	E84	W84	Dulaney
Loveicy	John Wheeler	18Nov1823	E57	W61	
Mary Ann	John McLaughlin	11Feb1840	E82	W83	Reed
Mary O.	Thomas B. Devoe	15Feb1842	E84	W85	Keech
Matilda	James F. Ashton	15Jun1864		W119	
Nathan	Sarah Wadsworth	24Feb1821	E53	W58	
Thomas	Delia Anderson	14May1807	E29	W39	
William K.	Margaret Ann Clark	25Jan1860		W111	

LYTTLETON [see Lyttleton Green, Lyttleton F. Morgan]

MAAGHER
Catharine	Andrew Gleason	26Jan1861	W113

MABBETT
A. Joseph	Annie S. Whitaker	26Sep1857	H12 W107	Finney

McADAW
James	Sarah Cottigan	01May1794	E5	W23
[see ret-AppA under McAdow and Cattigan]				

McADOO
Ann	Benjn Dixon	27Apr1779	B2	W1

McADOW
Andrew	Mary Mcfadden	08Dec1808	E32	W41	
Andrew J.	Sarah E. Henderson	11Apr1843	E86	W86	Finney
Ellen	Andrew Daily	02Mar1839	E80	W81	Finney
Margaret	Jehu Hare	07May1835	E75	E76	Finney
William	Mary Jane Henderson	01Feb1837	E77	W79	Dulany

MACATEE
Ann Maria	John Walter Streett	21Jan1862		W115	
Elizabeth	Jonathan Ady	04Aug1807	E30	W39	
Elizabeth A.	Henry Richardson	10Jan1837	E77	W78	Crosgery
Henry	Theresa Wheeler	28Jan1799	E15	W28	
Josiah J.	Geraldine Streett	25Dec1860		W113	

MACATEE, continued
Leonard	Juliet Morgan	26Nov1818	E50 W55	
Silvester	Jane Butler	23Feb1829	E65 W68	O'Brian
Thomas B.	Ruth E. Streett	10Jan1853	H3 W99	McNally

McATEE [* Mcatee]
Clement	Rachel Ann Quinlan	26Apr1841	E83 W84	Reed
George J.	Mary E. Brown	02Mar1835	E75 W76	Crosgy
Ignatius	Margaret Johnson	11Apr1836	E76 W77	Crosgay
Ignatius G.	Maria Butler	11Feb1824	E58 W62	
Mary Ann [*]	Francis A. Wheeler	04Jul1814	E42 W49	
Mary Ann	Stephen J. Raphell	26May1834	E74 W75	Todrig
Patrick	Ellen McFarlin	25Apr1839	E80 W82	Coskey
Samuel [*]	Elizabeth Green	05Jul1814	E42 W49	

McCABE
Catharine	Peter Sculley	13Jan1860	W111	
Patrick	Rose Feely	29Feb1860	W111	

McCAFFERTY
Michael	Alice Young	31Jan1855	H7 W102	Walter

McCAN
Margt	James Anderson	m. 1778		[ret-AppA]

McCANDELESS
Sarah	Joseph McCummins	06Feb1817	E46 W53

McCANDLESS
John	Sarah Spencer	21Aug1806	E28 W38
Ruth	William Bay	19Jan1808	E31 W40

McCANN
Lewis	Mary E. Markland	20Sep1861	W114	
Mary	Daniel Chipman	26Nov1817	E48 W54	
Mary J/I.	John Crawford	21Jul1854	H6 W101	Trout
William E.	Amanda M. Troutner	27Apr1853	H3 W99	Trout

McCARROLL
Ann	Timothy Shenaghen	06Dec1855	H8 W103	Walter

McCARTY
Owen	Elizabeth Flannagan	07Apr1779	B2 W1

McCASKEY
Hannah	William Johnson	25Oct1816	E46 W52

McCASKY
Sarah	Thomas Adlum	23Mar1799	E15 W28

McCAULEY
Mary Louisa	Joshua McLaughlin	12Dec1849	W94

McCAUSLAND
Henry	Mary Phipps	05Apr1809	E33 W42
Loucinda	Patrick Dinan	24Aug1847	W91
Maria	Joseph R. Hopkins	31Dec1864	W120
Sarah A.	George T. Davis	15Mar1849	W93

McCAVERTY
Biddy	Patrick Quinn	02Oct1830	E68 W70 O'Brian

McCAY
Henry S. J.	Margaret Christie	28Aug1854	H6 W101 Crampton

McCLASKEY
David	Ann Brownley	21Nov1805	E27 W37
Eliza	Joshua Guyton, Jr.	26Dec1822	E56 W60
Emily	Samuel Pyle	26Sep1844	E87 W87 Finney
Julyan	Ezekiel Morrison	26Jul1831	E69 W71 Morrison
Mary Matilda	Joseph Divers	09Feb1836	E76 W77 Morrison
Mernerva A.	Rich⁴ T. Fergurson	17May1841	E83 W84 Goldsbor

McCLEARY
Andrew	Esther Isreal	01Dec1800	E19 W30
Ann	John Judd	03Mar1824	E58 W62
John W.	Rebecca G. Enlows	17Mar1831	E68 W71 Keech

McCLENAHAN
Patrick	Matilda Brannan	04Jan1853	H3 McNally
[above lic. crossed out]			

McCLENTAN
Martha	Alexander Gordan	16May1780	C2 W4

McCLUIR
Tho.	Margᵗ McCoy	m. 1778	[ret-AppA]

McCLUNG
Charlotte A.	William Wright	22May1849	W93
Ephraim B.	Hannah E. Wiley	24Feb1857	H11 W106 Park
John	Elizabeth A. Heaton	27Jan1857	H11 W105 Dumm
Mary C.	William T. Strawbridge	19Jan1858	W108
Robert	Agnes Bell	20Feb1817	E46 W53
Robert	Mary Payne	03Feb1823	E56 W61
Robert	Elizabeth Bell	20Nov1847	W92
Robt. R.	Hannah A. Cathcart	27Dec1864	W120

McCLURE
Ann	James Spence	06Jan1779	B1 W1
Asenith Ann	Thomas Bay	26Mar1822	E55 W60
German	Charity Quinlan	04Feb1829	E65 W68 O'Brian
German	Ann Maria Garrison	25Oct1836	E77 W78 Dulany
James[?]	Mary Gollaher	m. 1789	[ret-AppA]
James	Sarah Watt	06Jan1823	E56 W61
Margᵗ	Aron McComas	07Jul1784	C9 W9

McCLURE, continued
Margaret	James Quinn	15Mar1827	E62 W66	Poteet
Rachel	William Richardson	30Apr1861	W114	
Thomas	Avarilla Streett	01Feb1825	E59 W63	Morrison

McCLURG
Jane	Patrick Logan	25Mar1840	E82 W83	Finney

McCLUSKEY
Bridget	Andrew Kearney	18Jul1862	W116	

McCOLLIC
And	Mary McDonall	11May1780	C2 W4	

MCOMAS
Clemency [Mcomas]	William Wilson	22Sep1819	E51 W57	
Elizabeth [MComas]	Joshua Rutledge, Senr	25Apr1820	E52 W57	

McCOMAS
Aaron, Jun.	Martha Gilbert	19Feb1798	E13 W27	Jno Allen
Adeline	James Poteet	20Mar1832	E70 W72	Sewall
[orig. lic. to Sewall; cr-Harf]				
Alexander	Mary Streett	17Feb1830	E67 W69	Park
Alexander	Hannah E. Cairnes	04Jan1864	W118	
Amos	Isabella Glenn	20Jun1807	E30 W39	
Ann B.	John W. Pearce	16Feb1854	H5 W100	Dunn
Aqa	Martha Amoss	10Jan1797	E10 W25	
Aquila	Sarah Montgomery	08Dec1807	E30 W40	
Aquila	Mary Ann Wetherall	05Apr1808	E31 W40	
Aron	Margt McClure	07Jul1784	C9 W9	
Caroline R.	Wm H. Calvert	14Jan1828	E64 W67	Finney
Casandra	James Anderson	12Feb1781	C4 W6	
Charles	Mary Gilbert	14Jun1800	E18 W29	
Danl	Martha Johnson	17Oct1781	C5 W7	
Daniel	Elizabeth Scott	18Feb1796	E11 W26	
Daniel	Sophia E. Hunter	24Jan1861	W114	ALJ1-94,142
Elizabeth	Robert Morgan	15Dec1791	E2 W21	
Elizabeth	Isaac Hays	17Aug1801	E20 W31	
Elizabeth	William Smith	10Aug1805	E26 W36	
Ellen	George Gilbert	16Oct1839	E81 W82	Finney
Gabriel A.	Rebecca J. Bradford	11Nov1834	E74 W76	Keech
George	Elizth Guyton	17Dec1827	E64 W67	Keech
Hannah	James Maddox	29Dec1802	E22 W33	
Hannah	James W. Slade	11Dec1813	E41 W48	
Henry	Kezia Araminta Cunningham	07May1840	E82 W83	Prettyman
James	Ann Amos	03Dec1780	C4 W5	
[entry after 19 Dec]				
James	Sarah Howard	27May1794	E5 W23	
James	Susan Green	19Oct1816	E46 W52	
James	Jamima Beaty	27Dec1825	E60 W64	Ewing
John C.	Ann Hunter	07Apr1835	E75 W76	Dulany
John E.	Elenora Sheckell	05Jan1843	E85 W86	Brown
John J.	Mary Martha Long	12Dec1861	W115	
Joshua	Rebecca J/I. Maul	23Sep1856	H10 W105	McCartny

McCOMAS, continued

Josiah S.	Charity Divers	22May1808	E31 W40	
Martha	Parker Gilbert	19Sep1797	E11 W26	[ret-AppA]
Martha	Dixon Slade	23Dec1817	E48 W54	
Martha A.	John J/I. Norris	19Jun1856	H10 W105	Monroe
Martha S.	Bennett Gilbert	03Jun1834	E74 W75	Finney
Mary	Washington M. Slade	06Feb1838	E79 W80	Keech
Mary A.	Robert Bowre	04Dec1849	W94	
Mary Jane	Elijah Hebner	31Dec1859	W111	
Milcah	William Amoss of Thos.	01Jan1803	E23 W33	
N. D.	Elizabeth Onion	23Jul1794	E5 W23	
Nathaniel	Susannah Bradford	05Jun1800	E18 W29	
Nicholas	Matilda Creigh	29Oct1818	E49 W55	
Preston	Hannah Eliza Gough	19Oct1809	E34 W43	
Sarah	Archibald Dorsey	10Oct1820	E53 W58	
Sarah	Christopher Hartman	12Sep1843	E86 W86	Maddox
Sarah E.	James T. Steen	06May1833	E72 W74	Lipscomb
Sarah Elizabeth	John W. Shields	06Mar1858	W108	
Soloman	Elizabeth Hughes	06Feb1837	E77 W79	Finney
Sophia	John Norris, Junr	24Dec1817	E48 W54	
Susan	Abraham Rutledge	03Apr1826	E61 W65	O'Brian
Susan	Robert Martin	29Oct1830	E68 W70	Morrison
Susanna	George Bradford	23May1801	E20 W31	
William	Clare Magness	09Dec1826	E62 W65	Pool

McCOMASS

Alexander	Clemency Presbury	19Apr1784	C8 W9	
Wm	Elizth Gilbert	11Jun1784	C8 W9	

McCOMMONS

Benj. L.	Matilda Ann Miller	20Jun1846	W90	
Edward	Elizabeth Ann Knight	29Jan1848	W92	
Edward	Ann R. Gallion	26Jan1857	H11 W105	Gallion
John	Hannah H. Plummer	25May1841	E83 W84	Gallion
John W.	Phoebe J/I. Grafton	14Feb1856	H9 W104	Cushing
Margaret A/H.	Jacob Bunce	18Aug1864	W119	
Rhody	Aquilla Galion	25Jun1839	E81 W82	Galion
William	Mary A. McMorris	29Apr1851	W96	
Zebulon	Margaret Walker	19Aug1833	E73 W74	Stephenson

McCONGALL

Daniel	Mary McLaughlin	07Oct1799	E16 W28	

McCONKEY

Eliza	Charles D. W. Johnson	11May1822	E55 W60	
Jno. Q. A.	Sarah S. Whiteford	06Dec1860	W112	
Stephen D.	Louisa G. Whiteford	22Feb1855	H7 W102	Lane
William	Susan R. Silver	26Dec1843	E86 W87	Finney

McCONKIE

James	Hetebila Baylis	05Nov1795	E8 W24	

McCORD

Thomas	Priscella Oliver	15Aug1816	E45 W52	

McCORMICK
Caroline H.   Mark A. Earle   24Jun1845 E88 W89
James   Elizabeth Henderson   19Oct1813 E40 W48
James T.   Julian B. Lee   13Jan1853 H3 W99 Cornelius

McCOY
Margt   Tho. McCluir   m. 1778   [ret-AppA]
Richard B.   Nancy Galbreath   16Feb1849   W93
Robt   Cassander Cole   09Jan1797 E10 W25

McCRACKEN
John   Sarah Smith   07Nov1792 E3 W22
Mary   William Magill   15Dec1802 E22 W33
Sally   Jonathan Sutton   15Nov1791 E1 W21
 [see ret-AppA; bn - Sarah]

McCRACKIN
Mary   James Hollingsworth   m. 1777   [ret-AppA]

McCRAKIN
James   Mary Smith   m. 1789   [ret-AppA]

McCREA
David   Bridget Nolan   29Aug1861   W114

McCREARY
Julian   Benjamin Sharp   20Feb1823 E56 W61

MCUBBIN
William   Ruth Cromwell[?]   m. 1803   [ret-AppA]

McCUBBIN
William   Elizabeth Donnond   07Mar1801 E19 W30

MCULBEN
Sarah   Peen Bartonslade   m. 1803   [ret-AppA]

McCULLCH
Ruth   Joseph Everit   30Nov1812 E39 W47

McCULLOUGH
Mary E.   John H. Myers   24Mar1851   W96
Robert   Lydia Yarnall   19Mar1823 E56 W61
William   Rachel Sheridine   04Feb1796 E8 W25

McCUMMINS
Joseph   Sarah McCandeless   06Feb1817 E46 W53

McCUNE
James   Sarah Reed   04Mar1817 E46 W53

McCURDY
Alexander C.   Mary Ann Turner   26Feb1831 E68 W71 Tippet

McCURLEY
Patrick   Sarah Webb   23Feb1780 C1 W3

McDANIEL
Eleanor   Alexander Harvey   m. 1777   [ret-AppA]

McDERMITT
John   Annie Ferry   03Oct1862   W116

McDERMODY
Edward   Matilda Bradley   15Sep1848   W93

McDERMOT
Thomas   Alice Farley   18Feb1853 H3 W99 McNally

McDERMOTT
Mary   Patrick Ghergaty   17Jan1858   W108
Patrick   Rosanna Kelly   23Sep1851   W97

McDONALD
Dennis   Ann Marann   28Jun1854 H6 W101 McNally

McDONALL
Mary   And McCollic   11May1780 C2 W4

McDONNALL
Ann   Andws Turner   [27?]Mar1780 C1 W3

McDOW
Ann Rebecca   William Townsley   15Nov1853 H4 W100 Dumb

McFADDEN [* Mcfadden]
Ann   Philip G. Bagley   22May1865   W121
Daniel [*]   Faithful Foster   15Jan1814 E41 W48
Eliza J.   Alex. Hamilton   11Feb1863   W117
Elizabeth [*]   Joseph Whitson   22Apr1822 E55 W60
Elizabeth   William Bay   01Mar1847   W91
Emily J.   James H. Day   31Jan1861   W113
Hannah   Nathan R. Stokes   13Jan1845 E88 W88 Parks
James A.   Martha M. Hardy   03Oct1864   W119
John   Mary Wann   05Apr1825 E59 W63 Morrison
Laura   William Bay   17Apr1865   W121
Mary [*]   Andrew McAdow   08Dec1808 E32 W41
Saml   Elisa Sharron   18May1857 H12 W106 Monroe
Sarah E.   James K. P. Neeper   08Oct1861   W114

McFADDIN
Saml   Eliza Bonar   m. 1778   [ret-AppA]
William C.[Mcfaddin] Rebecca McVey   17Jul1817 E47 W53

McFADDON
Charles   Elizabeth Wiles   21Jan1833 E72 W73 Stephenson
Robert   Eliza Stillings   24Apr1834 E74 W75 Donahay
Sarah E.   John C. McGaw   29May1856 H10 W105 McCartney

McFADEN [Mcfaden]
Ann   George Carnacle   10Oct1809 E34 W43

McFADON
Mary   Wm H. McGaw   13Nov1827 E63 W66 Finney
  [orig. lic. to Finny; cr-Harf; gn-William H. McGaw; bn-Mary Mcfadan]

McFARLIN
Ellen   Patrick McAtee   25Apr1839 E80 W82 Coskey

McFEELY
Susan   Patrick Boyd   22Jul1851   W96

McGAHEN
John   Ann Carroll   29Jul1794 E5 W23

McGATTAGAN
Thomas   Elizabeth McGavan   28Feb1812 E38 W46

McGAVAN
Elizabeth   Thomas McGattagan   28Feb1812 E38 W46

McGAW
Alice   Daniel Voshan   02Sep1793 E5 W23
Alizanna   Lawson W. Rodgers   05Oct1831 E69 W71 Webster
  [orig. lic. to Webster; cr-Harf]
Eliza A.   Fred. O. Mitchell   24May1864   W119
James   Sarah Bennett   09Aug1806 E28 W38
James   Mary Herbert   02Mar1831 E68 W71 Finney
James, Jnr.   Margaret Ranie   04Feb1834 E73 W75 Finney
Jane   William Hanna   26Mar1818 E49 W55
John   Phebe Gilbert   02Jul1801 E20 W31
John   Mary B. Keen   25Nov1828 E65 W68 Finney
John C.   Sarah E. McFaddon   29May1856 H10 W105 McCartney
Mary Ann   Lilbourn B. Rogers   12Feb1824 E58 W62
Rebecca   Amos Silver   19Jan1820 E52 W57
Robert   Elizabeth Hanson   16Dec1833 E73 W74 Finney
Robert F.   Mary Courtney   28Nov1837 E78 W79 Finney
Robt F.   Susan G. Trigger   06Jan1855 H6 W102 Reese
Samuel   Mrs. Jane Watters   06Jun1827 E63 W66 Finney
William   Caroline Cannon   19Apr1804 E25 W35
William Edward   Louisa A. Boyd   13Feb1862   W115
Wm H.   Mary McFadon   13Nov1827 E63 W66 Finney
  [orig. lic. to Finny; cr-Harf; gn-William H. McGaw; bn-Mary Mcfadan]

McGAY
Rebecca   Bennet Stewart   26Dec1811 E37 W45

McGEE
Sarah   James Jones Willmore   21May1782 C6 W8

McGILL
John   Martha Brazier   09Nov1796 E10 W25
Mary   William Shidle   28Jul1796 E9 W25

McGILTON Jane E.	James H. Hackett	12Oct1826	E62 W65	Pool	
McGIRLL Susanah	Isaac Whitaker	09Sep1794	E6 W23		
McGREGURY Rebecca	John Lee	29Dec1783	C8 W9	cr-Harf	
McGRIGER Lucinda	Edward Kerr	19Dec1810	E36 W44		
McGUIGAN John	Ann Blaney	15Oct1838	E79 W81	Finney	
McGUIRE Ann Patrick	Nathaniel Harpley Margaret Saunders	01Jul1801 18Mar1779	E20 W31 B1 W1		

McHENRY [see Sophia McHenry Hall]

McINTIRE Martha Eliz^th Peter	Sabastian Kurtz Bridget Broadly	17Aug1847 20Feb1852	W91 H1 W97	McNally	
McJILTON William	Ann Nevil	30May1804	E25 W35		
McKARNAN Michael	Martha Garrett	06Jul1802	E22 W32		
McKENDLESS James W.	Elizabeth Walker	02Dec1864	W120		
McKENLY Roger	Eliz^th Johnson	03Sep1780	C3 W4		
McKENNEY John [surname?] John	Mary Hanna Susan Burnes	23Aug1793 11Mar1818	E4 W23 E48 W54		
McKENNY Delia John	John W. Gordon Mary Clark	23Aug1832 12Jul1847	E71 W73 W91	Finney	
MACKEY Mary Ann	John Poole	25Aug1832	E71 W73	Finney	
MACKIE Mary	Nicholas Lewis	23Dec1800	E19 W30		
McKINDLESS Rebecca Ann	Thomas Miller	13Jan1852	H1 W97	Reed	

McKINLEY
Henry	Margaret Meehan	29Jan1855	H6 W102	
Richardrd F. [sic]	Sophia Wiles	02Jun1830	E67 W69	Stephenson

McKINNEY
Thomas	Christian Lancaster	11Apr1785	C10 W10

McKINNIE
William	Ann Maria Grovel	16Sep1834	E74 W75	Finny

McKINNON
Thomas	Eliza Jane Alexander	11Feb1834	E74 W75	Parke

MACKISON
Almira C.	Thomas Trafford	07May1859	W110

McKOEN
Hugh	Hannah Michael	02Jan1821	E53 W58

MACLAIN
Elizabeth	Nathan Hughes	22Sep1807	E30 W39

McLAUGHLIN
Ann	William Welch	16Jun1818	E49 W55	
Danl	Fras. Debrular	10Feb1779	B1 W1	
Danl	Cassandra Steel	06Sep1794	E6 W23	
Francis	John Crawford	16May1782	C6 W8	
George	Margaret Dixon	18Oct1817	E47 W54	
John	Mary Ann Lytle	11Feb1840	E82 W83	Read
Joshua	Mary Louisa McCauley	12Dec1849	W94	
Mary	Daniel McCongall	07Oct1799	E16 W28	
Patrick	Cathrine Campbell	28Sep1784	C9 W9	
Virginia J.	James A. Ward	21Dec1858	W109	

McLURE
William G.	Martha Tate	12Jan1820	E52 W57

McMAHON
Mary	John Fullum	15Jun1861	W114

McMATH
Mary	James Little, Jr.	17Aug1829	E66 W68	Keech
Wm	Sarah Moores	11Dec1792	E3 W22	

McMORRIS
Mary A.	William McCommons	29Apr1851	W96	
William	Mary Gallion	11Nov1830	E68 W70	Tippet

McMULLEN
Robert	Ann Touchstone	30Oct1784	C9 W10

[crossed-out entry for this couple 25Oct1779 B3 in different hand]

McNABB
Alice	John McVey	03Jun1833	E72 W74	Finney
Catharine A.	Joseph M. Harmer	27May1856	H10 W104	Lemmon
Robert	Ann Montgomery	06Jun1804	E25 W35	[ret-AppA]

McNEUSE
Catherine   John Porter   m. 1791   [ret-AppA]

McNIAL
Roger   Cassandra Linch   25Jan1802   E21 W32

McNIECE
Ann   James Harris   24Sep1803   E23 W34

McNIEL
Harriet   Hezekiah B. Smoot   27Jul1826   E61 W65   Keech

McNULTY
Ellen*   John Stanton   04Jan1831   E68 W70   Tippet
    [*Mary crossed out]

McNUTT
David	Susanna J/I. Acres	27Apr1855	H7 W102	Finney
Mary	Mordecai Orr	23Aug1817	E47 W53	
S. Gover	Mary M. Jones	16Jun1847	W91	

MACOMBER
John   Sarah E. Day   27May1862   W116

McPHAIL
Ann   Joseph Adlum   07Nov1798   E15 W27

McPHALA
Margaret   Samuel Scottin   15Jan1806   E27 W37

McVAY
Nancy   William Anderson   17Aug1815   E43 W50

McVEY
John	Alice McNabb	03Jun1833	E72 W74	Finney
Rebecca	William C. Mcfaddin	17Jul1817	E47 W53	
Sarah Ann	Albert Spicer	04Aug1836	E76 W78	Richardson
Sarah Ann	Benedict H. Wakeland	05Jun1856	H10 W105	Rankin

MADDEN
Elizabeth	Evan Evans	17Dec1817	E48 W54
James	Comfort Rigdon	10Dec1801	E21 W31
Jane	John Evans	23Jan1812	E37 W45
Mary	Abel Turner	19[?]Mar1797	E11 W25
(ret'd by Parson Luckie)			
Mary	James Townsley	19Jun1818	E49 W55

MADDOCK
Edward   Rachel Parsons   26Sep1805   E27 W36

MADDON
Hannah Ann   William Curry   02Oct1827   E63 W66   Finney
[orig. lic. to Finney; cr-Harf]

MADDOX
James   Hannah McComas   29Dec1802   E22 W33

MAGANIS
Mary   John Tredwell   05Jan1836   E76 W77   Richardson

MAGAW
Sally M.   John S. Maxwell   01Nov1858   W109

MAGILL
William   Mary McCracken   15Dec1802   E22 W33

MAGNES
Eleanore   Wm Adams   12Feb1782   C5 W7
Elizabeth   John Johnson   02Jan1800   E17 W29
James   Ann Baxter   24Dec1799   E17 W29
John   Martha Morris   30Jul1799   E16 W28

MAGNESS
Albert R.   Amanda F. M. Demoss   31Dec1860   W113
Amelia   William Treadway   21Dec1809   E34 W43
Amelia   William Griffin   07Oct1812   E38 W46
Ann   Wright Sparks   12Sep1805   E26 W36
Benjamin   Mary Turner   23Jun1825   E60 W64   Tidings
Benjamin   Sarah E. Magness   29Jul1830   E67 W70   Richardson
Cassandra   William Price   12May1827   E63 W66   Pool
Charity   William Sawyer   11Jan1819   E50 W56
Clare   William McComas   09Dec1826   E62 W65   Pool
Elijah   Frances M. Robinson   27Dec1855   H9 W103   Cushing
Elizabeth   Thomas Tredway   26Mar1828   E64 W67   Keech
[orig. lic. to Keech; cr-Harf]
James M.   Jane Smith Reed   30Aug1810   E35 W44
James M.   Mary Susan Demoss   01Dec1858   W109
John   Frances Williams   04Apr1837   E77 W79   Richardson
Otho W.   Lydia Bullock   23Aug1827   E63 W66   Keech
Parker   Rebecca Bramble   17Feb1853   H3 W99   Robey
Samuel   Elizabeth Flanagan   08Apr1805   E26 W36
Sarah   Rowland Rogers   03Dec1807   E30 W40
Sarah E.   Benjamin Magness   29Jul1830   E67 W70   Richardson
Temperance   Basil Watters   06Feb1808   E31 W40
Thomas   Mary Lee   15Oct1811   E37 W45

MAGNISS
Rachel   Binjamin Daws   06Apr1783   C7 W8

MAGRAW
Robert M.   Mary Ann Rogers   07Sep1837   E78 W79   Finney

MAHAN

Benjamin[?]	Sarah Gallion	03Oct1827	E63	W66	Finney
Elizabeth	John Criswell	18Mar1808	E31	W40	
Frenetta M.	John T. Cole	20Apr1861		W114	
George	Ann Cole	11Feb1817	E46	W53	
John	Mary Ann Mitchell	17Jul1835	E75	W76	Finney
Margaret	Joseph Townsley	04Jan1785	C10	W10	
Martin	Susan Hunter	09Apr1849		W93	
Sallie F.	James F. Taylor	10Dec1861		W115	
Thomas	Ann Clark	18Dec1851	H1	W97	McNulty
William	Agnes Jones	25Nov1800	E18	W30	
William	Maria Cummins	25Jun1827	E63	W66	Webster
[orig. lic. to Webster; cr-Harf; bn-Cummings]					
William	Mary Hawkins	21Dec1829	E66	W69	Webster
William	Frenetter Gilbert	04Mar1834	E74	W75	Dunahay

MAHON

Elizabeth	William Smith	05Jul1797	E11	W26
Susanna	Thomas P. Frisby	28Aug1811	E37	W45

MAHONEY

Florence	Caroline Burns	27Nov1843	E86	W87	Reid

MAJOR

Jones	Sarah E. Chenworth	07Apr1857	H11	W106	Cushing

MALCOLM

James C.	Elizabeth A. Walker	05Jun1855	H7	W102	Reese
Othman	Mary P. Stockham	26Jun1849		W94	

MALLICK

James	Susan Cullum	01Jan1862	W115
Thos. Wm.	Sarah A. Taylor	15Sep1863	W118

MALONE

Elizabeth	John Rodgers	28Dec1820	E53	W58
Hugh	Ann Cox	07Jun1779	B2	W2

MALSBY

Morris	Mary Lee	16Mar1802	E21	W32

MALTER

John Alphonso	Susan Rogers	06Apr1829	E66	W68	McGee

MANAHAN

Arthur	Ann H. Bay	19Feb1817	E46	W53
James	Maria Ann Brown	07Nov1822	E56	W60

MANAHON

Arthur	Mary Johnson	12Aug1819	E51	W56

MANHONE

Jesse	Susannah Brown	06Nov1802	E22	W33

Harford Co. Md. Marriage Licenses, 1777-1865

MANIFOLD			
Archibald T.	Gemima H. Meads	24Dec1864	W120
MANN			
Catherine	Samuel West	06Jan1820	E51 W57
Susanna	James Harwood	05Sep1811	E37 W45
MANSFIELD			
John	Ellen Cain	14Sep1859	W110
MANTEL			
Eli	Catharine Logue	20Apr1824	E58 W62
MARANN			
Ann	Dennis McDonald	28Jun1854	H6 W101 McNally
MARARTY			
Mary	John Brown	m. 1777	[ret-AppA]
MARKLAND			
Adward D.	Mary Forsythe	10Mar1856	H9 W104 Finney
Mary E.	Lewis McCann	20Sep1861	W114
MARKLEY			
John	Catharine Doxon	03Feb1853	H3 W99 Robey
MARKS			
Mary Minerva	William T. Lewis	18Oct1834	E74 W75 Keech
MARLEIN			
Caspar	Sophia Sitzler	08May1854	H5 W101 Smith
MARSH			
Frances	Silvester A. Silver	20Dec1854	H6 W101 Finney
Thomas	Persis R. Davenport	24Dec1859	W111

MARSHAL [see Marshal Baldwin]

MARSHALL [see Marshall Lee]			
Elizabeth	Andrew Wilson	01Dec1804	E25 W35
Jane	Amos Carman	23Feb1818	E48 W54
Thomas C.	Anna Baldwin	21Sep1858	W108
MARSHELL			
Mary	John Carman	08Feb1809	E33 W42
MARTHARS [marthars]			
Mary	Henry Ruff	26Apr1780	C2 W4
MARTIN			
Andrew	Elizabeth Evatt	23Jul1799	E16 W28
Annie Eliza	John Thos. Price	21Feb1863	W117
Catharine	Oliver Gallup	14Jan1828	E64 W67 Finney
Catharine	John Dana	17Feb1848	W92
Clara R.	Benjamin F. Carroll	06Nov1840	E82 W83 Finney

MARTIN, continued

Cynthia	Richard Everitt	27Nov1806	E29 W38	
Daniel	Priscilla Hopkins	13May1833	E72 W74	Finney
E.	John Bramble	02Mar1852	H2 W98	Norris
Elizabeth	Michael Cole	21Dec1819	E51 W57	
Jane L.	Joseph H. Sank	25Jan1859	W109	
John	Margaret Townsley	04Jun1800	E18 W29	
John	Providence Sheredine	26Aug1824	E58 W62	
John C.	Sarah J/I. Rohrhousen	16Sep1857	H12 W107	Brand
John H.	Susanna Hollis	06Feb1839	E80 W81	Collis
John J/I.	Minerva Jane Kennedy	30Jan1860	W111	
Joseph	Mary Jane Watson	21May1855	H7 W102	Brand
Lewis G.	Susan D. Cole	07Nov1864	W120	
Louisa	Daniel M. Swift	05Jan1839	E80 W81	Reese
Mary	James Miller[?]	30Oct1780	C3 W5	[or Milles?]
Mary	Daniel Swift	10Nov1825	E60 W64	Tidings
Mary	Peter Meehan	12May1855	H7 W102	Walter
Nancy	John Carroll	10May1859	W110	
Nathaniel	Hester Spence	29Sep1835	E75 W77	Gallion
Rebecca	Samuel Rigdon	27Nov1817	E48 W54	
Robert	Susan McComas	29Oct1830	E68 W70	Morrison
Robert L.	Elizabeth Ann Grafton	23Nov1861	W115	
Samuel	Elizabeth Bond	01Feb1860	W111	
Sarah	William Knight	29Jan1812	E37 W45	
Susan	Amos S. Osborn	07Mar1826	E61 W65	Finney
Thomas	Mary Grafton	21Dec1820	E53 W58	
Wakeman	Ann Maria Welch	26Jun1850	W95	
Walter	Nancy Vernay	28Jan1819	E50 W56	

MASK

Edward T.	Rebecca A. Keith	26Feb1855	H7 W102	Anderson

MASKELL [see Maskell C. Ewing]

MASON

Sarah	James Jones	16Mar1802	E21 W32

MASS

Samuel	Caroline Raine	24May1816	E45 W51

MASSEY

Alexander	Mary Bell	14Oct1818	E49 W55
John	Ann Birckhead	24Nov1798	E15 W27
John	Ann Burkhead	09Dec1802	E22 W33

MATHER

Jane	George Bradford	11Dec1804	E25 W35
Joannah	William Ryland	05Dec1796	E10 W25

MATHEWS [see Mathews Dyer]

Ann	Benedict Hanson	27Dec1807	E31 W40	
Carveel	Nancy Mathews	25Jan1796	E8 W24	
Cordelia Jane	William Osborn	24Mar1840	E82 W83	Anderson
Elizabeth	James Billingsley	11Sep1797	E11 W26	
Elizabeth	Jonathan Parsons	18Sep1819	E51 W56	

MATHEWS, continued
Ezekiel	Martha A. Beale	29Oct1855	H8 W103	Smith
Frances	Hudson Wood	20Dec1809	E34 W43	
Frances L.	Alonzo Hollis	18Jun1828	E65 W67	Pool
Harriott	William Paca	23Jun1808	E31 W41	
Josiah	Jane Forwod	16Jan1792	E2 W21	[ret-AppA]
Mary	Wm Hanson	04Nov1781	C5 W7	
Mary Jane	James H. Swartz	25Jan1856	H9 W104	Finny
Milcah L.	Benedict F. Watters	23Nov1818	E50 W55	
Nancy	Carveel Mathews	25Jan1796	E8 W24	
Roger	Elizth Maxwell	23Nov1782	C6 W8	
Roger	Constant Forwood	09Oct1800	E18 W30	
Sarah	John Gemmel	12Nov1849	W94	

MATTHEWS
I. G.	A. Helen Sappington	10Jun1864	W119	
Jacob F.	Catharine Hollis	15May1830	E67 W69	
Jesse	Ann Conn	30Jul1792	E2 W21	
John C.	Martha Hollis	02Aug1831	E69 W71	Sewell
Mary	Benjamin O. Hollis	13Oct1825	E60 W64	
[minister - Isaac Webster; orig. lic. to Isaac Webster; cr-Harf]				
William	Sarah Swart	03Apr1827	E62 W66	Pool
[orig. lic. to Pool; cr-Harf]				

MATTINGLY
John F.	Elizabeth J. Peters	21Nov1847	W92	

MAUL
Hannah	Silas Norris	08May1837	E77 W79	Richardson
Rebecca J/I.	Joshua McComas	23Sep1856	H10 W105	McCartney
Upton R.	Mary Jane Norris	10Nov1828	E65 W68	Keech

MAULSBY
Catherine	James Watkins	04Oct1810	E35 W44	
Elioner	Maurice Maulsby	22Mar1792	E2 W21	
Elizabeth Morris	John Brown	24Feb1808	E31 W40	
Hannah E.	James L. Hambleton	20May1843	E86 W86	Keech
Harriet B.	William Bouldin	13Oct1852	H2 W98	Keech
Israel D.	Jane Hall	08Feb1806	E28 W37	
Margaret M.	Thomas G. Howard	20Nov1823	E57 W61	
Mary C.	William H. Dallam	22Jan1852	H1 W97	Keech
Maurice	Elioner Maulsby	22Mar1792	E2 W21	
Sarah Ann	Thomas B. Amos	16Sep1841	E84 W84	Keech
Sarah Jane	John Yellott	31Jan1838	E79 W80	Keech

MAXWELL [see Maximitton Maxwell Strong, James Maxwell Day]
Ann	Meriken Bond	13Jun1807	E30 W39	
Charlotte	William Bowen	12Jan1819	E50 W56	
Elizth	Roger Mathews	23Nov1782	C6 W8	
Elizabeth	James Wood	08Apr1801	E20 W31	
Frances	Washington Stonebraker	14Mar1854	H5 W100	Finney
Jacob	Leanor Elizth Wilmer	25May1795	E7 W24	
James	Alice B. Gallion	28Dec1824	E59 W63	Webster
[orig. lic. to Webster; cr-Harf]				

MAXWELL, continued

John	Elizabeth Coen	03Nov1817	E48 W54	
John S.	Sally M. Magaw	01Nov1858	W109	
Martha	William Carsins	28Dec1847	W92	
Mary Ann	Benjamin S. Courtney	24Dec1832	E72 W73	Finney
Moses	Ann Wilmer	07Mar1796	E8 W25	
Phoebe	William Silver	06Jul1857	H12 W106	Finney
Ruthen G.	Mary J/I. Brandt	17Jan1853	H3 W99	Sanks
Sarah A.	Benjamin Ferrel	30Nov1857	H13 W107	Monroe
Thomas	Elizabeth G. Kerr	22May1841	E83 W84	Parke
William	Matilda Courtney	05Mar1827	E62 W66	Finny

MAYERS

Elizabeth	Casper Smith	15Jun1859	W110

MAYNADIER

Jer. Y.	Alice L. Fendall	18Apr1865	W121	
John H.	Laura M. Littig	13Dec1855	H8 W103	Poisell

MAYNARD [see Maynard Collins]

MAYNEDIER

Sarah	Amos Waters	03Oct1832	E71 W73	Keech

MAYNES

Sarah	James Laren	03Sep1863	W118

MAYS

Martha	John Hale	m. 1804	[ret-AppA]

MEADE

Mordecai	Mary Baker	20Nov1799	E17 W28

MEADS

Benedict	Mary Miles	25Nov1801	E21 W31	
Elizabeth	William Groves	m. 1788		[ret-AppA]
Gemima H.	Archibald T. Manifold	24Dec1864	W120	
Hannah	John Demoss	13Nov1816	E46 W52	
James B.	Emily Jane Hughes	07Jan1863	W117	
John D.	Sarah Ann Demoss	15Nov1848	W93	

MEANY

Ellen	John Connally	06Oct1848	W93

MECARTY

Hannah	Jacob Collins	25Jun1780	C2 W4

MECHEM

Jonathan E.	Ann Jane Smith	25Dec1860	W113	
Lucretia G.	John Calvin Hanna	22Dec1859	W111	
Naomi J.	Thomas E. Robinson	08Feb1853	H3 W99	Cornelius
Richard	Sarah Priscilla Jones	30Apr1831	E69 W71	Keech
Richard	Lucretia Alderson	03Dec1835	E76 W77	Scott
William	Ellen Moore	31Jan1832	E70 W72	Sewall

MEDCALF
Ann B.   James Potee   22Mar1808   E31 W40

MEECHEM
George   Amanda Ashton   13Dec1832   E71 W73 Keech

MEEHAN
Margaret   Henry McKinley   29Jan1855   H6 W102
Peter   Mary Martin   12May1855   H7 W102 Walter

MEEK
Jane   Robert Creswell   m. 1795   [ret-AppA]

MEEKS
Jane   John Ely   24Dec1792   E3 W22 [ret-AppA]
Martha   John Patterson   23Apr1782   C6 W7   br-Ceisul
Sarah   William Trigger   07Oct1812   E39 W46

MELIKEN
Alisanna   John Taylor   20Jun1779   B2 W2

MELVIL
Mary   John Molton   25Dec1820   E53 W58

MENSAL [see Mensal W. Fulton]

MEPHAM
Sarah M.   Robert Jennings   07Apr1856   H10 W104 Carter

MERCER
Prisilla   Peter B. Grace   04Apr1792   E2 W21

MERIKEN [see Meriken Bond]

MERL
Joseph   Elizabeth Waskey   26Mar1816   E45 W51

MERRETT
Mary   Absolum Galloway   04May1799   E16 W28

MERRICK [see Merrick Barron]

MERRYMAN [see Merryman Streett]
Catharine   Thomas Street   23Jan1813   E39 W47
Polly   Dennis Bond   m. 1787   [ret-AppA]
Rebecca   Lee Tipton   14Oct1818   E49 W55

METZGAR
Christiana F. C.   Clemence Francis Weber 18Jun1840 E82 W83 Golosbrog

METZGER
Caroline   George W. Rogers   14Jun1852   H2 W98 Chapman
Sarah Ann   Ringgold Smith   01May1832   E71 W72 Sargent

MICHAEL

Ann	Barnet Johnson	04Feb1819	E50 W56	
Bennett	Louisa Mitchell	10Jan1846	W89	
Caleb	Ann Eliza Swarts	07Jan1834	E73 W75	Dunahay
Charlotte	John Johnson	12Feb1816	E44 W51	
Daniel	Martha Horner	15Apr1807	E29 W39	
Daniel	Naomi Gilbert	13Jan1820	E52 W57	
Dan¹	Mary Greenfield	03Jul1841	E83 W84	Finney
Daniel G.	Sarah Elizabeth Oliver	19Apr1845	E88 W88	Finney
Elizabeth	John Miller	13Dec1806	E29 W38	
Hannah	Hugh McKoen	02Jan1821	E53 W58	
Henry	Sarah Griffith	10Oct1816	E45 W52	
Henry C.	Cornelia F. Courtney	17Jan1854	H5 W100	Cronin
Henry E.	Effa Courtney	22May1826	E61 W65	Finney
Henry E.	Maria Jane Hollis	28Sep1840	E82 W83	Prettyman
Henry J.	Sarah J. Michael	09May1857	H12 W106	Kinsey
Isabella	Thomas Gallup	07Mar1809	E33 W42	
Jacob	Susanna Crane	28Dec1808	E33 W41	
James	Semelia Cortney	m. 1788		[ret-AppA]
James	Neomi Taylor	25Oct1794	E6 W23	
James	Lizzie Keen	10Feb1863	W117	
James W.	Mary E. Stockham	15Mar1864	W119	
John C.	Ann M. Mitchell	14Apr1856	H10 W104	Finney
Laura E.	Edward R. Price	19Jan1865	W120	
Martha	John Fletcher	24Mar1823	E56 W61	
Martha	Robert L. Mitchell	25Feb1840	E82 W83	Anderson
Mary Ann	William H. Gilbert	29Jan1839	E80 W81	Finney
Mary Ann	James S. Lytle	22Dec1859	W111	
Matilda	William Fletcher	18Mar1830	E67 W69	Finney
Owen	Mary Ann Ashton	14Jan1839	E80 W81	Keech
Patty	Aquila Osborn	13Nov1801	E20 W31	
Sarah	Richard Everist	10Aug1804	E25 W35	
Sarah Ann	John Foy	03Apr1854	H5 W100	Wells
Sarah Elizth	Stephen W. Harkins	22Dec1859	W111	
Sarah J.	Henry J. Michael	09May1857	H12 W106	Kinsey
Skiss	Job Everist	12Mar1808	E31 W40	
William	Ann Judd	08Jul1797	E11 W26	
William	Sarah Johnson	31Mar1815	E43 W50	
William	Charlotte Lauder	29Nov1831	E70 W72	Sewell
William B.	Avarilla A. Courtney	19Dec1847	W92	

MICHELL

John	Issabella Taylor	m. 1789		[ret-AppA]

MIDDELDITCH

Catharine	William Baldwin	09May1849	W93	

MIDDENDORF

John H.	Casander E. Everitt	09Aug1859	W110	

MIDDLE

Elizabeth	James Lawson	06Feb1796	E8 W25	

MIDDLEDITCH

John	Jane Boomer	08Nov1856	H10 W105	Wilson
Lucy Ann	Richard S. Gallion	28Sep1832	E71 W73	Park
Sally	James Baldwin	18Jan1854	H5 W100	Clay

MIDDLETON

A. E. [br]	A. B. Hanson [gr]	29Nov1864	W120	
Theodore J. Webster				
Elizabeth Greenfield Debruler		26Jan1836	E76 W77	Dulaney
Walden G.	Mary Murphy	15Dec1813	E41 W48	
Waldon Gilbert	Avarilla Nabb	13Nov1809	E34 W43	

MIES

Christian	Miny Eck	09Nov1861	W114

MIFFLIN [see Mifflin Beaumont]

MILBURN

James	Elizth Collins	23Sep1782	C6 W8	[poss. Oct]

MILES

Ann C.	Wm Scarff	29Aug1843	E86 W86	Keech
Elanor *	Wm Hutchins	07[?]Mar1781	C4 W6	[or 11Mar]
[* Eleanora crossed out]				
Elizabeth	Ira Curtus	21Dec1826	E62 W65	Rockhold
Hannah	Henry Standiford	05May1865	W121	
Mary	Benedict Meads	25Nov1801	E21 W31	
Thomas	Ann Garrison	19Jun1805	E26 W36	

MILLAR

Mary	Jesse Coale	03Apr1817	E47 W53

MILLER

Adeline	Richard N. Allen	02Sep1828	E65 W68	Keech
Amos	Sally Ann Brannan	23Feb1865	W120	
Annetta	George Barnet	27Jun1828	E65 W67	Keech
[orig. lic. to Keeck; cr-Harf]				
Benjamin F.	Sarah A. Andrew	09Jun1847	W91	
Benjamin F.	Mary A. Andrew	14Apr1858	W108	
Caroline	Samuel Lawder	10Aug1847	W91	
Edward	Sarah Miller	03Mar1801	E19 W30	
Edward	Mary Coale	10May1817	E47 W53	
Eliza	Samuel Lauder	27Feb1833	E72 W73	Finney
Elizabeth	Henry Gilbert	23Jun1819	E51 W56	
Elizabeth	John Knight	23Apr1839	E80 W82	Galien
Elizabeth	Nathaniel Smithson	11Oct1856	H10 W105	Smith
Emeline	Thomas Charles Knight	12Jan1832	E70 W72	Sewall
[orig. lic. to Sewall; cr-Harf]				
George T.	Mary Elizth Andrew	14May1859	W110	
James	Mary Martin	30Oct1780	C3 W5	[or Milles?]
Jesep	Priscilla Robinet	02[?]Mar1798	E13 W27	
Jesse	Mary Lee	17Jun1832	E71 W73	Sewall

MILLER, continued

John	Elizabeth Michael	13Dec1806	E29 W38	
John	Elizabeth Jones	21Dec1808	E32 W41	
John	Mary Ryland	23Apr1822	E55 W60	
John	Mary Ann Baldwin	02Dec1837	E78 W79	Gallion
John	Margaret Shanahan	06Mar1859	W110	
Jo:	Sus^a Chew	05Sep1779	B3 W2	
Joseph	Fra^s Wilson	14Sep1785	C10 W10	
Joseph Henry	Sarah Jane Dorney	22Aug1859	W110	
Leatty	Joseph Hopkins	07Oct1817	E47 W54	
Margaret	William Stump	09Dec1807	E30 W40	
Margaret	Richard Sappington	04Nov1813	E40 W48	
Margaret	Randel Brannen	16Dec1829	E66 W69	Stephenson
Martha	James Russell	02Nov1825	E60 W64	Stephenson
[orig. lic. to Stephenson; cr-Harf]				
Martha J.	John W. Gallion	28May1839	E81 W82	Gallion
Mary Ellen	Samuel Streett	13Feb1855	H7 W102	Carter
Mary Jane	William Henry Wells	13Feb1843	E85 W86	Dulany
Matilda	Chenoweth Tredway	07Feb1827	E62 W66	Webster
[orig. lic. to Webster; cr-Harf]				
Matilda Ann	Benj. L. McCommons	20Jun1846	W90	
Priscilla	Jeremiah Rodgers	26Jan1804	E24 W34	
Rachel	Bennet Fletcher	16Oct1841	E84 W84	Myers
Rachel	William Hawkins	04Feb1852	H1 W97	Cadden
Rebecca	John Hederick	15Dec1835	E76 W77	Richardson
Robert	Margaret Hopkins	12Jan1813	E39 W47	
Robert	Annie Logran	13May1856	H10 W104	Littleton
Samuel	Mary Ann Spencer	06May1830	E67 W69	Stephenson
Sarah	Edward Miller	03Mar1801	E19 W30	
Sarah	Hindley Wilson	21Feb1812	E38 W46	
Thomas	Elizabeth Robinson	10Nov1806	E29 W38	
Thomas	Rebecca Ann McKindless	13Jan1852	H1 W97	Reed
Thomas	R. Caroline Ebaugh	28Dec1859	W111	
William	Elizabeth Spencer	04Apr1809	E33 W42	
William	Rebecca Bowen	09Mar1815	E43 W49	
William	Elizabeth Barton	11Feb1818	E48 W54	
William F.	Catharine Maria Stake[?]	25Feb1822	E55 W60	
[bn-poss. Slake]				

MILLIGAN

Annie	Richard T. Howlett	05Jan1858	W107	

MILLS

Sabina	John Vanzant	15Jul1795	E7 W24	
Thomas	Mary Thomas	m. 1786		[ret-AppA]
Thomas	Harriot Rockhold	12May1814	E42 W49	

MILLWAY

Mary	Michael Farrall	04Dec1837	E78 W79	Crosgay

MILWAKE

John	Sarah Ann Doxon	24Nov1852	H2 W98	Robey

MINNICK
Adaline   John Doyle   01Mar1856 H9   W104 Cushing

MIRIAM
Erastus   Caroline M. Hithcock   24May1853 H4   W99   Smith

MISKIMMON
Elizth Jane Abel Kirkwood   12Jun1843 E86 W86   Cross
Ruth Ann   John H. Kirkwood   25Nov1843 E86 W87   Cross

MISKIMMONS
Rosa   John Donavan   31May1845 E88 W88

MISKIMON
Margaret   Joshua Davis   14Jan1822 E55 W59
William   Mary Carman   08Aug1814 E42 W49

MITCHELL
Alfred   Harriett Bailey   09Feb1835 E75 W76   Finney
Amos A.   Emily J. Gilbert   21Mar1862   W115
Ann   Robert Hawkins   20Jul1797 E12 W26
Ann   John Chesney   27Nov1815 E44 W50
Ann Catherine   Amos Barnes   29Jan1817 E46 W52
Ann E.   Everitt Gilbert Hughes 20Dec1831 E70 W72   Sewall
Ann E.   John C. Michael   14Apr1856 H10 W104 Finney
Anna   William G. Gorrell   27Aug1840 E82 W83   Finny
Avarilla   John Boyd   09Jan1797 E10 W25
Avarilla   John Lilly   10Apr1834 E74 W75   Todrig
Bernard   Elizabeth Anderson   19Jun1827 E63 W66   McElhiney
Catherine   Thos Hutchins 03Oct1779 B3   W2
Catherine   William Yarnel   16Apr1832 E70 W72   Finney
Clemency   John Courtnay   17Mar1801 E19 W30
Clemency   Joseph Hopkins   19Dec1803 E24 W34
Clemency   Gideon Gilbert   09Apr1856 H10 W104 Rankin
Clemency G.   Thomas Brown   01Jul1820 E52 W58
Corbin L.   Christina Ann Gilbert   12Feb1839 E80 W81   Finney
Edward   Margaret Williams   29Mar1821 E54 W59
Edward   Martha Jane Streett   04Dec1844 E87 W88   Keach
Eleanor   John Barnes   29Apr1818 E49 W55
Elijah   Ann Boardsman   01Jun1795 E7   W24
Elisha   Eliza Gilbert   22Mar1832 E70 W72   Finny
Elizth   Samuel Nevel   18Aug1784 C9   W9
Elizabeth   Thomas Herbert   16Feb1807 E29 W39
Elizabeth Sophia   James Ruff   16Oct1816 E45 W52
Evan   Elizabeth Webster   29Dec1807 E31 W40
Evan   Frances Morgan   19Feb1839 E80 W81   Finney
Francis   Mary Jane Hawkins   25May1850   W95
Frederick   Permelia Trago   28Feb1801 E19 W30
Fred. O.   Eliza A. McGaw   24May1864   W119
Geo. W.   Emma C. Willey   15Dec1863   W118
Gerrard   Sarah Ann Gilbert   28Dec1841 E84 W85   Finey
Hannah   Thomas Chesney   18Feb1806 E28 W37
Harriet   John Osborn   25Jan1825 E59 W63   Finney
Harriot   David Silver   03May1815 E43 W50

MITCHELL, continued

Henry	Catharine Larbourd[?]	11Dec1827	E64	W67	Keech
Henry	Susan Holly	27Sep1851		W97	
Henry T.	Mary F. Mitchell	02Aug1850		W95	
James H.	Mary Ann James	07Jun1856	H10	W105	Cushing
John	Hannah Davis	15Jan1806	E27	W37	
John	Ann Martha Gilbert	04Dec1821	E55	W59	
John	Cordelia Arnold	30Apr1828	E64	W67	Webster
[orig. lic. to Webster; cr-Harf]					
John	Eliza Silver	19Mar1831	E68	W71	Finney
John	Ann Eliza Lovett	28Oct1850		W95	
John Adrean	Mary Adalisa White	08Jun1854	H5	W101	Smith
John C.	Sophia Patterson	14Apr1862		W116	
John H.	Telitha Jeffery	29Jan1827	E62	W66	Finney
Joseph G.	Frances A. Davenport	28Oct1863		W118	
Kent	Julia Ann Osborn	01Sep1840	E82	W83	Finney
Louisa	Bennett Michael	10Jan1846		W89	
Lucretia F.	John Craig	12Jan1861		W113	
Lydia	John Fulton	10Dec1799	E17	W28	
Maggie A.	John Harvey	30Jun1864		W119	
Martha	Wm B. Gould	26Oct1792	E3	W22	[ret-AppA]
Martha	Jonathan Dorset	23Jul1807	E30	W39	
Mary	Thomas Walsh	m. 1788			[ret-AppA]
Mary	William James	17Jan1796	E60	W64	Finney
Mary	Samuel Hopkins	24Nov1801	E21	W31	
Mary	George Hoey	20Apr1833	E72	W74	Donahay
Mary A.	John L. Williams	23Jan1864		W118	
Mary Ann	Joseph Dulany	30Dec1820	E53	W58	
Mary Ann	Jacob T. Mohler	19Oct1829	E66	W69	Finney
Mary Ann	John Mahan	17Jul1835	E75	W76	Finney
Mary Eliza	Silas L. Spencer	11Aug1857	H12	W106	Tustin
Mary F.	Henry T. Mitchell	02Aug1850		W95	
Mary Jane	John W. Hamby	25Jan1856	H9	W104	McDaniel
Mary S.	Isaac Willey	08Mar1825	E59	W63	Finney
Minerva Ann	John W. Waram	22Jan1847		W91	
Paca	Charity A. Cole	01Jan1814	E86	W87	Thomas
Rachael	Benjn Everett	01Apr1780	C1	W3	
Rachel	Richard Webster, Junr.	14Apr1800	E17	W29	
Rachel	Thomas Mitchell	24Sep1834	E74	W75	Stephenson
Rachel Elizth	Wm. H. Ewing	04Aug1863		W117	
Rebecca	Ebenezer Brown	03May1832	E71	W72	Finney
Richard	Priscilla Gilbert	12Feb1798	E13	W27	Jno Allen
Richard	Martha Gorrell	26Feb1833	E72	W73	Finney
Robert	Avarilla Hawkins	27Jun1831	E69	W71	Webster
Robert L.	Martha Michael	25Feb1840	E82	W83	Anderson
Sarah	Joshua Guyton	12Jan1781	C4	W5	
Sarah	William Mitchell	20Dec1796	E10	W25	
Sarah	John N. Gilbert	20Feb1839	E80	W81	Finney
Sarah Ann	George Saunders	28Jan1852	H1	W97	Gallion
Sarah E.	William J. Keen	21May1864		W119	
Susan F.	Noah Webster	12Jan1832	E70	W72	Sewall
Susanna	Amos Osborn	30Sep1807	E30	W39	
Sylvester	Sarah Ann Dawson	23Oct1839	E81	W82	Goldsborough

MITCHELL, continued
Thomas	Eleanor Morgan	07Dec1796	E10 W25	
Thomas	Susan Anderson	04Apr1815	E43 W50	
Thomas	Rachel Mitchell	24Sep1834	E74 W75	Stephenson
William	Sarah Mitchell	20Dec1796	E10 W25	
William	Mary Arnold	26Feb1822	E55 W60	

MOFFETT
Hannah   Daniel Ruff   08Dec1801 E21 W31

MOFFIT
Sarah E.   William T. Thompson   22Jan1859 W109

MOFFITT
John T.   Harriett Cullum   26Mar1859 W110

MOHLER
Jacob T.   Mary Ann Mitchell   19Oct1829 E66 W69 Finney

MOHRLEIN [see MOHRLIN, MARLEIN]

MOHRLIN
John   Anne Gebe   06Oct1854 H6 W101 Smith

MOLTON
Elizabeth	Joseph Patterson	23Sep1818	E49 W55	
John	Mary Melvil	25Dec1820	E53 W58	
Mary	Samuel Jones	22Jan1822	E55 W60	
Sarah	John Levi	20Dec1836	E77 W78	Reese

MONAHAN
John	Darkney[?] Waldrom	26Jan1780	C1 W3	
Martha	David Waldrom	11Jun1781	C5 W6	

MONJAR
William   Mary Jones   09Jan1793 E3 W22 [ret-AppA]

MONK
Elizabeth	William York	22May1817	E47 W53	
Jacob Lewis	Caroline Pitt	11Dec1858	W109	
William	Elizabeth Simpson	27Dec1792	E3 W22	[ret-AppA]

MONKS
Elecia M.	Ebenezer N. Allen	19Nov1821	E54 W59	
Eliza	Thomas Grier[?]	13Jan1854	H4 W100	Keech
Eliza C.	Ralph Clark	19Nov1821	E54 W59	
Francis E.	Ann Dawes	05Feb1825	E59 W63	O'Brien
James H.	Gertrude Ecoff	25Jul1857	H12 W106	Keech
James P.	Mary A. Tredway	10Feb1828	E64 W67	Keech
John	Sarah R. Lewis	25Feb1805	E26 W36	
Mary	James G. L. Presbury	27Nov1815	E44 W50	
Sophia	James Lee Morgan	06Apr1802	E22 W32	
William	Elizabeth Ziers	09Jan1807	E29 W38	

MONOHON
Blanch	Moses Preston	06Apr1819	E51 W56
Charlotte	Joseph Price	10Jun1819	E51 W56
John	Elizabeth Thompson	04Aug1810	E35 W44

MONTGOMERY
Ann	Robert McNabb	06Jun1804	E25 W35 [ret-AppA]
Ann	Isaac Stansbury	13Jan1818	E48 W54
Asael	Harriet Ann Wells	23Jul1857	H12 W106 Monroe
Elizth	John Webb	13May1779	B2 W2
Elizabeth	Aquila Amoss	25Apr1804	E25 W35
Ellen	George Moore	06Feb1816	E44 W51
Isaac	Ruth Hargrove	01Oct1798	E15 W27
James, M.D.	Caroline A. Kennedy	06Apr1831	E69 W71 Park
Jane	Nathaniel Durham	15May1854	H5 W101 Wilson
John	Ann Wood	17Jan1822	E55 W60
Mary Ann	William Streett	18Jun1841	E83 W84 Reid
Orpah Ellen	Robert Glenn	11Nov1818	E50 W55
Sarah	Aquila McComas	08Dec1807	E30 W40
William	Mary Ann Butler	08Feb1820	E52 W57

MONTOOTH
Henry	Lucy Ann Rigdon	07Feb1860	W111

MOOBERRY
William	Elisabeth Reardon	09Dec1784	C9 W10
William	Elizabeth Morris	19Sep1796	E9 W25

MOON
Catharine	James Self	20Sep1855	H8 W103 Smith

MOONEY
Hugh	Sarah Ann Bouldin	13Apr1844	E87 W87 Alexander

MOORE [see Ann Moore Baker]
Amanda	Benjamin Shears	18Aug1862	W116
Arsamus	Elizabeth Ann O'Donnell	05Feb1849	W93
Charles	Eliza S. Enfield	26Jan1858	W108
Eleanor	George Woolsey	02Mar1802	E21 W32
Elijah J. B.	Elizabeth L. Cole	11Mar1856	H9 W104 Alexander
Elizabeth	John St. Clair	05Mar1808	E31 W40
Ellen	William Mechem	31Jan1832	E70 W72 Sewall
George	Sarah Rhodes	08Aug1811	E37 W45
George	Ellen Montgomery	06Feb1816	E44 W51
George	Elizabeth Gilbert	15Oct1829	E66 W69 Finney
Hannah C.	William T. Curry	11Dec1857	W107
Harriott	Parker Forwood	04Oct1821	E54 W59
James	Elizabeth Walker[?]	20Jul1780	C2 W4
Jarrett B.	Sarah Cole	23Jan1865	W120
Jason	Deborah Woolsey	30Apr1799	E76 W28
John	Mary Scarbrough	03Aug1797	E11 W26 [ret-AppA]
(Ret'd by Rev. John Coleman)			
John T.	Louisa Wareham	17Oct1855	H8 W103 Smith
Joseph	Mary Ann Boarman	21Apr1828	E64 W67 O'Brien
Leedom B.	Letitia Lemmon	13Sep1853	H4 W100 Lemmon

MOORE, continued
Martha	John Neiper	19Aug1835	E75	W76	Finney
Permelia	William Thompson	20Jan1817	E46	W52	
Robert*	Elizabeth Cameron	23Nov1855	H8	W103	Smith

[*George crossed out]

Sarah	Robert Bryerly	30Dec1782	C7	W8	cr-Harf
Sophia	Jesse Thompson	08Jan1828	E64	W67	Pool
Susan	John Thompson	23Jul1834	E74	W75	Finney
William	Mary Davis	08Nov1810	E36	W44	
William S.	Mary O'Neil	05Dec1845		W89	

MOORES
Daniel	Sally Budd	03Dec1792	E3	W22	[? 3Jan1793]
Mary	James Bryarly	08Dec1817	E48	W54	

[marginal note - "Mr. Clendinen pay^d"]

Sallie R.	Philip Gover	23Feb1854	H5	W100	Keech
Sarah	W^m McMath	11Dec1792	E3	W22	

MORAND
Bridget	James Riley	09Feb1861		W113

MORATTA
Matthew	Cassander Scott	m. 1788[?]		[ret-AppA]

MORDEW
Jame L.	Henry Scarff	14Apr1856	H10	W104	Robey

MORE
John	Elizabeth Brown	11Sep1780	C3	W5

MORETON[?] [see also MOUTON]
Nathaniel	Sarah Copeland	23Feb1798	E13	W27	Jno Allen

MORGAN [see Morgan Richardson]
Ammfield[?]	Benjamin Ward	30Oct1815	E43	W50	
Cassandra Lee	Zacheus Onion Bond	19Jan1797	E11	W26	[ret-AppA]

(Returned by Rev. John Coleman)

Catharine	Charles L. Heck	08Apr1857	H11	W106	Crawford
Eleanor	Thomas Mitchell	07Dec1796	E10	W25	
Eleanor	John Hopkins	15Apr1798	E13	W27	
Eliza	David Carmack	30May1810	E35	W43	
Elizabeth	Henry Richardson	20Mar1782	C5	W7	
Elizabeth Hawkins	John Elliott	11Jun1810	E35	W44	
Frances	Evan Mitchell	19Feb1839	E80	W81	Finney
Hannah	Benjamin Silver of Gersham	14Sep1830	E67	W70	Finny
James	Mary Jane Holland	12Mar1856	H9	W104	Keech
James Lee	Sophia Monks	06Apr1802	E22	W32	
James Lee	Susan Wheeler	19Feb1811	E36	W44	
John C.	Alice M. Payne	14Feb1865		W120	
Josias	Louisa Fink	08Apr1847		W91	
Julia	Edward D. Richardson	13Nov1847		W92	
Juliet	Leonard Macatee	26Nov1818	E50	W55	
Luraner	Josias Slade	20Apr1802	E22	W32	

MORGAN, continued

Lyttleton F.	Susan R. Dallam	25Mar1840	E82 W83	Morgan
Martha H.	Thomas H. Morgan	27Jan1845	E88 W88	Keech
Mary	Ephraim Hopkins	19Oct1802	E22 W33	
Mary	Joseph Rodgers	30Mar1813	E40 W47	
Peggy	Josias Johnson	10Jan1792	E2 W21	
Robert	Elizabeth McComas	15Dec1791	E2 W21	
Robert E.	Mary Johns	03Jan1857	H11 W105	Crawford
Sarah	Joseph Hopkins	12Apr1799	E16 W28	
Sarah	Samuel Richardson	24Mar1805	E26 W36	
Thomas	Hannah Smith	02Feb1813	E39 W47	
Thomas H.	Martha H. Morgan	27Jan1845	E88 W88	Keech
Wakeman F.	Fannie C. Prigg	08Jan1861	W113	
William B.	Sarah Ann Stiles	07Feb1842	E84 W85	Finney

MORRIS [see Elizabeth Morris Maulsby, E. Morris Jenkins, Morris Maulsby]

Ann	William P. Edwards	12Jun1861	W114	
Elizth	Daniel Lain	03Sep1779	B3 W2	
Elizabeth	William Mooberry	19Sep1796	E9 W25	
Elizabeth	Nicholas Allender	29Sep1806	E28 W38	
Elizabeth	Bennet Hopkins	27Mar1848	W92	
Elizabeth	William Brewer	12Sep1860	W112	
Ellen	William Hopkins	07Jan1852	H1 W97	Reed
Isaac	Emily Sweeney	06Jul1814	E42 W49	
Jarrett	Eliza Wright	31Jan1850	W94	
John	Patience Collins	10Apr1781	C4 W6	
Joshua B.	Jane D. Alderson	20Mar1839	E80 W81	
Lizzie	John Botts	09Nov1864	W120	
Lloyd	Rebecca Shordan	24Jul1816	E45 W52	
Martha	John Magnes	30Jul1799	E16 W28	
Mary E.	Ed. H. Amos	11Nov1864	W120	
Phebe	Thomas Turner	09Nov1801	E20 W31	
Rebecca Jane	James O. Jones	13Apr1861	W114	
Susan M.	Charles B. Gilbert	26Sep1859	W110	
William	Susan Norris	30Jan1808	E31 W40	
William	Ann Wilson	30Jul1836	E76 W78	Dulany

MORRISON

Daniel S.	Mary H. Howlett	08Nov1824	E59 W63	Sark
Elizabeth	Robert Bowen	17Oct1816	E46 W52	
Ezekiel	Julyan McClaskey	26Jul1831	E69 W71	Morrison
Jacob	Elizabeth Hunter	03Jan1839	E80 W81	Finney
Jane Ann	Evans Deckman	21Sep1864	W119	
John	Mary Wright	24May1836	E76 W78	Parks
Hannah	Benjamin Willson	[15?]Nov1779	C1 W3	
William	Elizabeth Spicer	16Sep1816	E45 W52	

MORRISSON

John	Frances Webster	01Sep1791	E1 W21	
Martha	Alexander Nower	13Feb1794	E5 W23	

MORSELL

Elizabeth	Thomas J/I. Robinson	25Aug1855	H8 W103	Reese
James S.	Ann Maria Sewell	02Jun1831	E69 W71	Higby

MORTON
Samuel			Ann Harkins		10Nov1849	W94

MOSCOW
Andrew			Eliza Jack		21Mar1818	E49 W55

MOSER
Samuel D.		Margaret Harvey		19Nov1859	W111

MOTT
Daniel A.		Betsy Ann B. Rhodes	31Mar1831	E69 W71 Richardson

MOTTSON
Thomas			Blanche James		14Nov1861	W114

MOULTON
Amelia E.		Joseph H. Wilkinson	06Dec1854	H6 W101 Dumm
Charles W.		Caroline Wilkinson	20Dec1856	H11 W105 Cushing
William			Sarah Taylor		20Dec1826	E62 W65 Robb

MOUTON [or Moreton?]
William			Sarah West		10Nov1784	C9 W10

MOWBRAY
Margaret Ann		James Burkins		26Dec1861	W115

MOXLEY
Basil			Rachel Greenlee		05Oct1808	E32 W41

MULHERN
Margaret		James Murphy		11Jan1843	E85 W86
Michael			Susan Murphy		24Oct1835	E76 W77 Higbee

MULHORN
George			Nancy Bratcher		11Jul1780	C2 W4

MUMFORD
William			Margaret White		28Sep1818	E49 W55

MUMMA
John Thomas		Sarah C. Lemmon		20Oct1852	H2 W98 Yerkes

MUNGER
Peter			Rachel Rigdon		20Feb1813	E40 W47

MUNK
William			Susannah Heirs		23Mar1781	C4 W6

MUNNIKHUYSEN
John A.			Ann Bond		15Dec1829	E66 W69 Richardson
Priscilla E.		Howard B. Bond		14Jan1861	 W113

MUNROE
Rebecca Ann	John Nelson	20Sep1800	E18 W30	

MURPHEY
William	Sophia West	m. 1777		[ret-AppA]

MURPHY
Ephriam H.	Mary Brown	29Jan1842	E84 W85	Cunningham
George W.	Mary D. Keen	31Dec1855	H9 W103	Crampton
Henry	Elizabeth Norris	30Mar1781	C4 W6	
Isaac Thomas	Hannah Bond Bolton	20Dec1848	W93	
James	Margaret Mulhern	11Jan1843	E85 W86	Reid
John	Martha Groenlee	24Sep1806	E28 W38	
John	Mary Crow	26May1853	H4 W99	McNally
John B.	Hester Ann Barnes	28Jul1843	E86 W86	Maddon
Mary	Walden G. Middleton	15Dec1813	E41 W48	
Mary	Michael Murphy	31May1857	H12 W106	Walter
Michael	Mary Murphy	31May1857	H12 W106	Walter
Sarah	James West	24Feb1801	E19 W30	
Simon E.	Susan Scarff	27May1820	E52 W57	
Susan	Michael Mulhern	24Oct1835	E76 W77	Higbee
William L.	Sarah A. Sutton	27May1845	E88 W88	

MURRALL
Joseph	Sarah Neal	18Feb1819	E50 W56

MURRAY
James	Margaret Guyton	18Aug1800	E18 W29	
James	Sarah Biays Stump	30Jan1838	E79 W80	Goldsbrough
John	Mary O'Brian	25Jan1861	W113	
Mary	Samuel Forwood	28Oct1794	E6 W23	
Peter	Elizabeth Bear	26Jan1805	E26 W36	
Sarah	William Carr	05Feb1803	E23 W33	[ret-AppA]

MURRY
John	Sarah Forwood	20Jan1782	C5 W7

MUTCHMER
Susanah	Zachariah Amoss	23Jan1792	E2 W21

MYERS
Ann	William Lievy	22Dec1812	E39 W47	
Elizabeth	John Hutchenson	16Jun1802	E22 W32	
Elizabeth	Joshua Green	10Oct1805	E27 W36	
Harriett	John Whitaker	27Jul1822	E56 W60	
Henry	Elizabeth Bartley	23Oct1816	E46 W52	
Henry [gr]	Allen Scottland [br]	12Jan1847	W91	
John F.	Martha P. Bush	06Sep1852	H2 W98	Robey
John H.	Mary E. McCullough	24Mar1851	W96	
Lavinia	Edward E. Thompson	17Mar1862	W115	
Mary	Richard Barnes	27Sep1808	E32 W41	

NABB
Avarilla	Waldon Gilbert Middleton	13Nov1809	E34 W43	
Catherine	Horatio Strong	04Mar1833	E72 W73	Sewell
Mary	Thomas Spencer	09Jun1801	E20 W31	
Rebecca	James Maxwell Day	03Dec1804	E25 W35	

NACE
John A.	Sally R. Scarff	18Feb1857	H11 W106 Cushing

NAILOR
Thomas	Ann Dale	16Aug1814	E42 W49

NAIMIER
Amelia M.	Jacob Coonrod	21Mar1851	W96

NALOR
Ann	John Herbert	29Jun1822	E56 W60

NASH
Wm	Elizth Davis	12May1782	C6 W7

NEAL
Sarah	Joseph Murrall	18Feb1819	E50 W56

NEEDHAM
William	Jane Pogue	28Aug1795	E7 W24

NEEPER
James K. P.	Sarah E. McFadden	08Oct1861	W114
William A.	Sallie A. Davis	07Jan1863	W117

NEILL
Ann	Thomas Sheredine	19Mar1797	E10 W25	[ret-AppA]
William	Mary Sheredine	02Nov1797	E13 W26	Jno Coleman

NEILSON
James C.	Rosa Williams	29May1840	E82 W83	Goldsbrough

NEIPER
John	Martha Moore	19Aug1835	E75 W76	Finney

NELSON [see Nelson Bedford, Thomas Nelson Binns, Nelson Rosha]
Aqua	Frances Vansickle	14Feb1792	E2 W21	
Bennet	Elizabeth Harris	13Jan1845	E88 W88	Wysong
David	Rachel Baker	16Nov1780	C3 W5	
Elizabeth	John Ruff	01Mar1814	E41 W48	
Elizabeth	Robert Nelson	10Dec1833	E73 W74	Morrison
Geo.	Sarah Watt	19Jun1781	C5 W6	
George A.	Elizabeth A. Gallup	31Dec1860	W113	
James B.	Sarah E. Jarrett	23Jan1860	W111	
James H.	Missouri Wiley	09Apr1859	W110	
John	Rebecca Ann Munroe	20Sep1800	E18 W30	
John M.	Ann Jane Fullerton	27Oct1825	E60 W64	Tidings
Lydia A.	Francis Chafman	11Nov1852	H2 W98	Smith

NELSON, continued
Martha	Aquila Drew	21Jan1812	E37 W45	
Martha E.	Nicholas Hutchins	29Nov1847	W92	
Rebecca	Matthew Wiley	22May1781	C5 W6	
Robt	Sarah Johnson	20May1781	C5 W6	
Robert	Sarah Johnson	20Jun1781	C5 W6	
Robert	Elizabeth Nelson	10Dec1833	E73 W74	Morrison
Sarah	Cyrus Osborn	17Dec1805	E27 W37	
Sarah	William Glenn, Junr	29Nov1824	E59 W63	Morrison
Sarah	James Hope	24Feb1836	E76 W77	Morrison
Sarah E.	Abraham Cole	07Jun1847	W91	
William	Elizabeth Stansbury	16Apr1838	E79 W80	Cross

NEPER
Susan	Joshua R. Streett	29May1848	W92	

NEVEL
Samuel	Elizth Mitchell	18Aug1784	C9 W9	

NEVIL
Ann	William McJilton	30May1804	E25 W35	

NEVILL
Ann	Preston D.[?] Parke Taylor			
		14Mar1842	E84 W85	Finney
John	Elizabeth Bateman	09Nov1818	E50 W55	
Martha C.	Jonas Coale	06Feb1844	E87 W87	Thomas
Rachel	Samuel Norton	05Jun1824	E58 W62	
[orig. lic. to Webster; cr-Harf]				
Rebecca	Gilbert Holloway	31Dec1812	E37 W45	
Susana R.	John W. Wells	28Oct1840	E82 W83	Prettyman
William	Cassandra Davis	18Jan1809	E33 W42	

NEVILLE
Elizabeth W.	Samuel H. Bateman	19Dec1853	H4 W100	Dumb
Sarah	Thomas B. Bateman	02Jan1849	W93	

NEWGENT
Sylvester	Eliza Ann Aldridge	13Dec1826	E62 W65	Richardson

NICHOLS
James	Charlotte Saunders	28Jul1784	C9 W9	
Thomas	Martha Carter	16Jun1796	E8 W25	
William E.	Sarah H. Rickey	21Nov1861	W114	

NICOLS
Drucilla Durbin	Isaac Kelly	02Apr1801	E20 W31	

NOBLE [see Noble Cannon, Noble Rider]
Elizabeth	Scott Griffith	21May1812	E38 W46	
James	Mary West	12Dec1780	C3 W5	"Wheat"
James	Mary Fletcher	24Jan1823	E56 W61	
James	Elizabeth Gilbert	27Sep1837	E78 W79	Finney

Harford Co. Md. Marriage Licenses, 1777-1865   183

NOBLE, continued
Mary F.	Richard A. Barnes	13Mar1861	W113	
Pamelia	William Wilson	01Apr1826	E61 W65	Webster
[orig. lic. to Webster; cr-Harf]				
Thomas	Sarah Tuston	08Feb1826	E61 W64	Stephenson

NOGGLE
Daniel	Rebecca Buxster	24Mar1839	E80 W81	Dulaney
Manuel	Deborough Shannon	15Oct1846	W90	

NOLAN
Bridget	David McCrea	29Aug1861	W114

NOONAN
Sidney Almira	Washington Chinoworth	04Dec1845	W89

NORRINGTON
Mary	Joshua Wakelin	10Mar1819	E50 W56	
Mary Ann	Jesse Grafton	26Aug1829	E66 W69	Richardson

NORRIS [see Norris Chinworth, Norris Lester]
Alexander	Cornelia Norris	27Nov1832	E71 W73	Richardson
Amanda A.	William B. Norris	25Jun1827	E63 W66	Morrison
Aqa	Sarah Norris	25Nov1778	B1 W1	
Aquila	Mary Dutton	22Dec1804	E25 W35	
Cardiff D.	Mary F. Dutton	28Jun1834	E74 W75	Richardson
Catherine T.	Richard F. Hollis	21Oct1813	E40 W48	
Cecilia	Hiram Beaumont	02May1854	H5 W101	Finney
Charles	Mary Gafford	26May1810	E35 W43	
Cornelia	Alexander Norris	27Nov1832	E71 W73	Richardson
Cornelia	Daniel Scott	17Nov1863	W118	
Daniel	Frances Hughs	18Aug1792	E3 W21	
David	Mary Clowman	05Nov1829	E66 W69	Finney
David Lee	Laura A. Calwell	12Oct1857	H12 W107	Myers
Davis	Cecelia White	09Nov1815	E43 W50	
Edward	Rebecca Lee	14Dec1799	E17 W28	
Eliza Ann H.	William B. Smith	27Nov1855	H8 W103	Dumm
Elizabeth	Henry Murphy	30Mar1781	C4 W6	
Elizabeth	Franklin Hazlet	30Dec1857	W107	
Elizabeth Ann	Charles Duer	31Jan1826	E60 W64	Keeck
George	Margaret Riely	01Jun1809	E34 W42	
Hannah	George W. Anderson	22Jul1812	E38 W46	
Isaac	Elizabeth Jordan	27Apr1807	E29 W39	
Jacob	Avarilla Gallion	30Mar1784	C8 W9	
James	Ann Everett	19Apr1782	C6 W7	cr-Harf
John	Sarah Richardson	18Feb1784	C8 W9	cr-Harf
John	Ann Wadsworth	10Sep1799	E16 W28	
John, Junr	Sophia McComas	24Dec1817	E48 W54	
John C.	Caroline S. Calwell	26Nov1827	E63 W66	
[minister - Breckenridge?]				
John J/I.	Martha A. McComas	19Jun1856	H10 W105	Monroe
John W.	Susan E. Billingslea	14Jan1860	W111	
Joshua	Elizabeth Smith	30Sep1813	E40 W48	
Lathen	James Tyrrell	12Dec1801	E21 W31	

NORRIS, continued

Luther Augustus	Mary Hollis	22Jul1819	E51 W56	
Martha	Wm Norris	24Dec1779	C1 W3	
Martha	Enoch Churchman	01[?]Feb1792	E2 W21	
Mary	John Stockdale	06Oct1806	E28 W38	
Mary	William J. Wann	03Dec1835	E76 W77	Keech
Mary Ann	James Gammel	19Dec1837	E78 W80	Park
Mary Elizabeth	Geo. W. Hunter	26Oct1843	E86 W86	Mattox
Mary Jane	Upton R. Maul	10Nov1828	E65 W68	Keeck
Moses	Nancy Ruff	29Dec1845	W89	
Otho	Cornelia Wright	21Dec1824	E59 W63	Morrison
Rachel	Samuel Stubbins	06May1851	W96	
Reese	Susan Dutton	29Oct1804	E25 W35	[ret-AppA]
Robert W.	Catharine Young	06May1844	E87 W87	Little
Samuel	Frances Ann Sanders	22Jan1861	W113	
Sarah	Aqa Norris	25Nov1778	B1 W1	
Septimus	Cassandra Stump	27May1837	E78 W79	Goldsborough
Silas	Hannah Maul	08May1837	E77 W79	Richardson
Silas	Elizabeth Cunningham	28Feb1861	W113	
Sophia	John Johnson	08Jan1827	E62 W65	Richardson
Sophia C.	Benjamin F. Ebaugh	14May1831	E69 W71	Finney
Susan	William Morris	30Jan1808	E31 W40	
Susan	Daniel Cunningham	08Feb1815	E42 W49	
Susan G.	Wm P. Taylor	04Jan1843	E85 W86	Wilson
Susanna	John Duer	13Sep1811	E37 W45	
Thomas	Elizabeth Shaw	12Mar1827	E62 W66	Rockhold
Wm	Martha Norris	24Dec1779	C1 W3	
William	Eleanor Knight	13Jun1826	E61 W65	Stephenson
William	Elizabeth Payne	02Dec1864	W120	
William B.	Amanda A. Norris	25Jun1827	E63 W66	Morrison

NORTH

Edward	Emma P. Paul	10Sep1863	W118	

NORTON

Elizabeth [B.] * [*"B" crossed out]	Philip A. Barton	03Feb1803	E23 W33	[ret-AppA]
Samuel [orig. lic. to Webster; cr-Harf]	Rachel Nevill	05Jun1824	E58 W62	

NOWER

Alexander	Martha Morrisson	13Feb1794	E5 W23	

NOWERS

Ann	Jacob Hanson	02[?]Sep1793	E5 W23	

NOWLAND

Elias	Charlotte Collins	26Oct1809	E34 W43	
Eliza	George Starck	13Nov1810	E36 W44	
John	Ann Gassaway	28Jan1802	E21 W32	
Nancy	Nathan Swain	27Oct1801	E20 W31	
Perrgrine	Naomi Kimble	02Jul1816	E45 W51	

Harford Co. Md. Marriage Licenses, 1777-1865

NUMBERS
James	Mary Griffin	23Dec1817	E48 W54	
James	Sarah J. Taylor	24May1858	W108	
Margaret	Alanson Cole	02Jun1847	W91	
William	Emeline Griffin	05Aug1844	E87 W87	Eggy
Zena	Joshua Griffin	22Jul1846	W90	

NUN [see Richard Nun Allen]

NURSE
William	Isabella Bond	03Sep1840	E82 W83	Prettiman

NUTTERVILLE
Aramenta	George Debruler	11Jul1791	E1 W21

OATMAN
John	Sarah Lee	19May1825	E60 W63	Webster

[orig. lic. to Webster; cr-Harf]

O'BRIAN
Mary	John Murray	25Jan1861	W113	
Patrick	Julia Ann Hayes	15Aug1856	H10 W105	Walter
Thomas	Ann Wilson	05Aug1862	W116	

O'BRIEN
Catharine	John Rogers	26May1849	W94	
Charles	Mary Young	10Mar1806	E28 W37	
Cornelius	Margaret Gilbert	26Feb1835	E75 W76	Hoopman
Hanora	Daniel Holmes	07Jan1851	W96	
James	Mary Wareham	24Mar1810	E35 W43	
Margaretta [Obrien]	Samuel J/I. Riley	04May1821	E54 W59	
Mary H.	Harry D. Gough	31Dec1822	E56 W60	
Owen	Anne Oneale	07May1814	E42 W49	
Richard	Ellen Cruise	03Sep1850	W95	

O'CONNOR
John	Ann Hall	17Jun1813	E40 W47

O'DONNELL
Edward	Ann Maria Green	08Feb1836	E76 W77	Crosgay
Elizabeth Ann	Arsamus Moore	05Feb1849	W93	
George	Ann Wann	20Nov1845	W89	
John	Martha Turk	13May1807	E29 W39	
John	Mary E. Rider	27May1847	W91	
Martha Ann	John M. Blake	09Feb1861	W113	
Martha E.	Benedict T. Bussey	17Aug1857	H12 W106	Walter

O'HENRY
Henry	Ann Price	27Jul1797	E11 W26	[ret-AppA]

O'KEEF
Thomas	Catharine Ward	01Apr1856	H10 W104	Walter

OLDHAM
L or S ---[?]   Robt Willson   18Apr1782 C6 W7   cr-Harf

OLIVER
Ann   William T. Stewart   21Sep1846   W90
Frances Ellen   Benjamin S. Hastings   12Jun1860   W112
Priscella   Thomas McCord   15Aug1816 E45 W52
Sarah Elizabeth   Daniel G. Michael   19Apr1845 E88 W88 Finney

OLLIVER
James   Susannah Armstrong   25Feb1780 C1 W3
James   Sarah Cord   m. 1788   [ret-AppA]
Susannah   Garrett Garrettson   18Sep1784 C9 W9

ONEALE [Oneale]
Anne   Owen O'Brien   07May1814 E42 W49

O'NEIL
Mary   William S. Moore   05Dec1845   W89
Wiliam   Eliza J. Leator   22Nov1843 E86 W87 Billup

O'NEILL
Barney   Mary Donohoo   30Oct1860   W112
John H.   Mary W. Greene   24May1849   W94
Matilda   John Wood   31May1815 E43 W50

ONINS[?]
Thomas   Mary Dunn   02Sep1797 E11 W26 [gn Annis?]

ONION [see Zacheus Onion Bond]
Charity   John Divers   03Jan1804 E24 W34 [ret-AppA]
Corbin L.   Minerva Temple   02Apr1855 H7 W102 Keech
Corbin Lee   Mary Smithson   18Mar1806 E28 W37
Elizabeth   N. D. McComas   23Jul1794 E5 W23
Lloyd Day   Elizabeth Rouse   22Oct1825 E60 W64 O'Brien
Mary S.   Samuel A. Temple   19Jan1860   W111
Patty   Harry Gough, Esq.   m. 1788[?]   [ret-AppA]
Rebecca Weston   John C. Watters   10Nov1812 E39 W46

ORAM
Lizzie   George Dillman   26Jan1865   W120
Samuel   Charity Ledley   m. 1803   [ret-AppA]

ORCHARD
William H.   Sophia Belton   29Apr1834 E74 W75 Orchard

ORR
Jonathan   Mary Ann Foster   15Jan1841 E83 W84
  [minister - Goldsborough?]
Mordecai   Mary McNutt   23Aug1817 E47 W53
Robt   Ruth Crawford   09Aug1794 E5 W23 [ret-AppA]
Sarah   David Wilson   14May1816 E45 W51

ORTH
John P.	Catharine Kaiser	19Sep1856	H10	W105	Alexander

OSBORN
Adaline	Charles G. Baker	22Jan1849		W93	
Amos	Susanna Mitchell	30Sep1807	E30	W39	
Amos	Phoebe Silver	19Jan1835	E75	W76	Finney
Amos S.	Susan Martin	07Mar1826	E61	W65	Finney
Ann	John Wood	01May1797	E10	W26	
Ann	Elisha Greenland	23Feb1826	E61	W64	Stephenson
Anna Mary	Richard H. Carr	19Jan1850		W94	
Aquila	Patty Michael	13Nov1801	E20	W31	
Benjn	Elizth Garrison	08Apr1780	C1	W3	
Benjamin	Elizabeth Garrettson	22Apr1780	C2	--	
Bennet	Harriet M. Jackson	22Apr1858		W108	
Caroline M.	James Riley	16Jun1819	E51	W56	
Charles	Annie M. Wells	03Oct1861		W114	
Cyrus	Martha Warfield	25Nov1795	E8	W24	
Cyrus	Sarah Nelson	17Dec1805	E27	W37	
Cyrus	Sarah S. Silvers	26May1840	E82	W83	Finney
Elisha	Hannah Birckhead	30Jul1804	E25	W35	
Eliza	John Galloway	06Apr1831	E69	W71	Finney
Elizabeth	Gregory Barnes	m. 1788			[ret-AppA]
Elizabeth	William H. Divers	29Nov1827	E63	W67	Webster
Elizabeth	Thomas M. Wilkinson	02Dec1850		W95	
Eugenia A.	Lewis H. Todd	28Dec1843	E86	W87	Finney
Frances	Amos Hollis	22Mar1823	E56	W61	
George	Susanna Hawkins	08Feb1827	E62	W66	Stephenson
George V.	Martha Thompson	08May1863		W117	
Harriet C.	Mensal W. Fulton	18Apr1850		W95	
Jacob	Elizabeth Johnson	30Jun1847		W91	
James H.	Sarah White	06Jul1820	E53	W58	
John	Elizabeth Stewart	27Oct1794	E6	W23	
John	Harriet Mitchell	25Jan1825	E59	W63	Finney
Julia Ann	Kent Mitchell	01Sep1840	E82	W83	Finney
Louisa	Luther M. Stuart	01Dec1848		W93	
Martha	James Garrison	05Jan1780	C1	W3	
Martha	Cornelius Cole	09Jun1808	E31	W41	
Martha Rebecca	Daniel B. Chesney	11Feb1845	E88	W98	Rohr
Mary Ann	Ford Barnes	01Jan1822	E55	W59	
Mary Elizth	James L. Donohoo	27Jan1862		W115	
Owen	Sarah E. Taylor	02Dec1851	H1	W97	Gibson
Rebecca	Aquila Deaver	17Dec1805	E27	W37	
Sarah	Samuel B. Silver	15Dec1832	E71	W73	Finney
Sarah Ann	William Z. Silver	23Apr1850		W95	
Susanna	David Crane, Junr	17Mar1795	E7	W24	
Susanna	Richard Barnes	21Jan1832	E70	W72	Finney
Wm	Ann Lytle	16Dec1780	C3	W5	"Wheat"
William	Harriot Barnes	30May1809	E34	W42	
William	Cordelia Jane Mathews	24Mar1840	E82	W83	Anderson

OSBORNE
Harriet	Edwin Ewing	12Jul1843	E86	W86	Finney
Robert A.	Mary M. Silver	01Apr1851		W96	

OSMOND
Mary E.   George W. Fletcher   13Mar1865   W121

OTHMAN [see Othman Malcolm]

OTLEY
Jehue   Lydia Dean   22Mar1796 E8 W25

O'TOOLE
Bridget   Patrick Foley   22Sep1853 H4 W100 McNally

OWENS
Robert   Susannah Green   06Jan1800 E17 W29

OZMAN
Henry   Ann Wareem   14Nov1832 E71 W73 Finney
Mary Matilda   Henry C. Johnson   11Feb1862   W115

PACA [see Paca Mitchell, Paca Smith]
James   Ann Rieley   16Jan1810 E34 W43
John   Sarah Winston Dallam   13Sep1804 E25 W35
John W.   Cassandra Gilbert   06Dec1858   W109
Margaret   Jesse Cromwell   16Nov1799 E17 W28
Priscilla   Richard B. Dallam   25Mar1799 E15 W28
William   Harriott Mathews   23Jun1808 E31 W41
William   Elizabeth Wilges   14Aug1833 E73 W74 Dunahay
William   Ann Flowers   13Sep1838 E79 W80 Richardson

PAGE
Joseph   Charity Gallion   20Dec1861   W115

PAIN
John   Ellen Bosley   12May1834 E74 W75 Parks

PALMER
John, Jr.   Victoria Billingslea   16Jan1859   W111

PANNELL
Ann   James Silver   21Oct1846   W90
Emily M.   Benjamin Silver   02Feb1846   W89
Isabella W.   A. Henry Strasbaugh   30Oct1862   W116
Jane   John A. Silver   04Jan1845 E87 W88 Finney
Susan S.   Silas B. Silver   25Nov1857 H13 W107 Finney
William F.   Mary Ellen Slee   13Jan1852 H1 W97 Finney

PARKE [see Preston D. Parke Taylor]

PARKER [see Parker Gilbert, Samuel Parker Hopkins,
          Parker Hall Lee, Parker Magness]
Aq^a Sarah Amoss   03Mar1779 B1 W1
Eleanor   Charles Burkin   m. 1778   [ret-AppA]
Elizth Edmund Talbott   10Oct1779 B3 W2
Hester S.   Charles Watters Jacobs   02May1833 E72 W74 Hinkle
Hesther   Wm Stevenson   04Apr1796 E8 W25

PARKER, continued
James H.	Alice Lee	25Jun1861	W114	
John	Sarah Jones	26Aug1779	B3 W2	
Joseph C.	Sarah Stephenson	03Jun1835	E75 W76	Furlong
Margaret A.	Edward Wilson	11Jan1856	H9 W104	Finney
Mary R.	John H. Price	24Nov1838	E80 W81	Johns
Robert	Ann Stephenson	29Jan1800	E17 W29	
Robert	Rachel Price	29Apr1828	E64 W67	Stephenson
Samuel	Martha Pike	12Mar1810	E35 W43	
Sarah	Lewis H. Barron	25May1855	H7 W102	Finney

PARKS
Frederick	Elizabeth Cross	30Jul1817	E47 W53

PARLETT
Elizabeth E.	Thomas H. Poteet	28Jul1862	W116	
James	Mary Pearce	28Nov1837	E78 W79	Richardson
Washington	Ariel Standiford	06Dec1836	E77 W78	Richardson

PARMER
Elizabeth	Jehu Brown	29Dec1824	E59 W63	Finney
John[?]	Sarah Smith	27Jan1780	C1 W3	

PARR
Tamer	Jacob Lustater	31Jul1795	E7 W24

PARROTT
David	Rebecca Jane Gildea	12Oct1824	E58 W63

PARSONS
Amanda	John Holley	20Apr1846	W90
Caroline	Isaac Watters	11Sep1823	E57 W61
John	Elizabeth Street	29Aug1815	E43 W50
Jonathan	Elizabeth Mathews	18Sep1819	E51 W56
Mary	James Riggin	04Apr1810	E35 W43
Rachel	Edward Maddock	26Sep1805	E27 W36

PARTRIDGE
William	Rosanna Wilmer	29Mar1806	E28 W37

PATHRE
Samuel	Hannah Brannan	28Mar1864	W119

PATTEN
John	Matilda Ayres	01May1827	E63 W66	Barton

PATTERSON [see Patterson Bane]
Armintus T. [poss. 09Mar1857]	Hannah E. Hanna	11Mar1857	H11 W106	Finney
Fras	James Hammond	23Apr1781	C4 W6	
George	Bethia Presbury	m. 1778		[ret-AppA]
John	Avarilla Hall	08Feb1780	C1 W3	
John	Martha Meeks	23Apr1782	C6 W7	cr-Ceisul
John C.	Laura A. Webster	18Jun1861	W114	
John N.	Elizabeth Watkins	31Mar1851	W96	

PATTERSON, continued
Joseph	Elizabeth Molton	23Sep1818	E49 W55	
Joshua S.	Delila Grafton	17Oct1816	E45 W52	
Mary Frances	William Fulford	18Jun1804	E25 W35	
Matilda	John Whitaker	16Aug1827	E63 W66	Keech
Robert	Elizabeth Wheeler	03Jul1816	E45 W51	
Sophia	John C. Mitchell	14Apr1862	W116	
Susan	Aquila Thompson	22Nov1810	E36 W44	
William P.	Frances Gould	19Feb1810	E35 W43	

PATTON
John	Mary Ann Ely	19Oct1857	H13 W107	Kethcart
William H.	Frances Elizth Gilbert	26Apr1862	W116	

PAUL
Emma P.	Edward North	10Sep1863	W118	
Fanny	William Booth	18Jun1856	H10 W105	Smith
John	Sarah Hooper	22Jun1822	E55 W60	
Martha	William G. Dove	16Jan1816	E44 W51	
Rebecca	William Tucker, Junr	25Jan1816	E44 W51	
Susan N.	James Spicer	10Jan1822	E55 W59	

PAULT
Anthony	Agnes Stonerider	19Jun1846	W90

PAYNE
Alice M.	John C. Morgan	14Feb1865	W120	
Benjamin N.	Mary Cathcart	16Jan1829	E65 W68	Park
Elizabeth	William Norris	02Dec1864	W120	
Henry C.	Margaret J. Baldwin	26Dec1862	W117	
Josias	Amanda Z. Hutchins	09Mar1837	E77 W79	Parks
Mary	Robert McClung	03Feb1823	E56 W61	
Mary E.	David A. Edie	25Feb1856	H9 W104	Smith
Sophia C.	Jesse Riston	20May1844	E87 W87	Jones

PEARCE
Cassandra	Isaac Webster	29Jan1783	C7 W8	cr-Harf
George E.	Harriett Burnett	22Feb1864	W118	
John W.	Ann B. McComas	16Feb1854	H5 W100	Dunn
Margarett	William Robinson, Jn^r	20Jan1820	E52 W57	
Mary	James Parlett	28Nov1837	E78 W79	Richardson
Sarah	David Gillaland	19Dec1834	E74 W76	Richardson
Stephen	Catharine Allen	21Feb1825	E59 W63	Allen

PEARSE
Andrew	Cloe Everit	15May1799	E16 W28

PEARSON [see Elisha Pearson Amos]
Enoch	Margaret Reese	01Jan1818	E48 W54
Enoch, Junr	Ann Jay	22Jan1819	E50 W56
Marjarum	Ralph Ady	17Nov1812	E39 W47

PENDERGAST
Alisannah	Ja^s Coaleman	27Dec1780	C4 W5

Harford Co. Md. Marriage Licenses, 1777-1865

PENDIGAST
Margaret   James Tweedale   30May1854 H5 W101 McNally

PENNELL
Jonathan   Mary Ann Sunderland   30Apr1841 E83 W84 Cullum

PENNIMAN
Thomas   Delia M. Hall   05May1829 E66 W68 Keech

PENNINGTON
Ann   John Vanzant   12Mar1804 E24 W35
Harriot   William Foard   25Mar1817 E47 W53
Isaac   Cassandra Cummins   17Mar1802 E21 W32
Lambert   Hannah E. Wetherall   09Jun1864   W119
Samuel W.   Jane Herbert   25Jan1815 E42 W49
William C.   Henrietta Reed   26May1846   W90

PEPOO
Amanda A. C.   John Casper Hohn   14May1861   W114

PERDUE
Elizabeth   John Ayres   15Apr1847   W91

PERINE
Margt   Aqa Grafton   08Aug1779 B3 W2

PERKINS
Ann   Samuel Forwood   13Jun1795 E7 W24
Wm   Sarah Knight   09Jan1779 B1 W1

PERRY
Fras   John Saunders   19Aug1779 B3 W2
William   Mary Griffith   13Aug1799 E16 W28

PERRYMAN
Caroline E.   Jacob A. Preston   29Apr1834 E74 W75 Higbee
Elizabeth   Nathaniel Henderson   12Sep1792 E3 W22 [ret-AppA]
Emily   George Griffith   16Nov1813 E41 W48
George H.   Isabella A. Gover   11Dec1832 E71 W73 Higby
Isabella   Savington W. Crampton   28Jan1858   W108
John   Cassandra Horner   17Oct1791 E1 W21 [ret-AppA]
Martha   Mathew Hawkins   27Jul1815 E43 W50
Sarah R.   George Finley   21May1821 E54 W59

PETERMAN
Mottelenor   Joseph C. Carver   07Nov1820 E53 W58

PETERS
Elizabeth J.   John F. Mattingly   21Nov1847   W92
Ephemia   James W. Poplar   09Aug1849   W94
Sarah A.   George W. Carver   09May1853 H3 W99 Brill

PETERSON
James   Rennis Judd   06Mar1861   W113
Thomas J/I.   Sarah R. Criswell   05Apr1853 H3 W99 Keeck

PHELPS
Francis P.   Mary R. Springer   09May1853 H3 W99   Finney

PHESAY
Sarah   Evan Thomas   06Mar1784 C8 W9

PHILIPS
James M.   Eliza E. Troutner   19Dec1864   W120
Stephen J.   Lucretia Arthur   26Aug1861   W114

PHILISON
Sarah   Anthony Debruler   m. 1778   [ret-AppA]

PHILLIPS
Cordelia   Jacob Edward Giles   23Dec1808 E32 W41
Elizabeth   Thomas Archer   08Jun1803 E23 W33
Isaac   Sarah Phillips   30May1783 C7 W8   cr-Harf
James   Sarah Wilmer   18Aug1808 E32 W41
Jane   William N. Cathcart   20Oct1863   W118
Martha   Jacob Washington Giles   15Nov1802 E22 W33
Sarah   Isaac Phillips   30May1783 C7 W8   cr-Harf
Sarah P.   Francis J. Dallam   02Mar1815 E42 W49
Susannah   William Smith   26Nov1792 E3 W22   [ret-AppA]

PHIPPS
Mary   Henry McCausland   05Apr1809 E33 W42

PHISON
John   Martha Armstrong   16Jun1779 B2 W22

PHRISBY
Sarah   John Ferrell   05Sep1792 E3 W22
     [ret-AppA; gn poss. Fevrel or Fenell]

PICKET
Francis   Cathrine larkin [sic]   13May1780 C2 W4

PIERCE
John Y.   Rachel Ady   09Nov1850   W95
Mary   Jno Debruler   m. 1778   [ret-AppA]
Rebecca   Norris Chinworth   20Feb1822 E55 W60
Richard   Mary L. Sherdan   15Aug1860   W112

PIERSE[?]
Thomas   Mary Wilson   09Mar1793 E4 W22

PIKE
John Lewis   Martha Webster   06Aug1801 E20 W31
Martha   Samuel Parker   12Mar1810 E35 W43
Mary Ann   Benjamin Ford   27Apr1825 E59 W63   Tidings
Sarah J.   William J. H. Coale   13Sep1832 E71 W73   Sewell

PILKINGTON
Thomas   Cyrena Dorset   16Nov1812 E39 W47

PILLIPS
Sarah   Paca Smith   04Feb1799 E15 W28

PINING
John   Sarah Rigdon   03Dec1782 C6 W8

PINKNEY
William   Ann M. Rogers   m. 1789   [ret-AppA]

PINIX
Sarah   William Linam   05Dec1797 E13 W26   John Coleman

PITCOCK
Eleanor   William Woodards   25Jan1804 E24 W34   [ret-AppA]

PITT
Caroline   Jacob Lewis Monk   11Dec1858   W109

PLATT
John   Levinah Williams   28Dec1782 C7 W8   cr-Harf

PLUMER
Robert L.   Comfort Anderson   03Dec1859   W111

PLUMMER
Hannah H.   John McCommons   25May1841 E83 W84 Gallion

POCOCK
David   Mary Smith   14Aug1794 E6 W23
Eleanor   Charles Rockhold   02Dec1791 E1 W21
Elijah   Catharine Hughes   25Jul1808 E32 W41
Mary Ann   Phillip Amos   29Apr1824 E58 W62

POGUE
Daniel   Alice Crapson   16Oct1805 E27 W36
Jane   William Needham   28Aug1795 E7 W24
John   Ann Greenfield   23Jan1802 E21 W32

POLL
John   Emely P. Carroll   08Apr1835 E75 W76 Keech

POOL
Mary Ann   James F. Barclay   08Aug1831 E69 W71 Stephenson

POOLE
John   Mary Ann Mackey   25Aug1832 E71 W73 Finney
Thomas   Isabella Wright   15Feb1862   W115

POPLAR
James W.   Ephemia Peters   09Aug1849   W94
John   Henrietta Barnard   09Mar1858   W108
William   Henrietta Webb   01Aug1827 E63 W66 Reynolds

PORTER
Bathia	Cornelius Prall	08Feb1827	E62 W66	Richardson
Eleanor	Andrew Evett	13Apr1780	C1 W4	
John	Catherine McNeuse	m. 1791		[ret-AppA]
Marg^t	Joseph Steel	17Jan1795	E6 W24	
Mary Ella	Elihu H. Gillispie	01Feb1842	E84 E85	Reid
Robert	Mary Cowan	20Oct1803	E24 W34	

POTEE
James	Ann B. Medcalf	22Mar1808	E31 W40

POTEET
Cassandra	Thomas Smithson	17Jun1814	E42 W49	
Cathrine [Poteet?]	John Dooley	23Jul1781	C5 W7	
Delia	James Lee	08Jan1807	E29 W38	
Elizabeth	Abraham Whitaker	02Feb1804	E24 W34	
James	Adeline McComas	20Mar1832	E70 W72	Sewall
[orig. lic. to Sewall; cr-Harf]				
Jane	Jesse Gorsuch	11Nov1815	E44 W50	
Thomas H.	Elizabeth E. Parlett	28Jul1862	W116	
William	Eleanor Greenfield	16Feb1819	E50 W56	
William E.	Mrs. Emeline Scarff	05Dec1864	W120	

POTEETT
Adaline	Edward Rutledge	10Feb1862	W115

POTTS
Cath^a	Joseph Reese	m. 1778		[ret-AppA]
Jacob	Susannah Coard	31Oct1781	C5 W7	
Jonas John	Elizabeth J. Davis	24Dec1845	W89	

POWELL
Cordelia	Jonas Crew	18May1824	E58 W62
Mary	Hosea Barnes	11Nov1815	E44 W50
William	Sarah Stallians	28Apr1805	E26 W36

POWER
William G.	Lulia Zollinger	12Apr1849	W93

PRALL
Cornelius	Bathia Porter	08Feb1827	E62 W66	Richardson
Isaac R.	Ann B. Rhodes	07Feb1828	E64 W67	Keech

PRATER
William	Eleanor Grover	04Jul1812	E38 W46

PRATT
Adam	Anna Beagnar	01Mar1847	W91

PRESBURY [see Priscilla Presbury Day]
Bathia C.	John Sanders	02Feb1826	E61 W64	Richardson
Bethia	George Patterson	m. 1788		[ret-AppA]
Clemency	Alexander McComass	19Apr1784	C8 W9	
Delia	John Baker	13Aug1779	B3 W2	

PRESBURY, continued

Elizth	Michael Gilbert	18Nov1782	C6	W8	
Geo.	Betsy Lytle	06Nov1793	E5	W23	
Greenberry	Sarah Davis	18Jun1803	E23	W34	[ret-AppA]
Isabella	Thos Hall	19Mar1793	E4	W22	[ret-AppA]
Isabella	Ralph Higinbotham	23Feb1799	E15	W28	
James	Martha Baker	23Dec1800	E19	W30	
James G. L.	Mary Monks	27Nov1815	E44	W50	
Martha	Samuel Griffith	19Nov1778	B1	W1	
Mary	William Weatherall	19Sep1797	E11	W26	[ret-AppA]
Rachel C.	John Watters	04Nov1818	E49	W55	
Sophia	William Hall	m. 1788			[ret-AppA]

PRESTON [see Preston D. Parke Taylor]

Chloe A.	Daniel Loflin	10Nov1839	E81	W82	Finney
Clemency	Walter Billingsley	26Jan1782	C5	W7	
Elijah	Caroline Barton	11Feb1852	H1	W97	Cadden
Eliza	Jesse Cullum	24Dec1838	E80	W81	Rese
Elizth W.	Henry Ruff	19Feb1845	E88	W88	Jones
George	Elizabeth B. Beckingham	21Jun1858		W108	
Jacob A.	Caroline E. Perryman	29Apr1834	E74	W75	Higbee
John	Rebecca Ady	04Oct1804	E25	W35	
Louisa	Thomas Acres	18Feb1854	H5	W100	Finney
Martha Ann	William H. Preston	23Feb1853	H3	W99	Finney
Moses	Blanch Monohon	06Apr1819	E51	W56	
Rachel	William Bailey	26Jul1809	E34	W42	
Rachel	William Williams	31Dec1835	E76	W77	Dulany
Sarah	James Barton	26Apr1819	E51	W56	
Sarah	Joseph W. Shroff	05Dec1835	E76	W77	Park
Sylvester B.	Anna W. West	05Mar1827	E62	W66	Pool
Thomas	Jemima Barton	19Nov1817	E48	W54	
William H.	Martha Ann Preston	23Feb1853	H3	W99	Finney
William Smith	Eliza Ann Smith	11Jan1848		W92	

PRETZMAN

Eliza Ann	William Jacob Ewing	04Nov1862		W116

PREWIT

Benjamin	Ann Gaimes	25Apr1821	E54	W59

PRICE

Ann	Henry O'Henry	27Jul1797	E11	W26	[ret-AppA]
Aquila S.	Margaret J/I. Tignor	01Oct1856	H10	W105	Monroe
Cassandra	Samuel Jackson	01Dec1837	E78	W79	Richardson
Cassandra	George Knight	11Jun1846		W90	
Charles	Hannah Swart	02Jan1805	E26	W36	
Charles	Mary Elizabeth Flowers	11Nov1840	E82	W83	Prettyman
David	Rachel Smith	31May1803	E23	W33	
Edward R.	Laura E. Michael	19Jan1865		W120	
Eliza Ann	William Henry Knight	19Mar1839	E80	W81	Finney
Elizabeth	John Chisholm	08Apr1841	E83	W84	Cullum
George	Sarah Ann Hughes	07Jan1852	H1	W97	Gallion
Hannah	Amos Currey	26Jul1820	E53	W58	
Hannah	William Gough	26Dec1833	E73	W74	Finney
Hannah Jane	Kent M. Chesney	01Dec1830	E68	W70	Tippit

PRICE, continued

James	Isabella Armstrong	16Nov1801	E20 W31	
James	Cassandra Keen	11Feb1833	E72 W73	Sewall
Jesse	Sarah Ann Kelly	06Mar1855	H7 W102	Gallion
Job A.	Kate Andrews	25Feb1858	W108	
John	Nancy Kean	26Sep1811	E37 W45	
John	Margaret Corbin	04Apr1829	E65 W68	Richardson
John H.	Grace Williams	27Nov1829	E66 W69	Sephenson
John H.	Mary R. Parker	24Nov1838	E80 W81	Johns
John Thos.	Annie Eliza Martin	21Feb1863	W117	
Joseph	Charlotte Monohon	10Jun1819	E51 W56	
Margaret Ann	William Gilpin	19Apr1833	E72 W74	Stephenson
Mary	Thomas Turner	03Mar1810	E35 W43	
Preshoshy	Nicholas Gore	m. 1804		[ret-AppA]
Rachel	John Robinson	23Dec1816	E46 W52	
Rachel	William Wilson	02Jan1822	E55 W59	
Rachel	Robert Parker	29Apr1828	E64 W67	Stephenson
Rebeca	Samuel Howel	11Jul1780	C2 W4	
Robert	Mary Gubbin	15May1810	E35 W43	
Sarah	William Touchstone	27Mar1807	E29 W39	
Sarah	Samuel E. Wilson	17Mar1824	E58 W62	
Smith	Maria Ricker	15Oct1831	E70 W71	Sewall
Sophronia Ann	Christopher Johnson	24Jun1841	E83 W84	Wilson
Stephen C.	Elizabeth Standiford	14Dec1813	E41 W48	
Temperance	Benjamin Benson	28Mar1812	E38 W46	
William	Eleanor* Corbin	08Nov1802	E22 W33	
[*Susanna crossed out]				
William	Elizabeth Turner	05Jun1803	E23 W33	[ret-AppA]
William	Cassandra Magness	12May1827	E63 W66	Pool

PRIESTLY

William	Ellen Cave	28Jan1843	E85 W86	Alexander

PRIGG

Amanda M.	John S. Dallam	17Jun1845	E88 W88	
Carvill Hall	Christene Wheeler	09Nov1819	E51 W57	
Cassandra	Edward Brooke	20Dec1795	E8 W24	
Edward	Ann Johnson	12Feb1816	E44 W51	
Edward T.	Sarah Ann Cox	15Mar1836	E76 W77	Stevenson
Eliza	Henry Johns	02Feb1814	E41 W48	
Fannie C.	Wakeman F. Morgan	08Jan1861	W113	
Henrietta	John Jordan	02Feb1841	E83 W84	Reid
Joseph	Mary Cox	03Feb1801	E19 W30	
Joseph	Sarah Templin	13Jan1804	E24 W34	
Margaret S.	Joseph E. Bateman	20Mar1843	E85 W86	Finney
Martha J.	Michael J/I.[?] Wheeler	20Nov1851	W97	
Mary C.	Samuel S. Robinson	10Nov1857	H13 W107	Walter
Samuel T.	Sarah Ann Ely	21Dec1847	W92	
William H.	Eleanora Robinson	12Mar1856	H9 W104	Walter

PRINE

Martha	Abraham Durham	23Sep1813	E40 W48	

PRINTER

John H.	Elizabeth Ann Brown	13Dec1847	W92	

PRITCHARD

Ann	James Gorrell	20Jan1806	E27 W37	
Asael	Elizabeth Botts	06Jan1825	E59 W63	Finney
Benjamin H.	Elizth Holloway	07Apr1854	H5 W100	Finney
Cordelia V.	Henry Silver	04Dec1858	W109	
Elizth	John Williams	05Nov1781	C5 W7	
George	Susan Kimble	18Dec1832	E71 W73	Han--[?]
George W.	Ann E. Herbert	10Mar1828	E64 W67	Keech
James	Sarah Santee	m. 1778		[ret-AppA]
Louisa	John A. Watts	18Sep1854	H6 W101	Reese
Mary F.	George T. Groome	04Dec1858	W109	
Obediah	Sarah Baley	22Oct1782	C6 W8	
Sarah	William Kimble	21Oct1809	E34 W43	
Sarah Amanda	William W. R. Hall	29Oct1860	W112	
Susan	George Gray	30Jul1825	E60 W64	Tidings
William G.	Christian Rawhouser	26Jan1857	H11 W105	Monroe

PRITCHEL

Elizabeth	John W. Scarborough	18May1846	W90	

PROCTER

William G.	Sarah Bodnum	02Aug1827	E63 W66	Keech

PROCTOR

Ann	Peragrine Brown	28Jul1780	C2 W4	
Catherine	Peter Eisenbrey	20Sep1837	E78 W79	Goldsborough
Elizth H.	James H. Carr	04Feb1862	W115	
Israel	Catherine Travis	13May1837	E77 W79	Richardson
M. Alice	Alphonzo Swart	04Feb1865	W120	
Rebecca J.	William C. Glasgow	24Dec1864	W120	
Susan A.	Hanson Cole	22Nov1859	W111	
Thomas S.	Lucy Ann Loman	05May1832	E71 W73	Richardson

PROSER

John	Sarah Hall	09Feb1798	E13 W27	Jno Allen

PUE

Caleb	Harriott Bond	23Apr1822	E55 W60	
Caleb	Eliza Kennard	08Feb1831	E68 W70	Tippit
Joseph	Sarah Ann Thomas	10Jul1838	E79 W80	Richardson
Mary E.	George Kennard	24Sep1838	E79 W80	Collins
Rebecca	Franklin Whitaker	04Feb1846	W89	

PUMMEL[?]

Hanah	Joseph Hugston	27Aug1780	C3 W4	

PURCELL

Anastaria	Patrick Shannon	12May1862	W116	
Larence	Anna Rielly	17Aug1864	W119	

PURNELL

Martha E.	James T. Wilson	16Oct1857	H13 W107	Monroe

PURSEL
Edward   Mary Carroll   17Jul1781   C5 W7
  [after later dates in July]

PUSEY
Joel   Lida L. Crane   04Aug1863   W117

PYE
Margaret   Henry Queen   m. 1779   [ret-AppA]

PYLE
Amer   Mary R. Wann   20Aug1862   W116
David   Sarah Smith   04Jan1814   E41 W48
Edith   John Smith   24Apr1780   C2 W4
Elizabeth   Thomas M. James   09Mar1846   W90
Elizabeth   John Divers   20Dec1850   W95
Hannah   Philip Standiford   01May1828   E64 W67 Richardson
Herman   Sarah Jane Harkins   03Jan1845   W89
Isaac L.   Mary E. Welsh   30Jan1849   W93
Samuel   Emily McClaskey   26Sep1844   E87 W87 Finney
Samuel S.   Rebecca Robinson   10Mar1851   W96
William   Ann Johnson   01Dec1804   E25 W35
William, Junr   Susanna Baxter   07Oct1811   E37 W45

QUANLAND
Polly   James Daugherty   21Nov1803   E24 W34

QUARLES
Edward   Virginia P. Davis   23Feb1853   H3 W99 Waugh
John   Elizabeth Husbands   13May1797   E10 W26 [ret-AppA]

QUEEN
Henry   Margaret Pye   m. 1779   [ret-AppA]

QUIGGLE
George B.   Elenor Jane Sutor   29Dec1855   H9 W103 Smith

QUIGLEY
Mary Ann   Thomas B. Griffin   24Oct1859   W110

QUIGLY
Adeline A.   Robert Anderson   21Apr1842   E85 W85 Park

QUIMBY
Ezra   Mary Chesney   08Nov1821   E54 W59

QUINLAN
Charity   German McClure   04Feb1829   E65 W68 O'Brian
Charity   Edward A. Boarman   12Feb1857   H11 W106 Walter
Philip   Anna Maria Wheeler   19Aug1811   E37 W45
Philip T.   Elizabeth H. Taylor   24Mar1857   H11 W106 Crawford
Rachel Ann   Clement McAtee   26Apr1841   E83 W84 Reid

QUINLEN
James L.   Lavinia M. Rider   25Feb1840 E82 W83 Anderson

QUINLIN
Benjamin   Patty Green   06Dec1800 E19 W30
James   Susanna Cooper   07Apr1798 E13 W27

QUINN
Annestasia   Patrick Bradley   28Oct1856 H10 W105 Walter
James   Margaret McClure   15Mar1827 E62 W66 Poteet
Mary   Thomas Wilson   05Jun1860   W112
Patrick   Biddy McCaverty   02Oct1830 E68 W70 O'Brian

RABURGH
John   Rebecca Chandley   15Jul1807 E30 W39

RAGAN
Ann   John Butler   16Nov1829 E66 W69 Poisel

RAINE
Caroline   Samuel Mass   24May1816 E45 W51

RAITT
Charles H.   Cassandra Whitaker   07Jun1830 E67 W69 Keech

RAMPLEY
Elizabeth   John Amos   14Feb1824 E58 W62

RAMSAY
Alexander C.   Hannah E. Forwood   26Oct1846   W90
James M.   Martha S. Streett   01Jan1846   W89
James O.   Eliza M. Glasgow   08Jan1863   W117
Laura Louisa   Hugh Bay   13Jan1857 H11 W105 Crafford
Mary   William P. C. Whitaker   17Nov1845   W89
R. N.   Mary Martha Heaps   12May1860   W112
Samuel J.   Susana G. Stump   16Oct1838 E79 W81 Stephenson
William White   Eleanor Brooke Hall   04Mar1816 E44 W51

RAMSEY
Cunningham S.   Ann H. Bagley   20Apr1825 E59 W63 Sample
Elizth   Jacob Slack   22Dec1780 C4 W5
Hannah   Robert Scotland   08Jul1780 C2 W4
Hugh C.   Elizabeth Whiteford   23Nov1833 E73 W74 Martin
Robert   Jane Whiteford   28Feb1821 E54 W58
Thomas   Rody Austen   09Jun1807 E30 W39

RANDALL [see Randall Wallis]

RANDEL [see Randel Brannen]

RANDSOME [see Randsome Fayerweather]

RANIE
Margaret   James McGaw, Jnr.   04Feb1834 E73 W75 Finney

RAPHELL
Stephen J.   Mary Ann McAtee   26May1834 E74 W75 Todrig

RATHERS
Jas   Abigal Henderson   20Sep1781 C5   W7

RAWHOUSER
Christian   William G. Pritchard   26Jan1857 H11 W105 Monroe

RAYMOND
Daniel   Sarah Eliza Amos   18Feb1830 E67 W69 Keech
Saml Wilson   Mary Louisa F. Lenox   01Nov1842 E85 W85 Reid

REARDAN
James   Eliza Birckhead   06Oct1817 E47 W54

REARDON
Elisabeth   William Mooberry   09Dec1784 C9   W10
James   Mary Sutton   m. 1777   [ret-AppA]

REASIN
Amanda E.   Alexander S. Adams   20Jan1859   W109
Mary   John T. Bradberry   --May1857 H12 W106 Monroe
  [before 9 May]
Samuel H.   Emily M. Barns   17Mar1841 E83 W84 Myers

REASON [see Reason Dorsey, Reason Gorrell, James Reason Rockhold]
Avarilla   William Simmons   20Apr1812 E38 W46

REDDINGTON
Catharine   James Reddington   04May1853 H3   W99 McNally
James   Catharine Reddington   04May1853 H3   W99 McNally

REDMAN [see Redman Kane]
Mary   James Greenlee   08Apr1800 E17 W29

REED
Charles   Caroline Elizth Lester   04Aug1858   W108
Hannah   John Burgoin   25May1808 E31 W40
Henrietta   William C. Pennington   26May1846   W90
Hugh   Martha Hamby   26Feb1780 C1   W3
James   Elizabeth Sanders   08Nov1853 H4   W100 Hamilton
James W.   Mary E. Gorsuch   18Feb1858   W108
Jane Smith   James M. Magness   30Aug1810 E35 W44
Martha   Wm F. A. Kessler   10May1855 H7   W102 Hersey[?]
Robert W.   Sarah R. Watters   27Feb1841 E83 W84 Reese[?]
Sarah   James McCune   04Mar1817 E46 W53
Susan   Francis Alexander Linton 22Dec1849   W94
Thomas W.   Ann Eliza Jarrett   30Dec1851 H1   W97 Reed
William   Susan R. Wood   16Dec1828 E65 W68 Webster
  [orig. lic. to Webster; cr-Harf]

REEDS
Robt   Mary Carr[?]   13Mar[?]1781 C4 W6

REESE [see Reese Davis]
Annie	Samuel W. James	08Oct1861	W114	
Hester	Enoch Williams	06Sep1848	W93	
John	Elizabeth Brown	23Aug1780	C3 W4	
John	Cassandra Crawford	14Oct1823	E57 W61	
Joseph	Cath^e Potts	m. 1778		[ret-AppA]
Margaret	Enoch Pearson	01Jan1818	E48 W54	
Margaret	Samuel Henry	21Aug1823	E57 W61	
Martha	David Wiggers	13Apr1861	W114	
Sarah	Will. Evans	m. 1778		[ret-AppA]
Sarah	William Sykes	21May1828	E64 W67	Parks

REIREC[?]
Adam   Julian Gross   03Mar1856   H9 W104 Young

RENSHAW
Frances	John Johnson	22Jun1809	E34 W42	
John	Sarah Thompson	10Nov1810	E36 W44	
Joseph	Neoma Calder	07Jul1808	E32 W41	
Martha	Bernard Thompson	03Jan1811	E36 W44	
Mary Ann	James Thompson of Ja^s.	29Aug1818	E49 W55	
Otho N.	Elizabeth Amos	02Nov1830	E68 W70	Uwing
Robert	Mary Anderson	12Feb1781	C4 W6	
Salinah	Jones Bailey	19Dec1780	C3 W5	

REYNOLDS
Edward	Elizabeth Johnson	22Feb1842	E84 W85	Keech
Elizth	James Herron	03Jun1863	W117	
Lewis Franklin	I. Ann Whitelock	13Aug1860	W112	

REZIN
William D.   Sarah Jones   20Feb1813 E40 W47

RHOADS [see also RHODES, ROADS]
Susan   John Scarff   07Jul1811 E36 W45

RHODENHESEN [see also RODENHEISER]
Elizabeth   Thomas Knight   13Aug1831 E69 W71 Sewell

RHODES [see also ROADS, RHOADS]
Ann B.	Isaac R. Prall	07Feb1828	E64 W67	Keech
Betsy Ann B.	Daniel A. Mott	31Mar1831	E69 W71	Richardson
Eliza	Luke Lang	20Aug1810	E35 W44	
Harriet	George Boozer	23Jul1827	E63 W66	Richardson
Sarah	George Moore	08Aug1811	E37 W45	

RICA
Fredericka   George Swarp   23Aug1864 W119

RICDKERT
George   Anna Beagnar   07Dec1847 W92

RICE
Elizabeth	Michael Devin	09Jan1781	C4	W5
Martha R.	Thos. M. Treadway	01Jun1863		W117

RICHARDS
Benjamin	Elizabeth Howard[*]	14Jun1795	E7	W24	
[* surname written over another]					
John C.	Elizabeth Jarrett Thomas	27Oct1834	E74	W75	Higbee
Sarah Rebecca	William Jones	08Aug1842	E85	W85	Briscoll

RICHARDSON
Anne W.	William M. Chew	16Feb1814	E41	W48	
Benj.	Elizabeth Eaton	02Feb1797	E11	W25	
(Return by Parson Luckie)					
Caroline	Jesse G. Dance	19Oct1859		W110	
Charlotte H.	William B. Bond	20Apr1837	E77	W79	Richardson
Cyntha [sic]	Abraham Rutledge	08Apr1817	E47	W53	
Cynthia	John Bond of Saml	18Jan1794	E5	W23	
Daley	Peter Waldrin	15Oct1779	B3	W2	
E. Hall	Alice A. Wilson	19Nov1855	H8	W103	Rankin
Edward A.	Elizabeth Cunningham	28Apr1836	E76	W77	Richardson
Edward D.	Julia Morgan	13Nov1847		W92	
Edward M.	Hannah Jones	04Aug1819	E51	W56	
Elias Green	Sarah Ann Carsin	29Nov1849		W94	
Eliza	Freeborn Garretson	28Dec1811	E37	W45	
Elizabeth	Jacob Forwood	14Jul1818	E49	W55	
Ezekiel J/I.	Ann Ayres	09Mar1846		W90	
Francis A.	Margaret Howard	10Jan1861		W113	
Henry	Elizabeth Morgan	20Mar1782	C5	W7	
Henry	Elizabeth A. Macatee	10Jan1837	E77	W78	Crosgery
James A.	Margaret C. Jones	27Oct1860		W112	
James L.	Mary E. Courtney	10Jan1859		W109	
John	Sarah Lettie Johnson	07Jul1864		W119	
John S.	Mary R. Rouse	30May1860		W112	
Marg^t	Wm. Bradford	m. 1778			[ret-AppA]
Mary	Thomas Cowan	19Feb1785	C10	W10	
Mary	John Bond of W^m.	27May1802	E22	W32	[ret-AppA]
Mary	Nathaniel Yearly	08Dec1810	E36	W44	
Mary	James Carroll	18Dec1823	E57	W62	
Mary A.	Amos G. Day	07Jan1862		W115	
Morgan	Mary Welch	26Sep1816	E45	W52	
[bride's possible middle initial crossed out]					
Rebecca	William Worthington	12May1808	E31	W40	
Samuel	Sarah Morgan	24Mar1805	E26	W36	
Samuel	Prscilla[sic] Worthington	01Mar1830	E67	W69	Poisal
Samuel P.	Sally Ann Wiley	19Dec1857		W107	
Sarah	John Norris	18Feb1784	C8	W9	cr-Harf
Sophia T.	William T. Collins	09Oct1837	E78	W79	Finney
Susan	William Amoss	01Nov1815	E43	W50	
William	Rachel McClure	30Apr1861		W114	
William	Martha C. Crevensten	09Jan1862		W115	
William S.	Lizzie R. Bissell	08Feb1864		W118	

Harford Co. Md. Marriage Licenses, 1777-1865

RICHIE
John   Lavina Barnes   26Dec1808   E33 W41

RICKER
Maria   Smith Price   15Oct1831   E70 W71   Sewall

RICKETS
Ann   John Wilie   01Aug1804   E25 W35
Benjamin   Julian Watters   29Dec1823   E57 W62
Thomas M.   Caroline E. Strong   27Jan1824   E57 W62
Vincents   Elizabeth Evans   14Jan1815   E42 W49

RICKETTS
Lydia J/I.   William K. Galloway   02Mar1858   W108
Mary Ann   George Allender   12Jan1825   E59 W63   Richardson
Samuel   Elizabeth Watters   08Nov1824   E59 W63   Richardson
Samuel J.   Belinda Bowen   28Jan1858   W108
Winston   Sarah Taylor   07Nov1836   E77 W78   Keech

RICKEY
Emeline   William H. Allen   22Nov1858   W109
Sarah H.   William E. Nichols   21Nov1861   W114

RIDDLE
John Thomas   Mary E. Ward   21Dec1854   H6 W101   Trout
Mary   James Gordon   30Jul1782   C6 W8

RIDER
Artreque   Baltice Fie   01Feb1825   E59 W63   Webster
Ellen Frances   Michael J. Wheeler   27Dec1860   W113
Lavinia M.   James L. Quinlen   25Feb1840   E82 W83   Anderson
Mary E.   John O'Donnell   27May1847   W91
Noble   Artreque Cannon   28Dec1808   E33 W41

RIDGELY [see Rebecca Ridgely Coleman]

RIDGEWAY [see Ridgeway Thomas]

RIELEY
Ann   James Paca   16Jan1810   E34 W43

RIELLY
Anna   Larence Purcell   17Aug1864   W119

RIELY
Margaret   George Norris   01Jun1809   E34 W42

RIESTON
Sarah   John Kidd   15Mar1779   B1 W1

RIFFLE
Mathias   Elizabeth Bell   11Jan1831   E68 W70   Stephenson

RIGBIE
James	Mary Srader	18Jul1810	E35 W44	
Margaret	James Barnett, Junr	04Nov1805	E37 W36	

RIGDON
Alexander	Ann Johnson	11Dec1780	C3 W45	
Ann	Asberry Cord	21Nov1806	E29 W38	
Ann	James Bussey Amoss	04Jan1808	E31 W40	
Benjamin	Mary T. Watters	13Jan1847	W91	
Benjamin	Sarah Ann Amoss	24Oct1857	H13 W107	Wilson
Comfort	Thomas Chisholm	25Jan1796	E8 W24	
Comfort	James Madden	10Dec1801	E21 W31	
Elizabeth	Abraham Amoss	19Apr1821	E54 W59	
Elizabeth	Barnet J. Clark	12Jan1836	E76 W77	Richardson
Franklin	Priscilla Harkins	11Dec1848	W93	
Helen D.	William T. Amoss	24Jan1857	H11 W105	Wilson
Jass	Rebecca Jarvis	30Dec1779	C1 W3	
John B.	Miranda Deflora Rigdon	21Oct1836	E77 W78	Wilson
John F.	Sarah Weeks	29Sep1825	E60 W64	Webster
Lucy Ann	Henry Montooth	07Feb1860	W111	
Mary	Wm Catril	29Feb1780	C1 W3	
Mary	Samuel Everit	19Oct1805	E27 W36	
Miranda Deflora	John B. Rigdon	21Oct1836	E77 W78	Wilson
Rachel	Peter Munger	20Feb1813	E40 W47	
Robert Amos	Helen Dalby Bailey	20Feb1852	H1 W97	Wilson
Samuel	Rebecca Martin	27Nov1817	E48 W54	
Sarah	John Pining	03Dec1782	C6 W8	
Sarah Ann	William Smithson	01Jan1844	E86 W87	Wilson
Stephen	Martha Amoss	05Jun1813	E40 W47	

RIGGIN
James	Mary Parsons	04Apr1810	E35 W43	

RILEY
Catharine	William Stewart	28Mar1859	W110	
Dr. David	Drucilla Scarborough	07Sep1861	W114	
Emeline	William Wood	02Aug1851	W96	
James	Caroline M. Osborn	16Jun1819	E51 W56	
James	Matilda Waream	27Oct1830	E68 W70	Tippet
James	Margaret Wiggers	03Apr1858	W108	
James	Bridget Morand	09Feb1861	W113	
Jane	Robert Foster	m. 1787		[ret-AppA]
John	Nancy Kemble	31Dec1839	E81 W82	Hoopman
John H.	Mary A. Ross	03Apr1855	H7 W102	Gallion
John Thomas	Elizabeth Bowen	20Sep1862	W116	
Joseph	Elizabeth Ewing	29Apr1836	E76 W77	Dulany
Mary	John Darlin	24Jan1835	E75 W76	Danahay
Mary S.	Isaac Vanhorn	08Feb1865	W120	
Patrick	Alice Handly	14Jun1859	W110	
Rebecca	Samuel Jones	29Jun1837	E78 W79	Finy
Samuel J/I.	Margaretta Obrien	04May1821	E54 W59	
Samuel J.	Charlotte Combess	08Apr1823	E57 W61	

Harford Co. Md. Marriage Licenses, 1777-1865 205

RILEY, continued
Sarah	Richard H. Ruff	26Feb1818	E48	W54
Sarah	Isaac Way	02Sep1826		
[orig. lic. to Webster; cr-Harf]				
Thos	--[?] Campbell	05Jan1780	C1	W3

RINGGOLD [see Ringgold Smith]

RISTON
Jesse	Sophia C. Payne	20May1844	E87	W87	Jones

ROADS [see also RHODES, RHOADS]
Martha	Alexander Scott	17Oct1779	B3	W2
Thomas	Rachel West	23May1781	C5	W6

ROBB
Levi	Emeline Everist	27May1837	E78	W79	Hoffman

ROBERTS
Ellen	Salathiel Legoe	28Dec1838	E80	W81	Richardson
Isaah [sic]	Mary Standiford	11Apr1801	E20	W31	
James	Mary James	13Feb1802	E21	W32	
John	Clarissa Smith	09Mar1813	E40	W47	
John	Eliza Anthony	14Jul1813	E40	W48	
John	Priscilla Duley	31Jul1813	E40	W48	
John J.	Mary Elizabeth Evans	24Mar1838	E79	W80	Finney
Margaret	St Clair Streett	09Jan1844	E86	W87	Bon--
Marjary	William Holloway	04Mar1818	E48	W54	
Martha	David Swift	07Dec1803	E24	W34	
Owen	Jane Vansickle	02Jun1798	E15	W27	
Peter	Mary Slown	17May1779	B2	W2	
Rachael	Andrew Slown	03Jun1779	B2	W2	
Sarah	Matthew Beck	02Dec1778	B1	W1	
Sarah	Benjamin Hill	02Mar1803	E23	W33	
William G.	Mary F. Butler	01Jan1859		W109	
Zachariah	Ann Amos	09Jun1804	E25	W35	

ROBINET
Priscilla	Jesep Miller	02[?]Mar1798	E13 W27

ROBINSON
Eleanora	William H. Prigg	12Mar1856	H9	W104	Walter
Elizabeth	Thomas Miller	10Nov1806	E29	W38	
Elizabeth	John S. Huff	08Dec1845		W89	
Elizabeth B.	John R. King	27May1858		W108	
Frances M.	Elijah Magness	27Dec1855	H9	W103	Cushing
George	Mary Amanda Hitchcock	03Apr1860		W111	
Hannah H.	George Huff	26Nov1849		W94	
James	Martha Johnson	05Mar1804	E24	W35	
James C.	Susan S. Beeman	02Oct1863		W118	
Jane	Eneas West	22Jan1780	C1	W3	

ROBINSON, continued

John	Rachel Price	23Dec1816	E46 W52	
John	Sarah E. Boarman	07Jun1831	E69 W71	Wheeler
John	Elizabeth Birnard	30Dec1844	E87 W88	Rha--
John B.	Martha Ady	14Mar1812	E38 W46	
Joseph G.	Hannah Hughes	30Dec1847	W92	
Joseph S.	Eliza Howlett	30[?]Mar1843	E85 W86	Car--
[damaged page]				
Laura C.	Franklin C. Baldwin	21Nov1863	W118	
Minerva	James Demoss	01May1863	W117	
Rachel	James Guyton	30Jun1813	E40 W48	
Rachel	Abraham Knight	16Oct1827	E63 W66	Finey
Rachel L.	Nathan Dean	02Jan1854	H4 W100	Trout
Rebecca	Aaron Holland	04Apr1811	E36 W44	
Rebecca	Samuel S. Pyle	10Mar1851	W96	
Rebecca Jane	Matthew Wm. N. Wiley	05Feb1861	W113	
Samuel S.	Mary C. Prigg	10Nov1857	H13 W107	Walter
Sarah	William Knight	29Sep1797	E12 W26	
(Ret'd by John Allen)				
Solomon	Matilda Brannan	29Jul1854	H6 W101	Keech
Thomas E.	Naomi J. Mechem	08Feb1853	H3 W99	Cornelius
Thomas E.	Priscilla Spencer	24Oct1861	W114	
Thomas J/I.	Elizabeth Morsell	25Aug1855	H8 W103	Reese
William	Ann Walker	05Feb1818	E48 W54	
William, Jnr	Margarett Pearce	20Jan1820	E52 W57	
William	Jane Kirkwood	23May1832	E71 W73	Morison

ROCKEY

Samuel	Ariel H. Spicer	22Apr1852	H2 W98	Robey
W. H.	Sarah A. Stamm	01Mar1852	H1 W98	Robey

ROCKHOLD

Ann	Samuel Haythorn	29Jun1800	E18 W29	
Ann Ellen	Nathan Carman	19Jun1824	E58 W62	
Charles	Eleanor Pocock	02Dec1791	E1 W21	
Elijah	Rachel Hitchcock	08Nov1815	E43 W50	
Elijah, Junr	Margaret M. Ayres	30Dec1851	H1 W97	Elderdice
Harriot	Thomas Mills	12May1814	E42 W49	
Hariott	Henry Foy	01Jul1820	E52 W58	
James Reason	Martha Hollis	25Nov1813	E41 W48	
Lysias	Mina Curry	14Mar1865	W121	
Mary Ann	Samuel Haines	11Jul1833	E73 W74	Donahay

RODENHEISER [see also RHODENHESEN]

Kitty	Thomas Wann	27Nov1824	E59 W63	Webster
[orig. lic. to Webster; cr-Harf]				

RODGERS

Alexander	Delia Christie	13Oct1801	E20 W31	
Ann	Garratt Thompson	05Oct1808	E32 W41	
Elizth	John Beshang	13May1783	C7 W8	cr-Harf
Jane	William Rodgers	07Apr1802	E22 W32	
Jeremiah	Priscilla Miller	26Jan1804	E24 W34	

RODGERS, continued

Comdr John	Minerva Dennison	21Oct1806	E29	W38	
John	Elizabeth Malone	28Dec1820	E53	W58	
Joseph	Mary Morgan	30Mar1813	E40	W47	
Kitty	Rowland Rodgers	03Dec1800	E19	W30	
Lawson W.	Alizanna McGaw	05Oct1831	E69	W71	Webster
[orig. lic. to Webster; cr-Harf]					
Mary	Howes Goldsborough	12Oct1812	E39	W46	
Philip	Polly Johns	17Mar1804	E25	W35	
Rebecca	Andrew Gray	23Feb1802	E21	W32	
Rebecca	John Crawford	26Apr1809	E33	W42	
Rowland	Kitty Rodgers	03Dec1800	E19	W30	
Samuel	Sarah Young	30Nov1813	E41	W48	
Sarah R.	Harvey S. Jones	01Jan1853	H3	W98	Robey
William	Mary Hanna	20Mar1800	E17	W29	
William	Jane Rodgers	07Apr1802	E22	W32	

RODHAM

Mary	Thomas Siddell	28Jan1864		W118

ROGERS

Ann	John Hanna	22Mar1796	E8	W25	
Ann M.	William Pinkney	m. 1789			[ret-AppA]
Anna Mary	William T. Eva	04Mar1847		W91	
Benjamin	Mary Edwards	02Mar1826	E61	W64	Stephenson
Cassandra	Elisha Johnson	09Apr1821	E54	W59	
Catherine W.	William M. Grant	21Dec1839	E81	W82	Hunt
Elizth	John T. Hall	12May1828	E64	W67	Finny
George W.	Caroline Metzger	14Jun1852	H2	W98	Chapman
Hannah Ann E.	Joel S. Thrap	15Jul1845	E88	W89	
James	Emma Shemp	15Oct1856	H10	W105	Cushing
Jane	William Watters	22Jan1822	E55	W60	
John	Rachel Ely	07Jan1818	E48	W54	
John	Catharine O'Brien	26May1849		W94	
Joseph	Sarah Scarbrough	09Sep1780	C3	W5	
Lilbourn B.	Mary Ann McGaw	12Feb1824	E58	W62	
Lucinda Ann	Isaac Hoopman	04Dec1823	E57	W61	
Margaret	Nathaniel Chew	m. 1793			[ret-AppA]
Mary	Philip Warnick	26Oct1780	C3	W5	
Mary Ann	Robert M. Magraw	07Sep1837	E78	W79	Finney
Rowland	Sarah Magness	03Dec1807	E30	W40	
Sarah	Isaac J. Ely	04Nov1828	E65	W68	Stephenson
Susan	John Young	08Nov1810	E36	W44	
Susan	John Alphonso Malter	06Apr1829	E66	W68	McGee
Susan Jane	Westley Gorsuch	28May1835	E75	W76	Reese
Thos	Sarah Young	23Jun1780	C2	W4	
Thomas	Magy Hanna	01Jan1795	E6	W24	

ROHRHOUSEN

Sarah J/I.	John C. Martin	16Sep1857	H12 W107	Brand

ROMAN

Ruth Ann	William T. West	25Dec1835	E76	W77	Rutter

RONAY
Nancy   Dennis Breslond   08Jul1801 E20 W31

ROSHA
Nelson   Amanda E. Treadwell   31Mar1864   W119

ROSS
Arabella   Elijah Tayson   10Nov1857 H13 W107 Gallion
Hugh   Rebecca Glenn   23Jun1829 E66 W68 Morrison
Mary   Peter Blancher   04Apr1780 C1 W3
Mary A.   John H. Riley   03Apr1855 H7 W102 Gallion
William   Amelia B. Ford   16Jan1833 E72 W73 Sewell

ROUSE
Christoper C.   Mary G. Day   14Apr1834 E74 W75 Donahay
Elizabeth   Lloyd Day Onion   22Oct1825 E60 W64 O'Brien
Mary L.   Robert A. Cochran   19Sep1837 E78 W79 Keech
Mary R.   John S. Richardson   30May1860   W112
Sarah   Samuel H. Birckhead   13Jan1834 E73 W75 Dunahay
Sarah L.   J. B. Hanway   21Nov1864   W120

ROUSSEY
John   Eleanora Boarman   17Oct1846   W90

ROWLAND [see Rowland Rodgers, Rowland Rogers]
Henry   Mary Carr   21Nov1778 B1 W1
William   Cassandra Hopkins   03Feb1836 E76 W77 Stephenson
Dr. Wm B.   Cassandra F. Sappington   10Apr1846   W90

RUCK
Jas   Ann Balies[?]   01Sep1781 C5 W7

RUFF [see Henry Ruff Gilbert]
Daniel   Hannah Moffett   08Dec1801 E21 W31
Elizabeth   William Bull   13Apr1809 E33 W42
Franklin   Elizabeth Alexander   10May1845 E88 W88 Park
George   Mary Gilbert   03Oct1837 E78 W79 Collins
Hannah   Howard Whitaker   30Nov1815 E44 W50
Henry   Mary marthars [sic]   26Apr1780 C2 W4
Henry   Elizth W. Preston   19Feb1845 E88 W88 Jones
Henry   Sarah A. Streett   18Jun1857 H12 W106 Keech
Henry P.   Elizabeth Hanson   08Feb1816 E44 W51
James   Elizabeth Sophia Ruff   16Oct1816 E45 W52
John   Elizabeth Nelson   01Mar1814 E41 W48
Nancy   Moses Norris   29Dec1845   W89
Priscilla Ann   John Streett   16Jan1844 E86 W87 Ke--
Richard H.   Sarah Riley   26Feb1818 E48 W54
Sarah   Phillip Gilbert   09Feb1782 C5 W7
Sarah   Daniel R. Watters   20Feb1821 E53 W58
Sarah   John W. Day   15Apr1830 E67 W69 Richardson
Sarah F.   John H. Baker   19Jan1852 H1 W97 Gibson

RULEY
Philip   Amelia Cooms   10Aug1792 E3 W21

RUMMELL
John H.	Sarah Holland	05Jun1855	H7 W102	Cushing

RUMSEY [see Mary Rumsey Divers]
Charles H.	Caroline B. Howard	18Dec1820	E53 W58	
Charlotte	Edward Aquila Howard	10Dec1798	E15 W27	
Hannah	Henry Rumsey, Esq.	m. 1788[?]		[ret-AppA]
Henry, Esq.	Hannah Rumsey	m. 1788[?]		[ret-AppA]
Martha [Rumsey?]	Archibald Gittings	30May1815	E43 W50	
Sebina	Wm Hall	02Dec1782	C6 W8	

RUSH
Arnold	Esther Conn	21Jun1813	E40 W48
Dr. D. G.	Mrs. Lyle Davis	24Dec1864	W120
Eliza	Abraham Spicer	21Feb1822	E55 W60
Hannah	Robert C. Amos	09Dec1846	W90
Jacob	Rachel Bull	04Feb1806	E27 W37

RUSK [see John Rusk Streett]

RUSSEL
Samuel	Elizabeth Jane Williams	23Jan1843	E85 W86	Briscold[?]

RUSSELL
Elizabeth	William Ewing	19Sep1821	E54 W59	
Elizabeth	Philip Smith	18Dec1846	W90	
James	Martha Miller	02Nov1825	E60 W64	Stephenson
[orig. lic. to Stephenson; cr-Harf]				
Margaret M.	William H. Thompson	09Dec1854	H6 W101	Finney
Martin	Susan R. Keener	06Apr1864	W119	
Matilda	John W. Hawkins	06Oct1860	W112	
William	Margaret Kinsley	17Jun1806	E28 W38	
William	Mary Ann Knight	29Apr1838	E79 W80	Greenbanks

RUTH
Francis Asbury	Mary H. Bageley	18Oct1824	E58 W63	
Henry F.	Mary A. Liveres	17Nov1849	W94	
John	Ann Spence	30May1820	E52 W58	
John W.	Elizabeth Wright	07Jan1843	E85 W86	Gallion

RUTLEDGE
Abraham	Cyntha [sic] Richardson	08Apr1817	E47 W53	
Abraham	Elizabeth Harper	05Feb1823	E56 W61	
Abraham	Susan McComas	03Apr1826	E61 W65	O'Brian
Abraham	Ariel Amos	01Jan1857	H11 W105	[min. n.s.]
Amanda	Tobias Stansbury	26Dec1849	W94	
Ann	John Street, Jr.	28Feb1820	E52 W57	
Ann Eliza	Henry Wilson	11Jan1840	E81 W82	Prettyman
Belinda	Bazel Cooper	18Jan1826	E60 W64	Poteitt
Clare	Edward Bradlee	17Mar1784	C8 W9	
Edward	Rebecca Garrison	24Sep1850	W95	
Edward	Adaline Poteett	10Feb1862	W115	
Elizabeth	John Iley	03Dec1818	E50 W55	
Elizabeth N.	James Stephenson	15Jun1860	W112	
Emma Jane	William Turner	06Jan1859	W109	

RUTLEDGE, continued

Ignatius	Mary Ann Rutledge	10Apr1823	E57 W61	
Jacob	Monica Wheeler	01Apr1799	E16 W28	
Jacob	Virginia Streett	15Feb1841	E83 W84	Holmead
Joshua, Senr.	Elizabeth MComas [sic]	25Apr1820	E52 W57	
Margaret	Elisha England	30Mar1829	E65 W68	Richardson
Mary Ann	Ignatius Rutledge	10Apr1823	E57 W61	
Penelope K.	William Welch	17Apr1838	E79 W80	Hoolmead
Shadrach, Jr.	Sarah Brindley	18Oct1820	E53 W58	
Thomas	Sarah Gorsuch	m. 1804		[ret-AppA]

RUTTER

Eliza Margaretta	Amons d. St. Victor	15Sep1813	E40 W48	

RYAN

John	Mary Ryan	31Jul1852	H2 W98	McNally
Mary	John Ryan	31Jul1852	H2 W98	McNally
Mary	Henry Cahill	14Apr1858	W108	

RYLAND

Mary	John Miller	23Apr1822	E55 W60
William	Joannah Mather	05Dec1796	E10 W25

RYLEY

James	Margaretta Lee	22Jun1826	E61 W65	Webster
[orig. lic. to Webster; cr-Harf]				

SADLER

Hannah	John W. Caldwell	09Apr1859	W110

SADTLER

Charles H.	R. Priscilla Webster	04Nov1863	W118

SAFFERTY

Susannah	Thos Stevenson	07Jun1780	C2 W4

ST. CLAIR [see StClair Streett]

Bailey	Elizabeth Verney	01Apr1818	E49 W55	
Elizabeth Ann [StClair]	William Slade	13[?]Nov1844	E87 W88	Cross
James [StClair]	Susannah Bosley	12Jun1797	E11 W26	[ret-AppA]
Jane [St. Clair]	Samuel St. Clair	26Apr1809	E33 W42	
Jane [St. Clair]	Stephen Slade	04Jul1818	E49 W55	
Jane	William St. Clair	20Nov1808	W93	
John [St. Clair]	Temperance West	18Dec1799	E17 W29	
John [St. Clair]	Charity Saunders	17Apr1802	E22 W32	
John [St. Clair]	Elizabeth Moore	05Mar1808	E31 W40	
John	Emily Jane Allen	31Jul1858	W108	
Mary [St. Clair]	William Carins	18Aug1808	E32 W41	
Mary Jane	William Slade	16Oct1855	H8 W103	Wilson
Moses [St. Clair]	Ann Blaney	28Sep1809	E34 W43	
Samuel [St. Clair]	Jane St. Clair	26Apr1809	E33 W42	

Harford Co. Md. Marriage Licenses, 1777-1865   211

ST. CLAIR, continued
Thomas [St. Clair]	Mary Blaney	03Jul1800	E18 W29	
Verney	Louisa Watt	16Jan1849	W93	
William [St. Clair]	Hannah Hughes	20Jan1803	E23 W33	
William	Jane St. Clair	20Nov1848	W93	

ST. VICTOR [St. Victor]
Amons d.	Eliza Margaretta Rutter	15Sep1813	E40 W48	

SAMPSON [see Sampson S. Duncan, Sampson Touchstone, Sampson Tutchton]
Elizabeth	John Hays	20Sep1808	E32 W41	
Elizabeth	Edward Cloman	10Nov1838	E80 W81	Gallion
Jane	William Wright	26Oct1839	E81 W82	Finney
Rich^d	Hannah Amoss	03Mar1781	C4 W6	
[same parties 3 Feb C4]				

SANDERS
Elizabeth	William Brazier	25Jul1805	E26 W36	
Elizabeth	James Reed	08Nov1853	H4 W100	Hamilton
Frances Ann	Samuel Norris	22Jan1861	W113	
Hester	James Taylor	30Sep1806	E28 W38	
Isaac	Mary Hanby	06Jun1827	E63 W66	Finney
James	Sarah Brannon	07Mar1820	E52 W57	
John	Bathia C. Presbury	02Feb1826	E61 W64	Richardson
Joseph	Matilda Ely	11Jun1822	E55 W60	
Thomas	Elizabeth Tucker	16Oct1822	E56 W60	

SANGSTER
Alexander	Mary Ann Gibson	12Dec1815	E44 W50

SANGSTURE
Mary	John Gifford	03Nov1781	C5 W7

SANK
Joseph H.	Jane L. Martin	25Jan1859	W109

SANKS
Sarah C.	Samuel Fernald	04Aug1852	H2 W98	Sanks

SANTEE
Sarah	James Pritchard	m. 1778	[ret-AppA]

SAPPINGTON
A. Helen	I. G. Matthews	10Jun1864	W119	
Cassandra F.	Dr. Wm B. Rowland	10Apr1846	W90	
Gorard H.	Elizabeth Bailey	13Jun1831	E69 W71	Stephenson
Mary E.	John H. Guyton	31Jul1856	H10 W105	Keech
Rebecca N.	John Evans	05Jun1854	H5 W101	Finney
Richard	Cassandra Durbin	02Oct1784	C9 W9	
Richard	Margaret Miller	04Nov1813	E40 W48	
Sallie C. K.	William K. Williams	09Apr1860	W112	

SAUIS[?]
Sarah	Michael Sudlusky	07Nov1838	E80 W81	Richardson

SAUNDERS

Ann	Amos Evans	16Dec1823	E57 W62	
Araminta	James F. Gibson	18Jan1841	E83 W84	Dulaney
Charity	John St. Clair	17Apr1802	E22 W32	
Charlotte	James Nichols	28Jul1784	C9 W9	
Edward	Clarissa Smith	16Feb1814	E41 W48	
Edward	Margaret Scarbrough	08Dec1818	E50 W55	
Edward	Rachel Sheredine	08Nov1827	E63 W66	Webster
[orig. lic. to Webster; cr-Harf]				
Elizabeth	Matthias Lynch	20Dec1779	C1 W3	
Elizabeth	Henry Dearholt	04Sep1824	E58 W62	
Elizabeth	John C. Timmos	17Nov1830	E68 W70	Tippet
Frances	William Brambell	21Nov1839	E81 W82	Prettyman
George	Sarah Ann Mitchell	28Jan1852	H1 W97	Gallion
John	Fras Perry	19Aug1779	B3 W2	
John	Charlotte Day	11Jul1796	E8 W25	[or 16Jul]
John	Ann Baker	25Jun1811	E36 W45	
John	Mary Ann Yarnall	01Jul1843	E86 W86	Rescold
Joseph	Harriet Bernard	04Apr1847	W91	
Margaret	Patrick McGuire	18Mar1779	B1 W1	
Margaret	John Bonner	24Sep1825	E60 W64	Tidings
Mary Elizabeth				
	Saml K. Jenning Greenfield	22Nov1856	H10 W105	Cushing
Rachel D.	William Andrew Forsythe	12Feb1863	W117	
Robert	Mary Chisholm	29May1823	E57 W61	
Sarah Jane	William J. Hart	30Sep1843	E86 W86	Switzer[?]
Sarah R.	Joseph Grafton	28Sep1857	H12 W107	Gallion
William	Mary Bramble	20Jan1836	E76 W77	Richardson

SAWYER

William	Charity Magness	11Jan1819	E50 W56	

SCANTLING

Elizabeth	Benjamin Finecum	02Jul1801	E20 W31	

SCARBOROUGH

Ann Elizabeth	Philip Jno. Scarborough	30Dec1861	W115	
Drucilla	Dr. David Riley	07Sep1861	W114	
Edmund	Sarah E. Hurst	25Sep1855	H8 W103	Smith
Elias	Mary Ann Adams	14Jan1848	W92	
Emeline S.	William Lewin Bailey	26Dec1860	W113	
Euclidus	Susanna James	12Apr1809	E33 W42	
Gulielma P.	Abraham Huff	23Mar1847	W91	
Hannah E.	John Cavender	30Jan1857	H11 W105	Cushing
John Barclay	Rachel Frances Lewin	18Dec1860	W113	
John W.	Elizabeth Pritchel	18May1846	W90	
John W.	Julia Ann Howlett	16Dec1846	W90	
Mary	Jacob Forwood	02Feb1848	W92	
Mary Elizth	Daniel L. Bailey	05May1863	W117	
Philip Jno.	Ann Elizabeth Scarborough	30Dec1861	W115	
Samuel S.	Ann Jane Bailey	27Feb1860	W111	
Sarah	William Thomas	23Apr1812	E38 W46	
Sarah	William Haburn	01Oct1823	E57 W61	
Sarah R.	Thomas D. Temple	21Oct1850	W95	

SCARBROUGH

Amos	Jane Kerr	17Dec1825	E60	W64	Park
Ann	Edward Sweeney	22Oct1838	E79	W81	Cosgray
Hezekiah	Elizabeth Albert	01Feb1814	E41	W48	
Isaac	Rachel Weeks	08Jan1812	E37	W45	
Josiah	Sarah Smith	23Jan1838	E79	W80	Keech
Margaret	Edward Saunders	08Dec1818	E50	W55	
Mary	John Moore	03Aug1797	E11	W26	[ret-AppA]
(Ret'd by Rev. John Coleman)					
Mary Elizabeth	Andrew Howlet	11Dec1843	E86	W87	Thomas
Rachel	Michael Huff	31Dec1803	E24	W34	
Rachel	Nicholas Boyd	06Jan1819	E50	W56	
Rebecca	Daniel Jones	16Jan1813	E39	W47	
Rebecca	Robert Duley	26Jun1816	E45	W51	
Samuel	Letitia Warner	27May1809	E34	W42	
Sarah	Joseph Rogers	09Sep1780	C3	W5	

SCARFF

Amanda	Andrew J. Badders	15Aug1855	H8	W103	Hinsey
Charles T.	Martha Rebecca Hitchcock	30Jan1855	H7	W102	Trout
Mrs. Emeline	William E. Poteet	05Dec1864		W120	
Hannah E.	Archibald W. Guyton	02May1856	H10	W104	Myers
Henry	Sarah Kidd	10Dec1806	E29	W38	
Henry	Hannah Garrison	17Oct1815	E43	W50	
Henry	Jane L. Mordew	14Apr1856	H10	W104	Robey
John	Susan Rhoads	07Jul1811	E36	W45	
John	Martha Garretson	15Jun1815	E43	W50	
John	Dorcas Cecelia Slade	30Nov1859		W111	
Juliann	Luther M. Jarrett	02Mar1830	E67	W69	McGee
Margaret	William Grainger	03May1812	E38	W46	
Sally R.	John A. Nace	18Feb1857	H11	W106	Cushing
Sarah	George Hamilton	06Jul1818	E49	W55	
Susan	Simon E. Murphy	27May1820	E52	W57	
William	Elizabeth Whitaker	16Oct1809	E34	W43	
Wm	Ann C. Miles	29Aug1843	E86	W86	Keech

SCHAEFFER

Jonas	Ann Buckingham	07Dec1812	E39	W47

SCHECKLE

Solivia	John Knight	09Dec1845	W89

SCOTLAND

Robert	Hannah Ramsey	08Jul1780	C2	W4

SCOTT [see Scott Griffith, Scott Hamby, Scott Hughes]

Alexander	Martha Roads	17Oct1779	B3	W2	
Ann	John Long	21Feb1779	B1	W1	
Cassander	Matthew Moratta	m. 1788[?]			[ret-AppA]
Daniel	Margaret Short	06Apr1797	E11	W26	[ret-AppA]
(Ret'd by Rev. John Coleman)					
Daniel	Cornelia Norris	17Nov1863		W118	
Elizabeth	George Davis	13Jul1795	E7	W24	
Elizabeth	Daniel McComas	18Feb1796	E11	W26	

SCOTT, continued

George L.	Martha Caroline Acres	10Feb1863	W117	
James E.	Anna E. James	10May1859	W110	
Jane	William Knight	17Oct1851	W97	
John	Rebecca Baity	09Aug1830	E67 W70	Finney
Mary	Wm Willson	07Jan1779	B1 W1	
Mary	John Willson	30Mar1779	B1 W1	
Otho	Louisa M. Boarman	29Oct1823	E57 W61	
Sarah	Luke Dempster	m. 1788		[ret-AppA]
Sarah Y.	Thomas Bond	27Jan1806	E27 W37	

SCOTTEN

Joel	Martha Singleton	18Jan1812	E37 W45	
Martha E.	William Giles	10Sep1849	W94	
Rosena	Robert H. Haslam	11Apr1833	E72 W74	Damphoux
Squire	Sarah Ely	24Aug1816	E45 W52	

SCOTTIN

Samuel	Margaret McPhala	15Jan1806	E27 W37

SCOTTLAND

Allen [br]	Henry Myers [gr]	12Jan1847	W91

SCULLEY

Peter	Catharine McCabe	13Jan1860	W111

SEAGER[?]

Mary	Saml Lynch	24Mar1784	C8 W9

SEDGWICK [see Sedgwick James, Junr]

SEEMANN

Christine	Charles S. M. Besler	06Jan1845	E87 W88	--

SELF

James	Catharine Moon	20Sep1855	H8 W103	Smith

SENNOTH

Michael	Mary Hawkins	17Jun1828	E65 W67	O'Brien

SESSIONS

Mary	John Harden	13May1779	B2 W2

SEWELL

Ann Maria	James S. Morsell	02Jun1831	E69 E71	Higby
Catharine E.	Josiah Lee	02Jun1831	E69 W71	Higby
Cornelia Olivia	Alexander Sumerville	05Nov1832	E71 W73	Higby
James H.	Lucinda Johnson	02Jan1811	E36 W44	
Mary Harrison	John Howard	06Apr1802	E22 W32	[ret-AppA]
Rebecca	William Smith	m. 1777		[ret-AppA]
William H.	Rebecca Lewis	15Feb1803	E23 W33	[ret-AppA]

SHADE

Naoma	John P. Wainwright	08Nov1864	W120

SHAFFER
Catharine   George Emory   28Oct1863   W118

SHANAHAN
Margaret   John Miller   06Mar1859   W110

SHANBARGAR
William   Cristian Cornwell   28Aug1857   H12 W107 Wilson

SHANE
George H.   Nancy J. Heaps   28Apr1863   W117
Hannah   John Smith Hollingshead   30Nov1822   E56 W60
Henry W.   Nancy Deaver   03Oct1815   E43 W50

SHANNON
Deborough   Manuel Noggle   15Oct1846   W90
Geo.   Elizth Touchstone   03Jun1779   B2 W2
Jane   James Wood   23May1806   E28 W38
Jane   Joseph Johnson   05Jan1835   E75 W76 Dunahay
Patrick   Anastaria Purcell   12May1862   W116
Samuel   Mary Taylor   14Jun1825   E60 W64 Webster
Thomas   Ann Tutchstone   01Sep1821   E54 W59
Thomas   Hannah Loftin   28Mar1831   E69 W71 Tippet
Thomas   Margaret Tuchstone   27Dec1841   E84 W85 Cullen

SHARESWOOD
Frances   William Kimball   06Nov1834   E74 W76 Donahay
Lydia   Thomas Armstrong   29Apr1812   E38 W46
Mary   Greenberry Gallion   23Feb1809   E33 W42

SHARP
Benjamin   Julian McCreary   20Feb1823   E56 W61
Martha   John Denbow   09Mar1819   E50 W56
Susan   Thomas W. Ayres   07Nov1820   E53 W58

SHARRON
Elisa   Saml McFadden   18May1857   H12 W106 Monroe
William J.   Elizabeth Way   17Nov1863   W118

SHARTLE
John   Jane D. Kilgour   18Mar1854   H5 W100 Herron

SHAW
Elizabeth   Thomas Norris   12Mar1827   E62 W66 Rockhold
Harrison   Ann Hutchins   03Mar1835   E75 W76 Morrison
Joshua   Issabella Lindsey   01Nov1831   E70 W71 Sewall
Martha Rebecca   George Bradfield   19Aug1857   H12 W107 Gallion

SHAY
Bennet   Alice Brasfield   17Jan1831   E68 W70 Tippet
Catharine C.   George Larrew   05Jun1865   W121
Louisa   George Foard   12Jun1865   W121
Thomas   Clarissa Everist   28Feb1810   E35 W43

SHEARS
  Benjamin   Amanda Moore   18Aug1862   W116

SHEARWOOD
  Sarah   Matthew Denison   12Aug1798 E15 W27
  William   Hannah Brazier   22Mar1803 E23 W33

SHECKELL
  Elenora   John E. McComas   05Jan1843 E85 W86 Brown

SHECKLE
  Anna W.   Henry H. Bradford   21Jun1865   W121
  William   Ann Watters   26Aug1805 E26 W36

SHECKLES
  Mary   Samuel G. Taylor   13Nov1827 E63 W66 Keech

SHEILDS
  George   Elen Jane Courtney   23Jan1838 E78 W80 Finny

SHEKEL
  Richard   Mary Spencer   26May1814 E42 W49

SHEMP
  Emma   James Rogers   15Oct1856 H10 W105 Cushing

SHENAGHEN
  Timothy   Ann McCarroll   06Dec1855 H8 W103 Walter

SHENBERGER
  Eliza   James Baldwin   15Feb1851   W96

SHERADINE
  James   Eliz[th] Gorthrop   04Dec1794 E6 W23
  Sarah   John Gorthrop   30Jan1794 E5 W23

SHERDAN
  Elizabeth A.   Elijah Kirk   20Feb1865   W120
  Mary L.   Richard Pierce   15Aug1860   W112

SHEREDINE
  Asbury   Mahala Gallion   27Dec1853 H4 W100 Gallion
  John   Nancy Allen   17Apr1805 E26 W36
  Mary   William Neill   02Nov1797 E13 W26 Jno Coleman
  Mary   Richard Cain   02Jan1823 E56 W61
  Phoebe   John Allen   14Nov1805 E27 W37
  Providence   John Martin   26Aug1824 E58 W62
  Rachel   Edward Saunders   08Nov1827 E63 W66 Webster
       [orig. lic. to Webster; cr-Harf]
  Ruth Ann   James Baldwin   18Feb1835 E75 W76 Gallion
  Tho.   Mary Socust[?]   23Apr1784 C8 W9   [bn-Locust?]
  Thomas   Ann Neill   19Mar1797 E10 W25 [ret-AppA]

SHERIDAN
Richard   Margrett Ann Walker   04Feb1840   E81 W82   Prettiman

SHERIDINE
Eleanor   Stephen Treadwell   24Oct1805   E27 W36
Margaret J.   Samuel R. Knight   22Nov1859   W111
Rachel   William McCullough   04Feb1796   E8 W25

SHERLEY
Joseph   Elizabeth Bartol   22Feb1813   E40 W47

SHERMAN
Cecelia   William A. Guyton   17Apr1860   W112

SHERREN
Mary J.   George H. Highfield   31Aug1859   W110

SHETZLINE
John D.   Martha Rebecca Stockham   29Jan1861   W113 gr-Phila.

SHEWELL
Eliza   Daniel Long   19Mar1821   E54 W58

SHIDLE
William   Mary McGill   28Jul1796   E9 W25

SHIELDS
Elizabeth   Joseph Cox   26Jun1798   E15 W27
James   Elizabeth Thomas   23Mar1801   E19 W30
James   Elizabeth Green   25Jul1836   E76 W78   Crosgry
John W.   Sarah Elizabeth McComas   06Mar1858   W108

SHIERY
George   Margaret Townsley   28May1847   W91

SHINEFLUE
Conrod   Elizabeth Louge   27Jun1797   E4 W26

SHINESUCKER
Barbara   Thomas Edward Timmons   08Nov1858   W109

SHINN
Henry S.   Mary Barbara Corbin   17Jan1853   H3 W99   Brand

SHIPLEY
Ely   Elizth Kingston   16Feb1781   C4 W6
John   Ann Doran   06Feb1830   E67 W69   O'Brian
Joshua   Catherine Doran   01Feb1820   E52 W57

SHIRREN
Catharine   William W. Griffin   28Oct1861   W114

SHODY
Frances   Ashberry Taylor   02Mar1802   E21 W32

SHOLTZ
Rodolph E.   Anne Maria Wilgis   13Aug1856   H10 W105 Cushing

SHORDAN
Rebecca   Lloyd Morris   24Jul1816   E45 W52

SHORT
Margaret   Daniel Scott   06Apr1797   E11 W26   [ret-AppA]
   (Ret'd by Rev. John Coleman)

SHRADER
Harriet   James Charlton   18Nov1824   E59 W63   McElhiney

SHRODES
Charles   Sarah Jane Taylor   11Mar1850   W94

SHROFF
Joseph W.   Sarah Preston   05Dec1835   E76 W77

SHULTZ
Catharine   Elisha Guyton   21Dec1812   E39 W47
Chas. Frederick Egidius
                     Rosa Barnes   07Oct1853   H4 W100 McNally
Elizabeth   Michael Hooper   08Jun1818   E49 W55
Julian [br]   Calisle Francis [gr]   26Jul1834   E74 W75   Keech
William F.   Susan Simon   19Feb1862   W115

SHURE
John P.   Edna Fisher   24Dec1861   W115
Josiah J/I.   Rebecca A. Jones   03Jun1858   W108

SIBOLD
Susanna   Conrad Heinlein   09Jun1863   W117

SIDDELL
Thomas   Mary Rodham   28Jan1864   W118

SIDNEY [see George Sidney Armstrong]

SILK
Thomas R.   Anne E. Campbell   30Oct1861   W114

SILLIN
Mary   William Ford   10Apr1785   C10 W10

SILLS
Jacob Henry   Mary Jane Timonds   13Mar1860   W111

SILVER
Amos   Rebecca McGaw   19Jan1820   E52 W57
Benjamin, Junr   Charity Warnick   19Nov1806   E29 W38
Benjamin of Gersham Hannah Morgan   14Sep1830   E67 W70   Finney
Benjamin   Emily M. Pannell   02Feb1846   W89
Cassandra   Hugh C. Whiteford   27Oct1834   E74 W75   Finney

SILVER, continued

David	Harriot Mitchell	03May1815	E43	W50	
David	Elizabeth Hawkins	15Jan1818	E48	W54	
David H.	Ann Galbreath	28Nov1842	E85	W85	Park
Eliza	John Mitchell	19Mar1831	E68	W71	Finney
Elizabeth Ann	Doddridge S. Whiteford	01May1839	E81	W82	Finney
Euphemia	Wm. Thomas Easter	11May1853	H4	W99	Hamilton
Henry	Cordelia V. Pritchard	04Dec1858		W109	
Henry	Susannah Kirk	17Mar1863		W117	
Henry A.	Hannah Jane Galbreath	16Nov1849		W94	
James	Jane Forsythe	19Dec1822	E56	W60	
James	Ann Pannell	21Oct1846		W90	
Jeremiah P.	Mary Eliza Hoopman	31Dec1851	H1	W97	Finney
John A.	Jane Pannell	04Jan1845	E87	W88	Finney
Margaret	George T. Groom	05Aug1851		W96	
Margaret	William Silver	30Oct1860		W112	
Margaret D.	George Hayes	06Sep1828	E65	W68	Finney
Mary F.	Samuel Bayless	27Apr1833	E72	W74	Finney
Mary M.	Robert A. Osborne	01Apr1851		W96	
Philip W.	Alice Harlan	18Dec1832	E72	W73	Finney
Phoebe	George Washington Courtney	11Feb1806	E28	W37	
Phoebe	Amos Osborn	19Jan1835	E75	W76	Finney
Samuel B.	Sarah Osborn	15Dec1832	E71	W73	Finney
Silas	Eliza Hanway	16Jul1829	E66	W68	Keech
Silas B.	Susan S. Pannell	25Nov1857	H13	W107	Finney
Silvester A.	Frances Marsh	20Dec1854	H6	W101	Finney
Susan R.	William McConkey	26Dec1843	E86	W87	Finney
William	Phoebe Maxwell	06Jul1857	H12	W106	Finney
William	Margaret Silver	30Oct1860		W112	
William F.	Mary R. Whiteford	10Oct1838	E79	W81	
William Z.	Sarah Ann Osborn	23Apr1850		W95	

SILVERS

Garshom	Elizabeth Bayles	25Jan1803	E23	W33	
Jno	Jane Asker	m. 1778			[ret-AppA]
Mary	Zephaniah Bayles	07Sep1802	E22	W32	
Mary D.	Francis D. Anderson	10Jun1833	E73	W74	Finney
Rebecca	Robert Hanna	25Jan1837	E77	W78	Finney
Sarah S.	Cyrus Osborn	26May1840	E82	W83	Finney

SIMMONS

Ann	John Brown	01Jan1838	E78	W80	Finy
Caroline	John Ewing	26Jun1846		W90	
Thomas	Sarah Hill	m. 1787			[ret-AppA]
William	Sarah Everist	29Dec1808	E33	W41	
William	Avarilla Reason	20Apr1812	E38	W46	
William	Elizabeth Garrett	26Jan1818	E48	W54	

SIMON

John Henry	Druy Elizabeth Dixon	15Jan1840	E81	W82	Prettiman
Susan	William F. Shultz	19Feb1862		W115	

SIMPSON

Elizabeth	William Monk	27Dec1792	E3	W22	[ret-AppA]

SIMS
George   Mary Lynch   m. 1778   [ret-AppA]

SINCLAIR
Mary   Wm Amoss   19Nov1778 B1 W1

SINGLETON
Amos   Martha Everist   06Jan1848   W92
Ann Maria   William H. Whiteford 02Feb1852 H1 W97   Cadden
Emely   Merrick Barron   08Sep1828 E65 W68   Finney
Herman   Martha Jane Weeks   27Jun1855 H8 W103 Smith
John   Mary Holly   10Aug1840 E82 W83   Finney
Margaret Ann   John Hopkins   02May1849   W93
Martha   Joel Scotten   18Jan1812 E37 W45
Mary J.   Jefferson Crew   30Jan1857 H11 W105 McCartney
Sarah Ann   Benjamin Everist   22Feb1832 E70 W72   Webster
Sarah Ann   James Griffin   23May1855 H7 W102 Gallion

SITZLER
Sophia   Caspar Marlein   08May1854 H5 W101 Smith

SKIPWITH [see Skipwith C. Gorrell]

SLACK
Jacob   Eliz^th Ramsey   22Dec1780 C4 W5

SLADE
Abraham   Rosetta Anderson   27Feb1816 E44 W51
Amanda Z.   Charles W. Howard   22Sep1834 E74 W75   Keech
Benjamin A.   Catharine C. Lochary 03Apr1851   W96
Dixon   Martha McComas   23Dec1817 E48 W54
Dorcas Cecelia   John Scarff   30Nov1859   W111
Elizabeth   James Streett   04Mar1836 E76 W77   Keech
Ezekiel   Nancy Vogan   20Oct1808 E32 W41
James W.   Hannah McComas   11Dec1813 E41 W48
Josias   Luraner Morgan   20Apr1802 E22 W32
Julia   Michael Lochary   08Sep1841 E83 W84   Reid
Manirva   John Watkins   21Oct1830 E68 W70   Tibbit
Mary Ann   Thomas M. Cathcart   08Feb1848   W92
Mary Jane   Thomas Amoss   17Feb1858   W108
Nancy   Martin Colder   12Jul1838 E79 W80   Keech
Rachel   Joseph W. Strong   15Jan1850   W94
Sallie J.   Charles A. Burkins   08May1864   W119
Sarah   George W. Wheeler   16Mar1847   W91
Stephen   Jane St. Clair   04Jul1818 E49 W55
Susan   John W. Hale   19Dec1837 E78 W79   Cross
Washington M.   Mary McComas   06Feb1838 E79 W80   Keech
William   Elizabeth Ann StClair 13[?]Nov1844 E87 W88 Cross
William   Mary Jane St. Clair   16Oct1855 H8 W103 Wilson

SLATER
Salley   John Guyton   06Feb1809 E33 W42

SLEE
Mary Ellen	William F. Pannell	13Jan1852	H1	W97	Finney
William	Mary Courtney	21[?]Mar1843	E85	W86	Finney

SLEMAKER
Areanea	H. Patrick Finnagan	25Apr1792	E2	W21

SLOAN
Jerry	Catharine Sullivan	16Feb1857	H11	W106	Walter
Wm	Betsey Ashmead	04Oct1795	E7	W24	

SLOFER
Henry	Ann Garrison	06Jan1829	E65	W68	Richardson

SLOWN
Andrew	Rachael Roberts	03Jun1779	B2	W2
Mary	Peter Roberts	17May1779	B2	W2

SLUBY
Eleanor	Alexander Boyd	20Aug1812	E38	W46

SMALL
David	Mary Dawson	05Sep1805	E26	W36
Elijah	Rebeccah Jemeison	21Feb1799	E15	W28
John	Annie Smith	09Mar1863		W117

SMITH [see Jane Smith Reed, John Smith Hamby, John Smith Hollingshead, William Smith Preston]
Alexander Lawson	Martha Griffith	28Aug1792	E3	W22	[ret-AppA]
Alice	Wm Woolsey	10Sep1795	E7	W24	
Ann	William Curry[?]	03Aug1780	C2	W4	
Ann	Jesse Davis	05Nov1817	E48	W54	
Ann	Joseph Warner	25Feb1828	E64	W67	Keech
Ann	John Barnes	30Oct1832	E71	W73	Finney
Ann Jane	Jonathan E. Mechem	25Dec1860		W113	
Annie	John Small	09Mar1863		W117	
Bazil	Elizth Dooley	14Aug1782	C6	W8	
Bazill	Ann Cunningham	01May1781	C4	W6	
Bernard	Eliza Davis	28Jun1838	E79	W80	Coskrey
Betsy	John Howlet	21Jun1804	E25	W35	
Casper	Elizabeth Mayers	15Jun1859		W110	
Catharine	William Hoofman	30Aug1783	C7	W9	
Charles C.	Catharine Gorrell	26Dec1861		W115	
Christopher	Mary Carroll	21May1817	E47	W53	
Clarissa	John Roberts	09Mar1813	E40	W47	
Clarissa	Edward Saunders	16Feb1814	E41	W48	
Eliza Ann	William Smith Preston	11Jan1848		W92	
Elizabeth	[groom not named]	30Sep1795	E7	W24	
Elizabeth	James Cooley	26Oct1808	E32	W41	
Elizabeth	Richard Holloway	27Nov1810	E36	W44	
Elizabeth	Joshua Norris	30Sep1813	E40	W48	
Emma Louisa	John C. Tucker	23Apr1860		W112	

SMITH, continued

Frances	William M. Dallam	31Aug1808	E32	W41	
Frances	Edward Jolley	17May1810	E35	W43	
Frances	Richard Hopkins	06Jun1816	E45	W51	
Francis C.	Alice Bussey	14Jan1856	H9	W104	McManus
George	Ann Hawkins	27Jan1802	E21	W32	
George	Martha Ellen Durham	01Dec1851	H1	W97	Wilson
Hannah	Archibald Hays	23Feb1780	C1	W3	
Hannah	Zachariah Huff	01Nov1804	E25	W35	
Hannah	Thomas Morgan	02Feb1813	E39	W47	
Hannah	William B. Stephenson	22Dec1830	E68	W70	Tippet
Henry	Mary Ann Herbert	17Oct1831	E70	W71	Finney
Hetty	Christopher Wilson, Jr.	18Sep1823	E57	W61	
James	Sarah Haley	20Sep1797	E11	W26	[ret-AppA]
James	Agness Calder	26Mar1845	E88	W88	Reid
James	Frances Walker	09Sep1856	H10	W105	Finney
James	Harriet E. Jewins	14Feb1857	H11	W106	Finney
Jane	Richd Ward	12Apr1779	B2	W1	
Jane	Jacob Botts	21Feb1781	C4	W6	
Jane	John Deaver	26Nov1812	E39	W47	
Jehu[?]	Lydia Weiser	20May1828	E64	W67	Finney
John	Edith Pyle	24Apr1780	C2	W4	
John	Frances Griffith	m. 1787			[ret-AppA]
John	Elizabeth Downs	09Sep1794	E6	W23	
John	Nansey Bryarly	13Jun1801	E20	W31	
John	Hannah Forwood	07Jun1837	E78	W79	Parks
John	Eve Fry	07Dec1857		W107	
John	Sarah Botts	21Jun1859		W110	
John	Eliza Sutor	24Jan1863		W117	
John C.	Mary J/I. Jackson	08Jan1856	H9	W104	Reese
Joseph	Mary Toalson	m. 1777			[ret-AppA]
Joshua	Ann Gorrell	29Mar1813	E40	W47	
Josiah	Claracy Glanville	23Feb1808	E31	W40	
Julia M.	John Exton	17May1826	E61	W65	Reynolds
Kasper	Mary Ann Barlin	23Dec1837	E78	W80	Collins
Marg^t	Hugh Deaver	12Apr1782	C6	W7	cr-Harf
Margaret	John Wilson	22Nov1799	E16	W28	
Margaret S.	John H. Barrow	19Jan1854	H5	W100	Dumm
martha [sic]	Francis Dallam	24Apr1780	C2	W4	
Martha	Samuel Jay	07Feb1812	E38	W46	
Martha	Benjamin W. Duncan	01Feb1830	E67	W69	Stevenson
Martha F.	John - Welch [sic]	19Dec1842	E85	W86	Furgurson
Mary	Edward Dooley	28Aug1781	C5	W7	
Mary	James McCrakin	m. 1789			[ret-AppA]
Mary	David Pocock	14Aug1794	E6	W23	
Mary	Samuel Bagley	21Dec1820	E53	W58	
Mary	Samuel Way	08May1821	E54	W59	
Mary	Elijah W. Barrett[?]	14Nov1826	E62	W65	Stephenson
Mary	Augustus Bornemen	20Oct1860		W112	
Mary A.	William Wilson	01Mar1865		W120	
Matilda	Thomas Loflin	03Sep1808	E32	W41	
Moses	Mary Berry	08Jan1795	E6	W24	

SMITH, continued

Nathaniel	Caroline Hopkins	16Nov1836	E77 W78	
[minister - Stephenson?]				
Nathaniel	Lydea Ann Holliway	29Jan1845	E88 W88	Eage
Nicholas	Susan Bordan	03Nov1838	E80 W81	Coskey
Paca	Sarah Pillips	04Feb1799	E15 W28	
Phebie	Thomas Gallop	01Feb1792	E2 W21	
Philip	Elizabeth Russell	18Dec1846	W90	
Rachel	David Price	31May1803	E23 W33	
Rachel	John Brown	23Sep1823	E57 W61	
Rebecca	John Clark	01Mar1815	E42 W49	
Rebecca Ann	Edward Sweeting	01Apr1844	E87 W87	Ege
Reuben	Ann Farmer	04Feb1824	E57 W62	
Richard	Eliza Ann Hanna	06Dec1849	W94	
Rich'd. G.	Cassandra Bird	11Apr1865	W121	
Ringgold	Sarah Ann Metzger	01May1832	E71 W72	Sargent
Ringold	Elizabeth Harryman	29Aug1836	E76 W78	Smith
Robert H.	Mary Moore Hall	05Dec1861	W115	
Ruth	Jacob Enfield	14May1861	W114	
Samuel	Laura Julian Greme	04Feb1823	E56 W61	
Sarah	Wm Brannon	23Dec1779	C1 W3	
Sarah	John[?] Parmer	27Jan1780	C1 W3	
Sarah[?]	John Wells	12Mar1781	C4 W6	
Sarah	John McCracken	07Nov1792	E3 W22	
Sarah	Thomas Worwick	31Dec1811	E37 W45	
Sarah	David Pyle	04Jan1814	E41 W48	
Sarah	Josiah Scarbrough	23Jan1838	E79 W80	Keech
Sarah	George Cloak	07Apr1857	H11 W106	Monroe
Sarah J.	Jacob Brown	30May1865	W121	
Stump	Laura Brannan	15Dec1862	W116	
Susan A.	George Steinberger	31Oct1857	H13 W107	Austin
Susan W.	Silas Brosiers	02Jan1865	W120	
Thomas	Hannah Barrett	02Jun1802	E22 W32	
Thomas	Margaret Hopkins	14Apr1838	E79 W80	Gallion
Thomas	Elizabeth Willey	02Jan1856	H9 W104	Smith
Thomas Henry	Laura Berry	09Feb1865	W120	
William	Rebecca Sewell	m. 1777		[ret-AppA]
Wm	Jane Daugherty	17Feb1779	B1 W1	
William	Martha Bond	24Apr1780	C2 W4	
Wm	Margarett Spence	11Apr1783	C7 W8	cr-Harf
William	Susannah Phillips	26Nov1792	E3 W22	[ret-AppA]
Wm	Sarah Visepworth[?]	12Mar1793	E4 W22	
William	Elizabeth Mahon	05Jul1797	E11 W26	
William	Mary Hughes	27Dec1803	E24 W34	
William	Elizabeth McComas	10Aug1805	E26 W36	
William	Nancy Long	23Jul1817	E47 W53	
William	Juliann Brown	16Aug1830	E67 W70	Tippit
William	Charlotte Baker	22Apr1831	E69 W71	Stephenson
William B.	Eliza Ann H. Norris	27Nov1855	H8 W103	Dumm
Wm. H.	Margaret A. Kirk	02Jun1863	W117	
Winston	Cassandra Dallam	26Oct1796	E9 W25	

SMITHSON [see W. Smithson Forwood]
Amelia	William Wright	02Apr1804	E25	W35	[ret-AppA]
Benjamin	Ann Howard	24Dec1792	E3	W22	
Daniel	Susannah Taylor	03Feb1784	C8	W9	cr-Harf
Eliz.	Henry Dorsey of Edwd	05Feb1795	E6	W24	
Elizabeth	Ralph Lee	15Jan1812	E37	W45	
Elizabeth	Samuel L. Bond	07Jan1834	E73	W75	porter
Elizabeth	William E. Bull	25May1847		W91	
George	Mary Amos	02Mar1842	E84	W85	Cross
Henry	Catherine Archer	11Jul1836	E76	W78	Finney
John	Hannah Amoss	27Mar1811	E36	W44	
Julia Ann	Parker Lee Forwood	03Oct1863		W118	
Mary	Corbin Lee Onion	18Mar1806	E28	W37	
Nathaniel	Mary Bull	24Jan1779	B1	W1	
Nathaniel	Elizabeth Miller	11Oct1856	H10	W105	Smith
Rachel	Thomas Durham of David	11Apr1807	E29	W39	
Rennis B.	Absalom Galloway, Jur	13Jun1833	E73	W74	Keech
Thomas	Cassandra Poteet	17Jun1814	E42	W49	
Thomas P.	Lucretia Bosley	12Feb1849		W93	
William	Margaret Lee	05Sep1805	E26	W36	
William	Elizabeth Lee	11Mar1818	E49	W55	
William	Sarah Ann Rigdon	01Jan1844	E86	W87	Wilson

SMOOT
Hezekiah B.	Harriet McNiel	27Jul1826	E61	W65	Keech

SNAVILS
John A.	Mary Spears	15Jun1854	H6	W101	Reese

SNODY
Matthew	Sarah Wood	m. 1790	[ret-AppA]

SNOGRASS
Sarah	James S. Davis	26Oct1854	H6	W101	Trout

SNYDER
B. B. [gr]	R. C. Knight [br]	27Sep1837	E78	W79	Roberts
Mary Ann	John P. Chenoweth	22Mar1856	H9	W104	Hoopman

SOCUST
Mary	Tho. Sheredine	23Apr1784	C8	W9	[or Locust?]

SOMERS
Mary Ann	John Taylor	11Oct1864	W119

SORAH
Tho.	Mary Cusick	m. 1778	[ret-AppA]

SOUTHWICK
Ire	Ann Ely	24Feb1820	E52	W57

SOWERS
Mary	Jesse Davis	31Mar1806	E28	W37

SPARKS
Wright	Ann Magness	12Sep1805	E26 W36	

SPEADEN
Rebecca	John Garrison	02May1864	W119	

SPEARS
Harvey D.	Rachel Dixon	30Dec1834	E74 W76	Dulany
Mary	John A. Snavils	15Jun1854	H6 W101	Reese

SPEDDEN
Mary Ellen	Henry Hild	20Dec1847	W92	

SPENCE
Ann	John Ruth	30May1820	E52 W58	
Elizabeth	Joseph Finch	21Jan1808	E31 W40	
Elizabeth	William Hopkins	16Nov1836	E77 W78	Hoopman
Henry	Ann Strolenger	23Dec1807	E31 W40	
Hester	Nathaniel Martin	29Sep1835	E75 W77	Gallion
James	Ann McClure	06Jan1779	B1 W1	
Margarett	Wm Smith	11Apr1783	C7 W8	cr-Harf
Mary	Joseph P. Gallian	03Dec1838	E80 W81	Gallian
Nancy L.	Alexander Gallion	09Aug1858	W108	
Rachel	Garsham Gorrell	02Jan1821	E53 W58	
Sarah	James Everist	21Oct1835	E76 W77	Reese
Serene	Thomas Knight of Wm.	13Jul1830	E67 W70	Stephenson

SPENCER [see Spencer Fletcher, Spencer Lego]
Amos	Rose Ann Bonis	11Sep1840	E82 W83	Finney
Ann	Jesse Vanhorn	05Mar1818	E48 W54	
Ann	William Wright	20Dec1821	E55 W59	
Ann	Samuel Jefferson Garrison	07Aug1823	E57 W61	
Daniel Dorsey	Rachel Bounce	28Aug1862	W116	
Elizabeth	William Miller	04Apr1809	E33 W42	
Elizabeth	George Bailey	27Jan1851	W96	
Emm. Avarilla	Thomas Bolster	11Dec1821	E55 W59	
Hugh E.	Sarah Ann Way	12Aug1828	E65 W68	Richardson
Jarrett	Elizabeth Cole Herbert	02Sep1844	E87 W87	Gallion
John R.	Sarah Bailey	12Jan1848	W92	
John W.	Rebecca Keen	21Jul1817	E47 W53	
Mary	Alexr Gallion	14Jan1800	E17 W29	
Mary	Richard Shekel	26May1814	E42 W49	
Mary Ann	Samuel Miller	06May1830	E67 W69	Stephenson
Nicholas	Eliza Carty	12Aug1822	E56 W60	
Priscilla	Thomas E. Robinson	24Oct1861	W114	
Richd	Eliza Wild	m. 1778		[ret-AppA]
Ruth	John Andrew	14Mar1826	E61 W65	Finney
Sarah	John McCandless	21Aug1806	E28 W38	
Sarah	Joseph Gallop	20Oct1810	E35 W44	
Sarah	David Atkinson	26Feb1821	E54 W58	
Sarah R.	Robert J. Walker	24Jan1857	H11 W105	Monroe
Silas L.	Mary Eliza Mitchell	11Aug1857	H12 W106	Tustin

SPENCER, continued

Sophia	George W. Hopkins	21Feb1842	E84 W85	Gallion
Thomas	Mary Nabb	09Jun1801	E20 W31	
William T.	Eliza S. Bowman	18Jun1853	H4 W99	Gallion

SPICER

Abraham	Eliza Rush	21Feb1822	E55 W60	
Albert	Sarah Ann McVey	04Aug1836	E76 W78	Richardson
Amos	Hannah Johnson	19Jan1831	E68 W70	Richardson
Ariel H.	Samuel Rockey	22Apr1852	H2 W98	Robey
Eleanora	Benjamin S. Guyton	18Jun1842	E85 W85	John Reese
Elizabeth	William Morrison	16Sep1816	E45 W52	
Guli Elma Maria	Jesse Hollingsworth	01Oct1821	E54 W59	
Isaiah J/I.	Felima Jane Duvall	09Jun1830	E67 W69	Richardson
James	Susan N. Paul	10Jan1822	E55 W59	
James, Jr.	Sarah P. Timmons	06Nov1857	H13 W107	Monroe
Jane R.	Edward F. Johns	09Jul1845	E88 W89	

SPIES

Louis	Mary E. Stengel	29Feb1864	W118	

SPINCE

Cathrine	Elisha Bowen	10Dec1783	C8 W9	cr-Harf

SPRINGER

Mary R.	Francis P. Phelps	09May1853	H3 W99	Finney

SPRUCEBANKS

Elizabeth	Thomas Brooks	29May1807	E30 W39	
Frances	Henry Cunningham	25May1796	E8 W25	
Martha	Aarom Hughes	09Feb1808	E31 W40	

SQUIRE [see Squire Scotten]

SRADER

Mary	James Rigbie	18Jul1810	E35 W44	

SREARK

Sam¹	Hannah Carter	16Mar1779	B1 W1	

SRODES

Charles	Julian Whiteford	05Feb1823	E56 W61	

STAKE

Catharine Maria	William F. Miller	25Feb1822	E55 W60	[or Slake?]
Thomas	Elizabeth Hawkins	06Jan1818	E48 W54	

STALL

Jacob	Mary Ann Hill	06Jan1841	E83 W84	Wilson

STALLIANS

Ann	Richard Jury	22Nov1780	C3 W5	
Sarah	William Powell	28Apr1805	E26 W36	

STALLINGS
Rebecca   William Bradley   24Dec1801 E21 W31

STALLIONS
Jacob   Icabird Cofman   25Jun1807 E30 W39
John   Ann Whiteford   18Jun1807 E30 W39
Nancy   Isaac Tolson   22Jul1780 C2 W4

STAMM
Sarah A.   W. H. Rockey   01Mar1852 H1 W98 Robey

STANDAFORD
Prissila   Joshua Gorsuch[?]   m. 1804   [ret-AppA]

STANDIFORD
Amelia Ann   William Turner   08Sep1835 E75 W77 Keech
Ann   William Johnson   02Feb1807 E29 W38
Ann   John H. Grafton   31Mar1846   W90
Ariel   Washington Parlett   06Dec1836 E77 W78 Richardson
Banjamin   Rachel Amoss   09Jan1798 E13 W27 Jno Coleman
Benjamin   Elizabeth P. Hatton   19Dec1831 E70 W72 Sewall
Charles   Cassandra Knight   20Feb1865   W120
Cladius   Delia Hitchcock   17Dec1805 E27 W37
Cordelia E.   John W. Drummond   20Nov1851   W97
Delia   John Bull   08Dec1782 C6 W8
Edmond   Catharine Garner   05Nov1803 E24 W34
Elizabeth   Stephen C. Price   14Dec1813 E41 W48
Hannah   Samuel Hawkins   04Feb1784 C3 W9   cr-Harf
Henry   Hannah Miles   05May1865   W121
Isaac   Ellen J/I. Williams   25Feb1856 H9 W104 Cushing
James   Sarah Stewart   27Dec1781 C5 W7
John   Sarah Carroll   08Jan1813 E39 W47
Lloyd   Mary Hendon   17Nov1812 E39 W47
Mary   Isaah Roberts   11Apr1801 E20 W31
Mina   Samuel Young   27Apr1836 E76 W77 Morrison
Philip   Hannah Pyle   01May1828 E64 W67 Richardson
Providence   William White   16Jun1812 E38 W46
Sophia   Joseph W. Wallis   05Mar1844 E87 W87 Thomas
William C.   Sarah Jane Knight   19Nov1860   W112

STANDLEY
Elizabeth   William Deaver   03Jan1785 C10 W10

STANSBERRY
Elizabeth   John Gorden   22Nov1803 E24 W34

STANSBURY [see Stansbury Gallion]
Charles G.   Guley Ann Cox   26Aug1802 E22 W32
Elizabeth   William Nelson   16Apr1838 E79 W80 Cross
Isaac   Ann Montgomery   13Jan1818 E48 W54
Tobias   Amanda Rutledge   26Dec1849   W94
William   Sarah Cox   05Dec1808 E32 W41

STANTON
John   Ellen* McNulty   04Jan1831 E68 W70 Tippit
[*Mary crossed out]

STAPLEFORD
Sarah Ann   Benjamin Jeffers   21Sep1855 H8 W103 Reese
Winlock   Ann K. Vanhorn   15Dec1825 E60 W64 Webster

STARCK
George   Eliza Nowland   13Nov1810 E36 W44

STARR
Catharine A.   Barnett Clark   04Feb1860   W111
Elizabeth A. *   James Harvey   26Dec1850   W95
[* bride's surname uncertain]
Georgiana   James Dowling   23Jun1856 H10 W105 Cushing
William H.   Sarah Jane Doxen   14Feb1860   W111

STAUFFER
Henry   Sallie S. Cairnes   27Sep1858   W109

STEARNS
Amanda M.   William H. Judd   03Nov1853 H4 W100 Wilson
Elizabeth   James F. Cunningham   23Dec1862   W117

STEEL
Cassandra   Dan¹ McLaughlin   06Sep1794 E6 W23
Joseph   Marg^t Porter   17Jan1795 E6 W24
Joseph   Susanna Wood   02Jan1802 E21 W32

STEEN
James T.   Sarah E. McComas   06May1833 E72 W74 Lipscomb

STEINBERGER
George   Susan A. Smith   31Oct1857 H13 W107 Austin

STEINRIDER
Elizabeth   Edward Tully   08Aug1844 E87 W87 Reid

STELLINGS
James   Mary Barnes   10Mar1813 E40 W47

STENGEL
Mary E.   Louis Spies   29Feb1864   W118

STEPHENS
Joshua, Junr Mary Ann Whitelock   10Jan1853 H3 W98 Gallion

STEPHENSON
Ann   Robert Parker   29Jan1800 E17 W29
George   Francina Christie   22Oct1836 E77 W78 McGrady
James   Priscilla Hopkins   30Jul1799 E16 W28
James   Charlotter Hopkins   26Jul1831 E69 W71 Stephenson

STEPHENSON, continued

James	Sarah A. Billingslea	03Nov1845	W89	
James	Cassandra M. Hopkins	23Apr1850	W95	
James	Elizabeth N. Rutledge	15Jun1860	W112	
Jemima	William Kimble	28Feb1821	E54 W58	
Jonah	Rachel Hughes	10May1799	E16 W28	
Jonas	Mary Dunsheath	16Jul1800	E18 W29	
Mary	Corbin Cooley	08Jan1833	E72 W73	Stephenson
Polly	Elijah Kimble	02Dec1795	E8 W24	
Sarah	Joseph C. Parker	03Jun1835	E75 W76	Furlong
William B.	Hannah Smith	22Dec1830	E68 W70	Tippet

STEPHONSON

John	Asabel Carter	20May1819	E51 W56	

STEVENSON [see Stevenson Archer, Stevenson Harkins]

Delia	Nathan Gorden	01Nov1797	E13 W26	Jno Allen
Geo.	Sarah Botts	05Oct1791	E1 W21	
John	Jane Stewart	22Feb1779	B1 W1	
Thos	Susannah Safferty	07Jun1780	C2 W4	
Wm	Hesther Parker	04Apr1796	E8 W25	

STEWART [see Stewart Homburger]

Ann	Isaac Baker	22Nov1780	C3 W5	
Bennet	Rebecca McGay	26Dec1811	E37 W45	
Elizabeth	John Osborn	27Oct1794	E6 W23	
Elizabeth Jane	William Forwood	05Feb1844	E86 W87	Finney
Jane	John Stevenson	22Feb1779	B1 W1	
Mary	Jas Boner	01Mar1779	B1 W1	
Matilda W.	Herman Stifler	21Aug1855	H8 W103	Walter
Sarah	James Standiford	27Dec1781	C5 W7	
Thomas R.	Sarah Jane Bay	17Jun1846	W90	
William	Catharine Riley	28Mar1859	W110	
William T.	Ann Oliver	21Sep1846	W90	

STIFLER

Herman	Matilda W. Stewart	21Aug1855	H8 W103	Walter

STILES

Betsy	Michael Gilbert	30Apr1794	E5 W23	[ret-AppA]
Edward	Mary Angell	14Jan1801	E19 W30	
Sarah Ann	William B. Morgan	07Feb1842	E84 W85	Finney
William	Hannah Carroll	24Dec1821	E55 W59	

STILLINGS

Eliza	Robert McFaddon	24Apr1834	E74 W75	Donahay
James	Ann Swart	11Sep1809	E34 W43	

STINBCH

Martin	Susan Sweetzer	25Jul1862	W116	

STINE

George	Ann Houze	22Apr1828	E64 W67	Keech

STINEREADER
Henry　　　　　　Mary Hartmann　　　　　13Dec1848　　　W93

STOCKDALE
Ann Elizth　　　　Mathew Dyer　　　　　　06Oct1863　　　W118
John　　　　　　　Mary Norris　　　　　　06Oct1806　E28 W38
Mary　　　　　　　James Jones　　　　　　29May1795　E7 W24
Patty　　　　　　 William Grafton　　　　26Aug1807　E30 W39
Thomas　　　　　　Sarah Baxter　　　　　 18Dec1797　E13 W26　John Coleman

STOCKHAM
Harriet E.　　　　William H. Ford　　　　01Apr1856　H9 W104 Smith
Martha Rebecca　　John D. Shetzline　　　29Jan1861　 W113 gr-Phila.
Mary E.　　　　　 James W. Michael　　　 15Mar1864　 W119
Mary P.　　　　　 Othman Malcom　　　　　26Jun1849　 W94
Thomas　　　　　　Martha Anthony　　　　 04Jun1831　E69 W71 Sewall

STOCKTON
Richard C.　　　　Eliza P. Hughes　　　　09May1814　E42 W49

STOKES
David　　　　　　 Sarah Johns　　　　　　09May1800　E18 W29
Elijah　　　　　　Elizabeth Galloway　　 11Sep1807　E30 W39
John R.　　　　　 Sarah Blaney　　　　　 20May1839　E81 W82 Park
Nathan R.　　　　 Hannah McFadden　　　　13Jan1845　E88 W88 Parks
William Brooks
　　　　　　　　　Henrietta Maria Chamberlain Hughes　27Jun1808　E31 W41

STOLINGER
Ann　　　　　　　 William Griffin　　　　06Jun1833　E73 W74 Finney

STOLLCUP
Sarah　　　　　　 William Frost　　　　　10Aug1802　E22 W32

STOLLINGER
Evan　　　　　　　Ann Dinsmore[?]　　　　10Feb1835　E75 W76 Hoopman

STONEBRAKER
John C.　　　　　 Margaret Priscilla Judd　02Dec1858　 W109
John S.　　　　　 Ellen E. Blake　　　　 10Jan1859　 W109
Washington　　　　Frances Maxwell　　　　14Mar1854　H5 W100 Finney

STONEFIEDER
Ferdinand　　　　 Mary Angeline Venault　20Jun1843　E86 W86 Bird

STONERIDER
Agnes　　　　　　 Anthony Pault　　　　　19Jun1846　 W90

STOVIR
Susannah　　　　　John Arthur　　　　　　03Dec1861　 W115

STRASBAUGH
A. Henry　　　　　Isabella W. Panbnell　 30Oct1862　 W116

STRAWBRIDGE
Henry M.	Elizabeth Almony	01Jan1851	W96	
Lydia Ann	John Woodrow	18Dec1858	W109	
William T.	Mary C. McClung	19Jan1858	W108	

STREDEHOOF
Peter	Elizabeth Baker	22Jan1830	E66 W69	Hewin

STREET
Ann Rebecca	William Ashton	04Dec1844	E87 W88	Keach
Charlotte	Silas Baldwin	06Feb1816	E44 W51	
Elizabeth	John Denbow, Junr	18Jan1808	E31 W40	
Elizabeth	John Parsons	29Aug1815	E43 W50	
John, Jr.	Ann Rutledge	28Feb1820	E52 W57	
John	Sarah Denbow	16Dec1839	E81 W82	Poteet
Mary	Josias Blaney	07Dec1800	E19 W30	
Mary Ann	Robert Cariens	28Sep1840	E82 W83	Cross
Robert	Elizabeth Gladden	08Aug1826	E61 W65	Keech
Shadrich	Elizabeth Watkins	14Nov1812	E39 W46	
Thomas	Sarah Kennaday	29May1800	E18 W29	
Thomas	Catharine Merryman	23Jan1813	E39 W47	
Thomas	Susan Aston	26Nov1816	E46 W52	
William	Sarah Cox	15Dec1799	E17 W28	

STREETT
Avarilla	Thomas McClure	01Feb1825	E59 W63	Morrison
Benjamin	Martha Grafton	14Sep1807	E30 W39	
David	Sarah Ashton	22Feb1827	E62 W66	Keech
Geraldine	Josiah J. Macatee	25Dec1860	W113	
Glenn	Keziah Ashton	10Feb1826	E61 W64	Keech
Gustein	Michael Whiteford	17Jan1848	W92	
Hannah	James Gemmill	17Feb1825	E59 W63	Poteet
Hannah	William Amoss	05Mar1859	W110	
Issabella	Clement Butler	05Feb1821	E53 W58	
James	Elizabeth Slade	04Mar1836	E76 W77	Keech
Jemima	John Bay	12Nov1828	E65 W68	Finney
John of Thos	Hannah Jones	04Jul1804	E25 W35	
John	Priscilla Ann Ruff	16Jan1844	E86 W87	Ke--
John	Drucilla A. Johns	02Jan1854	H4 W100	Smith
John Joshua	Kate M. Watters	21Dec1853	H4 W100	Keech
John Rusk	Elizabeth Hope	16Dec1845	W89	
John T.	Mary Ann Bay	24Nov1858	W109	
John Walter	Ann Maria Macatee	21Jan1862	W115	
Josephine V.	Wm. Henry Watters	11May1863	W117	
Joshua R.	Susan Neper	29May1848	W92	
Julia Ann	William J. Blaney	05Apr1842	E85 W85	Wilson
Margaret L.	William E. Whiteford	24Jan1863	W117	
Martha Jane	Edward Mitchell	04Dec1844	E87 W88	Keach
Martha S.	James M. Ramsay	01Jan1846	W89	
Mary	Henry R. Amoss	17Mar1803	E23 W33	
Mary	Alexander McComas	17Feb1830	E67 W69	Park
Mary	James Devoe	22Jan1834	E73 W75	Finney
Merryman	Priscilla Bull	06Jan1844	E86 W87	Keech
Rachel	James Grafton	04Jun1807	E30 W39	

STREETT, continued
Ruth A.	William A. Wilson	15Feb1858		W108	
Ruth E.	Thomas B. Macatee	10Jan1853	H3	W99	McNally
St Clair	Margaret Roberts	09Jan1844	E86	W87	Bon--
Samuel	Mary Ellen Miller	13Feb1855	H7	W102	Carter
Sarah	Frederick Swann	02Mar1825	E59	W63	Poteet
Sarah A.	Henry Ruff	18Jun1857	H12	W106	Keech
Sarah Jane	Hamilton Lefevre	09Oct1837	E78	W79	Holmeads
Thomas (of Thos)	Mary Ann Foster	27Mar1832	E70	W72	Finney
Thomas H.	Sarah A. Bull	25Oct1853	H4	W100	Keech
Virginia	Jacob Rutledge	15Feb1841	E83	W84	Holmead
William	Mary Ann Montgomery	18Jun1841	E83	W84	Reid
William H.	Sarah J. Warner	09Feb1842	E84	W85	Wilson

STREIGHTHOOF
Catharine   Baltice Fie   10Jun1825 E60 W63 Webster

STRICKER
Jona.   Catharine Wilson   21Mar1797 E10 W26

STRICKLEN
Eliza T.	Jesse M. Hutton	16Mar1841	E83	W84	Alexander
John Benjamin	Lydia Ann Hutton	18Mar1841	E83	W84	Cullum
Joshua	Elizabeth S. Cashman	03May1814	E42	W49	
Sarah	Samuel Taylor	23May1810	E35	W43	

STRICKLING
John   Elizabeth Timmons   04Jan1781 C4 W5

STRITE
John   Lucinda Hitchcock   16Feb1857 H11 W106 McCartney

STRITEHOOF
Catharine	Thomas Denbow	01Mar1852	H1	W98	Robey
Sarah	William H. Brown	11Jun1853	H4	W99	Keech
Susan Ann	James Barton	23May1854	H5	W101	Finney
William W.	Mary Louisa Foard	19Dec1857		W107	

STROBLE
William	Sarah Harper	05Jul1816	E45	W52
Zachariah	Cassandra Ann Amoss	07Jan1794	E5	W23

STROBRIDGE
Joseph   Rebecca Curtis   02May1832 E71 W72 Sewell

STROLENGER
Ann   Henry Spence   23Dec1807 E31 W40

STROND
Wm   Mary Kenny   m. 1778   [ret-AppA]

STRONG
Caroline E.	Thomas M. Rickets	27Jan1824	E57	W62	
Ellen	William Swift	16Aug1852	H2	W98	Sanks
Horatio	Catherine Nabb	04Mar1833	E72	W73	Sewell

STRONG, continued

James	Susan Combess	06Jun1810	E35 W44	
Joseph W.	Rachel Slade	15Jan1850	W94	
Mary E.	John P. Howard	07Sep1845	E88 W89	
Maximitton Maxwell	Frances Ann Allender	14Sep1825	E60 W64	
[minister - Benjn Richardson]				
Sarah	Wm Waltham	16Dec1779	C1 W3	
Sarah	William Chambers	15Dec1801	E21 W31	
Sarah	Jeremiah Bidison	16Mar1802	E21 W32	
Sarah Ann	Thomas J. Hill	24Nov1834	E74 W76	Dulany
Thomas Henry	Talitha E. Gilbert	29Jan1862	W115	

STROUD

Thomas	Mary Barnhouse	16Mar1779	B1 W1	

STUARD

Elinor	William Condrum	08May1780	C2 W4	

STUART

Luther M.	Louisa Osborn	01Dec1848	W93	

STUBBINS

Alice Amanda	William H. Andrews	04Mar1865	W121	
Samuel	Rachel Norris	06May1851	W96	

STULL

Margaret Jane	Isaac Erwin	25Apr1862	W116	

STUMP [see Mary Sophia Stump Thomas, Stump Smith]

Ann	John Archer, Jur.	15Nov1805	E22 W33	
Cassandra	Septimus Norris	27May1837	E78 W79	Goldsborough
Eliza C.	Stephen Boyd	15Feb1821	E53 W58	
Elizabeth	Abraham Jarrett	13Nov1804	E25 W35	
Esther	Jeremiah Harlon	08Sep1800	E18 W30	
Frederick	Mary A. Stump	18May1863	W117	
Hannah C.	James W. Williams	15Oct1817	E47 W54	
Hannah C.	John Lilley	13Jun1826	E61 W65	O'Brian
Hannah E.	Edward Griffith	15Feb1817	E46 W53	
Harman	Elizth Dallam	19Jun1793	E4 W22	
Hester Ann	Hugh S. Holloway	13Feb1843	E85 W86	Hoopman
Kezia C.	Richard I. Jackson	30Apr1833	E72 W74	Finney
Mary	James Williams	20Sep1808	E32 W41	
Mary	Abraham J. Thomas	29Jul1813	E40 W48	
Mary	Peter Hoofman	01Aug1825	E60 W64	Stephenson
Mary A.	Frederick Stump	18May1863	W117	
Priscilla	John L. Griffith	26Jun1837	E78 W79	Goldsborough
Rachel C.	Samuel Forwood of Jno.	04Apr1828	E64 W67	Stephenson
Reubin	Margaret Wilson	31Oct1854	H6 W101	Trout
Rubin	Margaret Wilson	11Mar1805	E26 W36	
Samuel	Hannah Carter	28Mar1822	E55 W60	
Sarah Biays	James Murray	30Jan1838	E79 W80	Goldsbrough
Susana G.	Samuel J. Ramsay	16Oct1838	E79 W81	Stephenson
William	Margaret Miller	09Dec1807	E30 W40	

STURDEVANCE
Susanna   Thomas Williams   19Oct1836   E77 W78 Furlong

STURGEN
Catharine   Benjamen Carter   m. 1777   [ret-AppA]

STURGEON
Eleanor   George Curry   19Oct1780. C3 W5
Jean   Jonathan West   02Nov1779   C1 W3

STURTS
John Christian   Catharine Hebner   21Nov1858   W109

SUDLUSKY
Michael   Sarah Sauis[?]   07Nov1838   E80 W81 Richardson

SULLIVAN
Catharine   Jerry Sloan   16Feb1857   H11 W106 Walter
Ja^{s.} T. Harriett M. Elliott   21Jan1835   E75 W76 Goldsborough
James   Catharine Croghan   10Jul1857   H12 W106 Walter
James   Johana Downing   03Jul1858   W108
Julia   William Gay   03May1861   W114

SUMERVILLE
Alexandria   Cornelia Olivia Sewell   05Nov1832   E71 W73 Higby

SUMMERS
Mary   Jeremiah Eden   02May1791   E1 W21

SUNDERLAND
Mary   Charles Johnson   25Jan1823   E56 W61
Mary Ann   Jonathan Pennell   30Apr1841   E83 W84 Cullum
Thomas   Avarilla Galloway   01Jan1856   H9 W104 Reineck

SUTER
Ann   Jacob Ergood   19Dec1821   E55 W59
Barbara   John Webb   06Jul1809   E34 W42
Judith   Richd Fitzgerald 25Jul1780 C2 W4
Nicholas   Mary Howlet   03Nov1840   E82 W83 Goldsbrough

SUTOR
Elenor Jane   George B. Quiggle   29Dec1855   H9 W103 Smith
Eliza   John Smith   24Jan1863   W117
George W.   Annie A. Jones   13Jun1861   W114
Henry P.   Mary C. Leattor   15Aug1843   E86 W86 Billup
Maria Frances   John C. Walker   09Oct1858   W109
Thomas   Frances Levy   11May1833   E72 W74 Higby

SUTTEN
Mary   William knight [sic]   22Jul1780   C2 W4

SUTTON [see Sutton Cullum]
Amanda M.	Timothy L. Keen	16Dec1850	W95	
Ann Eliza	George Warham	21Nov1825	E60 W64	Webster
[orig. lic. to Webster; cr-Harf]				
Benjamin	Lorenza Ayres	06Feb1830	E67 W69	O'Brian
Benjamin	Mary Ann Almony	01Feb1845	E88 W88	Reid
Jonathan	Sally McCracken	15Nov1791	E1 W21	[ret-AppA]
Margaret	Nicholas York	19Dec1798	E15 W27	
Mary	James Reardon	m. 1777		[ret-AppA]
Mary	Ignatius Gibson	04Apr1815	E43 W50	
Nicholas	Mary Ann Doran	05Jan1827	E62 W65	O'Brian
Reubin	Ann Armstrong	09Feb1804	E24 W34	
Ruth	William Amoss	06Jun1799	E16 W28	
Samuel	Susan Chauncey	26Mar1832	E70 W72	Hiby
Sarah	Benjamin Bruner	27Sep1819	E51 W57	
Sarah A.	William L. Murphy	27May1845	E88 W88	
Thomas	Henrietta Butler	25[?]Nov1844	E87 W88	

SWAIN
Bathias	Athur Coard	28Jul1783	C7 W8	
Nathan	Nancy Nowland	27Oct1801	E20 W31	

SWAINE
Elizabeth	Amos Cord	22Jan1798	E13 W27	Jno Allen

SWANN
Frederick	Sarah Streett	02Mar1825	E59 W63	Poteet

SWARP
George	Fredericka Rica	23Aug1864	W119	

SWART
Alphonzo	M. Alice Proctor	04Feb1865	W120	
Ann	James Stillings	11Sep1809	E34 W43	
Hannah	Charles Price	02Jan1805	E26 W36	
Sarah	William Matthews	03Apr1827	E62 W66	Pool
[orig. lic. to Pool; cr-Harf]				

SWARTS
Abraham B.	Ann B. Carroll	02Jul1816	E45 W51	
Ann Eliza	Caleb Michael	07Jan1834	E73 W75	Dunahay
David	Mary Lucas	12Apr1809	E33 W42	
Ephraim	Susannah Jones	25Nov1806	E29 W38	

SWARTZ
James H.	Mary Jane Mathews	25Jan1856	H9 W104	Finney
Mary Ann	Henry C. Bowman	24May1852	H2 W98	Gibson

SWEENEY
Daniel	Mary Magdalen Carty	24Dec1802	E22 W33	
Edward	Ann Scarbrough	22Oct1838	E79 W81	Crosgray
Emily	Isaac Morris	06Jul1814	E42 W49	
Milly	Asa Warner	04Aug1798	E15 W27	

SWEETING
Edward	Rebecca Ann Smith	01Apr1844	E87	W87	Ege
John	Mary Elizabeth Jeffers	06Dec1847		W92	

SWEETZER
Susan	Martin Stinboh	25Jul1862		W116

SWENEY
Ruth	Bernard Dailey	10Feb1843	E85	W86	Reid

SWIFT
Amanda M.	Thomas Godwin	09Apr1860		W112	
Daniel	Mary Martin	10Nov1825	E60	W64	Tidings
Daniel M.	Louisa Martin	05Jan1839	E80	W81	Reese
David	Lettice Biggs	23Feb1796	E8	W25	
David	Martha Roberts	07Dec1803	E24	W34	
Elizabeth	James Fisher	18Jan1807	E29	W38	
James	Eliz^th J/I. Wilson	04Aug1857	H12	W106	Monroe
Jane	John Knight	08May1833	E72	W74	Donahay
John	Rebecca Bennett	30Dec1830	E68	W70	Tippet
Joseph	Eadeth Everitt	15Jan1835	E75	W76	Sheppard
Margarett	James Weeks	21Feb1828	E64	W67	Finney
Martha	Thomas Carty	09Apr1816	E45	W51	
Susannah	Simon Brown	29Aug1855	H8	W103	Lemmon
Thomas	Sarah Brown	18Dec1852	H2	W98	Finney
William	Ellen Strong	16Aug1852	H2	W98	Sanks

SYKES
William	Sarah Reese	21May1828	E64	W67	Parks

SYMINGTON
Thomas	Mary A. Wilson	16Nov1864		W120

SYNOTT
Thomas	Martha Haithhorn	12Mar1794	E5	W23

TAFF
Ann	James Lawrance	01May1782	C6	W7	cr-Harf

TALBOOT
Mary	Wm Willson	06Dec1781	C5	W7

TALBOT
Elizabeth	Joseph Frazier	26Apr1823	E57	W61

TALBOTT
Edmund	Eliz^th Parker	10Oct1779	B3	W2
Marg^t	Geo. Bradford	20Apr1784	C8	W9

TARBET
Agnes	Patrick Curley	14Mar1814	E41	W49

TARDY
John	Ann Clark	04Apr1781	C4

TASKER					
Ann	Edwd Dillion	29Jun1792	E2	W21	[ret-AppA]
TASON					
Andrew J.	Emma Hinsey	23Aug1853	H4	W99	Wilson
TATE					
Martha	William G. McLure	12Jan1820	E52	W57	

TAYLOR [see Sarah Taylor Gilbert, J. Taylor Crawford, Taylor Cole, Taylor Gilbert, Taylor Hughes]

Abraham	Mary Foard	m. 1777			[ret-AppA]
Abraham S.	Nancy Touchstone	25Apr1820	E52	W57	
Amanda E.	William Billingslea	26Jun1839	E81	W82	Prettiman
Amasa	Jemimah Kimble	01Jan1780	C1	W3	
Ann	Lancelot Carlile	22Jul1781	C5	W6	
[before 17Jul entry]					
Asa William	Sarah Ann Everist	26Nov1846		W90	
Ashberry	Frances Shody	02Mar1802	E21	W32	
Bennet	Mary Deaver	13May1806	E28	W38	
Bennett	Rachel Weeks	20Jun1832	E71	W73	Sewell
Charity	Benj. Jones	13Sep1791	E1	W21	
Elizabeth	Thomas Johnson	12Nov1796	E10	W25	John Coleman
[ret-AppA]					
Elizabeth	William Temple	05Jun1820	E52	W58	
Elizabeth	Hiram Coale	12Aug1830	E67	W70	Webster
[orig. lic. to Webster; cr-Harf]					
Elizabeth	Ridgeway Thomas	13Jan1857	H11	W105	Kensey
Elizabeth H.	Philip T. Quinlan	24Mar1857	H11	W106	Crawford
Frances	Nathan Hughes	06Jan1813	E39	W47	
George	Florilla Kimble	24Jan1806	E27	W37	
George F.	Nancy Wright	29Apr1820	E52	W57	
Hannah	Stephen Kimble	11Feb1793	E4	W22	[ret-AppA]
Hannah	John Davison	m. 1793			[ret-AppA]
Helen	John Keithley	11May1846		W90	
Henry S.	Susan Timmons	23Dec1833	E73	W74	Dulaney
Isaiah	Catharine Kimble	01Jan1805	E26	W36	
Issabella	John Michell	m. 1789			[ret-AppA]
James	Jane White	26Aug1795	E7	W24	
James	Sarah Aitkin	25Jan1800	E17	W29	
James	Susannah Kimble	06Feb1804	E24	W34	
James	Hester Sanders	30Sep1806	E28	W38	
James of Stephn.	Charlotte Dulaney	03May1809	E33	W42	
James	Mary Cannon	07Apr1814	E41	W49	
James F.	Margaret Ashley	21Jun1858		W108	
James F.	Sallie F. Mahan	10Dec1861		W115	
John	Alisanna Meliken	20Jun1779	B2	W2	
John	Rebecca Landrum	01Jul1795	E7	W24	
John	Mary Ann Somers	11Oct1864		W119	
John M.	Sarah Ann Hopkins	21Jul1835	E75	W76	Furlong
Joseph E.	Rebecca Knight	18Oct1830	E68	W70	Tippit
Lehemiah	Samuel Beard	m. 1777			[ret-AppA]

TAYLOR, continued

Mary	Hesekiah Whitacare	18Jul1783	C7	W8	
Mary	Thomas Dorney	07Nov1808	E32	W41	
Mary	Stephen Jones	24Nov1808	E32	W41	
Mary	John Chisholm	05Dec1808	E32	W41	
Mary	Eli Bennett	16Feb1819	E50	W56	
Mary	Samuel Shannon	14Jun1825	E60	W64	Webster
Mary Ann	Richard Hopkins	21Jul1832	E71	W73	Finney
Mathia	William P. Willey	15Nov1850		W95	
Milcha	Cooper Boyd	22Feb1821	E53	W58	
Minerva J.	Allen Hoofman	06Jun1865		W121	
Naomi	Joshua H. Dulany	25Jan1821	E53	W58	
Naomi P.	Richard R. Cullum	24Mar1825	E59	W63	Morrison
Neomi	James Michael	25Oct1794	E6	W23	
Preston D.[?] Parke	Ann Nevill	14Mar1842	E84	W85	Finney
Richard	Eleanor Courtnay	19Dec1800	E19	W30	
Richard M.	Margaret Ann Hopkins	16May1861		W114	
Robert	Margt Wheeler	01Apr1794	E5	W23	
Robert G.	Sarah A. Deaver	16Aug1862		W116	
Samuel	July Walmsley	26Mar1804	E25	W35	
Samuel	Sarah Stricklen	23May1810	E35	W43	
Samuel	Milkey Hill	14Nov1825	E60	W64	Tidings
Samuel G.	Mary Sheckles	13Nov1827	E63	W66	Keech
Sarah	William Moulton	20Dec1826	E62	W65	Robb
Sarah	Winston Ricketts	07Nov1836	E77	W78	Keech
Sarah A.	Thos. Wm. Mallick	15Sep1863		W118	
Sarah E.	Owen Osborn	02Dec1851	H1	W97	Gibson
Sarah Elizth	Robert Wilson	12Dec1857		W107	
Sarah J.	James Numbers	24May1858		W108	
Sarah Jane	Charles Shrodes	11Mar1850		W94	
Susan Ann	Aquila Dulany	19Dec1827	E64	W67	Finey
[orig. lic. to Finney; cr-Harf]					
Susannah	Daniel Smithson	03Feb1784	C8	W9	cr-Harf
William	Sarah Ann Everist	03Nov1846		W90	
Wm P.	Susan G. Norris	04Jan1843	E85	W86	Wilson

TAYSON

Caroline J.	William Knight	26Jan1859		W109	
Elijah	Mary Ginet	02Nov1820	E53	W58	
Elijah	Arabella Ross	10Nov1857	H13	W107	Gallion

TEBBETT

James	Ann Turner	17Feb1832	E70	W72	Richardson

TEMPLE

Minerva	Corbin L. Onion	02Apr1855	H7	W102	Keech
Rebecca H.	John T. Lee	25Feb1864		W118	
Samuel A.	Mary S. Onion	19Jan1860		W111	
Thomas D.	Sarah R. Scarborough	21Oct1850		W95	
William	Elizabeth Taylor	05Jun1820	E52	W58	

TEMPLER

Emily C.	Francis H. Janney	13Apr1853	H3	W99	[min. --]

TEMPLETON
Susanna	John Burke	28Dec1796	E10 W25	

TEMPLIN
Sarah	Joseph Prigg	13Jan1804	E24 W34	

TENLY
Henry	Mary Curry	13Nov1847	W92	

TERRY
Joseph R.	Edith W. Livezey	10Sep1857	H12 W107	Cushing

THEFT
Rachel	John Thomas	02May1780	C2 W4	

THOMAS
Abraham J.	Mary Stump	29Jul1813	E40 W48	
Ann	Jas Ward	17Jul1781	C5 W6	
["costs c/o John Lee Gibson"]				
Clement	Elizabeth Duley	31Jul1805	E26 W36	
David	Sarah Johnson	08Jun1800	E18 W29	
Elizabeth	James Shields	23Mar1801	E19 W30	
Elizabeth Jarrett	John C. Richards	27Oct1834	E74 W75	Higbee
Evan	Sarah Phesay	06Mar1784	C8 W9	
Frances	Jacob Wilson	27Sep1803	E23 W34	
Hannah	David Ecoff	10Feb1813	E39 W47	
Herman	Elizabeth Turner	19Nov1822	E56 W60	
James	Arabella Barnes	01Feb1796	E8 W24	
James	Mary Henderson	03Apr1817	E47 W53	
Jane	Barnet Johnson	27Apr1791	E1 W21	
Jane	Joseph Ward	23Nov1801	E20 W31	
John	Rachel Theft	02May1780	C2 W4	
John	Jane Cetherwood	28Dec1807	E31 W40	
John	Catharine Greer	20Jan1846	W89	
Joseph	Hannah Carty	27Oct1799	E16 W28	
Joseph	Permelia Collins	14Aug1805	E26 W36	
Martha	Barney Currier	22Aug1780	C2 W4	
Mary	Robert Hannah	25Jan1779	B1 W1	
Mary	Thomas Mills	m. 1786		[ret-AppA]
Mary	John Lawrence	16May1854	H5 W101	Trout
Mary Elizabeth	William Dawson Wilson	02Jan1837	E77 W78	Dulany
Mary M.	Wm Jewell	29Jun1784	C8 W9	
Mary Sophia Stump	Edward Y. Higbee	14Oct1835	E75 W77	Goldsborough
Patty	Moses Hill	14Oct1823	E57 W61	
Ralph H.	Rebecca Finley	31Dec1857	W107	
Ridgeway	Elizabeth Taylor	13Jan1857	H11 W105	Kinsey
Sarah Ann	Joseph Pue	10Jul1838	E79 W80	Richardson
William	Sarah Scarborough	23Apr1812	E38 W46	

THOMPSON [see J. Thompson Frieze]
Alexander of Danl.	Elizabeth Kidd	27Nov1807	E30 W40	
Andrew	Mary Cunningham	26Dec1804	E25 W35	
Andrew	Frances Day	04Mar1805	E26 W36	
Aquila	Susan Patterson	22Nov1810	E36 W44	
Bernard	Martha Renshaw	03Jan1811	E36 W44	

THOMPSON, continued

Charles H.	Martha Jane Gorrell	12Jun1850	W95	
Charles H.	Matilda J. Whitaker	15Apr1857	H11 W106	Cushing
Cynthia	Wm Hays	11Feb1796	E8 W25	
Daniel of Alexr.	Hannah Long	30Jun1808	E32 W41	
David	Sarah Drew	01Apr1779	B2 W1	
Edwd	Elizth Hanson	08Feb1780	C1 W3	
Edward	Amelia Whitaker	13Jun1825	E60 W63	Stevenson
Edward B.	Elizabeth Greenfield	04Jan1825	E59 W63	Guest
Edward E.	Lavinia Myers	17Mar1862	W115	
Eleanor	Benjamin Tracey	04Oct1820	E53 W58	
Elijah	Martha J. Forsythe	25Sep1840	E82 W83	Finny
Elizth	William Bower	20Jun1782	C6 W8	
Elizabeth	Sampson Touchstone	09Aug1803	E23 W34	
Elizabeth	Thomas Coale	24Nov1807	E30 W40	
Elizabeth	John Monohon	04Aug1810	E35 W44	
Ellender	John D. Grafton	03Apr1862	W116	
Evan W.	Sarah Elizth Knight	19Aug1859	W110	
Frances A.	Benjamin Chesney	08Jan1853	H3 W98	Finney
Garratt	Ann Rodgers	05Oct1808	E32 W41	
James	Hannah Y. Jay	m. 1788		[ret-AppA]
James	Sarah Gladden	04Nov1815	E43 W50	
James of Jas.	Mary Ann Renshaw	29Aug1818	E49 W55	
James	Elizabeth F. Gilbert	11Apr1845	E88 W88	Gallion
James	Ann Jane Cullum	04May1853	H3 W99	Finney
James	Mary E. How	15Apr1861	W114	
Jane	William C. Kirkwood	30Jun1824	E58 W62	
Jesse	Sophia Moore	08Jan1828	E64 W67	Pool
Jno	Susannah Luckey	05[?]Jul1781	C5 W6	
[entry after 17Jul]				
John	Susan Moore	23Jul1834	E74 W75	Finney
Joseph	Margaret Jarvis	01Aug1805	E26 W36	
Joshua	Ann Everist	02Feb1825	E59 W63	Stephenson
Mahlon	Angeline Whitaker	15Dec1851	H1 W97	Huntington
Margaret	William Jarvos	24Aug1780	C3 W4	
Margaret	Philip Coale	13Jan1836	E76 W77	Keech
Martha	Samuel Arthur	19Apr1862	W116	
Martha	George V. Osborn	08May1863	W117	
Martha C.	Job. W. Lamberth	20Mar1848	W92	
Mary	Jeremiah Bennington	17Sep1818	E49 W55	
Mary E.	James R. Deckman	28Apr1865	W121	
Matthew A.	Mary Ellis	24Mar1806	E28 W37	
Precilla	John Kean, Junr.	12Oct1801	E20 W31	
Rachel	Benjamin Hobbs	01Dec1801	E21 W31	
Sarah	John Renshaw	10Nov1810	E36 W44	
Sarah	John D. Conley	22Nov1810	E36 W44	
Sarah	Elisha Johnson	27Jan1858	W108	
Sarah Ann	George H. Bayless	21May1859	W110	
Stephen J.	Mary B. Hayward	10Oct1826	E62 W65	Keech
Susan	John Hawkins	02Mar1826	E61 W64	Richarsdon
Thomas	Elizth Willmott	28Jan1779	B1 W1	
Thomas of Josa.	Ann Grafton	16Jan1805	E26 W36	
Thomas	Elizabeth Jackson	08Feb1809	E33 W42	

THOMPSON, continued

William	Permelia Moore	20Jan1817	E46 W52	
William	Mary Wood	13Dec1824	E59 W63	Guest
William H.	Mary Jones	25Feb1830	E67 W69	Keech
William H.	Margaret M. Russell	09Dec1854	H6 W101	Finney
William T.	Martha A. Greenland	15Jan1853	H3 W99	Chapman
William T.	Sarah E. Moffit	22Jan1859	W109	

THOMSON

Aq^a Hannah Woolsey   02Oct1781   C5 W7

THORNTON

John   Jane Dunstone   10Apr1779   B2 W1

THRAP

Joel S.   Hannah Ann E. Rogers   15Jul1845   E88 W89

THRIFT

Richard   Mary Daws   02Oct1801   E20 W31

TIGNOR

Margaret J/I.   Aquila S. Price   01Oct1856   H10 W105 Monroe

TIMMONS

Elizabeth	John Strickling	04Jan1781	C4 W5	
Elizabeth	William Foard	02Jun1827	E63 W66	McVey
Harriot	William R. Woollen	31Oct1818	E49 W55	
J. Edwin	Sarah Elizth Wilson	22Nov1859	W111	
Jane	Thos Cosley	20Sep1779	B3 W2	
John	Elizabeth Lee	11Feb1817	E46 W53	
John C.	Rebecca Timmons	03Dec1816	E46 W52	
Julia	James Hodge	06Feb1839	E80 W81	Collins
Mary	James Foard	28Apr1838	E79 W80	Richardson
Rachel	Samuel Vanhorne	24Mar1825	E59 W63	Tydings
Rebecca	John C. Timmons	03Dec1816	E46 W52	
Sarah P.	James Spicer, Jr.	06Nov1857	H13 W107	Monroe
Susan	Henry S. Taylor	23Dec1833	E73 W74	Dulaney
Thomas Edward	Barbara Shinesucker	08Nov1858	W109	

TIMMOS

John C.   Elizabeth Saunders   17Nov1830   E68 W70 Tippet

TIMONDS

Mary Jane   Jacob Henry Sills   13Mar1860   W111

TIPPET

Elizabeth   John Blaney   29Jun1810   E35 W44

TIPTON

James W.	Martha M. Frances	21May1857	H12 W106	Cushing
Lee	Rebecca Merryman	14Oct1818	E49 W55	
William	Catharine Deets	25Apr1849	W93	

TOALSON
Mary   Joseph Smith   m. 1777   [ret-AppA]

TOBIN
Ellen   Michael Farrell   08May1856 H10 W104 Walter
Hannah   Jeremiah Tobin   04Feb1861   W113
James   Martha Lingan   17Nov1857 H13 W107 Walter
Jeremiah   Hannah Tobin   04Feb1861   W113

TODD
John   Mary Ann Wood   15Nov1836 E77 W78 Finney
Lewis H.   Eugenia A. Osborn   28Dec1843 E86 W87 Finney

TOLLENGER
Daniel   Mary Ann Hopkins   12Apr1827 E63 W66 Stephenson

TOLLINGER
Clemency   John Trego   10Dec1851 H1 W97 Gallion
George   Elizabeth Brannan   03Feb1854 H5 W100 Gallion

TOLLY
Sarah   William G. Andrew   11Jun1861   W114

TOLSON
Isaac   Neomia Cord   01Jul1780 C2 W4
Isaac   Nancy Stallions   22Jul1780 C2 W4
Isaac   Ann Collins   26Oct1780 C3 W5
   [additional entry 20Nov1780; C3]

TOMLINSON
Elijah T.   Eleanor Kellough   21Jun1840 E82 W83 Finney

TOMPKINS
Angeline   John Fitzpatrick   08Apr1856 H10 W104 Smith

TOPPAN [see Toppan Webster]

TORRANCE
George   Eleanor Fulford   30Jun1829 E66 W68 Keech

TOUCHSTONE [see also TUCHSTONE, TUTCHSTON, etc.]
Ann   Robert McMullen   30Oct1784 C9 W10
   [this couple listed in different hand 25Oct1779 B3 and crossed out]
Elizth   Geo. Shannon   03Jun1779 B2 W2
Elizabeth   George Green   05Jan1839 E80 W81 Reese
Hester   Thomas Wm. Jackson   15Jun1814 E42 W49
Jemima   William Laurence   06Sep1830 E67 W70 Webster
Julian   Richard Hawkins   11Dec1813 E41 W48
Nancy   Abraham S. Taylor   25Apr1820 E52 W57
Sampson   Elizabeth Thompson   09Aug1803 E23 W34
Sarah   William Butler   01Apr1818 E49 W55
William   Sarah Price   27Mar1807 E29 W39

TOUCHTON
Henry	Eliza Wood	04Apr1831	E69	W71	Finney

TOUCHTONE
Martha J/I.	Andrew J. Curry	17Aug1863	W117

TOWLAND
Benjamin	Martha Denbow	06Dec1814	E42	W49

TOWNLEY
James	Letitia Kenley	26Jul1845	E88	W89

TOWNSEN
James	Cathrine Jones	12Sep1780	C3	W5

TOWNSLEY
James	Mary Madden	19Jun1818	E49	W55	
James	Lamiania[?] Acres	27Feb1837	E77	W79	Finny
Joseph	Margaret Mahan	04Jan1785	C10	W10	
Margaret	John Martin	04Jun1800	E18	W29	
Margaret	George Shiery	28May1847		W91	
Samuel	Ann Hutchison	05Apr1858		W108	
William	Ann Rebecca McDow	15Nov1853	H4	W100	Dumb

TOWSON
Jacob	Margaret Towson	13Nov1798	E15	W27
Margaret	Jacob Towson	13Nov1798	E15	W27
Margaret Ann	Jacob A. Keller	24Dec1863		W118
Rosanna	Joseph Lee	16Jan1851		W96

TOY
Isaac	Frances Dallam	18Mar1793	E4	W22
John	Mary Carlon	11Feb1793	E4	W22

TRACEY
Benjamin	Eleanor Thompson	04Oct1820	E53	W58
Edward	Elizabeth Amoss	03Mar1810	E35	W43
Mary	Michael Dunn	25Nov1808	E32	W41

TRACY
Charles	Margaret Gardnor	27Sep1816	E45	W52
Joshua	Rachel Dilworth	06Oct1817	E47	W53
Richard M.	Mary Ann Kennedy	03Feb1858		W108

TRAFFORD
Thomas	Almira C. Mackison	07May1859	W110

TRAGER
Philip	Alice Lester	08Mar1826	E61	W65	Webster
[orig. lic. to Isaac Webster; cr-Harf]					
Robert	Sarah Gallion	31Jan1809	E33	W42	

TRAGO
Permelia	Frederick Mitchell	28Feb1801	E19 W30	
Susanna	James Fulton	13Aug1803	E23 W34	
William	Ellen Brannon	22Jan1817	E46 W52	

TRAINOR
Mary L.	William L. Chalk	21Dec1861	W115

TRANAR
Catharine Eliz[th]	Martin Caulfor	16Jun1858	W108

TRAPNALL
Rebecca	James Hicks, Jun[r]	18Jan1806	E27 W37

TRAVERSE
John	Mary Sophia Cole	28Jul1845	E88 W89

TRAVIS
Catherine	Israel Proctor	13May1837	E77 W79	Richardson
John	Catherine Bodden	27Feb1817	E46 W53	

TREADAWAY
Dan[l]	Mary Young	30Jul1781	C5 W6
[above entry before others in July]			
Mary	Dan[l] Donahae	14Jun1779	B2 W2

TREADWAY
Thomas	Julian Gilbert	08Jan1806	E27 W37
Thos. M.	Martha R. Rice	01Jun1863	W117

TREADWELL
Amanda E.	Nelson Rosha	31Mar1864	W119	
Eliza Ann	Benjamin Hendon	03Jan1839	E80 W81	Crosgey
Henry	Harriet Bussey	08Jan1849	W93	
Joseph B.	Ann Lochary	17Feb1857	H11 W106	Walter
Stephen	Eleanor Sheridine	24Oct1805	E27 W36	

TREDAWAY
Amos	Margaret Jane Carroll	17Jun1847	W91

TREDWAY
Ann	James Anderson	06Jan1815	E42 W49	
Ann	Henry Woolen	27Jun1818	E49 W55	
Aquila	Nancy Anderson	18Dec1809	E34 W43	
Aquila E.	Sarah A. Barnes	13Jun1855	H7 W103	Finny
Chenoweth	Matilda Miller	07Feb1827	E62 W66	Webster
[orig. lic. to Webster; cr-Harf]				
Christeen	George Hawkins	29Jan1838	E79 W80	Finy
Edward	Elizabeth Anderson	20Mar1810	E35 W43	
Elizabeth	Martin T. Gilbert	02Apr1805	E26 W36	
James	Mary Baxter	23Mar1808	E31 W40	
Martha	Rezin Gorrell	19Dec1831	E70 W72	Finney
Mary	Benjamin Warren	21Sep1807	E30 W39	
Mary A.	James P. Monks	10Feb1828	E64 W67	Keech

TREDWAY, continued
Ruth	Joseph Cathcart	15Nov1836	E77 W78	Jordan[?]
Sarah	Baily Warn	07Feb1801	E19 W30	
Thomas	Elizabeth Magness	26Mar1828	E64 W67	Keech

[orig. lic. to Keech; cr-Harf]

Thomas	Martha Bull	31Oct1850	W95	
William	Amelia Magness	21Dec1809	E34 W43	

TREDWELL
Helena	William Wright	22Sep1863	W118	
John	Mary Maganis	05Jan1836	E76 W77	Richardson

TREGO
Hannah	John D. Alderson	20Dec1838	E80 W81	Scott
John	Clemency Tollinger	10Dec1851	H1 W97	Gallion

TREUSCH
Charles	Laura A. Buckingham	16Sep1850	W95	

TRIGGER
Susan G.	Robt F. McGaw	06Jan1855	H6 W102	Reese
William	Sarah Meeks	07Oct1812	E39 W46	

TRISLER
Mary	Aaron Carver	17Mar1812	E38 W46	

TROUTNER
Amanda M.	William E. McCann	27Apr1853	H3 W99	Trout
Ann	Caleb Gallion	12Jun1823	E57 W61	
David	Jane Jones	03Jul1861	W114	
Eliza	Walter Cunningham	15Dec1847	W92	
Eliza E.	James M. Philips	19Dec1864	W120	
John H.	Margaret Burkins	24Oct1861	W114	

TRULAP
Isaac	Mary Hitchcock	19Jan1781	C4 W5	

TRUNDLE
James T.	Rachel M. Folk	03Jul1850	W95	

TUCHSTONE
Johel	Frances Armstrong	25Sep1838	E79 W80	Sheperd
Marg^t	Wm Carroll	14Nov1782	C6 W8	
Margaret	Thomas Shannon	27Dec1841	E84 W85	Cullen

TUCKER
Elisha R.	Hannah Ecoff	16Oct1854	H6 W101	Wilson
Elizabeth	Thomas Sanders	16Oct1822	E56 W60	
John C.	Emma Louisa Smith	23Apr1860	W112	
Mary	Thomas Waltham	22Oct1806	E29 W38	
William, Junr	Rebecca Paul	25Jan1816	E44 W51	
William H.	Sarah A. Jones	28Mar1848	W92	

TUDAR
John	Ann Inloes	29Mar1780	C1 W3	

TUDER
Elizabeth | Charles Baker | 12Sep1780 C3 W5

TULLY
Edward | Elizabeth Steinrider | 08Aug1844 E87 W87 Reid

TUNIS [see Martha Tunis Hill]
Martha | Richᵈ Horn | 27Jul1779 B3 W2

TURK
Cassandra | Walter Cunningham | 21Jun1804 E25 W35
Harriott | John Griffen | 09Nov1809 E34 W43
Jane | Walter Cunningham | 29Dec1814 E42 W49
Martha | John O'Donnell | 13May1807 E29 W39
Mary | Alvin Curtis | 07Apr1817 E47 W53

TURNER
Abel | Mary Madden | 19[?]Mar1797 E11 W25
  (Ret'd by Parson Luckie)
Alex^r. | Jane Johnson | 10May1780 C2 W4
Andrew | Julia Ann Whiteford | 16Jan1858 W107
Andw^s | Ann McDonnall | 27[?]Mar1780 C1 W3
Ann | James Tebbett | 17Feb1832 E70 W72 Richardson
Cathrine | John Johnson | 14Nov1780 C3 W5
Elizabeth | William Price | 05Jun1803 E23 W33 [ret-AppA]
Elizabeth | Herman Thomas | 19Nov1822 E56 W60
George | Mary Way | 03Oct1864 W119
Hannah | William Howlett | 03Feb1838 E79 W80 Collins
James | Sarah Calder | 22Apr1811 E36 W45
Martha E. | Nelson B. Campbel | 11Oct1864 W119
Mary | Benjamin Magness | 23Jun1825 E60 W64 Tidings
Mary Ann | Alexander C. McCurdy | 26Feb1831 E68 W71 Tippet
Mary Elizabeth | Alexander Grafton | 21Apr1852 H2 W98 Davis
Robert | Mary Vance | 16Nov1852 H2 W98 Parks
Sarah | Robt Allison | 09Jul1779 B3 W2
Sarah | Hugh Bay | 01Mar1785 C10 W10
Thomas | Delia Corbin | 24Oct1797 E11 W26
Thomas | Jemmima Hughes | 31Mar1801 E20 W31
Thomas | Phebe Morris | 09Nov1801 E20 W31
Thomas | Mary Price | 03Mar1810 E35 W43
Thomas | Margaret Johnson | 05Mar1816 E44 W51
William | Ann Allender | 13Nov1818 E50 W55
William | Amelia Ann Standiford | 08Sep1835 E75 W77 Keech
William | Emma Jane Rutledge | 06Jan1859 W109

TURPIN
Joseph A. | Laura S. Archer | 17Oct1836 E77 W78 Finney

TUSTON
Sarah | Thomas Noble | 08Feb1826 E61 W64 Stephenson

TUTCHSTON
John | Caroline West | 13Feb1839 E80 W81 Finney

TUTCHSTONE
Ann   Thomas Shannon   01Sep1821   E54 W59

TUTCHTON
Elizabeth   John Tutchton   07Mar1826   E61 W65   Richardson
John   Elizabeth Tutchton   07Mar1826   E61 W65   Richardson
Sampson   Sarah Ann Howard   07Jan1840   E81 W82   Prettyman

TUTCHTONE
Herman   Permelia Ann Carroll   14Dec1846   W90

TWEEDALE
James   Margaret Pendigast   30May1854   H5   W101 McNally

TYLER [see Tyler Baldwin]

TYRELL
Edwd N.   Ann Bosley   22Dec1835   E76 W77   Parks

TYRRELL
James   Lathen Norris   12Dec1801   E21 W31

TYSON
John   Anna Mary Gray   01Feb1848   W92

UMSHEAD[?]
Jean Favor   John H. Weaver   25Dec1841   E84 W85   Reid

UPP
Francis F.   Cecelia Blaney   30Sep1850   W95

VAN BIBBER
George L.   Hannah C. Archer   05Nov1839   E81 W82   Finney

VANCE
David   Mary Woolsey   03Oct1781   C5   W7
Elizabeth   William Cairns   13Jan1830   E66 W69   Morrison
Mary   Robert Turner   16Nov1852   H2   W98   Parks
Rebecca   Hugh Hannah   04Feb1781   C4   W6
Samuel   Mary Watters   08Oct1798   E15 W27
William   Martha Keeth   23Feb1781   C4   W6
William C.   Mary Hutchins   07May1832   E71 W73   Morison

VANDEGRIFT
Ann   Samuel Deaver   04Jan1809   E33 W42
Catharine   Josias Bailey   24Feb1823   E56 W61
George   Lydia Hawkins   15May1807   E29 W39
John W.   Matilda Williams   20Jan1813   E39 W47
Mary   John Hawkins   06Jan1807   E29 W38

VANHORN
Albert   Sarah Jane Kimble   24Nov1862   W116
Ann K.   Winlock Stapleford   15Dec1825   E60 W64   Webster

VANHORN, continued
Isaac	Mary Virginia Chalk	30Dec1861	W115	ALJ1-34,223
Isaac	Mary S. Riley	08Feb1865	W120	
Jesse	Ann Spencer	05Mar1818	E48 W54	
Sarah	John W. Hildt	19Oct1863	W118	

VANHORNE
Samuel   Rachel Timmons   24Mar1825   E59 W63   Tydings

VANSICKEL
Bennett	Mary Ann Everist	21May1817	E47 W53
Cordelia	John Chauncey	30Jan1816	E44 W51
Mary Ann	Henry Austin Greenfield	14May1821	E54 W59

VANSICKLE
Bennett	Susanna Chauncey	02Feb1807	E29 W38
Elizabeth G.	Garret Chauncey	24Jan1809	E33 W42
Frances	Aqua. Nelson	14Feb1792	E2 W21
Henry	Cordelia Chauncey	01Feb1804	E24 W34
Jane	Owen Roberts	02Jun1798	E15 W27

VANZANDT
William   Ann Hill   12Feb1822   E55 W60

VANZANT
John	Sabina Mills	15Jul1795	E7 W24
John	Ann Pennington	12Mar1804	E24 W35

VEAZEY
George   Mary Webster   10Jun1828   E64 W67   Finney

VEAZY
George   Rebecca Barnes   05Feb1813   E39 W47

VENAULT
Mary Angeline   Ferdinand Stonefieder   20Jun1843   E86 W86   Bird

VERNAY
Jane [Vernay?]	Israel Curry	27Dec1825	E60 W64	Richardson
Nancy	Walter Martin	28Jan1819	E50 W56	

VERNEY [see Verney St. Clair]
Elizabeth   Bailey St. Clair   01Apr1818   E49 W55

VINCENT
Charles   Cassandra Webster   03Dec1811   E37 W45

VISEPWORTH[?]
Sarah   Wᵐ Smith   12Mar1793   E4 W22

VOGAN
Nancy   Ezekiel Slade   20Oct1808   E32 W41

VOSHALL
Elizth   Arch^d Johnson   23Sep1783   C7   W9

VOSHAN
Daniel   Alice McGaw   02Sep1793   E5   W23

WADSWORTH
Ann	John Norris	10Sep1799	E16 W28
Elizabeth	Samuel Hughes	23Apr1821	E54 W59
Sarah	Nathan Lytle	24Feb1821	E53 W58

WAINWRIGHT
John P.   Naoma Shade   08Nov1864   W120

WAKELAND
Benedict H.	Sarah Ann McVey	05Jun1856	H10 W105 Rankin
Benjamin	Mary Ann Bay	29Dec1821	E55 W59
Hannah	John Wann, Junior	28Feb1809	E33 W42
James	Mary Susan Greenland	17Mar1856	H9 W104 Finney
Juliann	Thomas Lilly	02Feb1828	E64 W67 Keech
[orig. lic. to Keech; cr-Harf]			
Mary	John Evans	02Nov1822	E56 W60
William P.	Amanda E. Greenland	29Jan1850	W94

WAKELIN
Joshua   Mary Norrington   10Mar1819   E50 W56

WAKEMAN [see Wakeman Bryarly, Wakeman B. Hopkins, Wakeman Martin, Wakeman F. Morgan]

WALDER
Theo.   Mary Harman   10Mar1865   W121

WALDON [see Waldon Gilbert Middleton]

WALDRIN
Peter   Daley Richardson   15Oct1779   B3   W2

WALDROM
Darkney[?]	John Monahan	26Jan1780	C1 W3
David	Martha Monahan	11Jun1781	C5 W6

WALKER
Ann	William R. Brookes	27May1802	E22 W32
Ann	William Robinson	05Feb1818	E48 W54
Anna J.	William H. Gale	28Sep1858	W109
Christian H.	Cornelia A. Coale	22Jun1857	H12 W106 Littleton
Elizabeth	James Moore	20Jul1780	C2 W4 [bn Walks?]
Elizabeth	William E. Woodhouse	26Mar1831	E68 W71 Stephenson
Elizabeth	James W. McKendless	02Dec1864	W120
Elizabeth A.	James C. Malcolm	05Jun1855	H7 W102 Reese
Frances	James Smith	09Sep1856	H10 W105 Finney

WALKER, continued

George	Elizabeth Bailey	29Jan1806	E27 W37	
George, Junr	Susanna Coale	01Nov1837	E78 W79	Finney
George F.	Laura H. Elliott	25Nov1862	W116	
James	Elizabeth Brown	28Sep1826	E61 W65	Finney
James	Elizabeth Keen	17Jan1831	E68 W70	Tippet
James W.	Sarah Ann Wilson	16Sep1833	E73 W74	Finney
John	Harriet Bartol	18May1825	E60 W63	Finney
John	Eliza Herbert	15Nov1848	W93	
John C.	Maria Frances Sutor	09Oct1858	W109	
John R.	Annie E. Wiles	26Oct1861	W114	
Joseph R.	Sarah Jane Harman	20Dec1861	W115	
Lucinda A.	George Baldwin	25Sep1862	W116	
Margaret	Zebulon McCommons	19Aug1833	E73 W74	Stephenson
Margret	James Everett	09Feb1793	E4 W22	
Margrett Ann	Richard Sheridan	04Feb1840	E81 W82	
Robert	Catharine Hoopman	04Dec1821	E55 W59	
Robert J.	Sarah R. Spencer	24Jan1857	H11 W105	Monroe
Sarah Ann	Aquila D. Keen	22Apr1833	E72 W74	Finney
Thomas	Eleanor Gorsuch	03Feb1852	H1 W97	Reed
Thomas J.	Sarah L. Carr	20Apr1864	W119	
William P.	Eliza A. Howlett	07Jan1851	W96	

WALLACE

Archibald	Sarah Jane Heaps	30Dec1828	E65 W68	Park
John	Louisa C. Jolley	27Jun1815	E43 W50	
Joseph	Ann C. Curry	16Jul1855	H8 W103	Beatty
Sarah	Richard Dallam	14Oct1815	E43 W50	
William	Mary A. Heape	28May1859	W110	

WALLIS [see John Wallis Hopkins]

Joseph W.	Sophia Standiford	05Mar1844	E87 W87	Thomas
Mary Ann	George Bevard	20May1820	E52 W57	
Mary Jane	Joseph T. Johnson	20Feb1856	H9 W104	Finny
Randall	Ann Worthington	01[?]Jun1795	E7 W24	
Samuel	Margaret W. Dallam	27May1833	E72 W74	Donahay
Samuel	Sarah Ann Wilson	14Mar1842	E84 W85	Park
William	Mary Farmer	26Nov1817	E48 W54	

WALMSLEY

July	Samuel Taylor	26Mar1804	E25 W35

WALSH

Thomas	Mary Mitchell	m. 1788	[ret-AppA]

WALSTRUM

Mary	John Lee	22Feb1832	E70 W72	Gallion

WALTAM

Angeline	Robert Wilson	17Dec1839	E81 W82	Sheppard

WALTER

Mary	John Gross	28Jul1864	W119

WALTERS
William	Ann Foard	02Oct1817	E47 W53	

WALTHAM
Clement	Alisanna Webster	27Jan1801	E19 W30	
Elizabeth	William Billingslea	16Nov1802	E22 W33	
Mary	Robert Dutton	22Mar1784	C8 W9	
Sarah	James York	10May1796	E8 W25	
Susan	Robert Henry	22Sep1849	W94	
Thomas	Patty Greenfield	21May1795	E7 W24	
Thomas	Mary Tucker	22Oct1806	E29 W38	
Wm	Sarah Strong	16Dec1779	C1 W3	

WANN
Ann	George O'Donnell	20Nov1845	W89	
Benjamin	Elizabeth Ann Holland	21Dec1841	E84 W85	Keech
Benjamin	Sarah Rebecca Chillitte	04Jul1855	H8 W103	Brand
Charles	Sarah Brooks	24Nov1831	E70 W72	Sewell
Elizabeth	John Kennedy	12Apr1832	E70 W72	Keech
Jacob	Minerva Brooks	09Jan1823	E56 W61	
James	Mary Ann Billingslea	06Feb1832	E70 W72	Keech
John, Junior	Hannah Wakeland	28Feb1809	E33 W42	
Miss Lizzie	John F. Lingan	11May1859	W110	
Mary	John McFadden	05Apr1825	E59 W63	Morrison
Mary R.	Amer Pyle	20Aug1862	W116	
Rebecca	James C. Holland	24Feb1831	E68 W70	Tippet
Susanna	Samuel Ecoff	25Nov1830	E68 W70	Keeck
Thomas	Kitty Rodenheiser	27Nov1824	E59 W63	Webster
Thomas	Hester Grafton	07Dec1826	E62 W65	Keech
William J.	Mary Norris	03Dec1835	E76 W77	Keech

WARAM
John W.	Minerva Ann Mitchell	22Jan1847	W91	

WARD
Aesha	Joseph Herbert	09Mar1815	E43 W49	
Avis	Richard Kenley	25Mar1781	C4 W6	
Benjamin	Martha Dorset	16Apr1807	E29 W39	
Benjamin	Ammfield[?] Morgan	30Oct1815	E43 W50	
Catharine	Thomas O'Keef	01Apr1856	H10 W104	Walter
Charles	Elizabeth White	14Jun1832	E71 W73	Sewall
Edward	Deborah Cromwell	18Oct1808	E32 W41	
Eliza J/I.	Andrew A. W. Bannister	31Jan1856	H9 W104	Cushing
George	Catharine Blake	07Mar1859	W110	
J. Thomas	Sophia Bramble	12May1857	H12 W106	Cushing
Jas	Ann Thomas	17Jul1781	C5 W6	
("costs c/o John Lee Gibson")				
James A.	Virginia J. McLaughlin	21Dec1858	W109	
Jarrett	Elizabeth Barnes	03Feb1841	E83 W84	Finney
John	Hannah Harkins	09Jun1829	E66 W68	McGee
John S.	Sarah Wells	05May1825	E60 W63	Tidings
Joseph	Jane Thomas	23Nov1801	E20 W31	
Joseph	Martha Forwood	22Jun1841	E83 W84	Wilson

WARD, continued
Mary	William Hobbs	29Nov1811	E37 W45	
Mary	Henry Hazelett	22Aug1857	H12 W107	Finney
Mary A.	Michael G. Anderson	22Nov1862	W116	
Mary E.	John Thomas Riddle	21Dec1854	H6 W101	Trout
Peggy	Robert Crawford	04Jul1784	C9 W9	
Rich^d	Jane Smith	12Apr1779	B2 W1	
Richard	Elizabeth Forwood	15Feb1814	E41 W48	
Richard, Jr.	Sarah Boyd	15Jan1820	E52 W57	
Rosa	Elisha Johnson	20May1864	W119	
Sarah J/I.	Joseph Gorrell	20Dec1855	H8 W103	McCartney
Soloman	Nancy Bond	30May1837	E78 W79	Keech
Thomas	Sarah Billingslea	05Oct1863	W118	

WARE
John	Elizth Kidd	20Mar1779	B1 W1	
John W.	Sarah Ann Hopkins	21Dec1853	H4 W100	Dumm
[gn may be Ward]				

WAREAM
Matilda	James Riley	27Oct1830	E68 W70	Tippet

WAREEM
Ann	Henry Ozman	14Nov1832	E71 W73	Finney

WAREHAM
Anna E.	Robert Evans	20Jun1855	H7 W103	Tustin
Elizabeth	William G. Burk	19Feb1827	E62 W66	Reynolds
John	Louisa Cole	03Aug1844	E87 W87	Finney
John T.	Susan E. Keen	05Jul1853	H4 W99	Smith
Louisa	John T. Moore	17Oct1855	H8 W103	Smith
Margaret	Jacob Hoopman	16Dec1818	E50 W56	
Mary	James O'Brien	24Mar1810	E35 W43	
Mary E.	Benedict H. Keen	01Dec1852	H2 W98	Smith

WARFIELD
Martha	Cyrus Osborn	25Nov1795	E8 W24	

WARHAM
George	Ann Eliza Sutton	21Nov1825	E60 W64	Webster
[orig. lic. to Webster; cr-Harf]				

WARN
Baily	Sarah Tredway	07Feb1801	E19 W30	

WARNER [see William Warner Forwood]
Asa	Milly Sweeney	04Aug1798	E15 W27	
Hannah	John C. Forwood	22Dec1828	E65 W68	Keeck
Joseph	Ann Smith	25Feb1828	E64 W67	Keech
Letitia	Samuel Scarbrough	27May1809	E34 W42	
Lucinda	Robert Wright	20Mar1856	H9 W104	Wilson
Lucinda	Jacob Iley	05Dec1859	W111	
Maria Jane	David Harry	05Feb1861	W113	

WARNER, continued

Mary Ann	David Hanway	27Jan1836	E76 W77	Keech
Mary Elizabeth	George W. Eggleston	18Oct1851	W97	
Sarah J.	William H. Streett	09Feb1842	E84 W85	Wilson

WARNICK

Charity	Benjamin Silver, Junr	19Nov1806	E29 W38
Philip	Mary Rogers	26Oct1780	C3 W5

WARREN

Benjamin	Mary Tredway	21Sep1807	E30 W39

WARRICK

Mary	William Everitt	29Apr1820	E52 W57

WARRINER

Elizabeth	Jacob Forwood	07[?]May1781	C5 W6

WASKEY

Elijah	Delia Debruler	25May1819	E51 W56
Elizabeth	Joseph Merl	26Mar1816	E45 W51
Julian	Gabriel Lastaker	04Feb1806	E27 W37

WATERS

Amos	Sarah Maynedier	03Oct1832	E71 W73	Keech
Henry	Grace Wilson	21Feb1792	E2 W21	
Henry	Patience Bond	17[?]May1793	E4 W22	
James	Ellen Gibson	14Sep1816	E45 W52	
Stephen	Sarah Dorsey	24Feb1794	E5 W23	

WATKINS

Abel	Rachel James	13Feb1810	E35 W43	
Elizabeth	Shadrich Street	14Nov1812	E39 W46	
Elizabeth	John N. Patterson	31Mar1851	W96	
Hannah	James Jenkins	29May1820	E52 W58	
Isaiah	Elizabeth D. England	09May1842	E85 W85	Keech
James	Catherine Maulsby	04Oct1810	E35 W44	
John	Elizth Evans	16Aug1779	B3 W2	
John	Margaret Creal	30Oct1817	E47 W54	
John	Manirva Slade	21Oct1830	E68 W70	Tibbit
Mary Ann	Joseph Gafford	15Feb1813	E39 W47	
Melissa A.	William J. Davis	21Jan1853	H3 W99	Wilson
Susanna	Zacheus Cord	06Apr1801	E20 W31	
Vincent J.	Elizabeth Aldridge	16Sep1812	E38 W46	

WATSON

Ann	Andrew Alexander	27Jan1814	E41 W48	
Ellen R.	John T. Evans	05Dec1842	E85 W86	Brown
Hannah	Samuel Harper	03Apr1833	E72 W73	Finney
John	Elizabeth Connolly	07Mar1859	W110	
Mary Ann	William Hanna	13Aug1828	E65 W68	Finney
Mary Jane	Joseph Martin	21May1855	H7 W102	Brand

WATT
James	Martha Wilson	10Feb1824	E58 W62	
James	Mary Amos	08Jul1831	E69 W71	Sewall
John	Martha Amos	09Jan1828	E64 W67	Keech
Joseph	Mary Hitchcock	07Sep1817	E47 W53	
Louisa	Verney St. Clair	16Jan1849	W93	
Mary	Thomas Carlen	27Nov1816	E46 W52	
Peggy	John Davis	24Mar1804	E25 W35	
Sarah	Geo. Nelson	19Jan1781	C5 W6	
Sarah	James McClure	06Jan1823	E56 W61	

WATTERS [see Charles Watters Jacobs]
Ann	William Sheckle	26Aug1805	E26 W36	
Ann Amelia	Thomas J. Calwell	01Dec1834	E74 W76	Webster
Basil	Temperance Magness	06Feb1808	E31 W40	
Benedict F.	Milcah L. Mathews	23Nov1818	E50 W55	
Benedict F.	Julia H. Watters	09Feb1835	E75 W76	Lyon
Daniel R.	Sarah Ruff	20Feb1821	E53 W58	
Deborah	William Whitson	07Jan1818	E48 W54	
Eliza K.	James A. Amoss	19Jan1846	W89	
Elizabeth	Samuel Ricketts	08Nov1824	E59 W63	Richardson
Elizabeth	David Flowers	02Nov1844	E87 W88	Keech
Elizabeth	George Wilgis	01Apr1852	H2 W98	Davis
Elizabeth Ann	Henry Jas Bully	22May1855	H7 W102	Cushing
Francinia	Arnold Williams	04Mar1858	W108	
Henry	Mary Bradford	31Dec1800	E19 W30	
Henry	Jane Hanna	09Mar1815	E43 W49	
Henry G.	Mary Clendinen	04Feb1823	E56 W61	
Isaac	Caroline Parsons	11Sep1823	E57 W61	
Mrs. Jane	Samuel McGaw	06Jun1827	E63 W66	Finney
John	Esther Young	08Jan1805	E26 W36	
John	Rachel C. Presbury	04Nov1818	E49 W55	
John	Eunice Low	04Apr1853	H3 W99	Gailey
John C.	Rebecca Weston Onion	10Nov1812	E39 W46	
Jonas	Bathia Galloway	05Jan1813	E39 W47	
Julia H.	Benedict F. Watters	09Feb1835	E75 W76	Lyon
Julian	Benjamin Rickets	29Dec1823	E57 W62	
Kate M.	John Joshua Streett	21Dec1853	H4 W100	Keech
Laura Jane	Dr. Robert Dickey	19Dec1862	W116	
Mary	Samuel Vance	08Oct1798	E15 W27	
Mary	Francis Delmos	01Apr1806	E28 W38	
Mary	John R. Gittings	17Oct1849	W94	
Mary T.	Benjamin Rigdon	13Jan1847	W91	
Rhoda	David Flowers	01Jul1803	E23 W33	
Robert A.	Elizabeth Harlan	21Feb1846	W90	
Ruth	Marshal Baldwin	14Mar1816	E45 W51	
Sarah	Hezekiah Harriman	28Jan1806	E27 W37	
Sarah R.	Robert W. Reed	27Feb1841	E83 W84	Reese[?]
Stephen	Mary Ann Brown	31Mar1802	E21 W32	
Walter	Mary Kennard	06Jun1822	E55 W60	
William	Elizabeth Brown	01Jul1799	E16 W28	
William	Sarah Wilson	14Apr1808	E31 W40	
William	Jane Rogers	22Jan1822	E55 W60	
Wm Henry	Josephine V. Streett	11May1863	W117	

WATTLE
Isaac　　　　　　　　Mary Griffy　　　　　　　　04Nov1834　E74 W76　Hoopman

WATTS
John A.　　　　　　　Louisa Pritchard　　　　　18Sep1854　H6　W101　Reese
Maria　　　　　　　　Benjamin Lego　　　　　　　27Nov1843　E86 W87　Lurtzer
Walter W.　　　　　　Sarah E. Wells　　　　　　14Jun1854　H6　W101　Reese

WAULSTRUM
Sarah Jane　　　　　　John W. Carter　　　　　　25Sep1852　H2　W98　Lemon

WAY
Caleb P.　　　　　　　Mary J. Devoe　　　　　　　04Mar1845　E88 W88　Wilson
Caleb P.　　　　　　　Ann Devoe　　　　　　　　　25Jun1849　　　W94
David　　　　　　　　Ann Lukins　　　　　　　　11Dec1801　E21 W31
Elizabeth　　　　　　William J. Sharron　　　　17Nov1863　　　W118
Hannah　　　　　　　　Thomas J. Ely　　　　　　　17May1836　E76 W77　Richardson
Isaac　　　　　　　　Sarah Riley　　　　　　　　02Sep1826
　[orig. lic. to Webster; cr-Harf]
Job　　　　　　　　　Ann Harry　　　　　　　　　03Sep1806　E28 W38
John　　　　　　　　　Mary Amoss　　　　　　　　22Jun1806　E28 W38
Mary　　　　　　　　　George Turner　　　　　　03Oct1864　　　W119
Samuel　　　　　　　　Mary Smith　　　　　　　　08May1821　E54 W59
Sarah Ann　　　　　　Hugh E. Spencer　　　　　　12Aug1828　E65 W68　Richardson

WEARHAM
Elizabeth　　　　　　Hutson Woods　　　　　　　19Dec1838　E80 W81　Galien

WEARIM
Rachel　　　　　　　　Danl Anderson　　　　　　29Feb1784　C8　W9　cr-Harf

WEATHERAL
Henry　　　　　　　　Charlotte E. Day　　　　　27Apr1797　E10 W26　[ret-AppA]

WEATHERALL
James　　　　　　　　Sarah Chancey　　　　　　　19Feb1783　C7　W8
Mary Ann　　　　　　　John Day　　　　　　　　　24Jan1783　C7　W8
Sarah　　　　　　　　Wm Copeland Goldsmith　　m. 1778　　　　　[ret-AppA]
William　　　　　　　Mary Presbury　　　　　　　19Sep1797　E11 W26　[ret-AppA]

WEAVER
Catharine Mary　　　　Henry Frederick　　　　　25Nov1852　H2　　　McNally
Isaac　　　　　　　　Rachel Husband　　　　　　25Dec1811　E37 W45
John H.　　　　　　　Jean Favor Umshead[?]　　25Dec1841　E84 W85　Reid

WEB
Julian　　　　　　　　Joshua D. Wright　　　　　03Dec1828　E65 W68　Finney

WEBB
Barbara　　　　　　　George Laurance　　　　　　19Aug1812　E38 W46
George　　　　　　　　Margaret Baughman　　　　05Nov1798　E15 W27
Henrietta　　　　　　William Poplar　　　　　　01Aug1827　E63 W66　Reynolds

WEBB, continued

John	Elizth Montgomery	13May1779	B2	W2
John	Barbara Suter	06Jul1809	E34	W42
Margaret	Richard Downing	16Jul1780	C2	W4
[above entry after 22July]				
Prissilla	Samuel Downing	15Jul1784	C9	W9
Samuel	Elizabeth Dawney	07Jul1814	E42	W49
Sarah	Patrick McCurley	23Feb1780	C1	W3

WEBER

Clemence Francis	Christiana F. C. Metzgar	18Jun1840	E82	W83	Golosbrog
Clemence Francis	Anna Lenigan	15Jul1850		W95	

WEBLEY

Annie	William Bush	16Jun1862		W116

WEBSTER [see John Webster Johnson, Theodore J. Webster Middleton]

Alisanna	Clement Waltham	27Jan1801	E19	W30	
Augustus	Ann Calwell	22Mar1828	E64	W67	Richardson
Caroline	William Brown	11Nov1815	E44	W50	
Cassandra	Charles Vincent	03Dec1811	E37	W45	
Elizabeth	Joseph Downing	23Apr1799	E16	W28	
Elizabeth	Evan Mitchell	29Dec1807	E31	W40	
Frances	John Morrisson	01Sep1791	E1	W21	
Isaac	Cassandra Pearce	29Jan1783	C7	W8	cr-Harf
Isaac	Clemency Hughes Gilbert	27Apr1809	E33	W42	
Isaac	Susan Dixon	05Aug1813	E40	W48	
Ja^s	Mary Brice	01Mar1780	C1	W3	
John Luster	Susan Brown	19Dec1839	E81	W82	Finney
Joseph	Martha Chauncey	30May1792	E2	W21	[ret-AppA]
Josephine	William Dallam	24Apr1843	E86	W86	Finney
Laura A.	John C. Patterson	18Jun1861		W114	
Margaret	John Holland Barney	05Nov1825	E60	W64	Finney
Martha	John Lewis Pike	06Aug1801	E20	W31	
Mary	George Veazey	10Jun1828	E64	W67	Finney
Mary A.	Algernon S. Dorsey	03Jun1851		W96	
May	Nathan Lufborough	23Apr1795	E7	W24	
[see ret-AppA, bn *Mary* Webster]					
Miram	Scott Hamby	29Dec1829	E66	W69	McGee
Noah	Susan F. Mitchell	12Jan1832	E70	W72	Sewall
Phebe	John Davis	26Dec1822	E56	W60	
R. Priscilla	Charles H. Sadtler	04Nov1863		W118	
Rachel Cassandra	Francis A. Bond	26Oct1859		W111	
Richard, Junr	Rachel Mitchell	14Apr1800	E17	W29	
Samuel	Mary Baker	03Aug1780	C2	W4	
Sarah F.	Thomas J. Keating	11Jun1862		W116	
Toppan	Mary Chauncey	14Apr1817	E47	W53	
William	Mary Hollis	29Feb1804	E24	W35	

WEEKS

Ann	Nicholas Cox	12Aug1820	E53	W58
Anna	Thomas Everist	16Feb1813	E40	W47
Catharine	Amos Cord	27Jul1822	E56	W60
Elizabeth A.	Benjamin Calhoun	18Mar1846		W90

WEEKS, continued

James	Margarett Swift	21Feb1828	E64 W67	Finney
John	Mary Gilbert	05Nov1816	E46 W52	
Martha Jane	Herman Singleton	27Jun1855	H8 W103	Smith
Mary	Ezekiel Everist	13Mar1823	E56 W61	
Rachel	Isaac Scarbrough	08Jan1812	E37 W45	
Rachel	Bennett Taylor	20Jun1832	E71 W73	Sewell
Sarah	John F. Rigdon	29Sep1825	E60 W64	Webster
Tacy Ann	William Enfield	26Nov1862	W116	

WEIR

Abraham	Ruth Blaney	27Jun1807	E30 W39
Eleanor	David Bell	10Mar1801	E19 W30

WEISER

Lydia	Jehu[?] Smith	20May1828	E64 W67	Finney

WELCH

Ann Maria	Wakeman Martin	26Jun1850	W95	
Bridget	Stephen Crow	31Oct1864	W119	
Catharine F.	William H. Harward	18Jan1842	E84 W85	Reid
Elizth Ellen	Alexander Carthain	28Aug1845	E88 W89	
Elizabeth L.	John Wilson	31May1847	W91	
Harriot	Joseph Davis	11Dec1810	E36 W44	
John --	Martha F. Smith	19Dec1842	E85 W86	Furguson
Mary [*]	Morgan Richardson	26Sep1816	E45 W52	
[* an initial crossed out]				
Thomas	Martha Groves	21May1793	E4 W22	
W^m	Elizth Horton	29Jul1794	E5 W23	
William	Ann McLaughlin	16Jun1818	E49 W55	
William	Penelope K. Rutledge	17Apr1838	E79 W80	Hoolmead

WELLS

Annie M.	Charles Osborn	03Oct1861	W114	
Benjamin N.	Avarilla Hollis	31Dec1831	E70 W72	Sewall
Charles W.	Elizabeth Hopkins	06Jan1858	W107	
Derias W.	Louisa Green	09Jun1838	E79 W80	Burrows
Elizabeth	Wm J. Hollis	05Mar1845	E88 W88	Dulaney
Ellen	Thomas J. Gorsuch	17Nov1859	W111	
Harriet Ann	Asael Montgomery	23Jul1857	H12 W106	Monroe
James	Semelia Hollis	25Feb1839	E80 W81	Dulaney
James B.	Charlotte Conner	15Dec1851	H1 W97	Huntington
John	Sarah[?] Smith	12Mar1781	C4 W6	
John	Harriet Courtney	10Aug1832	E71 W73	--
John W.	Susana R. Nevill	28Oct1840	E82 W83	Prettiman
Martha	Rev. Edward Kinsey	27Oct1860	W112	
Mary Ann	William Coale	23Dec1834	E74 W76	Dunaha
Mary Ann	John L. Criswell	26Dec1854	H6 W102	Herron
Sarah	John S. Ward	05May1825	E60 W63	Tidings
Sarah E.	Walter W. Watts	14Jun1854	H6 W101	Reese
William H.	Elizabeth Cole	22Jan1849	W93	
William Henry	Mary Jane Miller	13Feb1843	E85 W86	Dulany
Zenas	Elizabeth Flanagan	04Sep1799	E16 W28	

WELSH
Falix	Margaret Barnes	27May1781	C5 W6	
Mary Ann	John Glackin	22Dec1862	W116	
Mary E.	Isaac L. Pyle	30Jan1849	W93	
Sarah J.	George A. Crevenstin	29Jun1858	W108	

WEST
Anna W.	Sylvester B. Preston	05Mar1827	E62 W66	Pool
Caroline	John Tutchston	13Feb1839	E80 W81	Finney
Eneas	Jane Robinson	22Jan1780	C1 W3	
Enos	Rebecca Hanaway	18Dec1800	E19 W30	
James	Sarah Murphy	24Feb1801	E19 W30	
John G.	Mary Eliza Dick	29Mar1858	W108	
Jonathan	Jean Sturgeon	02Nov1779	C1 W3	
Luke	Sarah Bryon	27May1779	B2 W2	
Martha	Reason Gorrell	18Nov1819	E51 W57	
Mary	James Noble	12Dec1780	C3 W5	"Wheat"
Rachel	Thomas Roads	23May1781	C5 W6	
Ruth	Henry Long	13Dec1831	E70 W72	Sewell
Samuel	Catherine Mann	06Jan1820	E51 W57	
Sarah	William Mouton[Moreton?]	10Nov1784	C9 W10	
Sophia	William Murphey	m. 1777		[ret-AppA]
Stacy	Ann Whitaker	07Mar1805	E26 W36	
Stacy	Mary Dallam	09Feb1832	E70 W72	Keech
Susannah	John Connard	13Oct1783	C8 W9	cr-Harf
Temperance	John St. Clair	18Dec1799	E17	W29
Thomas	Ellen E. Carroll	29May1833	E72 W74	Richardson
William T.	Ruth Ann Roman	25Dec1835	E76 W77	Rutter

WESTON [see Rebecca Weston Onion]

WETHERALL
Catharine	Wm Wilmer	05Jun1797	E10 W26	
Charlotte E.	Mathew Birckhead	18Oct1815	E43 W50	
Francina H.	Elisha Pearson Amos	21Jan1858	W108	
Hannah E.	Lambert Pennington	09Jun1864	W119	
James H.	Susan Hill	29Aug1833	E73 W74	Donahay
Mary	Joshua Brown	m. 1777		[ret-AppA]
Mary Ann	Aquila McComas	05Apr1808	E31 W40	

WETHERILL
Elizabeth M.	William Gladden	26Nov1858	W109

WHALAND
Robert W.	Harriet H. Hays	10Nov1835	E76 W77	Finney

WHALEN
Michael	Bridget Carroll	14Aug1854	H6 W101	McNally

WHEAT
James C.	Mary A. Haynes	23Oct1838	E79 W81	Reese

WHEELER

Ann	Daniel Foster	05Aug1824	E58 W62	
Anna Maria	Philip Quinlan	19Aug1811	E37 W45	
Benjn	Elizth Green	04Feb1793	E4 W22	
Caroline	Francis Ady	19Nov1841	E84 W84	Reid
Christene	Carvill Hall Prigg	09Nov1819	E51 W57	
Clare	Joseph Everett	21Nov1795	E8 W24	
Eleanor	John G. Grindall	17Nov1807	E30 W39	
Elizabeth	Robert Patterson	03Jul1816	E45 W51	
Elizabeth	Robert Boarman	13Oct1835	E75 W77	Crausgay
Francis A.	Mary Ann Mcatee	04Jul1814	E42 W49	
George W.	Sarah Slade	16Mar1847	W91	
Harriet S.	Augustus F. Brown	30Dec1857	W107	
Henry G.	Mary Ann Cairnes	01May1854	H5 W101	Carter
John	Loveicy Lytle	18Nov1823	E57 W61	
Joseph A.	Henrietta Green	13Apr1820	E52 W57	
Juliana	Edward F. Bussey	23Aug1811	E37 W45	
Margt	Robert Taylor	01Apr1794	E5 W23	
Mary	Robert Bowman	01Feb1796	E8 W24	
Mary Ann	Josias Wilson	07Aug1844	E87 W87	Reid
Michael J/I.	Martha J. Prigg	20Nov1851	W97	
Michael J.	Ellen Frances Rider	27Dec1860	W113	
Monica	Jacob Rutledge	01Apr1799	E16 W28	
Sarah	Nathan Horner	09Dec1794	E6 W23	
Susan	James Lee Morgan	19Feb1811	E36 W44	
Theresa	Henry Macatee	28Jan1799	E15 W28	

WHISTLER

Lee M.	Mary A. Jackson	09Jan1865	W120

WHITACRE

Hesekiah	Mary Taylor	18Jul1783	C7 W8
John	Rachel Johnson	06Sep1780	C3 W4

WHITAKER

Abraham	Elizabeth Poteet	02Feb1804	E24 W34	
Amelia	Edward Thompson	13Jun1825	E60 W63	Stevenson
Angeline	Mahlon Thompson	15Dec1851	H1 W97	Huntington
Ann	Stacy West	07Mar1805	E26 W36	
Annie S.	A. Joseph Mabbett	26Sep1857	H12 W107	Finney
Cassandra	Charles H. Raitt	07Jun1830	E67 W69	Keech
Dorsey H.	Sarah Galloway	26Oct1826	E62 W65	Keech
Elizabeth	William Scarff	16Oct1809	E34 W43	
Frances	Jacob Kirk	23Jan1838	E79 W80	Keech
Franklin	Rebecca Pue	04Feb1846	W89	
Howard	Hannah Ruff	30Nov1815	E44 W50	
Isaac	Susanah McGirll	09Sep1794	E6 W23	
Isaac	Margaret Everist	09Feb1798	E13 W27	Jno Allen
Isaac	Catharine Blake	18Mar1848	W92	
John	Harriett Myers	27Jul1822	E56 W60	
John	Matilda Patterson	16Aug1827	E63 W66	Keech
Margaret	William Cronan	23Apr1806	E28 W38	
Martha H.	John Kean	18Aug1834	E74 W75	Todrick
Mary Elizabeth	James Heathcote	10Jul1843	E86 W86	Reid

WHITAKER, continued

Matilda J.	Charles H. Thompson	15Apr1857	H11 W106	Cushing
Rachel	Aquila Carroll	11Jan1815	E42 W49	
Samuel	Elizabeth Anderson	15Jun1809	E34 W42	
Samuel	Margaret Whitelock	25Dec1850	W95	
Sarah B.	Henry Barnes	28Aug1822	E56 W60	
Thomas	Charlotte Durham	22Feb1800	E17 W29	
William P. C.	Mary Ramsay	17Nov1845	W89	

WHITE [see Sophia White Hall, Charlotte White Hall, William White Ramsay]

Abraham	Martha Bussey	03Jun1797	E10 W26	
Cecelia	Davis Norris	09Nov1815	E43 W50	
Charles	Mary Herbert	07Sep1809	E34 W43	
Delia	Philip Gordon	14Jul1797	E11 W26	
Delilah	Wm Godwin	15Jul1797	E11 W26	[ret-AppA]
Elizth	George Cousins	10Sep1794	E6 W23	
Elizabeth	Charles Ward	14Jun1832	E71 W73	Sewall
Grafton	Margaret Denny	03Jan1781	C4 W5	"Wheat"
James	Hannah Bull	05Jun1798	E15 W27	
Jane	James Taylor	26Aug1795	E7 W24	
Margaret	William Mumford	28Sep1818	E49 W55	
Mary	Paltus Fie	08Dec1782	C6 W8	
Mary Adalisa	John Adrean Mitchell	08Jun1854	H5 W101	Smith
Mary E.	Levi S. Jennis	25Dec1850	W95	
Sarah	William Anderson	18Feb1818	E48 W54	
Sarah	James H. Osborn	06Jul1820	E53 W58	
William	Agnes Adams	05Sep1797	E11 W26	
William	Providence Standiford	16Jun1812	E38 W46	

WHITEFORD

Ann	John Stallions	18Jun1807	E30 W39	
Ann	Robert Kerr, Junior	01Mar1819	E50 W56	
Ann	James Christie	10Jul1834	E74 W75	Finney
Belina C.	William H. Wilson	23Apr1860	W112	
Doddridge S.	Elizabeth Ann Silver	01May1839	E81 W82	Finney
Eliza	Hugh Whiteford	21Mar1827	E62 W66	Park
Elizabeth	Esrom Hughes	01Apr1800	E17 W29	
Elizabeth	Hugh C. Ramsey	23Nov1833	E73 W74	Martin
Henry S.	Elizabeth Jane Conley	01Jun1841	E83 W84	Myers
Hugh	Eliza Whiteford	21Mar1827	E62 W66	Park
Hugh C.	Cassandra Silver	27Oct1834	E74 W75	Finney
James	Ann Beatty	17Mar1826	E61 W65	Ewing
Jane	Robert Ramsey	28Feb1821	E54 W58	
Julia Ann	Andrew Turner	16Jan1858	W107	
Julian	Charles Srodres	05Feb1823	E56 W61	
Louisa G.	Stephen D. McConkey	22Feb1855	H7 W102	Lane
Mary R.	William F. Silver	10Oct1838	E79 W81	
Michael	Gustein Streett	17Jan1848	W92	
Robert	Nancy Kerman	02Feb1796	E11 W26	
Robert	Elizabeth Henry	14Apr1818	E49 W55	
Samuel	Elizabeth Butler	02Mar1799	E15 W28	
Sarah Jane	Henry C. Amoss	20Oct1860	W112	
Sarah S.	Jno. Q. A. McConkey	06Dec1860	W112	

WHITEFORD, continued
William	Catherine Johnson	11Dec1854	H6 W101	Crawford
William E.	Margaret L. Streett	24Jan1863	W117	
William H.	Ann Maria Singleton	02Feb1852	H1 W97	Cadden

WHITELOCK
Andrew J.	Sarah Dixon	02Nov1863	W118	
Charles	Catherine Herbert	18Jun1839	E81 W82	
[minister - Goldsborough?]				
Eveline	William Brown	25Dec1850	W95	
I. Ann	Lewis Franklin Reynolds	13Aug1860	W112	
James	Caroline Bowman	02Nov1842	E85 W85	Gallion
John	Jane Gorrell	12Jan1839	E80 W81	Reese
John	Ann Eliza Wilson	22Dec1846	W91	
Margaret	Samuel Whitaker	25Dec1850	W95	
Mary Ann	Joshua Stephens, Junr	10Jan1853	H3 W98	Gallion

WHITMAN
Martin	Catharine Wise	06Mar1863	W117	

WHITSON
Burt	Mary Ann Knight	10Apr1824	E58 W62	
Joseph	Elizabeth Mcfadden	22Apr1822	E55 W60	
Joseph B.	Laura Garrettson	28Dec1860	W113	
Sarah	George Jewel	02Apr1803	E23 W33	
Thomas	Isabella Criswell	02Apr1812	E38 W46	
William	Deborah Watters	07Jan1818	E48 W54	

WHITTEMAN
Michael	Hannah Creamer	05Jun1846	W90	

WHITTEMORE
Henry	Mary Ann Bell	20Nov1821	E54 W59	

WIGGERS
Anna J/I.	Thomas Cannon	27Aug1853	H4 W99	Trout
David	Martha Reese	13Apr1861	W114	
Margaret	James Riley	03Apr1858	W108	
Rebecca	John Garrison	26Nov1833	E73 W74	Keech

WILD
Eliza	Richd Spencer	m. 1778		[ret-AppA]

WILES
Aquila	Mary Bayless	08Dec1829	E66 W69	Finney
Elizabeth	Charles McFaddon	21Jan1833	E72 W73	Stephenson
George N.	Julia Ann Clark	27Feb1856	H9 W104	Lemmon
Hannah	Constance C. Green	29Aug1855	H8 W103	Wiles
Hariet	Daniel M. Cooley	28Sep1839	E81 W82	Finney
Sophia	Richardrd[sic] F. McKinley			
		02Jun1830	E67 W69	Stephenson
William, Jnr.	Ann Chesney	24Feb1832	E70 W72	Sewall
William	Nancy Hopkins	25Mar1834	E74 W75	Gallion
William, Jr.	Blanch W. Davis	29Jul1836	E76 W78	Smith

WILEY [see Wiley Jones]
Ann	Joseph C. Bosley	13Feb1847	W91	
Caroline	John Wiley	30Jan1863	W117	
David	Ellen Cathcart	10Oct1845	W89	
David	Mary Amanda Wiley	29Dec1863	W118	
Eliza	John N. Kilgore	01Feb1851	W96	
Elizabeth	William Evatt	m. 1794		[ret-AppA]
Elizabeth	Aaron Keech	29Aug1850	W95	
Hannah	William Duncan	29Dec1852	H3 W98	Smith
Hannah	John F. Wright	29Jan1853	H3 W99	Smith
Hannah E.	Ephraim B. McClung	24Feb1857	H11 W106	Park
Isabella	James Kirk	23Dec1804	E25 W35	
John	Rachel Ann Wilson	19Dec1835	E76 W77	Parks
John	Ann Ayres	29Jan1857	H11 W105	Lee
John	Caroline Wiley	30Jan1863	W117	
Mary Amanda	David Wiley	29Dec1863	W118	
Matthew	Rebecca Nelson	22May1781	C5 W6	
Matthew Wm. N.	Rebecca Jane Robinson	05Feb1861	W113	
Missouri	James H. Nelson	09Apr1859	W110	
Rebecca	William Heapes	13Jan1834	E73 W75	Parke
Rebecca Ann	Thomas H. Wiley	13Feb1854	H5 W100	Carter
Sally Ann	Samuel P. Richardson	19Dec1857	W107	
Thomas H.	Rebecca Ann Wiley	13Feb1854	H5 W100	Carter
William	Caroline Bradford	15Jun1836	E76 W78	Smith

WILGES
Elizabeth	William Paca	14Aug1833	E73 W74	Dunahay

WILGIS
Anne Maria	Rodolph E. Sholtz	13Aug1856	H10 W105	Cushing
George	Elizabeth Watters	01Apr1852	H2 W98	Davis
James	Susanna Conley	07Feb1839	E80 W81	Collis
Jemima	John Conolly	08Apr1841	E83 W84	Cullum
Margaret	John Wright	05Dec1827	E63 W67	Webster
[orig. lic. to Webster; cr-Harf]				
Sarah	Christian Blessing	07Aug1856	H10 W105	Cushing

WILIE
Jane	James Kirk	31Dec1799	E17 W29
John	Ann Rickets	01Aug1804	E25 W35

WILKERSON
Elizth	John Greenland	23Feb1848	W92

WILKINSON
Caroline	Charles W. Moulton	20Dec1856	H11 W105	Cushing
Hannah Jane	James Henry Jennis	26May1839	E81 W82	Wilson
Joseph H.	Amelia E. Moulton	06Dec1854	H6 W101	Dunm
Rachel	Isaac Broomell	19Mar1838	E79 W80	Willson
Thomas M.	Elizabeth Osborn	02Dec1850	W95	

WILLEY

Charles	Eliza Hopkins	12Jan1821	E53	W58	
Charles L.	Francis J. Herbert	19Dec1848		W93	
Elizabeth	Thomas Smith	02Jan1856	H9	W104	Smith
Emily	William Bell	06Jan1818	E48	W54	
Emma C.	Geo. W. Mitchell	15Dec1863		W118	
Harriett	Peter Codes	14Sep1859		W110	
Isaac	Mary S. Mitchell	08Mar1825	E59	W63	Finney
Isaac E.	Ann M. Cummins	26Feb1856	H9	W104	Reineck
Mary S.	Jera[?] Herbert	08Oct1856	H10	W105	Galion
Rebecca	Thomas Allen	09Aug1808	E32	W41	
William P.	Mathia Taylor	15Nov1850		W95	

WILLIAMS

Abigail L.	Arthur Woolford	26Nov1829	E66	W69	Stephenson
Ann	James Hamby	13Jan1800	E17	W29	
Arnold	Francinia Watters	04Mar1858		W108	
Benjamin	Keziah Elliott	26Feb1847		W91	
Editha H.	William H. Cullum	15Aug1864		W119	
Eliza R.	Robert E. Fairbank	06Dec1849		W94	
Elizabeth Jane	Samuel Russel	23Jan1843	E85	W86	Briscold[?]
Ellen J/I.	Isaac Standiford	25Feb1856	H9	W104	Cushing
Enoch	Hester Reese	06Sep1848		W93	
Frances	John Magness	04Apr1837	E77	W79	Richardson
George	Elizabeth B. Hawkins	30May1815	E43	W50	
Grace	John H. Price	27Nov1829	E66	W69	Sephenson
Henry W.	Frances A. Barnes	22Jan1844	E86	W87	Reese[?]
James	Mary Stump	20Sep1808	E32	W41	
James A.	Ruth Eliza Wilson	15Nov1845		W89	
James W.	Hannah C. Stump	15Oct1817	E47	W54	
John	Elizth Pritchard	05Nov1781	C5	W7	
John	Mary Coulson	23Nov1783	C8	W9	cr-Harf
John	Mary Billingslea	01Jan1806	E27	W37	
John L.	Mary A. Mitchell	23Jan1864		W118	
Levinah	John Platt	28Dec1783	C7	W8	cr-Harf
Lewis J.	Harriet H. Archer	17Jun1850		W95	
Margaret	John Ely	21May1817	E47	W53	
Margaret	Edward Mitchell	29Mar1821	E54	W59	
Mary	William W. S. Greenway	05Jun1843	E86	W86	Billup
Mary	James Fairbank	24Jan1844	E86	W87	
Matilda	John W. Vandegrift	20Jan1813	E39	W47	
Nancy	Reubin Leigh	21May1806	E28	W38	
Pelitha	David Davis	19Mar1822	E55	W60	
Rosa	James C. Neilson	29May1840	E82	W83	Goldsbrough
Sarah	James Allen	06Jan1781	C4	W5	
Sarah Elizth	Nicholas B. Greenland	08Sep1863		W118	
Thomas	Susanna Sturdevance	19Oct1836	E77	W78	Furlong
Thomas	Sarah Ann Barton	18Nov1840	E82	W83	Finney
Wm	Ruth Barnes	m. 1778			[ret-AppA]
William	Syna Andrews	19Jan1804	E24	W34	
William	Mary Jeffery	03Jan1817	E46	W52	
William	Rachel Preston	31Dec1835	E76	W77	Dulany
William H.	Mary Hunter	18Jan1827	E62	W66	Poole
William K.	Sallie C. K. Sappington	09Apr1860		W112	

WILLIAMSON
John S.	Mercy Cox	24Sep1832	E71 W73	Park
William T.	Margaretta Andrews	08Nov1858	W109	

WILLMORE
James Jones	Sarah McGee	21May1783	C6 W8

WILLMOTT
Eliz[th]	Thomas Thompson	28Jan1779	B1 W1

WILLS
Kate	Nicholas B. Gilbert	27Mar1854	H5 W100	Reese
Sarah Ann	Ephraim G. Hopkins	21Dec1855	H9 W103	Reese

WILLSON
Benjamin	Hannah Morrison	15[?]Nov1779	C1 W3	
Isabella	Wm Bennington	12Jan1779	B1 W1	
James	Hannah Ady	08Oct1783	C8 W9	cr-Harf
Jane	Sam[l] Kenley	05Sep1779	B3 W2	
John	Mary Scott	30Mar1779	B1 W1	
John	Letitia Kenley	27Aug1779	B3 W2	
Mary	John Dallam	13May1780	C2 W4	
Rob[t]	L.[or S.] Oldham	18Apr1782	C6 W7	cr-Harf
Wm	Mary Scott	07Jan1779	B1 W1	
Wm	Mary Talboot	06Dec1781	C5 W7	

WILMER
Ann	Moses Maxwell	07Mar1796	E8 W25	
Benjamin	Margaret Crawford	28May1800	E18 W29	
Hannah	Edward Day of John	01Aug1801	E20 W31	
James J.	Letitia Day	m. 1803		[ret-AppA]
Leanor Eliz[th]	Jacob Maxwell	25May1795	E7 W24	
Rebecca	James Wilson	14Mar1818	E49 W55	
Rosanna	William Partridge	29Mar1806	E28 W37	
Sarah	James Phillips	18Aug1808	E32 W41	
Wm	Catharine Wetherall	05Jun1797	E10 W26	

WILMOT
Mary	Jacob Hall	20May1784	C8 W9

WILSON [see Sam[l] Wilson Raymond]
Alice A.	E. Hall Richardson	19Nov1855	H8 W103	Rankin
Allen	Rebecca M. Hewett	20Jan1851	W96	
Andrew	Elizabeth Marshall	01Dec1804	E25 W35	
Ann	William D. Lee	14Feb1810	E35 W43	
Ann	William Morris	30Jul1836	E76 W78	Dulany
Ann	Thomas O'Brian	05Aug1862	W116	
Ann Eliza	John Whitelock	22Dec1846	W91	
Cassandra A.	James Kean	03Feb1829	E65 W68	O'Brian
Catharine	Jon[a] Stricker	21Mar1797	E10 W26	
Christopher, Jr.	Hetty Smith	18Sep1823	E57 W61	
Christopher	Mary Bagley	08Jun1852	H2 W98	Cornelius
Clarissa	John Kean, Jun[r]	27Dec1831	E70 W72	O'Brien

WILSON, continued

David	Sarah Orr	14May1816	E45 W51	
David E.	Mary S. Wilson	11Jan1856	H9 W104	Finney
Edward	Margaret A. Parker	11Jan1856	H9 W104	Finney
Elizabeth	Ephraim Cox	30Nov1802	E22 W33	
Elizabeth	John Wilson	09Jun1824	E58 W62	
Elizabeth	Joseph Anderson	11Feb1831	E68 W70	Park
Elizth J/I.	James Swift	04Aug1857	H12 W106	Monroe
Fra^s	Joseph Miller	14Sep1785	C10 W10	
Frances	Zachariah Durham	01Jan1817	E46 W52	
Grace	Henry Waters	21Feb1792	E2 W21	
Harriet	James Alexander	21Dec1839	E81 W82	Keech
Harriet A.	Samuel M. Dickson	14Jun1865	W121	
Henry	Ann Eliza Rutledge	11Jan1840	E81 W82	Prettyman
Hesther A.	Charles Holland	25Dec1850	W95	
Hindley	Sarah Miller	21Feb1812	E38 W46	
Humphy	Sarah Ann Durham	10Feb1844	E87 W87	Keech
Isaac	Elizabeth Gilbert	m. 1792		[ret-AppA]
Isaac	Mary Brooke	16Nov1807	E30 W39	
Jacob	Frances Thomas	27Sep1803	E23 W34	
James	Rebecca Wilmer	14Mar1818	E49 W55	
James	Frances Evans	06May1826	E61 W65	Finney
James	Letetia Wilson	24May1827	E63 W66	Keech
James	Elizabeth Hill	11Feb1834	E74 W75	Dulaney
James T.	Martha E. Purnell	16Oct1857	H13 W107	Monroe
Jane	William Yarley	22May1806	E28 W38	
Jane	Jacob Gladden	07Apr1830	E67 W69	Parke
Jane	John Holland	11Dec1850	W95	
Jane	James Baker	21May1864	W119	
John	Margaret Smith	22Nov1799	E16 W28	
John	Sarah Bacon	17Sep1811	E37 W45	
John	Frances Irvin	27Jan1817	E46 W52	
John	Elizabeth Wilson	09Jun1824	E58 W62	
John	Jane Knight	20Mar1843	E85 W86	Dulany
John	Elizabeth L. Welch	31May1847	W91	
Joshua	Rebecca Lee	20Apr1824	E58 W62	
Josias	Mary Ann Wheeler	07Aug1844	E87 W87	Reid
Letetia	James Wilson	24May1827	E63 W66	Keech
Louisa	Joseph M. Clay	27[?]Jun1855	H8 W103	Crampton
Margaret	Rubin Stump	11Mar1805	E26 W36	
Margaret	Reubin Stump	31Oct1854	H6 W101	Trout
Maria	William Carty	16Mar1841	E83 W84	Cullum
Martha	Charles Lee	16Jan1792	E2 W21	
Martha	James Watt	10Feb1824	E58 W62	
Martha Maria	James Galbreath	17Jun1845	E88 W88	
Mary	David Dick	17Dec1780	C3 W5	
Mary	Thomas Pierse[?]	09Mar1793	E4 W22	
Mary	Robt Kilgor	12Dec1843	E86 W87	Park
Mary A.	Thomas Symington	16Nov1864	W120	
Mary Jane	Thomas Wm Debruler	29Mar1855	H7 W102	Reese
Mary S.	David E. Wilson	11Jan1856	H9 W104	Finney
Nicholas	Sarah Elizth Debruler	02Apr1846	W90	
Rachel	Archer Lee	06Apr1807	E29 W39	
Rachel Ann	John Wiley	19Dec1835	E76 W77	Parks

WILSON, continued

Rebecah	John Cord	13Feb1797	E10 W25	
Robert	Susannah Wilson	28Oct1819	E51 W57	
Robert	Lydia Hollaway	07Jan1828	E64 W67	Finney
Robert	Angeline Waltam	17Dec1839	E81 W82	Sheppard
Robert	Sarah Elizth Taylor	12Dec1857	W107	
Ruth	John Amoss	14Jun1810	E35 W44	
Ruth Eliza	James A. Williams	15Nov1845	W89	
Saml	Prissilla Gover	08Dec1794	E6 W23	
Samuel E.	Sarah Price	17Mar1824	E58 W62	
Sarah	Thomas Jinney	03Nov1799	E16 W28	
Sarah	Thomas Lofton	22Feb1802	E21 W32	
Sarah	William Watters	14Apr1808	E31 W40	
Sarah	John Hopkins	29May1809	E34 W42	
Sarah	William Divers	09Jun1829	E66 W68	McGee
Sarah Ann	James W. Walker	16Sep1833	E73 W74	Finney
Sarah Ann	Samuel Wallis	14Mar1842	E84 W85	Park
Sarah E.	Edward M. Allen	02Dec1852	H2 W98	Keech
Sarah Elizth	J. Edwin Timmons	22Nov1859	W111	
Sarah Louisa T.	George T. Gilbert	16Jul1835	E75 W76	Finney
Solomon	Hetty York	25Dec1813	E41 W48	
Susan	William Bolster	27Jan1818	E48 W54	
Susannah	Robert Wilson	28Oct1819	E51 W57	
Thomas	Elizabeth Hickman	11Sep1797	E11 W26	
Thomas	Mary Quinn	05Jun1860	W112	
William	Sarah Lee	28Feb1798	E13 W27	Jno Coleman
William	Margaret Winstanley	24Mar1801	E19 W31	
William	Clemency Mcomas	22Sep1819	E51 W57	
William	Rachel Price	02Jan1822	E55 W59	
William	Pamelia Noble	01Apr1826	E61 W65	Webster
[orig. lic. to Webster; cr-Harf]				
William	Caroline P. Hawkins	15Jan1846	W89	
William	Mary A. Smith	01Mar1865	W120	
William A.	Ruth A. Streett	15Feb1858	W108	
William C.	Susan G. Adams	28Nov1848	W93	
William Dawson	Mary Elizabeth Thomas	02Jan1837	E77 W78	Dulany
William H.	Belina C. Whiteford	23Apr1860	W112	
William W.	Ann Ferguson	06May1853	H3 W99	McMullin

WINLOCK [see Winlock Stapleford]

WINSTANLEY
Margaret	William Wilson	24Mar1801	E19 W31

WINSTON [see Sarah Winston Dallam, Winston Ricketts, Winston Smith]

WISE
Catharine	Martin Whitman	06Mar1863	W117

WITHERS
Joseph	Eudosia Chocke	[25Mar]1843	E85 W86

WOLLEN
Margaret A.	William S. Herman	13Jan1857	H11 W105	Cushing

WOOD

Ann	John Montgomery	17Jan1822	E55 W60	
Eliza	Henry Touchton	04Apr1831	E69 E71	Finney
Elizabeth	John Donahoo	18Feb1812	E38 W46	
George	Cloe C. Ady	28Nov1848	W93	
George W.	Mary E. Hawkins	31Aug1850	W95	
Hudson	Frances Mathews	20Dec1809	E34 W43	
Jacob	Honer Kidhey[?]	22Mar1779	B1 W1	
James	Ann Gooding	07May1781	C4 W6	
James	Susanah Fields	24Jan1792	E2 W21	
James	Elizabeth Maxwell	08Apr1801	E20 W31	
James	Jane Shannon	23May1806	E28 W38	
John	Charlotte Abbott	30Jun1808	E32 W41	
John	Matilda O'Neill	31May1815	E43 W50	
John	Elizabeth Holland	03Jan1861	W113	
Joshua	Mary Botts	21May1779	B2 W2	
Joshua	Ann Osborn	01May1797	E10 W26	
Joshua	Hannah Bradford	08Jan1813	E39 W47	
Joshua	Susan Frisby	02Mar1816	E44 W51	
Mary	Hosia Barnes	m. 1778		[ret-AppA]
Mary	William Thompson	13Dec1824	E59 W63	Guest
Mary Ann	John Todd	15Nov1836	E77 W78	Finney
Moses	Margaret Bowen	28Jan1803	E23 W33	
Rebecca	Amos Barnes	12May1782	C6 W7	
Richard	Ann Jemison	10Jun1802	E22 W32	
Sarah	Daniel Donahoe	18Jan1785	C10 W10	
Sarah	Matthew Snody	m. 1790		[ret-AppA]
Sarah	John Young	27Jul1824	E58 W62	
Sarah Rebecca	Benjn Chauncey	31May1843	E86 W86	Aggey
Susan R.	William Reed	16Dec1828	E65 W68	Webster
[orig. lic. to Webster; cr-Harf]				
Susanna	Joseph Steel	02Jan1802	E21 W32	
William	Ann Maria Bond	29Jan1798	E13 W27	
William	Ann Chesney	28Mar1812	E38 W46	
William	Emeline Riley	02Aug1851	W96	

WOODARDS

William	Eleanor Pitcock	25Jan1804	E24 W34	[ret-AppA]

WOODHOUSE

Kate	John P. Adams	29Nov1859	W111	
William E.	Elizabeth Walker	26Mar1831	E68 W71	Stephenson

WOODROW

John	Lydia Ann Strawbridge	18Dec1858	W109

WOODS

Hutson	Elizabeth Wearham	19Dec1838	E80 W81	Galien
James A.	Mary F. Carpenter	31Jan1859	W109	

WOOLEN

Harriott	Henry Dorney, Junr	06Mar1827	E62 W66	Richardson
Henry	Ann Tredway	27Jun1818	E49 W55	

WOOLEY
Joseph	Hannah Lynch	10May1816	E45 W51	

WOOLFORD
Arthur	Abigail L. Williams	26Nov1829	E66 W69	Stephenson

WOOLLEN
Rachel	William Ford	04Feb1806	E27 W37	
William R.	Harriot Timmons	31Oct1818	E49 W55	

WOOLSEY
Deborah	Jason Moore	30Apr1799	E16 W28	
George	Eleanor More	02Mar1802	E21 W32	
Hannah	Aqa Thomson	02Oct1781	C5 W7	
Henry	Rebecca Cochran	08Jun1803	E23 W33	
Joseph	Sarah Johnson	28Nov1784	C9 W10	
Mary	David Vance	03Oct1781	C5 W7	
Wm	Alice Smith	10Sep1795	E7 W24	

WORK
Mary E.	Robert Bonfield Gorrell	30Dec1857	W107	

WORTHINGTON
Ann	Randall Wallis	01[?]Jun1795	E7 W24	
Charles	Hannah Yellott	17Apr1806	E28 W38	
Elizabeth	George D. Fitzhugh	01May1832	E71 W72	Wyatt
Hannah R.	Wakeman B. Hopkins	20Oct1829	E66 W69	Stephenson
James	Margaret Amos	01Jan1838	E78 W80	Park
James	Rebecca Evans	05Oct1850	W95	
James C.	Blanch H. Lee	08Apr1846	W90	
John Yellott	Margaret Elgar Coale	03May1832	E71 W73	Magraw
Joseph	Mary Johnson	30May1793	E4 W22	
Mary	Joseph Dallam	22Sep1803	E23 W34	
Priscilla W.	Thos C. Hopkins	28May1834	E74 W75	Finney
Prscilla [sic]	Samuel Richardson	01Mar1830	E67 W69	Poisal
Samuel	Sarah Chew	11Apr1809	E33 W42	
Susan J.	William B. Bateman	07Dec1813	E41 W48	
William	Rebecca Richardson	12May1808	E31 W40	

WORTHY [see John Worthy Cunningham]

WORWICK
Thomas	Sarah Smith	31Dec1811	E37 W45	

WRIGHT [see Wright Sparks]
Caleb	Elizabeth Gilbert	24Feb1825	E59 W63	Rockhold
Caleb	Ann Gilbert	22Dec1828	E65 W68	Finney
Cornelia	Otho Norris	21Dec1824	E59 W63	Morrison
Eliza	Jarrett Morris	31Jan1850	W94	
Elizabeth	John W. Ruth	07Jan1843	E85 W86	Gallion
Isabella	Thomas Poole	15Feb1862	W115	

WRIGHT, continued

John	Cathrine Coldham	20Dec1780	C4	W5	
John	Ann Keets	08Feb1808	E31	W40	
John, Junr	Agness Gordon	24Jan1820	E52	W57	
John	Margaret Wilgis	05Dec1827	E63	W67	Webster
[orig. lic. to Webster; cr-Harf]					
John	Martha J/I. Irvin	15Dec1855	H8	W103	Smith
John F.	Hannah Wiley	29Jan1853	H3	W99	Smith
Joshua D.	Julian Web	03Dec1828	E65	W68	Finney
Joshua L.	Mary Wright	30Aug1847		W91	
Mary	John Morrison	24May1836	E76	W78	Parks
Mary	Joshua L. Wright	30Aug1847		W91	
Mary Jane	Edward Lingan	29Jan1861		W113	
Nancy	George F. Taylor	29Apr1820	E52	W57	
Rachel Ann	Benjamin Jones	17Mar1862		W115	
Robert	Lucinda Warner	20Mar1856	H9	W104	Wilson
Thomas	Ann Green	16Mar1791	E1	W21	
Thomas	Rachel Jamison	03Feb1805	E26	W36	
Thomas	Elizabeth Biards	24Feb1824	E58	W62	
William	Amelia Smithson	02Apr1804	E25	W35	[ret-AppA]
William	Ellen Henderson	28Sep1815	E43	W50	
William	Ann Spencer	20Dec1821	E55	W59	
William	Jane Sampson	26Oct1839	E81	W82	Finney
William	Charlotte A. McClung	22May1849		W93	
William	Helena Tredwell	22Sep1863		W118	

WYLE

Joshua	Rachel Gallion	30Nov1815	E44	W50

YACKETT

William	Sally Jamison	27Mar1806	E28	W37

YARLEY

William	Jane Wilson	22May1806	E28	W38

YARNALL

John B.	Eliza Jane Jeffery	02Jan1826	E60	W64	Webster
[orig. lic. to Webster; cr-Harf; no month stated]					
Lydia	Robert McCullough	19Mar1823	E56	W61	
Mary Ann	John Saunders	01Jul1843	E86	W86	Rescold

YARNEL

Rebecca W.	James Carroll	01Nov1830	E68	W70	Tippet
William	Catherine Mitchell	16Apr1832	E70	W72	Finney

YEARLY

Nathaniel	Mary Richardson	08Dec1810	E36	W44
Rachel	Henry Divers	17May1815	E43	W50

YEIT

Michael	Barbary Fox	10Aug1855	H8	W103	Alexander

YELLIOTT

Mary	Francis Hollingsworth	24Dec1801	E21	W31

YELLOTT [see John Yellott Worthington]
Hannah	Charles Worthington	17Apr1806	E28 W38	
John	Rebecca Ridgely Coleman	01May1806	E28 W38	
John	Sarah Jane Maulsby	31Jan1838	E79 W80	Keech

YOAKLY
Mary	Edward Cotty	12May1780	C2 W4	

YOKELY
John	Sally Hendrick	21Dec1795	E8 W24	[ret-AppA]
Rebecca	John Cannon	15Jun1814	E42 W49	

YOKUM
Charles	Ann Evatt	03Jan1798	E13 W27	

YORK [see Sarah York Howard]
Ann	Samuel James	29Dec1824	E59 W63	Richardson
Blanch	Benedict Hill	13Jul1811	E36 W45	
Edward [york]	Mary Hughes	29Dec1781	C5 W7	
Edward	Ann Bennett	06Feb1817	E46 W53	
Elizabeth	Benjamin Lego	02Apr1806	E28 W38	
Hannah	Jno Gold Howard	m. 1778		[ret-AppA]
Hannah	John York	22Dec1784	C9 W10	
Harris	Rachel Bennet	29Dec1818	E50 W56	
Hetty	Solomon Wilson	25Dec1813	E41 W48	
James[poss. George]	Letty Daugerty	03Apr1781	C4 W6	
James	Sarah Waltham	10May1796	E8 W25	
John	Hannah Deaver	m. 1777		[ret-AppA]
John	Hannah York	22Dec1784	C9 W10	
Mary	William Hill	10Feb1806	E28 W37	
Nicholas	Margaret Sutton	19Dec1798	E15 W27	
Oliver	Sarah Groves	09Nov1779	C1 W3	
Statia	John Carty	18Jun1823	E57 W61	
William	Elizabeth Monk	22May1817	E47 W53	

YORKE
Lydia	Robert Ingham	18Apr1800	E17 W29	

YOUNG
Alice	Michael McCafferty	31Jan1855	H7 W102	Walter
Catharine	Robert W. Norris	06May1844	E87 W87	Little
Elizabeth	John Worthy Cunningham	09Jan1846	W89	
Esther	John Watters	08Jan1805	E26 W36	
Geo.	Elizth Husbands	18Mar1780	C1 W3	
George	Elizabeth Bull	31Jul1781	C5 W7	
Hugh	Amelia Barton	22Dec1806	E29 W38	
John	Susan Rogers	08Nov1810	E36 W44	
John	Sarah Wood	27Jul1824	E58 W62	
Mary	Danl Treadaway	30Jul1781	C5 W6	
[before other July entries]				
Mary	Charles O'Brien	10Mar1806	E28 W37	
Robert	Alice Farley	23Sep1854	H6 W101	McNally
Samuel	Mina Standiford	27Apr1836	E76 W77	Morrison

Harford Co. Md. Marriage Licenses, 1777-1865

YOUNG, continued
Sarah	Thos Rogers	23Jun1780	C2	W4	
Sarah	Samuel Rodgers	30Nov1813	E41	W48	
Susannah	Christian Heir	05Aug1851		W96	
Wm	Annaballa Loney	16Jan1783	C7	W8	cr-Harf

ZEARS
| Martha Agnes | James Wm. Carty | 24Jan1860 | W111 |

ZIERS
| Elizabeth | William Monks | 09Jan1807 | E29 W38 |

ZIMMERMAN
| Eliz. J. | John E. Bennett | 16Feb1863 | W117 |
| John C. | Margaret A. Harman | 03Nov1864 | W120 |

ZOLLINGER
| Henry A. | Elizabeth M. Courtney | 19Apr1843 | E86 W86 |
[minister - Happersett?]
| Lulia | William G. Power | 12Apr1849 | W93 |

* * * * * * * * * * * * *

Example of Marriage License Issued in Harford County

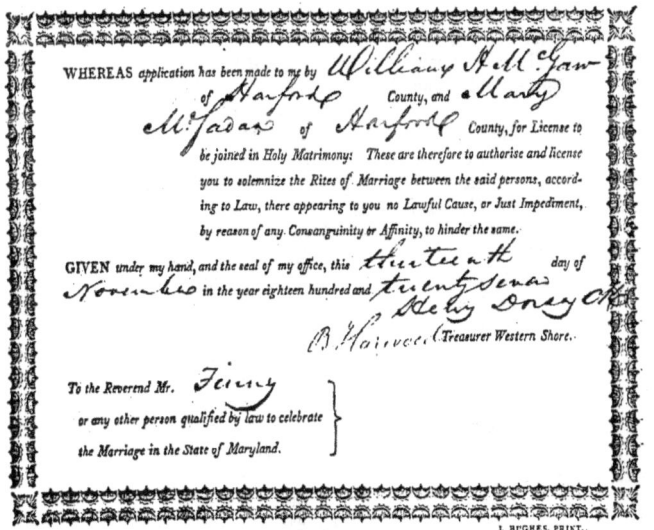

APPENDIX A

HARFORD COUNTY RETURNS OF MINISTERS TO TREASURER

Included in the Scharf Collection, now at the Maryland State Archives, are some minister's returns of marriages performed. They had been sent to the state Treasurer pursuant to Chapter 12, article 8, of the Session Laws of the Maryland General Assembly for February 1777. (Since 1865, they have been reported to the clerk of the county court who issued the license.) Eliza Hay Leisenring published these in 1900 in *Maryland Marriages, 1777-1804*. The entries designated as pertaining to Harford County are reproduced here, having been compared with the originals, and are indexed by cross-references in the main body of the text.

<u>By Rev. William West</u>, Rector of St. George's Parish:

June 12, 1777	Abraham Taylor	was married to Mary Foard
June 13, 1777	Alexander Harvey	to Eleanor McDaniel
June 18, 1777	Joseph Smith	to Mary Toalson
June 21, 1777	William Fizzee	to Sarah Dematt
July 24, 1777	Peter Duzan	to Keziah A-- [illeg.]
July 26, 1777	John Barnet	to Elizabeth Hill
July 27, 1777	Nehemiah Baily	to Mary Hobbard
July 30, 1777	Joseph Hunter	to Elizabeth Durham
Aug. 7, 1777	James Reardon	to Mary Sutton
Aug. 14, 1777	William Smith	to Rebecca Sewell
" "	Joshua Brown	to Mary Wetherall
Sept. 16, 1777	Samuel Beard	to Lehemiah Taylor
Oct. 16, 1777	John York	to Hannah Deaver
Oct. 19, 1777	John Buckley	to Frances Hanby
1777 Dec. 23	William Murphey	& Sophia West
	James Hollingsworth	& Mary McCrackin
24	Asa Taylor	& Hannah Kimble
25	Tho. Lancaster	& Christian Gordin
	John Brown	& Mary Mararty
30	Hollis Hanson	& Avarilla Hollingsworth
1778 Jany. 20	John Beedle Hall	& Sarah Hall
Feb. 1	Tho. Sorah	& Mary Cusick
5	Will. Harris	& Ann Barrett [Barrelt?]
8	James Anderson	& Marg^t McCan
10	Wm. Copeland Goldsmith	& Sarah Wetherall
17	George Sims	& Mary Lynch
26	Tho. McCluir	& Marg^t McCoy
March 5	Wm. Bradford	& Marg^t Richardson
8	Jno Debruler	& Mary Pierce
	James Bevard	& Rachael Jones
22	Anthony Debruler	& Sarah Philison
23	Richd Spencer	& Eliza^a Wild
April 7	Charles Burkin	& Eleanor Parker
May 5	Will. Evans	& Sarah Reese
19	George Lytle	& Catharin Chansey

("These [next two couples] were married by the Rev:d Mr. White in my absence:")

June 18	Dan:l Donnavin	& Eliza. Covey
	Francis Deacon	Judah Conner
22	John Blackburn	& Mary Kirkpatrick
23	Joseph Reese	& Cath:a. Potts
25	Jno Gold Howard	& Hannah York
Aug:t. 9	James Hannah	& Rebecca Hanson
11	John Forward	& Eliza Deane
13	James Pritchard	& Sarah Santee
	Peter Jones	& Jane Hines
19	Jno Silvers	& Jane Asker
20	Jno Gold Howard	& Hannah Carty
27	W:m. Strond	& Mary Kenny
	Jacob Denovin	& Sus:a Gilbert
	W:m Williams	& Ruth Barnes
	W:m Jones	& Sus:a Dixon
Oct. 27	Sam:l McFaddin	& Eliza Bonar
Nov. 1	Tho. Brown	& Mary Clark
30	Rich:d Greenland	& Jane Hearn

By Rev. John Clark: 8 Dec 1777, Baltimore County
("certifies only marriages since American States were declared independent")

Oct. 9, 1777   Benjamen Carter   Catharine Sturgen
("both of Harford County"; "by lic. granted by John Lee Gibson")

By Rev. Sewal:

Feb. 15, 1779   Henry Queen   Margaret Pye

By Rev. William Tilghman Ringgold:

March 25, 1786   Thomas Mills   Mary Thomas

By Rev. John Ireland, Protestant Episcopal;
[Cecil County items in list not included]

1787	{Thomas Simmons	Sarah Hill
(June 10)	{Aquila Bailey	Rachael Barnes
	{John Smith	Frances Griffith
	Josias Hall	Martha Garretson
	Dennis Bond	Polly Merryman
	Greenbury Dorsey	Frances Copeland
	William Barnes	Margaret Armstrong
	Robert Foster	Jane Riley

("Sion Hill 3 Nov 1790")

Jan. 6, 1788	Gregory Barnes	Elizabeth Osborn
Jan. 24, 1788	Ford Barnes	Mary Gilbert
Feb. 27, 1788	George Patterson	Bethia Presbury
Mar. 6, 1788	James Michael	Semelia Cortney
April 6, 1788	James Thompson	Hannah Y. Jay
May 11, 1788	Thomas Walsh	Mary Mitchell
May 15, 1788	William Hall	Sophia Presbury

June 10, 1788	Hosia Barnes	Mary Wood	
Oct. 2, 1788	James Olliver	Sarah Cord	
Dec. 18, 1788	Elijah Davis	Mary G. Garretson	
Feb. 26, 1789	James McCrakin	Mary Smith	
Mar. 16, 1789	William Pinkney	Ann M. Rogers	
June 7, 1789	John Michell	Issabella Taylor	
July 26, 1789	Benjamin Brucebanks	Mary Daugherty	
Dec. 31, 1789	Chrispian Cunningham	Elizabeth Horner	
June 8, 1790	Thomas Cowan	Sarah Barnes	
Sept. 12, 1790	Mathew Snody	Sarah Wood	

("Sion Hill, 1 Nov. 1791-23 Nov 1792")

Oct. 28, 1790	Samuel Jackson	Elizabeth Hanson	

("all since Nov. 1, 1790")

Jan. 27, 1791	John Porter	to Catherine McNeuse	
Oct. 18, 1791	John Perryman	Cassandra Horner	

("Since 1 Nov 1791 till 1 Nov 1792 returned")

Nov. 24, 1791	Jonathan Sutton	Sarah McCracken	
Dec. 21, 1791	Samuel Griffith	Elizabeth Garrettson	
Jan. 19, 1792	Josiah Matthews	Jane Forwood	
June 8, 1792	Joseph Webster	Martha Chauncy	
July 1, 1792	Edward Dillion	Anne Tasker	
Aug. 30, 1792	Alexander Lawson Smith	Martha Griffith	
Sept. 6, 1792	John Ferrel [or Fevrel]	Sarah Phrisby	
Sept. 13, 1792	William Kimble	Nelly Kimble	
Sept. 13, 1792	Nathaniel Henderson	Elizabeth Perryman	

("A.A. Co., 31 Dec 1795, Nov. 15, 1792 to Dec. 22, 1795")
 [returns duplicated Nov. 1, 1792-Nov. 1, 1793; variations noted]

Oct. 28, 1792	William Budd Gould	Martha Mitchell	
Nov. 15, 1792	John Guest (of Phila)	Rebecca Hall	
Nov. 27, 1792	William Smith	Susannah Phillips	
Dec. 6, 1792	Isaac Wilson	Elizabeth Gilbert	
Dec. 25, 1792	John Ely	Jane Meek	{Meeks}
Jan. 3, 1793	William Monk	Elizabeth Simpson	{Dec. 27, 1792}
Jan. 17, 1793	Augustine Boyer	Sabina Hall	{16th}
Jan. 22, 1793	William Munger	Mary Jones	{19th, Monjar}
Feb. 28, 1793	Stephen Kimble	Hannah Taylor	{11th}
March 21, 1793	Thomas Hall	Isabella Presbury	{19th}
March 31, 1793	John Davison	Hannah Taylor	{30th}
May 30, 1793	William Jolley	Sarah Chew	{28th}
Aug. 8, 1793	Ezekiel Cole	Sarah Courtenay	{5th}
Nov. 21, 1793	Nathaniel Chew	Margaret Rogers	
May 1, 1794	Michael Gilbert	Betsey Stiles	
[no date given]	James McAdow	Sarah Cattigan	
July 3, 1794	Charles Gilbert	Mary Horner	
Aug. 12, 1794	Robt Orr	Ruth Crawford	
Dec. 4, 1794	William Gilbert	Jane Ewen	
Dec. 23, 1794	William Evatt	Elizabeth Wiley	
April 20, 1795	Nathan Lufborough	Mary Webster	
Sept. 22, 1795	Robert Creswell	Jane Meek	
Nov. 3, 1795	John Hasson	Rachael Barrett	
Dec. 22, 1795	John Yokeley	Sally Hendrick	

Harford Co. Md. Marriage Licenses, 1777-1865 275

By Rev. Levy Heath of St. John's Parish, Joppa, H. Co.:
("lic. granted by Mr. Gibson"; oath Joppa Nov. 4, 1788)

Dec. 20, 1787	James Carrol Esq.	Sophia Gough	
April 17, 1788	William Groves	Elizabeth Meads	
June 4	Luke Dempster	Sarah Scott	
Feb. 27	John Day	Sarah Allender	
Jan. 26	William Galley	Grace Cashman	"manuscript"
April 19	Thos Lucas	Sarah Lynch	
May 16	Harry Gough Esq.	Patty Onion	
Mar. 22	Matthew Moratta	Cassander Scott	
Nov. 13	Henry Rumsey Esq.	Hannah Rumsey	

By Rev. Ezekiel Cooper:

1789	James McClure {?}	Mary Gollaher
	Alex. Ford	Rachel Barnes
	Andrew Doyle	Elizabeth Fields

By Rev. John Coleman, Rector St. John's Parish, Balto. & Harf. Counties:
("14 in all from Nov 1st 1796 to Nov 1st 1797")
[Baltimore County items not reproduced here]

Nov. 17, 1796	Thomas Johnson	Elizabeth Taylor	lic. H Co.
Jan. 19, 1797	Zaccheus Onion Bond	Cassandra Lee Morgan	Harf Co.
26	John Hambleton	Aley Gafford	Harf. Co.
March 9, 1797	Thomas Sheredine	Ann Neil	Harf. Co.
April 6, 1797	Daniel Scott	Margaret Short	Harf. Co.
May 2, 1797	Henry Wetherall	Charlotte E. Day	H. Co.
May 18, 1797	John Quarles	Elizabeth Husbands	H. Co.
June 29, 1797	James St. Clair	Susanna Bosley	H. Co.
July 22, 1797	William Godman	Delilah White	H. Co.
July 27, 1797	Henry O'Henry	Ann Price	H. Co.
Aug. 3, 1797	John Moore	Mary Scarbrough	H. Co.
Sept. 21, 1797	James Smith	Sarah Haley	H. Co.
" " "	William Wetheral	Mary Presbury	H. Co.
" " "	Parker Gilbert	Martha McComas	H. Co.
Oct. 19, 1797	Daniel Cunningham	Ann Amoss	H. Co.

By Rev. Benjamin Richardson of H. Co.:
("Nov. 6, 1802 for the year 1802 since Novr 1801")
[Baltimore County couple excluded]

April 6, 1802	John Howard	Mary Harrison Sewell
May 27, 1802	John Bond (of Wm)	Mary Richardson

Returned 3 Nov 1803:

Dec. 23, 1802	Edwd Allender	Nacky Enlowes
Jan. 30, 1803	James Huggins	Sally Barett
Feb. 3, 1803	Philip A. Barton	Elizth Norton
Feb. 6, 1803	William Carr	Sarah Murrey
Feb. 15, 1803	William H. Sewell	Rebecca Lewes
March 20, 1803	James J. Wilmer	Letitia Day
March 27, 1803	William Johnson	Mary Fleeharty

May 19, 1803	William MCubbin	Ruth Cromwell [-boll?]
June 9, 1803	William Price	Elizth Turner
June 25, 1803	Greenbury Presbury	Sarah Davis
July 25, 1803	Samuel Bradford	Jane Bond
Sept. 1, 1803	Samuel Oram	Charity Ledley
Oct. 13, 1803	Richd Ayres	Elizth Baxter

Returned 5 November 1804:

Nov. 17, 1803	Thomas Allender	Sarah Barton
	Peen Bartonslade	Sarah MCulben
Dec. 20, 1803	Edward B. Bussey	Sarah Howard
Dec. 25, 1803	John Hatton	Sarah Collings
Jan. 3, 1804	John Divers	Charity Onion
Jan. 19, 1804	Isaac Holland	Ruth Hatton
Jan. 26, 1804	William Woodard	Ellenor Pitcock
March 21, 1804	Joshua --[illeg.*]	Prissila Standaford

[*looks like Tacxcick; Leisenring reads as Gorsuch]

June 7, 1804	Robert MNab	Ann Montomery
June 26, 1804	James Husbands	Margrate Galleher
Oct. 29, 1804	Rhesa Norris	Susannah Dutton

By Rev. Edmund Rockhold in Baltimore Co., 25 October 1804:
("by license that Couple marked these of Harford")

Dec. 15, 1803	William Bull	Polly Hicks	
Jan. 31, 1804	John Hale	Martha Mays	
April 8, 1804	Nicholas Gore	Preshoshy Price	
April 8, 1804	William Wright	Amilia Smithson	Harford
May 17, 1804	Thomas Rutledge	Sarah Gorsuch	

APPENDIX B

SOME MISCELLANEOUS MARRIAGE RETURNS

Beginning in 1865, the newly required returns by ministers to the Clerk were recorded in Volume A.L.J. No. 1, which contains marriage records to 1886. The original returns themselves are stored in file boxes in the Clerk's office.

While there was no requirement until 1865 for locally recording marriage ceremonies performed, the Rev. Mr. Swentzel of Harford County [Frederick Swentzell was pastor of the Deer Creek Methodist Protestant Circuit for 1861-1862 and 1877-1879] in 1880 belatedly recorded four from 1861 and 1862, all performed in Harford County, where all parties resided. References to these appear in the main text and the data is fully set out here. [There are two page references because returns are recorded by first letter of surname both for the bride and for the groom.] Note some slight variations with the names as recorded in the main text. (The first recorded 9 April, the rest 8 May 1880).

ALJ#1 pp.	Groom	Bride	Date
94 & 142	Daniel M. McComas	Sophia E. Hunter	24 Jun 1861
34 & 223	Isaac Vanhorn	Virginia Chalk	30 Dec 1861
21 & 34	Samuel H. Bageley	Martha M. Ewing	28 Jun 1862
94 & 106	Thomas Johnson	Mary Ann Hayghe	21 Nov 1862

APPENDIX C

CLERGY TO WHOM LICENSES WERE DIRECTED

For the periods 1824 through 1845 and 1851 through 1857, the extant original license books state the surname (and in a few instances also the given name or initial) of the minister or priest whom the applicant indicated was to perform the ceremony. As the license also authorized any other clergyman to act, the name is not proof that the named individual was the officiant. Similarly, as pointed out in the introduction, the existence of a license is not in itself proof of a marriage, although in the vast majority of cases, there will have been a marriage ceremony and the named clergyman will have performed it.

A number of the ministers are mentioned only once or twice, but many more frequently. The Rev. William Finney of Churchville Presbyterian Church was by far the most frequently designated minister in the time period covered.

Following is an alphabetical list of the names of clergy cited in the records, with many identified, some only tentatively, by means of reviewing pastoral rosters from individual church histories and from regional denominational sources, such as Clarence V. Joerndt's *St. Ignatius and her Missions* and Armstrong's *Old Baltimore Conference*. The list was submitted to the late Edna A. Kanely when the compilers learned of her then forthcoming *Directory of Ministers and the Maryland Churches They Served, 1634-1990*. Readers may wish to consult that work, published just before her death, and her earlier *Directory of Maryland Church Records*. Miss Kanely was able to make some additional identifications, but surprisingly there are many names which did not appear in her research. There was no way to identify clergy bearing commonly held surnames when none of the name were found among local clergy rosters. Some names may be of "local" Methodist preachers, who are not listed in any formal record. Others may have been clergy from Baltimore or elsewhere, temporarily in the area or chosen to officiate at a relative's nuptials. Also included are the clergy who made the marriage returns to the Treasurer which are set out in Appendix A. No attempt has been made to list or reconcile all the variant spellings in the records.

AGGEY (presumably = EGE)
ALEXANDER
ALLEN
ANDERSON
AUSTIN (perhaps = TUSTIN)
BARTON (perhaps Thomas, Bapt.)
BEATTY (could be James Beaty of the Balto. M. E. Conf.)
BILLOPP, Thomas Farmer, P.E., St.George's, 1841-1845
BINADE
BIRD
BLANCE
BOLTON
BON--
BOND, D.
BOSWORTH, E(liphalet?) N., Pres., Franklinville & Bel Air, 1849-1853
BRAND, William Francis, St.Mary's P.E., 1851-1907
BRECKINRIDGE (could be Robert Jefferson or John, both Pres., of Baltimore)

BRISCOLL,-COLD (perhaps = RESCORL)
BROWN, Richard, M.E., W. Harf. Cir., 1843
BULL, John W., M.E., E. Harf. Cir., 1848
BURROWS (perhaps George, Pres., West Nottingham & Port Deposit)
CADDEN, Robert, M.E., E. Harf. Cir., 1851
CARTER, John Pym, Pres., Bethel, 1853-1856
CHAPMAN, William H., M.E., E. Harf. Cir., 1849
CHESNEY, Jesse, M.E.
CLARK, John, Pres., Bethel, 1769-1775 and later
CLAY, Jeremiah, M.P., Deer Creek Cir., 1853
COLEMAN, John, P.E., St. John's, Joppa-Kingsville, 1789-1800, 1812-1816
                 Christ, Rock Spring, 1803-1816
COLLIER, William, M.P., Deer Creek Cir., 1837-1838
COLLINS, Isaac, M.E., Harf. Cir., 1837-1838
      Levin A., M.P., Deer Creek Cir., 1837
COLLIS (perhaps = COLLINS)
COOKER, Ezekiel
CORNELIUS (perhaps John W. or Thomas, M.E.)
COSKERY, Henry Benedict, R.C., St. Ignatius, 1834-1838
CRAMPTON, Savington Warren, St, George's P.E., 1845-1872
CRAWFORD, Thomas M., Pres., Slateville, 1851-1872
CRONIN (presumably Cornelius C. or John Wesley, M.E.)
CROSGAY see COSKERY
CROSS, Andrew B., Pres., Bethel, 1837-1845
CULLUM, J. Wesley, M.E., Harf. Cir., 1841
CUNNINGHAM (perhaps N. P. of Balto. M.E. Conf.)
CUSHING, Henry Caleb, M.P., Deer Creek Cir., 1855-1857
DAMPHOUX, Edward J., R.C., Baltimore
DAUGHERTY (perhaps B.W., M.E.)
DAVIS
DONAHAY, James W., M.E., Harf. Cir., 1833-1834
DORSEY, Dennis B., M.E., Harf. Cir., 1826
     Edwin, M.E., Harf. Cir., 1828
DULANEY
DUMM, William Thomas, M.P., Deer Creek Cir., 1843-1844, 1853-1854
EAGY (presumably = EGE)
EGE, Oliver, M.E., E. Harf. Cir., 1843-1844
ELDERDICE, John, M.P., Deer Creek Cir., 1847-1849
EMORY, Robert, M.E., Harf. Cir., 1839-1840
EWING (perhaps Alexander, M.E.)
FINNEY, William, Pres., Deer Creek (Churchville) 1813-1854
               Harmony 1855-1856
FOLEY, John S., Cath., St. Patrick's HdG, 1858
FOOBS (perhaps = FORBES)
FORBES (perhaps Matthew Lewis, P.E., St. James, Manor, 1842-1858)
FREY
FURGURSON (perhaps William, M.E.)
FURLONG, Henry, M.E., Harf. Cir., 1835-1836
GAILEY
GALLION, Stansbury, M.E. local
GAMBLE (perhaps James, M.E. missionary to Harford colored people, 1855-1857)
GIBSON, Alexander E., M.E., W. Harf. Cir., 1850
                   E. Harf. Cir., 1851-1852
GOLDSBOROUGH, Robert Lloyd, P.E., St. George's & H. de Grace, 1834-1841
GREENBANK (perhaps Richard M., M.E., Port Deposit, 1837-1838)

GUEST, Job, M.E. circuit rider
HAMILTON, George D., M.P., Deer Creek Cir., 1832
HAN--
HAPPERSETT, Reese, Pres., Havre de Grace, 1841-1844
HAWK (perhaps HANK, of whom there were several M.E.)
HEATH, Levi, St. John's P.E., Joppa, 1786-1789
HENKLE, Eli, M.P., Deer Creek Cir., 1829
       J. M., M.P., Deer Creek Cir., 1845
HERRON, James, M.E. local (or Levin D., M.E.)
HERSEY, John, M.E. local
HEWIN (see EWING)
HIBY (perhaps = HIGBEE)
HIGBEE, Edward Young, P.E., St. George's & Havre de Grace, 1829-1834
HINSEY
HOFFMAN (perhaps Henry, M.E., or = HOOPMAN)
HOLMEAD, Alfred, P.E., St. James, Manor, 1836-1842
HOOPMAN, Jacob, M.P.
       John, M.E.
HUNT, William, M.P., Deer Creek Cir., 1839-1840
HUNTINGTON, Cyrus, Pres., Havre de Grace, 1848-1852
IRELAND, John, St. George's, P.E., 1787-1792
JOHNS (John or Henry Van Dyke, P.E.)
JONES, John M., M.E., W. Harf. Cir., 1844
JORDAN
KEECH, John Reeder, P.E., St. John's P.E., Kingsville, 1819-1861
                       Christ, Rock Spring, 1819-1861
KETHCART (perhaps Robert, Pres. SE York Co., late 1700s)
KINSEY, Edward E., M.E., E. Harf. Cir., 1856-1857
LANE
LEE
LEMMON, Jonathan, Meth., Dublin area
LIPSCOMB, Robert M., M.E., Harf. Cir., 1832
LITTLE, George O., M.E., W. Harf. Cir., 1844
LITTLETON, Charles Humphrey, M.P., Deer Creek Cir., 1856
LUCKEY, George, Pres., Bethel & Centre, 1784-1824
LYON
McCARTNEY, Francis, M.E., W. Harf. Cir., 1855-1856
McDANIEL, H. C., M.E., E. Harf. Cir., 1855
McELHINEY (perhaps Dr. George, P.E.)
McGEE, Thomas, M.E., Harf. Cir., 1828-1829
McGRADY
McKAY
McMANUS (perhaps B. J. A., R.C.)
McKINSEY
McMULLIN, Solomon, M.E., W. Harf. Cir., 1846
McNALLY, John J., R.C., St. Ignatius, 1851-1854
McVEY
MADDOX, William W., M.P., Deer Creek Cir., 1843-1844
MAGRAW (perhaps James, Pres., W. Nottingham, Cecil Co.)
MARTIN
MEYERS, Thomas B., M.E., Havre de Grace, 1841-1842
MILLIGAN
MONROE, Jonathan, M.E., E. Harf. Cir., 1856-187
MORGAN
MORRISON, George, Sr., Pres., Bethel, 1825-1837

MYERS (see MEYERS)
NORRIS
O'BRIEN, Timothy, R.C., St. Ignatius, 1820-1832
ORCHARD
PAGE (perhaps Edward, M.E., of Cecil Co. 1826)
PARKE, Samuel, Pres., Slate Ridge, 1814-1860; Centre, 1820-1848
PENNELL
POISAL, John, M.E., Harf. Cir., 1826, 1829
POOLE, William C., M.E., Harf. Cir., 1826-1827
              M.P., Deer Creek Cir., 1832
PORTER, John W., M.P., Deer Creek Cir., 1833-1834
POTEET (perhaps Thomas, Bapt.)
PRETTYMAN, William, M.E., Harf. Cir., 1839-1840
RANKIN, William A., Pres., Bel Air and Churchville, 1855
REESE, Aquilla A., M.E., Harf. Cir., 1838
    Daniel Evans, M.P., Deer Creek Cir., 1830, 1835-1836, 1845-1846
    John Smith, M.P.
    Philip B., M.E., E. Harf. Cir., 1854-1855
REID, Charles A., M.E., W. Harf. Cir., 1850-1851
    James, M.E., Harf. Cir., 1820-1821
    James, R.C., St. Ignatius, 1839-1845
REINICK, William, M.P., Deer Creek Cir., 1848, 1855
RESCORL, Philip, M.E.
REYNOLDS, John, P.E., St. George's, 1825-1828
RHA--
RICHARDSON, Benjamin, M.E.
RICHARDSON
RINGGOLD, William Tilghman
ROBB (perhaps John, local Meth. or William, M.E., Zion, Cecil Co 1848)
ROBERTS
ROBY, Washington, M.P., Deer Creek Cir., 1850-1851
ROCKHOLD, Edmund
ROCKHOLD
ROCKWELL
ROHR
RUTTER (perhaps L. C., Pres.)
SAMPLE
SANKS, James, M.E., E. Harf. Cir., 1852-1853
SARGENT (perhaps Thomas B., M.E.)
SARK
SCOTT
SEWALL, Charles, R.C., St. Ignatius, 1779-1780
SEWELL, James, M.E., Harf. Cir., 1831-1832
SHEPHERD, Jacob R., M.E., Harf. Cir., 1827
SILL, Amos H., Pres., Churchville, 1856 and later
SMITH, Thomas Stuart Crowe, Pres., Havre de Grace, 1852-1855
                   Bethel & North Bend, 1857-1864
SMITH (perhaps Amos, M.E., Harf. Cir. 1835-1836)
STEPHENSON, James, local M.E.
STIER (perhaps Frederick, M.P.)
SWITZER, Thomas H., M.E., E. Harf. Cir., 1843
THOMAS, David, M.E., W. Harf. Cir., 1843
TIPPETT, Charles B., M.E., Harf. Cir., 1830
TODRIG, Francis Thomas, R.C., St. Ignatius, 1832-1834
TROTT (perhaps = TROUT)

TROUT, David, M.E., W. Harf. Cir., 1853-1854
TUSTIN, Septimus, Pres., Havre de Grace & Grove, 1854-1859
TYDINGS, Richard, M.E., Harf. Cir., 1824-1825
WALTER, Jacob A., R.C., St. Ignatius, 1854-1858
WAUGH ([Bishop] Beverly, Dr. John W., or J. Hoffman, all M.E.)
WEBSTER, Isaac, M.P., Deer Creek Cir., 1831
WELLS (perhaps Joshua of Balto. Conf. M.E.)
WEST, William, P.E., St. George's, 1772-1779
WHEELER
WHITE (perhaps [Bishop] William, P.E., acting at St. George's, 1778)
WHITTINGHAM, William Rollinson, P.E. Bishop of Maryland
WIGGINS
WILES, Alfed, M.E.
WILSON, John G., M.P., Deer Creek Cir., 1841-1842
   Victor T., M.P., Deer Creek Cir., 1835
WYATT, T. J., P.E., St. John's, Havre de Grace, 1846
  (or perhaps William Edward, P.E., St. Paul's, Balto.)
WYSONG, Thomas Turner, M.E., E. Harf. Cir., 1844
YERKES, Stephen, Pres., Bethel, 1845-1852
YOUNG, Charles B., M.E., E. Harf. Cir., 1845-1846

Notes on Methodist Circuits

Harford Circuit (Methodist Episcopal) consisted of the entire county prior to 1843 and would include Bel Air, Dublin, Calvary, Havre de Grace, Watters, Abingdon, and Bush Forest.

West Harford Circuit (Methodist Episcopal) was established in 1843 and included LaGrange Furnace, Thomas Run, Friendship, Darlington, Bel Air, Deans Schoolhouse, Jarettsville, Centre, McKendree, Ebenezer, Watters, and Dublin.

East Harford Circuit (Methodist Episcopal) was established in 1843 and included Aberdeen, Garrettson Chapel, Smiths Chapel, Rock Run, Calvary, Bush Chapel, Abingdon, and Gunpowder.

Deer Creek Circuit (Methodist Protestant, originally Associated Methodist) included Log Meeting, Bel Air, Watters, Wesleyan Chapel, Abingdon, Calvary, and Union Chapel.

www.ingramcontent.com/pod-product-compliance
Lightning Source LLC
Chambersburg PA
CBHW070726160426
43192CB00009B/1326